THE VOYAGE IN

THE VOYAGE IN

Published for Dartmouth College

by University Press of New England

HANOVER AND LONDON, 1983

Fictions of Female Development

EDITED BY

Elizabeth Abel,

Marianne Hirsch, and

Elizabeth Langland

UNIVERSITY PRESS OF NEW ENGLAND

LIBRARY OF CONGRESS CATALOGING IN PUBLICATION DATA
Main entry under title:

The Voyage in.

   Includes bibliographical references and index.
   1. English fiction—Women authors—History and
criticism—Addresses, essays, lectures.   2. Women in
literature—Addresses, essays, lectures.   3. Sex role in
literature—Addresses, essays, lectures.   4. Bildungsroman—
Addresses, essays, lectures.   5. American fiction—
Women authors—History and criticism—Addresses, essays,
lectures.   I. Abel, Elizabeth.   II. Hirsch, Marianne.
III. Langland, Elizabeth.
PR830.W6V69   1983   823'.009'9287   82-40473
ISBN 0-87451-250-6
ISBN 0-87451-251-4 (pbk.)

Contents

v

Preface

The Voyage In emerged from the growing recognition that our individual scholarly concerns—society in the novel, genre theory, and psychoanalytic theories of female identity—converged in the study of the female novel of development. We decided to pool our own thoughts and those of other feminist critics in a collection of essays on the various manifestations of a fictional form surprisingly neglected by critics. Although we initially planned to divide the collection according to our areas of expertise, we quickly found our most fruitful collaboration in pursuing together the multiple connections of our separate approaches. Our close and productive working relationship has extended to our contributors whose valuable insights and suggestions have enriched our own exchange. This book is the product of distinctive feminist collaboration, one that is particularly satisfying because of the personal friendships that have been fostered by a common scholarly endeavor. We shared the editorial duties equally, and the order of our names does not reflect the distribution of responsibility.

Many people have contributed directly or indirectly to this project. For financial assistance we thank the Dartmouth Research Committee, the Vanderbilt Research Council, the Converse Faculty Development and Research Fund and the University of California, Berkeley. We are grateful to the Addison Gallery of American Art at Phillips Academy, Andover, Massachusetts, for permission to use Mary Cassatt's *Mother and Child in Boat* on the cover of this volume. We also thank our companions, Jerald Jahn, Richard Meyer, and Leo Spitzer, for their continued support, and our children, Erika, Peter, Oliver, Alex, and Gabriel, for the insights they have given us into development. We are especially grateful to our parents for the working spaces they generously offered and which enabled us to overcome the geographic distance that makes collaboration difficult. Finally, we appreciate the help of many feminist scholars with whom we have shared our work on this project and whose insights are scattered anonymously throughout its pages.

E.A., M.H., and E.L.

I INTRODUCTION

There seems at present to be only partial
agreement between men and women about the
adulthood they commonly share.

—Carol Gilligan

Introduction

> The sights were all concerned in some plot, some adventure, some es-
> cape. . . . Now they were among the trees and savages, now they were on
> the sea; now they were on the tops of high towers; now they jumped; now
> they flew. . . . At last the faces went further away; she fell into a deep
> pool of sticky water, which eventually closed over her head. . . . There
> she lay, sometimes seeing darkness, sometimes light, while every now and
> then someone turned her over at the bottom of the sea.[1]

This painful hallucinatory illness and eventual death mark the end of
the voyage taken by Rachel Vinrace, the heroine of Virginia Woolf's
The Voyage Out. For Rachel, the journey to exotic South America offers the opportunity to break away from her limiting home and insufficient education, which have failed to instruct her about "the shape
of the earth, the history of the world, how trains worked, or money
was invested, which people wanted what, or why they wanted it"
(p. 34). Because a respectable twenty-four-year-old woman could not
travel alone, however, Rachel is chaperoned by her businessman father and by her beautiful aunt/surrogate mother, Helen Ambrose,
who wishes to complete her niece's one-sided education, which has
been confined almost exclusively to music, Rachel's only passion and
only access to truth and feeling.

Rachel's stay in South America allows her to encounter the challenges of maturity even as it presents her with the irresolvable conflicts that face many women as they come of age. Essential aspects of
adulthood are presented to Rachel in the microcosmic British society
of the hotel, in her friendship with Helen, in her meeting with a
young writer, Terence Hewett, and finally in her second journey up
the mysterious Amazon, a symbolic voyage into the dark landscapes
of the soul. In the heart of the South American continent, at a distance from the constraints of British society, Rachel and Terence discover that they love each other and imagine a harmonious union that
seems to satisfy their youthful desires. In this dreamy setting, they become engaged, but their return to the coast marks a return to their al-

legiances to British civilization and previously hidden antagonisms erupt. Here "love" means the social obligations of marriage, and Rachel's subordination to Terence. A seemingly playful struggle ensues when Terence interrupts Rachel's piano playing to suggest she write thank-you notes while he writes his novel. Rachel's dress is ripped: the sexual violence suggests that threats to her virginity are threats to her freedom and integrity as well. The engagement also forces her to choose between her loyalty to Helen and to Terence, to separate from one for an increasingly remote prospect of harmony with the other. Rachel wonders in frustration if it would ever be possible to integrate the different facets of her psyche or to blend with another human being: "Would there ever be a time when the world was one and indivisible?" (p. 296).

For Rachel death is that time. Faced with maturity, Rachel dies from a fever mysteriously contracted when she contracts to marry Terence. On the verge of entering adult life as Terence's wife in London, Rachel withdraws into a feverish inner landscape that dramatizes her fears about adulthood, fears possibly anticipated by her mother's premature death. Terence idealizes Rachel's death as a moment of perfect communion between them; but for Rachel the hallucinatory descent into the suffocating water provides her only escape from a violent and confining social world and from the female body that frustrates her spiritual and artistic cravings.

Woolf's plot raises crucial questions about fictions of female development: How typical is Rachel's course toward death? What psychological and social forces obstruct maturity for women? What are the prevailing patterns of women's development in fiction? How does gender qualify literary representations of development?

Development is a relative concept colored by many interrelated factors, including class, history, and gender. Theories of development tend to emphasize certain factors at the expense of others. Literature, especially the novel, offers the complexity of form necessary to represent the interrelationships shaping individual growth. The desire to translate these interrelationships into a coherent narrative has produced a distinctive genre, the *Bildungsroman,* or novel of formation. Since its origin in Goethe's *Wilhelm Meister's Apprenticeship,* the *Bildungsroman* has emphasized the interplay of psychological and social forces. Through further questioning, the definition of the genre has gradually been expanded to accommodate other historical and cultural variables. Gender, however, has not been assimilated as a pertinent category, despite the fact that the sex of the protagonist modifies every aspect of a particular *Bildungsroman:* its narrative structure, its implied psychology, its representation of social pressures.[2]

By examining fictional representations of female development, this volume integrates gender with genre and identifies distinctively female versions of the *Bildungsroman.* Our purpose requires that we first reexamine and revise generic definitions, beginning with the assumptions underlying the earliest examples of the form. Second, in order to understand the individual's relation to society, an interaction fundamental to the genre, we clarify the gender bias inherent in traditional accounts of this relationship. Next we examine the psychological conventions that have defined the goals of development and discover their failure to account for specifically female experience. Through this process of critical revision, we describe an alternative generic model that not only reveals common strategies in diverse and hitherto unclassified female narratives, but which also redefines and expands the definition of fiction of development.

The *Bildungsroman* emerged from the particular historical and intellectual circumstances of eighteenth-century Germany. According to Martin Swales, "it is a novel form that is animated by a concern for the whole man unfolding organically in all his complexity and richness."[3] The genre embodies the Goethean model of organic growth: cumulative, gradual, total. Originating in the Idealist tradition of the Enlightenment, with its belief in human perfectibility and historical progress, this understanding of human growth assumes the possibility of individual achievement and social integration. The goal of Goethe's prototypical hero, Wilhelm Meister, is to "develop myself just as I am," to realize the physical, intellectual, emotional, moral, and spiritual capacities inherent in his personality. The classic conception of *Bildung,* outlined by Wilhelm Dilthey, stresses this process:

A regulated development within the life of the individual is observed, each of its stages has its own intrinsic value and is at the same time the basis for a higher stage. The dissonances and conflicts of life appear as the necessary growth points through which the individual must pass on his way to maturity and harmony.[4]

Through careful nurturing, the hero should be brought to the point where he can accept a responsible role in a friendly social community. Clearly, successful *Bildung* requires the existence of a social context that will facilitate the unfolding of inner capacities, leading the young person from ignorance and innocence to wisdom and maturity.

In no single novel, however, does the developmental journey take such a smooth and uncomplicated course. Goethe's utopian Tower Society in *Wilhelm Meister's Apprenticeship* is meant to provide a harmonious and enabling context for growth. But in his travels, Wilhelm encounters people and experiences that the essentially rational Tower cannot fully subsume. The distance between the ideal *Bildung,* as outlined by Goethe and Dilthey, and actual human possibility within culture has led some theorists to deny the value of the *Bildungsroman* as a literary concept, for not even the prototypical *Wilhelm Meister* seems fully to correspond to the theoretical ideal.[5]

Other theorists have retained the literary category but with significant expansions, viewing the novel of development as a more comprehensive German genre, stretching from Wieland to Hesse, or even as a European genre that includes such novels as *Great Expectations, Père Goriot* and *Lost Illusions, Sentimental Education, Jude the Obscure, The Red and the Black,* and *A Portrait of the Artist as a Young Man.*[6] These expanded definitions move the genre away from German idealism, from the symbolic and socially conservative aspects of the German novel, toward a vision of individual development as a series of disillusionments or clashes with an inimical milieu. These clashes often culminate not in integration but in withdrawal, rebellion, or even suicide. Social integration in such novels can be achieved only by severe compromise.

By either definition, the *Bildungsroman* shares the "chief interest" of the novel as a genre, defined by literary theorists such as Northrop Frye as "human character as it manifests itself in society."[7] With few exceptions, the relationship between the individual and society, as it is represented in the novel, is marked by clashes of unique human possibility with the restraints of social convention. But critics have assumed that society constrains men and women equally. In fact, while male protagonists struggle to find a hospitable context in which to realize their aspirations, female protagonists must frequently struggle to voice any aspirations whatsoever. For a woman, social options are often so narrow that they preclude explorations of her milieu. Pacing the roof at Thornfield Hall, Charlotte Brontë's Jane Eyre expresses this frustration:

Women need exercise for their faculties and a field for their efforts as much as their brothers do; they suffer from too rigid a restraint, too absolute a stagnation, precisely as men would suffer; and it is narrow-minded in their more privileged fellow-creatures to say that they ought to confine themselves to making puddings and knitting stockings, to playing on the piano and embroidering bags.[8]

Even the broadest definitions of the *Bildungsroman* presuppose a range of social options available only to men. Only male development is marked by a determined exploration of a social milieu, so that when a critic identifies the "principal characteristics" of a "typical *Bildungsroman* plot," he inevitably describes "human" development in exclusively male terms.[9] Jerome Buckley's *Season of Youth* clearly demonstrates this limitation. The very starting point of Buckley's plot, "a child of some sensibility" who grows up in the country and encounters forces hostile to imaginative growth, occurs in few novels with female protagonists. *Jane Eyre, Villette, The Mill on the Floss,* and *Little Women* do begin with the heroine's childhood; more often, however, fiction shows women developing later in life, after conventional expectations of marriage and motherhood have been fulfilled and found insufficient. In contrast to most female protagonists, Buckley's hero receives a formal education that "may suggest options not available to him in his present setting." Even the repressive schooling portrayed by Dickens, for example, provides a context in which social rules and values can be acquired, internalized, and evaluated. Nineteenth-century heroines rarely benefit from formal schooling. Even those directly involved in formal education, such as Jane Eyre and Lucy Snowe, do not significantly expand their options, but learn instead to consolidate their female nurturing roles rather than to take a more active part in the shaping of society.

Once dissatisfied with his limited opportunities, Buckley's hero "leaves the repressive atmosphere of home . . . to make his way independently in the city. . . . There his real education begins." On the other hand, women in nineteenth-century fiction are generally unable to leave home for an independent life in the city. When they do, they are not free to explore; more frequently, they merely exchange one domestic sphere for another. While the young hero roams through the city, the young heroine strolls down the country lane.[10] Her object is not to learn how to take care of herself, but to find a place where she can be protected, often in return for taking care of others. Nor do women sever family ties as easily as men. When Austen's Emma marries, she marries her brother-in-law's brother and insists that they live in her father's house so that she may continue to take care of him. Although Rachel Vinrace ventures out, she is always accompanied or followed by either her father or her aunt. The "two love affairs or sexual encounters, one debasing, one exalting" that Buckley sees as the minimum necessary for the male hero's emotional and moral growth are clearly forbidden his sisters. Even one such affair, no matter how exalting, would assure a woman's expulsion from society. Although adulterous relationships may offer nineteenth-century heroines brief escapes from the constraints of marriage and family obligations, this option also guarantees punishment.

Buckley's *Bildungsroman* plot culminates with the hero's accommodation to society, a resolution achieved after "painful soul searching" and signaling the completed passage to maturity. Even the rebel's defiance and the artist's withdrawal are conventional arrangements with society. Novels of female development, by contrast, typically substitute inner concentration for active accommodation, rebellion, or withdrawal.[11] As Charlotte Brontë's narrator in *Villette* ironically observes: woman is supposed to spend her life quiescently "as a bark slumbering through halcyon weather, in a harbor still as glass—the steersman stretched out on the little deck, his face up to heaven, his eyes closed: buried, if you will, in a long prayer."[12] Confinement to inner life, no matter how enriching, threatens a loss of public activity; it enforces an isolation that may culminate in death. In Kate Chopin's *The Awakening,* Edna Pontellier succumbs to the lure of a spiritual landscape; isolated from society, starved for activity, Effi Briest in Fontane's novel looks toward the stars in search of a spiritual home, and dies. Turning away from marriage and adulthood, Rachel Vinrace sinks into a hallucinatory inner world that opens into death. Even if allowed spiritual growth, female protagonists who are barred from public experience must grapple with a pervasive threat of extinction.

In *Season of Youth*, Buckley does consider the development of one heroine. A chapter on *The Mill on the Floss* entitled "A Double Life" subsumes Maggie Tulliver's development to that of the symbiotic brother-sister pair. Neglecting the social conditions that thwart Maggie's emergence, Buckley attributes her failure to become self-determining to hereditary weakness in her personality and to artistic flaws that stem from Eliot's alleged overidentification with her protagonist. Viewed, however, in the context of nineteenth-century social possibilities, Maggie's death is a logical and artistically valid consequence of her situation.

Maggie Tulliver's "long suicide" suggests at least two ways in which the nineteenth-century heroine could not comply with what critics have defined as the typical developmental pattern.[13] Her complex fate both dramatizes the destructive effects of a parochial society and points to the inherently different psychological features of women's maturation. Maggie's strong allegiance to the parental home, for example, is usually seen as a developmental failure. Recent feminist psychoanalysis, however, casts a different light on Maggie's priorities and the life they shape. By helping to explain some of the apparent incongruities embedded in female plots—allegiances that repeatedly lead to death, for example—feminist theories of gender difference enable new readings of female fictions of development.

Drawing from the school of object relations, which emphasizes pre-Oedipal relationships, recent feminist psychoanalytic theorists such as Nancy Chodorow, Dorothy Dinnerstein, Jean Baker Miller, Jane Flax, and Carol Gilligan have revised the traditional, hierarchical account of psychosexual differences.[14] In contrast with Freudian orthodoxy, which links psychological to anatomical differences, these theorists trace the influence of gender on identity to the dynamics of the mother-infant bond. In Freudian theory the presence or absence of the phallus determines gender: the female is simply a defective male—castrated, lacking, rather than other. Only the male can achieve a full adulthood by his passage through the Oedipus complex, which fear of castration induces him to overcome. In the Freudian paradigm, fear promotes acceptance of the incest prohibition, thereby giving birth to the super-ego, which monitors desire in accord with social norms, signaling entry to the adult world. Girls, already "castrated" according to Freud, have less incentive to relinquish their Oedipal attachments and remain psychically embedded in family relationships, never developing a strong superego. In Freudian theory, women remain culturally marginal, passive, dependent, and infantile.[15] By shifting the focus from Oedipal to pre-Oedipal experience and by highlighting interpersonal relationships rather than anatomy, feminist theorists construct a picture of femininity as alternative, not inferior, to masculinity.

Mothers identify more closely with their daughters than their sons, according to this revisionist theory. Girls consequently learn to see themselves as partially continuous with their mothers, while boys learn early of their difference and separateness. Female identity is shaped primarily by the fluctuations of symbiosis and separation from the mother. Rather than being superseded by the Oedipal relation to the father, this process of identification and differentiation endures throughout adult life. Whereas boys define their identity by contrast, not relation, to the earliest caretaker, girls persist in defining themselves relationally and thus do not develop the precise and rigid ego boundaries common to males. Nancy Chodorow summarizes this difference succinctly: "The basic feminine sense of self is connected to the world; the basic masculine sense of self is separate."[16] In contrast with Freud's description of the ego as "something autonomous and unitary, marked off distinctly from everything else," Jean Baker Miller suggests that "women's sense of self becomes very much organized around being able to make and then to maintain affiliations and relationships."[17] Therefore, Miller concludes, "the ego, the I of psychoanalysis, may not be at all appropriate in relation to women."[18] Historically, only the masculine experience of separation and autonomy has been awarded the stamp of maturity; feminist theory suggests that the insistence on relationship reveals not a failed adulthood, but the desire for a different one.

A distinctive female "I" implies a distinctive value system and unorthodox developmental goals, defined in terms of community and empathy rather than achievement and autonomy.[19] The fully realized and individuated self who caps the journey of the *Bildungsroman* may not represent the developmental goals of women, or of women characters. Female fictions of development reflect the tensions between the assumptions of a genre that embodies male norms and the values of its female protagonists. The heroine's developmental course is more conflicted, less direct: separation tugs against the longing for fusion and the heroine encounters the conviction that identity resides in intimate relationships, especially those of early childhood. The deaths in which these fictions so often culminate represent less developmental failures than refusals to accept an adulthood that denies profound convictions and desires.

Specifying the influence of gender on the developing self and its social opportunities prepares us to identify some characteristic features of women's developmental fiction. We can describe this female version of the genre most dynamically in terms of recurrent narrative structures and thematic tensions.

Two narrative patterns predominate. The first, that of apprenticeship, is essentially chronological. In showing a continuous development from childhood to maturity, this paradigm adapts the linear structure of the male *Bildungsroman.* Although their protagonists travel through different stages, novels such as *Jane Eyre, Villette, The Mill on the Floss, Children of Violence,* and *Sula* conform to the convention of tracing development from childhood conflicts to (frequently imperfect) adult resolutions that provide some closure to the heroine's apprenticeship. The progression toward closure may assume diverse forms. Jane Eyre and Maggie Tulliver, for example, both interrupt their growth by periodic returns to the past, but Jane evolves, while Maggie is caught in a spiral whose coils return her to the river Floss.

Rachel Vinrace presents a somewhat different pattern, in which development is delayed by inadequate education until adulthood, when it blossoms momentarily, then dissolves. Rachel's deferred maturation points toward the second prevailing pattern of female growth in fiction: the awakening. For many heroines, development does not proceed gradually from stage to stage. In novels such as *The Awakening, Mrs. Dalloway, The Summer Before the Dark,* and such classic male-authored novels as *Madame Bovary* and *Effi Briest,* the time frame for development is doubly unconventional. First, the protagonists grow significantly only after fulfilling the fairy-tale expectation that they will marry and live "happily ever after." Because it frequently portrays a break not from parental but from marital authority, the novel of awakening is often a novel of adultery.[20] Second, development may be compressed into brief epiphanic moments. Since the significant changes are internal, flashes of recognition often replace the continuous unfolding of an action.[21]

The female developmental plot may engender other formal revisions of the *Bildungsroman.* Novels that depict female apprenticeship and awakening not only alter the developmental process, but also frequently change its position in the text. The tensions that shape female development may lead to a disjunction between a surface plot, which affirms social conventions, and a submerged plot, which encodes rebellion; between a plot governed by age-old female story patterns, such as myths and fairy tales, and a plot that reconceives these limiting possibilities; between a plot that charts development and a plot that unravels it.[22] The developmental tale may itself be concealed in coded memories, as in *Mrs. Dalloway,* or deflected through recurrent dreams, as in *Wide Sargasso Sea.* Fictions of female development may revise the conception of protagonist as well. Women characters, more psychologically embedded in relationships, sometimes share the formative voyage with friends, sisters, or mothers, who assume equal status as protagonists. Alcott's *Little Women* makes Meg, Beth, and Amy participants in Jo's development; Sula and Nel become the collective protagonists in Morrison's *Sula.*[23]

Describing how women come of age in fiction naturally has thematic ramifications. Women's developmental tasks and goals, which must be realized in a culture pervaded by male norms, generate distinctive narrative tensions—between autonomy and relationship, separation and community, loyalty to women and attraction to men. The social constraints on female maturation produce other conflicts, not unique to female characters, but more relentless in women's stories. Repeatedly, the female protagonist or *Bildungsheld* must chart a treacherous course between the penalties of expressing sexuality and suppressing it, between the costs of inner concentration and of direct confrontation with society, between the price of succumbing to mad-

ness and of grasping a repressive "normality." Rachel Vinrace's truncated life poignantly illustrates these diverse tensions. Marriage and
community mean sacrificing integrity and work; sexuality focuses the
frightening relations between men and women and spells the loss of
a nurturing female bond. Yet withdrawal to the inner life leads to fever, hallucination, and death.

Although identifying these formal and thematic characteristics enables us to propose generic status for a range of fictions of female development, our definition is not a static one. The interplay of tensions
shifts with history. The male *Bildungsroman,* according to David H.
Miles, has reached its "absolute end" in Grass's *The Tin Drum,* "the
uninhibited tale of a dwarf whose most remarkable growth is purely
phallic."[24] While the *Bildungsroman* has played out its possibilities
for males, female versions of the genre still offer a vital form. Wom-
en's increased sense of freedom in this century, when women's experience has begun to approach that of the traditional male *Bildungsheld,*
finds expression in a variety of fictions. Although the primary assumption underlying the *Bildungsroman*—the evolution of a coherent self—
has come under attack in modernist and avant-garde fiction, this
assumption remains cogent for women writers who now for the first
time find themselves in a world increasingly responsive to their needs.
It is no wonder, then, that the novel of development has become, in
Ellen Morgan's words, "the most salient form of literature" for contemporary women writing about women.[25] As women have moved actively into the public sphere, the outer world has featured more
prominently in their developmental fictions: the extensive travel and
political involvement of a Martha Quest, for example, substantially
expands the genre's topography. Whereas Miles charts a movement in
the male *Bildungsroman* from "the world without to the world within,"
from *Wilhelm Meister's Apprenticeship* to *The Notebooks of Malte
Laurids Brigge,* from the adventure tale to the confessional novel, and
finally to parody, we see, in fictions of female development, a movement from the world within to the world without, from introspection
to activity, from the "Confessions of a Beautiful Soul" to *The Adventures of Fanny Hackabout-Jones.*

It has become a tradition among critics of the *Bildungsroman* to
expand the concept of the genre: first beyond the German prototypes,

then beyond historical circumscription, now beyond the notion of *Bildung* as male and beyond the form of the developmental plot as a linear, foregrounded narrative structure. Our reformulation participates in a critical tradition by transforming a recognized historical and theoretical genre into a more flexible category whose validity lies in its usefulness as a conceptual tool. While emphasizing gender differences, our definition shares common ground with the presuppositions and generic features of the traditional *Bildungsroman:* belief in a coherent self (although not necessarily an autonomous one); faith in the possibility of development (although change may be frustrated, may occur at different stages and rates, and may be concealed in the narrative); insistence on a time span in which development occurs (although the time span may exist only in memory); and emphasis on social context (even as an adversary). Continuity, as well as significant difference, links our picture of developmental fiction to the conventions of the classic *Bildungsroman.*

The goal of this volume is twofold: to outline a female tradition and to demonstrate the diverse critical approaches it elicits. The texts discussed in this volume were not chosen to constitute a complete canon; rather, they illustrate the wide range of female stories of development. Our broad perspective preserves the cross-cultural context that the *Bildungsroman* has come to span, though our emphasis, by necessity, falls on the Anglo-American tradition in which women have most extensively appropriated the novel form, and this form in particular. Exploring a multinational tradition reveals similarities of women's experience across linguistic boundaries. To probe the tradition's formal boundaries, we include essays that examine the developmental narratives in fairy tales, short stories, and films. We also investigate gender boundaries through essays that include male representations of female development. These essays raise questions feminist critics have not yet resolved: do male versions of female experience differ intrinsically from female versions? Might the patterns of narrative convention and the varieties of individual perspective qualify gender distinctions?

The essays are arranged to delineate three historical stages. First, we consider nineteenth-century novels that redefine the tradition of the male *Bildungsroman.* The opening two essays, comparative in method and comprehensive in scope, establish two developmental paradigms. In "Spiritual *Bildung:* The Beautiful Soul as Paradigm," Marianne Hirsch discloses a female subplot within the prototypical male *Bildungsroman,* Goethe's *Wilhelm Meister's Apprenticeship.* The Beautiful Soul, Wilhelm's female counterpart, cuts herself off from the social world to foster a hermetically enclosed inner development. In her case, religion nurtures spiritual growth, but as this strategy of withdrawal evolves in more secular novels by Eliot, Fontane, and Chopin, it culminates inevitably in death. Susan J. Rosowski's "The Novel of Awakening," reprinted in this volume, is one of the first essays to have identified a female variation of the classic male form. Rosowski discovers the essence of female *Bildung* in a moment of simultaneous awakening to inner aspirations and social limitations; she traces the persistence of this pattern through Flaubert's *Madame Bovary,* Chopin's *The Awakening,* Cather's *A Lost Lady,* Smedley's *Daughter of Earth,* and Eliot's *Middlemarch.*

The next three essays in this section turn from general definitions to readings of important works by major nineteenth-century women novelists: one British and one American. In " 'Fairy-born and human-bred': Jane Eyre's Education in Romance," Karen E. Rowe criticizes the limited models that fairy tales offer women and demonstrates that Jane Eyre matures only by transcending fairy-tale scripts that are ultimately replaced in the novel with patterns of Christian romance. Jane Eyre, more than any other heroine, conforms to the male *Bildungsheld,* and perhaps for that reason her story reveals a balance between the developmental tensions of separation and relationship. Brontë does not allow her later heroine Lucy Snowe the same opportunities for social accommodation. In "The Reflecting Reader in *Villette,*" Brenda R. Silver argues that this heroine finds only a literary resolution to her dilemma. Lucy negotiates the conflict between concealing and revealing her unconventionality by constructing a narrative with two implied readers: one conventional, the other sympathetic to her unusual aspirations. Actual, not literary, sisterhood is central to Elizabeth Langland's "Female Stories of Experience: Alcott's *Little Women* in Light of *Work.*" Langland shows that *Work* can reveal *Little Women's* submerged plot, which uses the novel's multiple protagonists to challenge the overt emphasis on marriage as female destiny by lovingly depicting maternal and sororal relationships that foster adulthood.

We turn next to those twentieth-century works which continue to articulate a specifically female tradition, sometimes by revising major nineteenth-century novels by women. In "The Sisterhood of Jane Eyre and Antoinette Cosway," Elizabeth R. Baer explores *Jane Eyre* from the perspective of Jean Rhys's *Wide Sargasso Sea.* The common dreams of the survivor Jane and her double, the madwoman Bertha "Antoinette" Rochester, act as subversive narratives redefining the surface texts. Between these seemingly antithetical heroines Baer establishes a kinship that calls into question oppositions between bestiality and spirituality, madness and sanity, separation and relationship. Switching the context to the American West, Blanche H. Gelfant's "Revolutionary Turnings: *The Mountain Lion* Reread" traces the growing incompatibility between brother and sister, revealing telling similarities and differences between Stafford's novel and *The Mill on the Floss.* In *The Mountain Lion,* the brother's adoption of the frontier ethos divides him from his sister and finally destroys her. Unlike Maggie Tulliver's death, the accidental murder of Mollie Fawcett is not redeemed by the affirmation of a familial bond.

Whereas these two novels revise specific nineteenth-century texts, Virginia Woolf's *Mrs. Dalloway* more broadly revises the courtship plot central to nineteenth-century fiction. Using psychoanalytic theory, Elizabeth Abel in "Narrative Structure(s) and Female Development: The Case of *Mrs. Dalloway*" shows that the novel's retrospective developmental tale is located in a subtext that reveals the heroine's unresolved attachment to an adolescent female world. In the numerous volumes of *Children of Violence,* as Catharine R. Stimpson demonstrates in "Doris Lessing and the Parables of Growth," Doris Lessing sketches the totality of a female life that progresses from the traditional family to the cosmos, from childhood through maturity to death. Lessing's *Bildungsroman* offers the heroine an expanded outer and inner realm in which she perpetually reconstructs herself; the heroine's work centers not on career, but on achieving an integrated consciousness in a fragmented universe. Woolf's and Lessing's narrative choices illuminate the formal range of female developmental fiction in the twentieth century. While Woolf accentuates the tense interplay of multiple plots, making it the basis of self-conscious formal experimentation, Lessing creates an encyclopedic narrative that accords the female hero the scope and coherence traditionally reserved for the male protagonist of the nineteenth-century novel.

The essays in our final section on contemporary narrative expose many of the same oppositions and tensions that have shaped fictions of female development since the early nineteenth century; at the same time, they expand the genre's formal and thematic limits. In "Through the Looking Glass: When Women Tell Fairy Tales," Ellen Cronan Rose examines feminist revision of traditional fairy tales, those embryonic stories of development. She demonstrates how Anne Sexton, Olga Broumas, and Angela Carter reverse the gender biases inherent in the tales, which assign action and adventure to boys and quiescence and passivity to girls. Assertive, sexual, and active, these modern fairy-tale heroines are rescuers and fighters whose growth is enabled by strong female relationships. Like Rose, Mary Anne Ferguson discovers in contemporary fiction by women archetypal stories, specifically that of Psyche, in which she finds a model of a positive mother-daughter bond. In "The Female Novel of Development and the Myth of Psyche," Ferguson links Welty's "At the Landing," Alther's *Kinflicks,* and Jong's *The Adventures of Fanny Hackabout-Jones* as stories of trials from which women emerge triumphant. In "Exiting from Patriarchy," Bonnie Zimmerman identifies a variant of the novel of development, the lesbian coming-out story. Excluded from traditional female roles, the lesbian protagonist has greater mobility and freedom than the heterosexual woman: her story thus paradoxically approximates that of the nineteenth-century male *Bildungsheld.*

Female community, often the sustaining force for the lesbian heroine, becomes a goal in works that explore the development of a different political consciousness. In " 'Why are you afraid to have me at your side?': From Passivity to Power in *Salt of the Earth,*" Margo Kasdan reads this film of the 1950s as a developmental tale in which political community is the key to the heroine's personal growth. While the female community in *Salt of the Earth* is a liberating force, Esperanza's marriage hinders her developing sense of self. Yet the com-

mon struggle against racism enables the men to confront their own
prejudice, providing the couple and the community with a chance to
grow. The essays of Mary Helen Washington and Marta Peixoto continue to extend to other cultural contexts the exploration of family as
constraint. In "Plain, Black, and Decently Wild: The Heroic Possibilities of *Maud Martha*," Mary Helen Washington discusses the critical
neglect of even the strongest female heroes of Afro-American fiction.
In Washington's reading, however, Gwendolyn Brooks's Maud Martha,
even while she fails to achieve the freedom of an artistic identity, does
find a vital voice to express her sense of devaluation and her disappointment in love and marriage. Although her development "ends in
pregnancy and not a poem," Maud's artistic intentions and social consciousness do emerge, however covertly. Family ties also imprison the
protagonists in the short stories of the important Brazilian writer,
Clarice Lispector. In *"Family Ties:* Female Development in Clarice
Lispector," Marta Peixoto reads a collection of stories as segments of
a single developmental tale that places epiphanic moments of awakening against a return to family responsibility.

The final essay, Sandra Frieden's "Shadowing / Surfacing / Shedding: Contemporary German Writers in Search of a Female *Bildungsroman*," concludes the volume where it began, with the German tradition of the *Bildungsroman,* now revitalized and transformed by contemporary German writers who erase the boundaries between fiction
and autobiography. Through three novels by Ingeborg Bachmann,
Brigitte Schwaiger, and Verena Stefan, Frieden traces a progression
from restrictive gender roles to a futuristic vision of an unformed
female self.

The range of women writers—mainstream and minority, British,
American, European, and Latin American—who return to fictions of
development testifies to the enduring power of the genre. Honoring
this variety, our collection strives for an expansive rather than an
exclusive picture of a female tradition. Suggestive and multiple connections, rather than limited definitions of genre or national tradition,
assemble these essays into a collaborative description. Different critical
approaches join in identifying the formal and thematic traits that characterize the fiction of female development. In its course from the

earliest *Bildungsromane* to their contemporary transformations, the collection expands and modifies the notion of development in fiction to include distinctive female paradigms. Accentuating gender, the volume points toward a more dynamic, multivalent definition of a genre. By extending boundaries, *The Voyage In* enacts a voyage out.[26]

II NINETEENTH-CENTURY FORMULATIONS:

Changing a Tradition

MARIANNE HIRSCH

Spiritual *Bildung:* The Beautiful
Soul as Paradigm

Woman is the Sleeping Beauty, Cinderella, Snow White, she who
receives and submits. In song and story the young man is seen
departing adventurously in search of a woman; he slays the
dragon, he battles giants; she is locked in a tower, a palace, a
garden, a cave, she is chained to a rock, a captive, sound asleep;
she waits.

Simone de Beauvoir[1]

The struggle between Antigone and Creon represents that struggle
between elemental tendencies and established laws by which the
outer life of a man is gradually and painfully being brought into
harmony with his inner needs. Until this harmony is perfected,
we shall never be able to attain a great right without also doing
a great wrong.

George Eliot[2]

Beauvoir's image of the fictional heroine, of her passivity and confinement, suggests some of the difficulties surrounding the notion of female development in fiction. "In song and story," woman's role is to
wait: her life is static; ahistorical, the course it enacts is the antithesis
of *Bildung.* And yet we can find in Beauvoir's mininarrative a progression of sorts: woman's sleep and anticipation can be seen to outline a movement from tower to palace to garden to cave, a movement
opposite the young man's adventurous departure. Sleep and quiescence
in female narratives represent a progressive withdrawal into the symbolic landscapes of the innermost self. As such, they make possible a
form of development, albeit one-dimensional, far short of Goethe's
ideal formation of human totality. Excluded from active participation
in culture, the fictional heroine is thrown back on herself. The intense

inwardness that results allows her to explore and develop spiritually, emotionally, and morally, but often at the expense of other aspects of selfhood. In the traditional tale, female sleep is interrupted by the arrival of the prince who awakens the heroine to adulthood—that is, marriage—a reentry into external involvement and social activity, but only in the private sphere and in the role of one who continues to "receive and submit," who is willing to subordinate herself to husband and children. The tales to which Beauvoir refers do not consider the clash between the inner growth that might have occurred during the period of waiting and the subordinate and passive role woman is required to assume in her adult life.

It is this clash between outer laws and inner imperatives that Eliot sees as the crux of *Antigone*. In refusing the passivity attributed to her, in refusing marriage and allegiance to the state, Antigone brings that clash into the open. As she explains the overwhelming need to bury her brother, Antigone maintains she is following "the unwritten unalterable laws of God and heaven";[3] Creon, however, refusing to recognize them, calls them "woman's law." In following the laws of "the country of the dead,"[4] Antigone devotes herself and her life to affiliations from which she cannot and does not want to be free: the bond to her parents whose sins she must expiate and the bond to her brother or, as she calls him, her "mother's son."[5] She asserts the primacy of these "everlasting" ties over any others:

> O but I would not have done the forbidden thing
> For any husband or for any son,
> For why? I could have had another husband
> And by him other sons, if one were lost;
> But, father and mother lost, where would I get
> Another brother?[6]

In choosing old laws over new ones, family loyalties over civic duties, her (dead) brother over her (living) lover, childhood allegiances over adult loves, Antigone chooses death. Thereby she seeks a reunion with the dead family she prefers to a potential living one. Her affirmation of her "inner" self, of the past and her childhood, is both a form of rebellion and a form of extinction.[7]

Yet Antigone's resistance has broader consequences, challenging, as it does, the functioning of the state. For this reason, she must be punished. Ironically, her interment is but another version of the captivity that defines woman's lot; her premature death but an image for woman's interrupted growth. Calling her grave a "bridal bower,"[8] she merely exchanges one prison for another. Eliot interprets the choice with which Antigone is faced, the disjunction between the inner and the outer, as a cosmic disorder, one which affects all human endeavor, not only in Greek drama but also in the nineteenth-century novel, one which not only destroys Antigone but also diminishes Creon and the culture as a whole. Yet society recovers and Antigone's negation is ultimately directed against her own self.

Antigone's choice, circular and destructive as it may at first seem, can be seen as an affirmation of a deeper and more fundamental self, one that can find no actualization in the society Creon has constructed. Her choice can also be read as an emblem of woman's psychological needs as modern psychoanalysis defines them; it can be seen as a parallel of Freud's description, late in his career, of an older and more fundamental influence on female personality than the Oedipus conflict he once perceived as central for both men and women. Discovering the importance of what he called the "pre-Oedipus phase" in women, Freud was as surprised as archaeologists must have been upon discovering the Minoan-Mycenean civilizations behind the Greek.[9] Antigone's affirmation of the laws of her ancestors refers to pre-Oedipal laws, the laws of a civilization that was, at least according to myth, matriarchal, and in which child and parents might not have suffered the tragic separation that brings about Oedipus' double crime. For Antigone, symbolically, Creon represents the passage to patriarchy and post-Oedipal law: not only does he repudiate "woman's law," but he is also the father of the man she is engaged to marry.

Freud's outline of male and female psychological development is analogous to this historical progression from pre- to post-Oedipal law. *Antigone* demonstrates how devastating woman's refusal to follow that progression can be, how conflicted woman's developmental course is doomed to be. Even if she follows it from stage to stage, her strong attachment to the mother and to pre-Oedipal symbiosis, doubly repressed so that a transfer of attachment to the father and to other men can take place, is never fully superseded by adult heterosexual attachments, but remains a dominant influence on adult personality.[10] Recent feminist psychoanalytic theory views the pre-Oedipal phase, significantly different in impact for women than for men, as the source of all subsequent relationships, as the basis of female personality. The girl's relation to her mother, their interdependence and continuity, their lack of separation and differentiation, their fluid and permeable ego boundaries described in the work of Nancy Chodorow and other theorists,[11] are reflected not only in Antigone's choice of the "inner life" but in the struggles of nineteenth-century heroines, fellow victims of the disjunction defined in Eliot's essay.

This lack of "harmony" between the outer and the inner life, the dichotomization that propels man outside and confines woman inside, defines female development in the nineteenth-century novel. Woman's exclusively spiritual development is a death warrant, whether symbolically in the form of marriage and conformity, as for Cinderella, Snow White, and Sleeping Beauty, or literally in the form of resistance and willful withdrawal, as for Antigone. Using four works published between 1795 and 1899, I shall explore the outlines and implications of inner development both as the inevitable result of woman's quiescence and as the only area of development open to women in the nineteenth-century novel. The plot of inner development traces a discontinuous, circular path which, rather than moving forward, culminates in a return to origins, thereby distinguishing itself from the traditional plot outlines of the *Bildungsroman*. With this circularity, structures of repetition rather than structures of progression come to dominate the plot.

The most forceful, almost emblematic, illustration of how female development is channeled inward can be found in Goethe's "Confessions of a Beautiful Soul," an intratext contained in *Wilhelm Meister's Apprenticeship* (1795). Because Goethe's novel is generally considered the prototype of the *Bildungsroman*, it is important to find in it a paradigm for female *Bildung* as well as for male. The text very clearly reserves Wilhelm's type of development for young men, but it presents, in this self-contained insert, Wilhelm's female counterpart. Nonetheless, Goethe's novel is androcentric; Wilhelm's own development provides its central focus, and the story of the Beautiful Soul is important primarily in its reaction to Wilhelm.

The three subsequent novels I shall analyze illustrate important changes in the patterns that occur as a woman moves into the center of the text. George Eliot's *The Mill on the Floss* (1860), Theodor Fontane's *Effi Briest* (1895), and Kate Chopin's *The Awakening* (1899) are part of an alternative tradition of *female* novels of development, a tradition which, hitherto unrecognized as such, poses serious questions about the possibility of female *Bildung* in the nineteenth-century novel. Seen against the background of women's psychological needs (inner life) and the opportunities for women offered by the societies represented in these novels (outer life), these stories lead us to examine the conventions of the *Bildungsroman,* and the ability of these conventions to resolve the contradictions posed by these imperatives. A comparative study of this typically female pattern of growth demonstrates gender to be even more fundamental than national tradition in determining generic conventions.[12]

More fully than *Antigone,* these four novels dramatize the heroines' allegiance, both chosen and imposed, to a psychological reality that, in the imagery used to describe it, resembles the pre-Oedipal phase outlined in psychoanalytic writing. Attachment to this phase is characterized by fusion, fluidity, mutuality, continuity and lack of differentiation, as well as by the heroines' refusal of a heterosexual social reality that violates their psychological needs, a reality defined by images of fragmentation, separation, discontinuity, alienation, and self-denial. Faced with the break between psychological needs and social imperatives, literary convention finds only one possible resolution: the heroine's death.

How are we to read these deaths, however? It is here that feminist criticism faces one of its most difficult and value-laden questions. Seen in the context of the *Bildungsroman*'s valorization of progress, heterosexuality, social involvement, healthy disillusionment, "normality," adulthood, these deaths are pointless, violent, self-destructive. Yet if we look at what adulthood and maturity mean for the female protagonists of these texts, at the confinement, discontinuity, and stifling isolation that define marriage and motherhood, they do not present positive options. Traditional criticism sees the Beautiful Soul, Maggie, Effi, and Edna as neurotic women, afraid of adulthood and sexuality. To adopt this view is to ignore the limited possibilities offered by their societies. I submit that the heroines' allegiance to childhood, pre-Oedipal desire, spiritual withdrawal, and ultimately death is not neurotic but a realistic and paradoxically fulfilling reaction to an impossible contradiction. By showing death to be the only viable response to deep inner needs, these texts lead us to question the very values of *Bildung* itself, as it has traditionally been understood. Positing a different sexuality (one which erases the distinction between self and other, subject and object) and a different notion of self (marked by attachment rather than separation), this withdrawal, I would argue, is a renunciation in a limited sense only: in another, it emerges as a different kind of affirmation.[13]

These novels do lead us, however, to examine a pattern of spiritual development in male heroes, the *Künstlerroman*. Similarly dissatisfied and led to withdraw into the inner life, its male heroes find a solution that saves them from the heroines' death, the solution of art which is virtually unavailable to the young woman in the nineteenth-century novel. The story of female spiritual *Bildung* is the story of the potential artist who fails to make it.

"Confessions of a Beautiful Soul" is the story of a female development inside a male development, and it illustrates the possibilities open to the exceptional woman in Goethe's carefully constructed universe. The women in the novel, whether the weak Mignon and Aurelie, or the strong Therese and Nathalie, are either caretakers of men, nurturing mothers, or the victims of male inconstancy. Except for the mysterious free spirit Philine, none but the Beautiful Soul develops a sense of strength and independence. Yet she can do so only by negating the roles reserved for her and by withdrawing from all social intercourse.

The "Confessions," found at a turning point in the novel, play a crucial role in its structure. They provide the transition from Wilhelm's picaresque adventures in the theater, purely outward, to his *Bildung* by the Tower Society, which leads him to greater self-reflexiveness. In many ways, the Beautiful Soul is the antithesis of Wilhelm

who has an "aversion to reflection," is unable to write his own autobiography, and enjoys living in the present by repressing memory and
the past.[14] By balancing Wilhelm's "strangely *un*psychological"[15] nature, his growth through activity and social involvement, with the
Beautiful Soul's pure subjectivity and pure spirituality, Goethe creates
in his novel the human totality in which he believes. This equilibrium
is posited at the expense of the Beautiful Soul, however; she is no less
a victim of the novel's economy and ethic than the tragic Mignon with
her allegiance to the past and her pure emotion. The Beautiful Soul
represents one pole of human development—the purely subjective,
psychological, emotional, spiritual. This extreme is so deathly dangerous that it needs to be contained. Just as the Beautiful Soul herself
is ultimately isolated from the children of the next generation, so her
narrative is isolated from the novel, safely contained in its form as a
posthumous insert.

The Beautiful Soul's development cannot be described according
to the ideal standards of *Bildung* that Goethe's novel outlines, the
gradual organic unfolding of inner capacities, culminating in active
social involvement and civic responsibility. Her development is not
gradual, but consists of three violent transformations, three birth
processes from which, each time, she emerges as a new being. Instead
of developing her total personality, she concentrates only on her
spiritual, moral, and emotional side, to which even the intellect becomes subordinate. Her ultimate rebirth is also a death, a withdrawal
from any possibility of activity or social involvement. It is not a progression but a return to life before birth, to an undifferentiated, unbounded form of existence. Society lacks an arena where she might,
like Wilhelm, blossom and open, where she might have an effect.
Thrown back on herself, then, she takes her growth to the only fulfillment possible, the mystical fusion with God.

Her story, then, is a special kind of *Bildung*. It begins when at age
eight a nine months' illness, initiated by a severe hemorrhage, gives
her the occasion for introspection as well as education and awakens
her soul to "sensitivity and memory." We can see this illness as a
birth process, but it is a birth that takes her inward, to the quiescence
of a "snail which retreats into its shell." During the illness, she discovers suffering and love, and receives the help that enables her

"soul . . . to develop according to its own imperatives."[16] That help takes the form of a multifaceted education: her mother reveals the Bible to her, her father instructs her about nature, and her aunt reads her love stories and fairly tales. As she emerges from her illness, she is led to search for "creatures who would respond to [her] love" (p. 75). Her inability to find them in the external world fosters in her an "inclination for the invisible" (p. 75): God becomes her confidant—it is a God she invents according to her own needs for response and affirmation.

When she returns to social intercourse, she realizes that the roles reserved for her—fiancée, lover, wife, even daughter and sister—leave no room for that self she discovered and cultivated during her illness. Her quick intelligence and vivid curiosity prompt her father to call her his "defective son," and she quickly learns that women are excluded from all intellectual exchange. In spite of two negative experiences with men, the protagonist does fall in love under circumstances which, in their symbolic import, clearly delineate her subordinate female role. The second hemorrhage is not hers but her lover's and, as she rushes to help him, she too becomes covered with his blood, which she then ritualistically washes from her body. If this is an image of birth, it is a birth into love that casts her in the worldly role of caretaker of a man. This scene can also be read as a symbolic sexual initiation; yet as such, it underlines danger and violence. It is no accident that her fiancé's name is Narcissus—marriage, for women, involves total involvement with another and self-destruction. The protagonist comes to describe her engagement as a "bell jar which locked me into an airless room" (p. 93).

Gradually realizing that the development of her inner qualities— the sensitivity, memory, and love she discovered during her early illness—can take place only outside society, outside even the most intimate love and family relationships, the protagonist breaks off her engagement and gives up all worldly and sensual pleasures in favor of "exhilarating inner feelings" (p. 93). Her family, especially her mother who shares her longings, supports her in her withdrawal. The third (her second) hemorrhage fully convinces her to "give up life, in order to stay alive" (p. 100). This worldly death/spiritual birth coincides with "another test," her mother's slow and agonizing death, a parallel of her own childhood illness and a suggestion of the long and painful process that entry into the spiritual life entails.

The only context that can foster the Beautiful Soul's development is a religious and not a social one. Her withdrawal, even while being a strong statement of self-affirmation, must also be seen as a form of diminution. She literally becomes a beautiful soul, cut off from all human community, cut off as well from her own body: "It was as though my soul were thinking without the company of the body, it looked at the body as a strange being, as one looks at a piece of clothing" (p. 126). After this rebirth as a beautiful soul, she undergoes another full process of education: it begins with the realization of her total faith in God and the life of the soul, a realization that further isolates her because it is not shared in the same degree by her only friend, Philo, and because she finds it only in degraded form in the pietistic community she tries to join. This faith totally colors her subsequent learning: art, music, literature, and even nature are no more than occasions for self-reflection.

The Beautiful Soul's inwardness to an extreme self-absorption, to an inability to care for others that frightens those around her. Ironically, she herself has become a "Narcissus," forced into extreme self-involvement by the selflessness that is demanded of women.[17] The God she worships is in large measure her own imaginative creation, her "absent lover" and "invisible friend" (p. 103), the occasion to savor her "exhilarating feelings" and the outlet for her "inclination toward the invisible." As Beautiful Soul, she exists in a state where all boundaries between self and other, inner and outer, art and life, have been erased; her soul absorbs everything and becomes a "mirror . . . in which the external sun could be reflected" (p. 76). The withdrawal into the soul, her estrangement from her body, and the sense of fluidity and boundlessness that results from her withdrawal suggest a state of pre-Oedipal fusion, of romantic oneness with the universe, a lack of differentiation that keeps her separate from social adult existence.[18] This withdrawal is a return to her early illness, symbolically the state of gestation.

The Beautiful Soul's imaginative creation of a context capable of affirming her deepest needs is a creative response to impoverishing and diminishing social circumstances and not, as some critics have claimed, a neurotic form of regression, a flight from adult sexuality.[19] Like Antigone's, the Beautiful Soul's withdrawal is an active rebellion; ultimately, however, it is turned against herself. Like Antigone, she threatens society to such a degree that her uncle deems it necessary to keep her sister's children away from her. It is this enforced isolation that prompts her to write her confessions, as Suzanne Zantop says, *"against* the uncle, *against* society and *to* the children." We must see the heroine's adoption of the religious life as the only option; an accommodation to society would have meant an acceptance of herself as inferior and thus the antithesis of *Bildung.*

The Beautiful Soul does find in the Christian God an outlet for the values she discovered in her months of concentrated inwardness. Nevertheless, her resistance to woman's nurturing role takes her to an extreme of self-absorption, for which she pays a considerable price: she can exist only as a disembodied soul; no longer active in life, she is already living an afterlife. Her spiritual growth is a physical death; the independence and self-determination she gains is bought at the expense of relationship and community. The only form of communication she can establish is a posthumous one, through her writing. And here she is confined to play the role of other to Wilhelm's self: here, her voice is confined and contained, balanced in such a way as to make her experience no more than the example of one extreme of human development. By "killing" the emotional Mignon and the spiritual Beautiful Soul, by elevating the Amazon mother, Nathalie, as an ideal of femininity, Goethe protects society from the subversive extremes into which women are channeled. Pushed into absolute subjectivity, the exceptional woman is cut off from social intercourse; pushed into the role of posthumous confessor, her narrative remains virtually separate from the rest of the plot.

The Beautiful Soul's development, real and full as it is, must be circular if viewed within the context of the values that the entire novel upholds. Following the lure of the invisible, she both finds and loses herself, both affirms and dissolves her existence. Like Antigone, she is buried alive, confined in the structures of her inner self and in the structures of Goethe's novel.

Thus the "Confessions" situate themselves squarely on one side of the dialectic that defines the German *Bildungsroman* and preoccupies

German literary theory in the late eighteenth and throughout the nineteenth century: the debate between poetry and prose, the ideal and the everyday, the potential self and the limited, realized self, reflection and action, the symbolic and the realistic.[20] Whereas the traditional (male) German *Bildungsroman* generally (and *Wilhelm Meister* in particular) finds itself uneasily poised between the two poles of this dialectic, the "Confessions" demonstrate the rewards and the dangers of being locked into one—absolute inwardness, eternal potentiality, total "disponibilité," unlimited by the constraints of everyday experience. In the more realistic English and American traditions of the novel of development, the pattern of spiritual withdrawal seems all the more extreme.

The impasse of the Beautiful Soul exists for many nineteenth-century fictional heroines, but the religious option does not. In a secular context, inner *Bildung* proves to be a death warrant, not only metaphorically as for Goethe's Beautiful Soul, but literally. George Eliot's *The Mill on the Floss* provides a feminocentric counterpart to *Wilhelm Meister's Apprenticeship,* yet Maggie's development follows the paradigm of the Beautiful Soul. Whereas for the Beautiful Soul spiritual development carried to an extreme becomes dangerously antisocial and subversive, for Maggie Tulliver, it leads only to *self*-destruction. And, in the absence of a religious context, her worldly death is unredeemed by spiritual rebirth. In the absence, as well, of a surrounding narrative that balances the female extreme, her self-destruction becomes all the more unrelenting. Yet even Maggie's death is presented by the author as a different form of affirmation and redemption.

We see the absurd limitations of Maggie's social possibilities in an early scene where she is asked to explain a picture from Defoe's *History of the Devil* of an old woman submerged in water:

They've put her in to find out whether she's a witch or no, and if she swims, she's a witch, and if she's drowned—and killed, you know—she's innocent, and not a witch, but only a poor silly old woman. But what good would it do her then, you know, when she was drowned? Only, I suppose, she'd go to heaven, and God would make it up to her.[21]

Religious salvation means little to Maggie. The exceptional woman is doomed to destruction in any case: if she dares to transgress, to be a

witch, she will be burned at the stake; if she tries to conform, like Maggie, she will drown and die unredeemed.[22]

Like the Beautiful Soul's confessions, *The Mill on the Floss* allows us to compare a male and a female development, and thereby to assess the possibilities open to the exceptional young woman. Both women are unusually bright and curious; both learn that society will not reward them for being, as Mr. Tulliver calls it, "too 'cute." Both experience unusually strong emotional and spiritual desire in their childhood; both respond to the lure of an invisible spiritual realm, which in both novels is described in Edenic, paradisal imagery. Both, when thwarted, turn inward, developing a powerful subjective life ruled by memory, imaginative invention, spiritual hunger. In fact, if one were to trace Maggie's development, it would be the story of an inner growth, consisting of her unconditional adoration of her brother, her attic games, her flight to the gypsies, her adoption of Thomas à Kempis's program of renunciation. The landscape of the Red Deeps, where she walks in her most unhappy hours, best describes the disparity between the impoverished outer world and the rich inner world she creates:

. . . visions of robbers and fierce animals haunting every hollow. But now it has the charm for her which any broken ground, any mimic rock and ravine, have for the eyes that rest habitually on the level. [p. 260]

Maggie's inner life rests on one dominant feeling, her strong attachment to her brother Tom, an attachment she never transcends: "The first thing I ever remember in my life is standing with Tom by the side of the Floss, while he held my hand: everything before that is dark to me" (p. 268). That special relationship is already tainted when the novel begins; it is colored by the traditional sex roles Maggie and Tom are expected to assume and which separate them from one another. They are further separated by their different natures, Tom's pragmatism and Maggie's creativity. The lasting power of childhood and the desire for continuity derive from the positive memories of pre-Oedipal fusion, Maggie and Tom holding hands by the river (in the womb), as well as from the frustrating memories of pain, disappointment, and distance between them.[23] The past, which remains Maggie's prime value and motivating force throughout the novel, is remembered both as the time when "the outer world seemed only an extension of our own personality," when "joys were vivid" (p. 135), and when discipline, self-denial, and the duty to renounce her impulses and desires were paramount. For her desire to repair the loss, to reunite what has been severed, Maggie is made to feel wrong, immature.

Although, like the Beautiful Soul's, Maggie's education consists of a series of abrupt breaks and transformations that violate deeply her need for continuity, the quality of these changes is radically different: Eliot highlights the pain that is absent in Goethe's novel, the conflicts inherent in renunciation and withdrawal from the outer life. Maggie's loss of her home, her loss of Tom and of Philip, and finally her renunciation of Stephen will leave her depleted: no amount of spiritual and moral growth can compensate for what feels like death: "It is like death. I must part with everything I cared for when I was a child" (p. 263). Whereas the Beautiful Soul is protected from temptation, sheltered from suffering, and rewarded with salvation, Maggie is exposed to conflict and pain at every stage. Inner growth can only be bought at the cost of great anguish.

Like the Beautiful Soul, Maggie is traditionally seen by critics as neurotic, unnaturally attached to home and her brother, afraid of adulthood and sexuality. But Maggie's self-denial is a long habit, her only behavior ever rewarded, and ironically it becomes her only form of self-assertion. Maggie has gradually internalized all the crippling social forces that have taught her to repress and deny her full humanity. Her childhood anger, rage, and frustration, turned against herself, end up destroying her.[24]

The values she has adopted and internalized leave her only one option at the end of the novel, to turn against her desires by fleeing from Stephen to home: yet ironically that step of moral strength, which affirms the values of home and family, loyalty and tradition, is not recognized by the world of St. Ogg's. Eliot allows Maggie a moral *Bildung* based on self-sacrifice and renunciation; St. Ogg's insists that women must, like Mrs. Tulliver, like Lucy, simply *be*—no growth is allowed them at all: "for the happiest women, like the happiest nations, have no history" (p. 335).

The tremendous incongruity of that position in a world where all the conventional life-styles and traditions are crumbling is made apparent by Maggie's adult role models—Aunt Moss who is destitute and Mrs. Tulliver who is totally unable to cope with change in her life. The only strong woman is the unlikable and sterile Aunt Glegg, who is also the only one to understand the strength and the suffering required by Maggie's return. The lack of harmony between the outer and the inner life has here reached cosmic enough proportions to make survival for women like Maggie impossible.

Whereas the Beautiful Soul has to cut herself off from family and community ties in order to find self-actualization in the spiritual life, Maggie's spiritual development derives from her bond with her family. Self-denial and renunciation are strategies by which she can affirm the family and tradition over herself. Yet when both family and society reject her efforts and when religious salvation no longer provides a reward, Maggie drowns like the poor silly old woman in Defoe's book.

Maggie's return home constitutes a circular development like that of the Beautiful Soul: the inner landscapes she has explored and in which she has become lost have found no actualization in her work or in the love of Stephen. Their *only* outward analogue is home. Home has become her religion: her childhood is described as an "Eden before the seasons were divided and when the starry blossoms grew side by side with the ripening peach" (p. 166); her decision to leave Stephen is based on "memories, and affections, and longings after perfect goodness, that have such a strong hold on me" (p. 418), and which constitute "the divine voice within us" (p. 419); home itself is "the sanctuary where sacred relics lay" (p. 420). On her return to that home, Maggie is turned out by the brother she adores, yet accepted by her mother, who, despite her incomprehension, proves the depth of the value of home and family, the strength of a tie that precedes and supersedes even Maggie's bond to Tom. In fact, Maggie's final return to the Mill is a return to her mother and to Tom, a desire to save both and to find both.

Seen in this context, Maggie's drowning looks like the only possible fulfillment of her subjective development—like Antigone's resistance to social forces that deny family, links with the past, and woman's full humanity. In their death by drowning in the boundless river, Maggie and Tom return to a pre-Oedipal fusion untainted by those forces: "brother and sister had gone down in an embrace never to be parted: living through again in one supreme moment the days when they had clasped their little hands in love, and roamed the daisied fields together" (p. 456). Divided by social convention from the deepest parts of themselves, they find that "in their death they were not divided" (p. 457). The irony of this line underscores the ironic conjunction of social defeat and spiritual affirmation in the novel.

It is remarkable that Eliot should describe this accidental death in such positive ways. Death might, in fact, provide the only means to reverse the growth into limitation and subordination that is reserved for women "in song and story" and in nineteenth-century society. This is the argument of both Gillian Beer and Nancy Miller, who look at the circular plot of *The Mill on the Floss* as the creation of an extravagant and unusual, typically female, narrative logic. As Beer puts it:

George Eliot chose always to imprison her favorite women—Dinah, Maggie, Dorothea. . . . But at the end of *Mill* her obduracy fails. She allows Maggie the fulfillment of immersion and self-denial, the obliteration of self in familial love. . . . She allows them [the unassuageable longings of her heroine] fulfillment in a plot which simply glides out of the channeled sequence of social growth and makes literal the expansion of desire. . . . For women under oppression such needs can find no real form within an ordering of plot which relies upon sequence, development, the understanding and renunciation of the past, the acceptance of the determined present.[25]

Seen in this manner, the circular developments of Maggie and the Beautiful Soul lead us to question the equation of *Bildung* with separation, autonomy, social involvement. Maggie, especially, illustrates a different form of development—rooted in childhood, marked by her insistence on continuity, located in the inner self, culminating in death, it is nevertheless a development of a total individual, spiritual, moral, intellectual, emotional, even sexual. Maggie's values, like Antigone's, profoundly challenge the values of her culture.

Unlike *The Mill on the Floss, Effi Briest* is traditionally read not as a novel of development, but as a social novel (*Gesellschaftsroman*), as

Fontane's indictment of Prussian morality that lovelessly destroys the adulterous heroine, as his articulation of the conflict between natural and social law. Even though Fontane uses Effi to make a larger social point, her circular progression, culminating in extinction, does articulate a development that follows the paradigm of inner growth and return similar to that of the Beautiful Soul and Maggie Tulliver.

Unlike Maggie and the Beautiful Soul, Effi is exceedingly conventional; she values money, nobility, and diversion. Still, at the beginning of the novel, Effi possesses a very special, perhaps exceptional, zest for life, as well as a powerful and active imagination and a passionate nature. Her boyish physical activity is described as a yearning for freedom; she refuses to behave like a lady. She is childlike not only in her joyful play with her friends but also in her powerful attachment to her home, her parents, and her girlfriends. In the novel's first scene, we find Effi, aged sixteen, and her mother sitting in the garden quilting an altar rug: her attachment to home remains, as for Maggie, a kind of religion for Effi.

The marriage proposal she receives on that day constitutes a violent break in this idyll. Again, for Effi, growth is not a gradual process but a violent transformation. The interruption of her childish games recalls Hades' rape of Persephone: as Persephone innocently picks flowers with her friends, he abducts her to the underworld to be his wife and queen. As in the myth, marriage is a form of death in *Effi Briest*. This is symbolically obvious even to her husband, Instetten, as Effi, inside the dark house, is now unable to respond to her girlfriends' sunny call to play: "Come on, Effi!" Instetten's stern, unloving nature, the bleak setting of the distant Kessin where the couple go to live, the "underworld" atmosphere Effi encounters or creates there reinforce the parallel between marriage and death. Effi's marriage contrasts drastically with the dreams of exotic bedroom screens and red lamps that preoccupied her during her engagement. Instead, another dream world emerges, one ruled by fear and disappointment rather than by sensuality. In her imagination, the history of her house takes on ominous proportions, as do the cook's creepy black hen, the uncanny stuffed shark and crocodile in the entry way, and especially the Chinaman who died of a broken heart and is said to haunt the house. Here is the underside of Effi's yearnings for the exotic; yet, terrifying as she finds the spook, she still prefers it to the desperate loneliness and emptiness of her Kessin life that more and more directs her inward.

Effi's affair with Major Crampas is a symptom of her ennui and not of passionate love. She succumbs to him unwillingly, sinking as her carriage sinks into the slough. Her image of a "God's wall" of snow, which protects a poor widow from the fierce enemy she fears, indicates Effi's feeling of helplessness, her desire for protection. Yet the enemy Effi fears is both within and without, in herself as well as in Crampas: "She was strongly affected by all that was mysterious and forbidden."[26] Sexuality itself is described through Crampas's narratives of Heine poems as violent, dangerous, deathly. The protection Effi desires and desperately needs, however, was lost when she was so suddenly separated from her home at a point when she was yet unequipped for the strong conflicts and utter desolation of adult life, unprepared for its static and uneventful sameness.

The parental home, as Effi continues to maintain, comes first for her; even long after her marriage and the birth of her child, it remains the seat of her attachments and the object of her desire, the source of her inner world. As such, it is never superseded by her attachments to either husband, lover, or child. In fact, the inner longing for home motivates all of Effi's behavior. Yet, like Maggie's, Effi's relationship to her home is a problematic one. Her father, like Mr. Tulliver, is loving but highly ineffectual. (Even their expressions of helplessness are similar: Tulliver's "It's a puzzling world" and Briest's "That's *too* big a subject.") Her mother fails to understand her dissatisfactions; in fact, her mother is very much the cause of Effi's premature and mistaken marriage. *She* was initially in love with Instetten and, in suggesting so emphatically that Effi accept his proposal ("and if you don't say no, which I can hardly imagine my clever Effi doing, then by the age of twenty you'll have gone as far as others have at forty. You'll go much further than your mother" [p. 24]), she insists that her daughter both live out *her* fantasy and repeat her own decision of marrying a man who is suitable but whom she does not love. Mother and daughter are at the same time similar—Effi maintains that her vitality is her mother's legacy to her—and vastly different—Frau Briest has learned to control her energy by a strict and highly conventional demeanor. Her mother's stern distance and high ambitions leave Effi forever longing for warmth, nurturance, and understanding. She writes numerous frank letters about her fears and loneliness, letters that evoke from her parents no more than a helpless sadness. Effi is thus a Persephone who, lacking Demeter's protection, must fend for herself in the social underworld.

In response to her longings and fears, Effi finds Roswitha, for her the good natural maternal presence, untouched by the unnatural conventions that rule Frau Briest's maternal behavior. Effi meets Roswitha in the cemetery and talks to her about childbirth: acquainted with birth and death, Roswitha has the power to assuage Effi's fears. In hiring Roswitha to be her child's nurse, Effi also hires her to be her own mother: Effi immediately insists that Roswitha share her bedroom and removes Instetten to another room. Even more significant than this substitution is the playful substitution of Roswitha for Crampas; when Effi goes out walking to meet her lover, she always arranges to meet Roswitha as a pretext. They never meet, of course. In fact, nothing about the meetings between the lovers is revealed but this playful failure to find Roswitha. This ellipsis suggests that Roswitha, or the mother, is the actual object of Effi's desire. Both Instetten and Crampas are mere stand-ins for a much deeper longing for the maternal nurturance of home. Her preoccupation with it keeps Effi eternally confined to an inner landscape.

The misdirected nature of Effi's affair makes its discovery seven years later seem all the more meaningless. Yet, Effi's resulting banishment from marriage, motherhood, and her parental home, followed by her failed attempt to lead an independent life in Berlin, constitutes a second violent break in her development and occasions a gradual and progressive extinction. Imprisoned in her small apartment, devoid of any activity and any company except that of Roswitha, Effi spends most of her days staring at the cemetery outside her window. Society has ostracized her: there is no place for the adulterous woman. When she is almost dead, the only possible step forward is also a step backward: her return to Hohen-Cremmen. Her father's brief telegram, "Come, Effi," recalls her girlfriends' call to childhood games and Demeter's retrieval of Persephone from the underworld. Whereas Persephone's return is cyclical, Effi's is total; the novel's last scenes are almost identical and therefore ironic repetitions of the first. Wearing the same dress, swinging as high as she can, Effi resumes a childlike life in her parental family. At her age, however, that existence can only be fulfilled in death.

On her deathbed Effi confesses that the days of her final feverish illness were her best days. This acknowledged valorization of the inner over the outer life constitutes Effi's most meaningful *Bildung*. As she spends hours gazing at the stars, Effi expresses a longing for a heavenly home, one that precedes and surpasses even Hohen-Cremmen. It is not a longing for Christian redemption, but for a mystical fusion with the night. According to the text, this gazing into the cool night ends up killing her, but her death is described in unequivocally positive terms as a stillness, a feeling of liberation, peace.

Not the active rebellion of Antigone, not the decisive withdrawal of the Beautiful Soul, nor the heroic effort of Maggie, Effi's death is a slow extinction. And yet, it results from the same dislocation, the same cosmic disorder as the other three "deaths." Here, the "lack of harmony" between the inner and the outer life is defined as a disjunction between natural instinct and cultural codes and imperatives. Even the most intimate family relationships are tainted by this conflict: the Briests' confusion between parental love and social disapproval indirectly causes Effi's death.

In this context, Effi's forgiveness of Instetten, who most clearly exemplifies this disjunction, emerges as a device that weakens her own resistance to the values she ends up underwriting. In forgiving Instetten, she recognizes that her own allegiance to natural laws, to home and parents, that her longings for pre-Oedipal symbiosis are regressive and antisocial, and that only Instetten's cold and calculated ambition can serve the advancement of this society. Realizing that she herself has only death to offer, Effi is willing to let him raise their daughter: her influence, like the Beautiful Soul's, is dangerous to children. This recognition, however, is most ironic in relation to Effi's own mother who, subscribing fully to the codes of the Prussian culture, failed to produce a daughter who could survive in it. In letting Effi forgive (Antigone never does), Fontane neutralizes the potentially subversive power of her own spiritual development. This scene clearly demonstrates the novel's primary focus: not Effi herself, but Effi as an example. In this male-authored text, the woman serves as the optimal illustration of social injustice and deterioration.

Effi's death, like that of the other heroines, has been prepared by her "inclination for the invisible," by the inward direction of her life and growth and by her exclusively subjective activity. In this novel, too, female plots are described as static; the conventional romantic *Geschichte,* like that of her mother's youth told by Effi to her friends, is defined by renunciation, self-denial. Effi faces her death with equanimity, convinced, like the man in the anecdote she recounts, that should she be called away from the dinner table prematurely, she would "not really miss anything" (p. 265). If her only active participation is not in the outer but in the inner life, her early death is not an interruption but a culmination. This type of female plot becomes a reversal of the conventional male plot, as female *Bildung* is no longer marked by progress or linear direction, but by circularity and dissolution. In her ability to recover her interrupted past, Effi, like Maggie, is allowed a reversal of the conventional plot, but that reversal is an interruption of plot.

With death as her only possible fulfillment, Effi is clearly a victim; like the ancient pre-Christian victims who were sacrificed on the stones that so horrify her when she visits the Hertasee, Effi is the sacrificial victim of the conflict between "elemental tendencies and established laws." The removal of Effi leaves society intact.

Edna Pontellier in Kate Chopin's *The Awakening* is the oldest of the four protagonists discussed here: she is twenty-eight, has been married for several years, and is the mother of two children when the novel begins. Unlike the other three heroines, her familial attachments are to her children and to an extent to her husband more than to her family of origin. And yet, here too we find the pattern of inward growth, return, and eventual death. Chopin defines with great clarity the conflict that has ruled all the novels between "that outward existence which conforms" and "the inward life which questions."[27] In the course of the novel, Edna moves from this "dual life" more and more into the "inward life," primarily because her discovery of the inner self makes conformity more and more unbearable. Conformity, it is clear, would entail being a "mother-woman": "they were women who idolized their children, worshipped their husbands, and esteemed it a privilege to efface themselves as individuals and grow wings as ministering angels" (p. 8).

Edna's process of awakening, both to social limitation and to spiritual wealth, is connected to the sea, to her childhood, and to the love of Robert, who first makes her conscious of her soul by eliciting feelings of love. By channeling her more and more inward, the process of awakening ironically leads her to death: "A certain light was beginning to dawn dimly within her,—a light which, showing the way, forbids it" (p. 13). Edna can find no external person or place that could contain or comprehend her newfound self, and, ultimately, it is her utter solitude that kills her.

The awakening process is immediately defined as a movement inward and backward. Beginning with "dreams, thoughtfulness . . . shadowy anguish . . . tears," it is connected to Edna's childhood, when she "had lived her own small life all within herself" (p. 14). One particular image characterizes her childhood feelings, that of a small girl walking through a huge, seemingly endless green meadow "idly, aimlessly, unthinking and unguided" (p. 17). Edna relives this feeling of boundlessness during her summer at the seashore and especially during the night she ventures out to test her swimming skills, "reaching out for the unlimited in which to lose herself" (p. 30). This decisive moment is followed and deepened by the trip to Belle-Isle, her fairy tale sleep there, her response to Mlle. Reisz's music, which "sets her spirit free" (p. 84), her progressive disengagement from all social intercourse, even that of her husband and children, and her almost complete solitude.

Chopin highlights the deathly dangers of such pure subjectivity, dangers of dissolution, of absorption into the boundless. During her night swim, Edna hears the voice of death and must gather all her strength to return to shore. The danger is that to which the two lovers in Edna's anecdote (or dream) succumb, that of paddling· out to sea, never to return, of "drifting into the unknown" (p. 76). Edna, too, ends up succumbing to this danger, primarily because she loses touch with the outer life that could sustain her if it allowed her to actualize some inner longings. Her move to the "pigeon house" is such an at-

tempt, as is her work as a painter. Yet Edna depends primarily on
love, and when Robert so dismally fails to understand her, when she
sees, as Adele Ratignolle gives birth, that she is separated from and
yet attached to and constrained by her children, she seeks fusion and
freedom in the ocean where she first experienced it.

Edna's suicide has been the subject of much critical controversy. It
is a more active death than Maggie's or Effi's. It responds to more
varied needs—emotional, physical, spiritual. Yet it is described in
highly ambivalent terms. Chopin juxtaposes the "bird with broken
wing . . . reclining, fluttering, circling disabled down, down to the
water" (p. 124) with "some new-born creature, opening its eyes in a
familiar world that it had never known" (p. 124). In her conscious
ambivalence, Chopin skirts the issue of whether the suicide is a triumph or a failure. What she does emphasize very clearly, however,
is that it is a repetition and therefore a culmination of Edna's initial moment of awakening, a logical outcome of her inward growth.
The feelings of suicide are identical to those that define the initial
awakening:

The voice of the sea is seductive; never ceasing, whispering, clamoring,
murmuring, inviting the soul to wander for a spell in the abyss of solitude;
to lose itself in mazes of inward contemplation.

The voice of the sea speaks to the soul. The touch of the sea is sensuous,
enfolding the body in its soft, close embrace. [pp. 14, 123-24]

By means of this total circularity, the novel clearly suggests that
Edna's discovery of the inner life can lead to only one ending in this
society—her premature death. Edna's suicide is preceded by a feeling
of ennui similar to Effi's; she clearly sees that the only possible plot
for her would consist of endless repetition of frustration and passionless lovers. Death becomes an escape from female plot and the only
possible culmination of woman's spiritual development.

As she dies, Edna returns to her Kentucky home, hears the barking
of her dog and the hum of the bees. Childhood, in all these texts
about women, is not so much the beginning of a continuous progression, the source of a future, but a presence to return to, necessary precisely because female development is so fragmented and discontinuous. "The past . . . offered no lesson which she was willing to heed"

(p. 49). The absence of plot and progression locks woman into an endless moment from which she is incapable of emerging; beginning and end, origin and destination are identical. "But the beginning of things, of a world especially, is necessarily vague, tangled, chaotic, and exceedingly disturbing. How few of us ever emerge from such beginning! How many souls perish in its tumult!" (p. 14).

The novel does suggest, however tentatively, one possible means of avoiding death—the transformation of inner development into an artistic career. Of the four heroines, Edna is the only one who has a model of a female artist among her acquaintances. Yet Mlle. Reisz provides more of a deterrent than an incentive: personally, she is unpleasant and an outcast; in her music she interprets and improvises but is not an original creator. The life of the artist she represents is lonely, asexual, cut off from all human connection, an impossible one for Edna, whose awakening makes her long precisely for closer human contact.

Even more important than the absence of positive models for an artistic career, however, is the barrier that motherhood erects. Mme. Ratignolle, the "mother-woman," is at the opposite pole from Mlle. Reisz, and Edna finds herself between the two. Immediately preceding her suicide, Edna assists Adele in the birth of her child and is reminded to "think of the children." Watching the physical act of childbirth acts precisely as such a reminder for Edna:

The children appeared before like antagonists who had overcome her; who had overpowered and sought to drag her into the soul's slavery for the rest of her days. But she knew a way to elude them. [p. 123]

As she observes the birth, Edna comes to see herself as the originator of life; for her children she is the equivalent of the ocean in which she longs to be immersed. Birth (separation) is a "scene of torture"; suicide re-members the severed body. Paradoxically, Edna eludes her children by becoming herself a child as well as a mother in her fusion with the ocean.[28]

Edna's dislocation, like that of the other three heroines, is certainly not uncommon in the Romantic and post–Romantic traditions. It is not dissimilar to the Romantic poet's *mal du siècle,* to Fabrice del Dongo's withdrawal, Frederic Moreau's unease, Wordsworth's longing, Tonio

Kröger's ambivalence; even more closely does it approach the retreat of Marcel and Stephen Dedalus. Lukács calls this kind of novel a novel of disillusionment, where the inner self seems so much larger and richer than the outer.[29] The male texts are, like the female ones, governed by a longing for home, family, and childhood, by similar dissatisfactions with society and by the discovery of a rich inner life. Yet, with one or two exceptions, out of that inner richness emerges the power of creation. The male self, centered in the creative imagination which has the power to absorb, internalize, even to generate the outer world, need not be destroyed by inwardness. All of these writers emphasize the dangers of an immersion in the imagination—the danger of self-dissolution, be it through Wordsworth's Nature, which reclaims Lucy and the Boy of Winander, or through the dizzying freedom of imaginative creation, the absolute solipsism that blurs all boundaries in Joyce and Proust.

The four female novels I have analyzed follow to a point the pattern of the *Künstlerroman,* of the young artist's withdrawal into the inner life, which leads to a discovery of his vocation. Art offers a solution to the lack of "harmony" between "the outer life of man" and "his inward needs." For the young male artist, a retreat into the inner life leads to an organized creativity that is inconceivable for our four heroines. Marcel, Stephen, and Tonio gain in their process of introspection a knowledge and insight that can illuminate the "lack of harmony" for others. They are able to generate, from this knowledge, forms that can be actualized, communicated, shared. Art and the imagination provide the only means to transcend the dislocation that plagues all these characters. The celebration of the imagination is the celebration of individual power over otherness, over an unknowable nature and a dissatisfying social world. Stephen Dedalus, at the end of his *Bildung,* can depart on an adventure of the imagination, confident in his ability to "forge in the smithy of [his] soul, the uncreated conscience of [his] race."[30]

Just as religious salvation is unavailable to Eliot's, Fontane's, and Chopin's secular protagonists, so they are barred from the redemption of art. All three of these heroines are potential artists, yet all find that their artistic activity provides no way out of the inwardness into which they have withdrawn and in which they become lost. As Gilbert and

Gubar suggest, "Euridyce . . . abandoned in the labyrinthine caverns of Hades . . . is really (like Virginia Woolf's 'Judith Shakespeare') the woman poet who never arose from the prison of her 'grave cave.' "[31] Silent, Euridyce, who was killed on the very day of her marriage, has to depend on Orpheus's art to help her escape from the underworld. Yet his backward glance, his imprisoning look, kills her with even more finality than the viper's bite, condemning her to an eternal stay in the underground cavern. Orpheus alone has the medium through which he can both enter and return from the world of the dead, both gain insight and express what he has learned. Euridyce might inspire Orpheus's song (like his mother who is a muse), but she has no voice with which to assimilate and tell her own highly discontinuous story.

Like Euridyce, our four nineteenth-century protagonists remain forever trapped and lost in their underworld caverns. For them, inwardness affords no sustained insight, introspection no more than glimpses of self-knowledge.[32] Subjectivity is not an assertion of individual identity and imaginative power, but a dissolution, an extinction. The inner life thus becomes not the locus of knowledge and power but the place, in the words of Jane Austen, of "feelings unemployed."[33]

Orpheus himself, however, is also destroyed, in spite of the power of his song. Propelled outward into the world while Euridyce remains trapped in the underground maze, he is no more able to survive this tragic dichotomization than she is. It could be argued, in fact, that the male protagonists of these four novels, unlike the artist heroes of the *Künstlerroman,* are just as much the victims of the lack of harmony between the inner and outer life and that, although they are better able to survive it, their development is also stunted by that disjunction. Haemon dies without Antigone's allegiance to the past, Creon survives but is severely diminished. Tom Tulliver dies together with Maggie, also a victim of the past, although the reimmersion in it surely is less meaningful to him than to Maggie. Baron Instetten survives and achieves social success, but his momentous personal loss leaves him tired and cynical. Robert Lebrun remains the ineffectual and uncomprehending slave of convention. Even Wilhelm Meister, the prototypical hero of the *Bildungsroman,* fails to develop fully his spiritual side.

Neither the male nor the female protagonists of these novels are able to resolve a crippling dichotomization. Yet, in spite of the constraints posed by the cosmic disorder Eliot diagnoses, in spite of the limited possibilities offered by literary conventions that cannot transcend this disorder while allowing the heroine to survive, the female protagonists of these four nineteenth-century texts do achieve an individual, highly unconventional form of fulfillment. In the words of Nancy Miller, they "transcend the perils of plot with a self-exalting dignity."[34] Unless the tragic division of male from female plot, male from female development, is overcome, such dignity is as much as we as readers of the nineteenth-century novel can reasonably desire.[35]

SUSAN J. ROSOWSKI

The Novel of Awakening

The *Bildungsroman* or apprenticeship novel is defined by its theme. It is "a novel which recounts the youth and young manhood of a sensitive protagonist who is attempting to learn the nature of the world, discover its meaning and pattern, and acquire a philosophy of life and 'the art of living.' "[1] The definition and the examples that follow it are notably masculine, omitting developments of this theme in literature by and about women—the theme of awakening. The novel of awakening is similar to the apprenticeship novel in some ways: it also recounts the attempts of a sensitive protagonist to learn the nature of the world, discover its meaning and pattern, and acquire a philosophy of life, but she must learn these lessons as a woman. This difference results in other differences between the novel of awakening and the apprenticeship novel. The subject and action of the novel of awakening characteristically consist of a protagonist who attempts to find value in a world defined by love and marriage. The direction of awakening follows what is becoming a pattern in literature by and about women: movement is inward, toward greater self-knowledge that leads in turn to a revelation of the disparity between that self-knowledge and the nature of the world. The protagonist's growth results typically not with "an art of living," as for her male counterpart, but instead with a realization that for a woman such an art of living is difficult or impossible: it is an awakening to limitations. These elements of the novel of awakening may be illustrated by five representative novels: *Madame Bovary, The Awakening, My Mortal Enemy, Daughter of Earth,* and *Middlemarch.*

Flaubert's *Madame Bovary* is a prototype for the novel of awakening. Emma Bovary, a character who has learned the nature of the world through romantic fiction, struggles to acquire an art of living in accord with those fictional values.[2] Conflict is largely internal, between two selves: an inner, imaginative self of private value is at odds

Reprinted by kind permission of the editors of *Genre,* a quarterly published by the University of Oklahoma.

with an outer, conventional self of social value. Movement is from an initial childhood separation between the two selves to an illusion of synthesis in marriage, followed by an awakening to the impossibility of such a union and a return to separation. Finally, like many other protagonists in the novel of awakening, Emma Bovary is essentially passive. Tension results from the reader's awareness of the impossibility—even undesirability—of her efforts: we ask what will happen to Emma Bovary, not what will she bring about, and we measure her greatness—her soul—by the extent to which she awakens to impossibilities.

In her childhood, Emma Rouault experienced a separation between two basic elements in herself—her private, imaginative self and her public, social self. Early she began to live a dual life: at school, the outward asceticism of a convent was at odds with inner excesses of religious mysticism and romantic dreams; at home, the realism and simplicity of farm life conflicted with dreams of luxury and bliss. Romantic fiction promises that separation between these two lives will end with marriage, when a girl will combine passionate love with public duties as a wife and mother. And so Emma Rouault, believing "love, that marvelous thing which had hitherto been like a great rosy-plumaged bird soaring in the splendors of poetic skies, was at last within her grasp,"[3] marries Charles Bovary.

Almost immediately disparity between dream and reality is evident, for Emma "could not bring herself to believe that the uneventful life she was leading was the happiness of which she had dreamed" (p. 45). Tension builds as her imaginative self, shaped by romantic fantasies, finds no outlet in her role as a wife. By the time the Bovarys are invited to a ball given by a neighboring marquis at la Vaubyessard, Emma has recognized that all her efforts to insert passionate love into her marriage have failed. Bored with her everyday existence, she perceives the ball as an incarnation of her earlier fantasy life, but with a difference. At the ball, imaginative value is maintained only by a complete separation from the human reality of time, and Emma ceases to perceive herself in terms of a past and a future: "amid the splendors of this night her past life, hitherto so vividly present, was vanishing utterly; indeed she was beginning almost to doubt that she had lived it. She was here: and around the brilliant ball was a shadow that veiled all else" (p. 58).

It is against this fact of separation that Emma Bovary concentrates her resources. As a woman, however, her possibilities for action are limited: she believes her sex is dependent upon a man to initiate her "into the intensities of passion, the refinements of life, all the mysteries" (p. 46). No longer expecting to be satisfied by vicarious existence through her husband, Emma turns to other men—to a son and, finally, to lovers. While she is pregnant, she imagines the "idea of having a male child was like a promise of compensation for all her past frustrations. A man is free, at least—free to range the passions and the world, to surmount obstacles, to taste the rarest pleasures. Whereas a woman is continually thwarted. Inert, compliant, she has to struggle against her physical and legal subjection" (p. 101).

With the birth of a daughter, even this dream of vicarious extension is denied, and Emma turns to lovers for satisfaction of her romantic cravings. Entering an affair with a neighboring landowner, Rodolphe Boulanger, Emma revels "in the thought as though she were beginning a second puberty. . . . She was entering a marvelous realm where all would be passion, ecstasy, rapture" (p. 183). More specifically, Emma again imagines release from the limitations of space and time: "she was in the midst of an endless blue expanse, scaling the glittering heights of passion; everyday life had receded, and lay far below, in the shadows between those peaks" (p. 183). Separation between her two lives remains complete: Emma does not imagine joining her fantasy with everyday existence, but rather leaving everyday existence and entering a dream world of romantic love: "she was becoming, in reality, one of that gallery of fictional figures; the long dream of her youth was coming true" (p. 183).

Tension in the novel of awakening results from the reader's awareness that the protagonist's attempts to escape human realities are impossible. Flaubert reminds us of this impossibility by counterposing to Emma's dream of escape characters that represent worldly concerns. Lheureux, a usurer, pursues Emma as a hunter pursues his victim, tightening his net about her as she becomes ensnared in debts taken on in desperate attempts to reproduce the luxurious life of her imagination. The blind man's pursuit is symbolic, a stark reminder of the sickness, decay, and death that are inevitable elements of human existence.

Finally, then, change undoes Emma Bovary's dreams of romantic bliss. Her vision of a future with Rodolphe, "infinite, harmonious" (p. 221), ends when he abandons her. Her initial happiness with the clerk, Leon, ends when she rediscovers "adultery . . . could be as banal as marriage" (p. 330). Through change, Emma Bovary realizes the impossibility of her dream of everlasting bliss, for "everything was a lie! Every smile concealed a yawn of boredom; every joy, a curse; every pleasure, its own surfeit; and the sweetest kisses left on one's lips but a vain longing for fuller delight" (p. 322). Eventually, the tension between Emma's two lives becomes intolerable. Still seeking to satisfy the imaginative self formed in her childhood and wishing to escape "like a bird, to recapture her youth somewhere far away in the immaculate reaches of space" (p. 332), Emma takes poison. In her last moments, the narrator comments, she undoubtedly rediscovers "the lost ecstasy of her first mystical flights and the first visions of eternal bliss" (p. 368).

But Emma Bovary's final vision is not rendered directly, for the perspective here is the narrator's. Indeed, throughout the novel, Flaubert maintains ironic distance from his protagonist:[4] the reader more often observes than participates in Emma Bovary's awakening. In a later, American novel, *The Awakening,* Kate Chopin combines elements from *Madame Bovary* with a significant shift in focus. The ironic distance of *Madame Bovary* is replaced by a high degree of narrative sympathy. Written by a woman and focusing strictly upon changes of consciousness in its protagonist, *The Awakening* represents a distilled example of the novel of awakening.

The theme of limitation characteristic of the novel of awakening begins in the initial pages of *The Awakening,* in which the protagonist, Edna Pontellier, is presented as a passive embodiment of a social role. The omniscient narrator looks through Leonce Pontellier's eyes as he watches his wife approach, viewing her as he would "a valuable piece of personal property."[5] But Edna Pontellier is stirred to dreams, and with her dreams comes the tension that will be developed through the rest of the novel. For like Emma Bovary, Edna has a "dual life—

that outward existence which conforms, the inward life which ques-tions" (p. 893). Her outward existence is that of social roles—the roles of wife and mother. Her inner life, on the other hand, is that of imaginative release through dreams. Through dreams, one may be freed from arbitrary measurements, as Edna was when she dreamed of walking across a big field in which she " 'could see only the stretch of green before me, and I felt as if I must walk on forever, without coming to the end of it' " (p. 896).

However, underlying this sense of imaginative freedom is a reality of limitation. When a child, Edna distinguished between the outer world of reality and the inner life of dreams; with her marriage, she had expected to end this duality by severing her connection with a dream life, for "as the devoted wife of a man who worshiped her, she felt she would take her place with a certain dignity in the world of re-ality, closing the portals forever behind her upon the realm of ro-mance and dreams" (p. 898). As the novel progresses, the apparent calm of Edna's social role seen in the initial paragraphs is destroyed by her increasingly powerful responses to the sensuousness around her. With her emerging passions, Edna again becomes conscious of her own duality: her youthful romantic infatuations are transmuted into an adult combination of romance and sexuality. This revitaliza-tion climaxes when, while listening to piano music, Edna responds with her whole being: "the very passions themselves were aroused with her soul, swaying it, lashing it" (p. 906).

But, contrary to the illusion of independence offered by this revital-ized inner self, Chopin describes the release of Edna's imaginative life in passive terms. Edna "blindly" follows "whatever impulse moved her, as if she had placed herself in alien hands for direction" (p. 913). At the heart of this passivity is Edna's attempt to escape from the ob-jective world, for self-determination is impossible without taking into account the realities of human existence—time and change. Knowing the essential irreconcilability of her romantic dreams with reality, Edna carefully avoids any confrontation of the two. Her refrain that she will not think about the future runs like a motif throughout the novel. Attempting to protect her revitalized inner life, Edna physically and psychologically isolates herself, casting off family responsibilities, pursuing her solitary thoughts, and, finally, moving to her own house.

During this period, Edna's attempts to satisfy the need of her soul "for the unlimited in which to lose herself" (p. 908) take the classic feminine form of love. But her attempts to love are frustrated. Her emerging sexuality—the natural adult outgrowth of romantic long-ings—is developed by the rake, Arobin, in an alliance that leaves her dissatisfied, for it remains dissociated from love. Conversely, her love for the character most sympathetic in age and spirit to herself, Robert, leaves her dissatisfied also, for it remains dissociated from sex.

Finally, then, Edna, like Emma Bovary, completes the process of awakening by placing her romantic dreams for escape in the context of time and change. For the first time, she sees herself in terms of the past and the future: "she had said over and over to herself: 'To-day it is Arobin; to-morrow it will be some one else'" (p. 999). Edna's sui-cide represents her final attempt to escape—to escape her children, her lovers, and, most important, time and change. For only by complete isolation of self can Edna be truthful to her inner life. Any contact with external reality threatens this dream. Thus Edna, while swim-ming to sea and death, returns to her childhood dreams of limitless-ness, recalling the meadow of her youth and her belief that "it had no beginning and no end" (p. 1000).

Imagery describing Edna Pontellier's death is similar to that de-scribing Emma Bovary's death. Both characters, experiencing the ex-panding consciousness basic to the growth of the child into an adult, come to the age-old realization of the conflict between the soul's yearning for the infinite pitted against the body's imprisonment in the finite. But the protagonist for this realization is traditionally male: he must learn to concentrate his energies in work that, by having broad social and ethical implications, will transcend his own mortality. Flau-bert and Chopin, using women as their protagonists, add to thematic tension by including sexist roles that restrict the woman from the ex-pansion necessary to deal with her realization. Alternatives are se-verely limited to feminine options: the woman must choose between her inner life of romance and the outer world of reality. Either alter-native leaves her passive: when she is true to her romantic dreams, she is the passive pawn of her own moods; when she attempts to fol-low the outer world, she is the passive pawn of men—of a husband or a lover. More important, the dreams in which she attempts to lose herself are limited: she regresses to childhood dreams of limitlessness or she loses herself in romantic dreams of passion.

In her 1899 review of *The Awakening,* Willa Cather comments on Flaubert's and Chopin's limiting their characters' inner lives to the traditionally feminine mode of romantic love. Cather writes,

Edna Pontellier and Emma Bovary are studies in the same feminine type. . . . Both women belong to a class, not large, but forever clamoring in our ears, that demands more romance out of life than God put into it. . . . they are the victims of the over-idealization of love. . . . These people really expect the passion of love to fill and gratify every need of life, whereas nature only intended that it should meet one of many demands. They insist upon making it stand for all the emotional pleasures of life and art; expecting an individual and self-limited passion to yield infinite variety, pleasure, and distraction, and to contribute to their lives what the arts and the pleasurable exercise of the intellect gives to less limited and less intense idealists. So this passion, when set up against Shakespeare, Balzac, Wagner, Raphael, fails them. They have staked everything on one hand, and they lose. They have driven the blood until it will drive no further, they have played their nerves up to the point where any relaxation short of absolute annihilation is impossible. . . . And in the end, the nerves get even. Nobody ever cheats them, really. Then the "awakening" comes.[6]

Later, in *My Mortal Enemy,* Cather presents her own version of an awakening, concentrating upon the moral implications to women of this feminine type who are "the victims of the over-idealization of love." The awakening in *My Mortal Enemy* develops in an almost symmetrically inverse direction from that of *Madame Bovary* and *The Awakening.* Emma Bovary and Edna Pontellier move from reality to dream; Myra Henshawe moves from dream to reality.

This movement occurs in three stages, corresponding to the meetings between the narrator, Nellie Birdseye, and Myra Henshawe.[7] In the first stage, the dream is dominant as Nellie recounts the story of the elopement of Myra Driscoll and Oswald Henshawe. For this story, Cather draws heavily upon a stock romantic situation. Myra Driscoll is the one-dimensional romantic heroine, "an orphan" who "had been brought up by her great-uncle"[8] in a manner worthy of a fairy tale: she "had everything: dresses and jewels, a fine riding horse, a Steinway piano" (p. 12). The romantic pattern continues with her falling in love with the dashing Oswald Henshawe. The young lovers meet the opposition of their elders, the result of "an old grudge of some kind" (p. 13), and, although Myra's uncle threatens disinheritance, they secretly elope. In presenting this story, Cather foreshadows her thematic concern with the moral implications of the romantic myth. The story of Myra and Oswald's elopement becomes an enticing social convention for, as Nellie recalls, Myra "and her runaway marriage were the theme of the most interesting, indeed the only interesting, stories that were told in our family on holidays or at family dinners" (p. 3).

The serious thematic question about this process is identified by Nellie, who initiates the theme of awakening to be developed in the rest of the novel. Refusing to allow the romantic tale to remain in the distant past, she asks about the consequences of the lovers' actions: despite the fact that they were disinherited, have the lovers " 'been happy, anyhow' "? The rather off-hand reply to her question, " 'Happy? Oh, yes! As happy as most people,' " elicits Nellie's reflection, "That answer was disheartening; the very point of their story was that they should be much happier than other people" (p. 17). The question implicit in this response is similar to the objection Cather raises to Flaubert's and Chopin's protagonists: what is the "point" of the romantic legend that idealizes love?

In developing a response to the question, Cather makes two basic modifications in focus from *Madame Bovary* and *The Awakening:* the earlier two novels presented protagonists married to men obviously unsuited to them in both age and temperament. Only the thinnest illusion of love ever existed within marriage: they awaken both to the power and to the limitation of romantic love outside of marriage. Cather, however, places romantic love within marriage. And the earlier two novels present a relatively specific time in the lives of their protagonists: neither Emma Bovary nor Edna Pontellier lives to the full maturity of old age. Cather, however, gives temporal change a major role by taking Myra Driscoll Henshawe from childhood to old age. Indeed, the dominant reality within which the awakening of *My Mortal Enemy* occurs is the human reality of change.

In the opening scenes of *My Mortal Enemy,* the incongruity between the figures in the legend and the characters themselves stresses temporal change: the Myra Driscoll Henshawe of the romantic legend, an ageless heroine, is rather grotesquely unlike "the real Myra Henshawe" (p. 19), who, at "forty-five" (p. 4), is "a short, plump woman in a black velvet dress" (p. 5). Similarly, though not quite so obviously, in the initial pages Cather introduces change through Nellie Birdseye, for the naive young girl who had been told the romantic tale of Myra Henshawe "ever since [she] could remember anything at all" (p. 3) is strikingly different from the complex narrator, recounting her childhood memories with the human compassion possible only with adult understanding. The child Nellie represents the romantic perspective of escape from time: she thinks of the Driscoll place, for example, "as being under a spell, like the Sleeping Beauty's palace; it had been in a trance, or lain in its flowers like a beautiful corpse, ever since that winter night when Love went out of the gates and gave the dare to Fate" (p. 17); the narrator Nellie provides a counterpoint of reality by recalling, "I knew that this was not literally true" (p. 17).

This underlying discrepancy between romance and reality is defined sharply at the time of the second meeting between Myra and Nellie, now in New York. Here the emphasis is upon the disparity between the romantic legend and human reality: Myra emerges from the myth to become a complex character, directly questioning the morality of becoming involved in the loves of others. She reflects to Nellie, " 'See the moon coming out, Nellie—behind the tower. It wakens the guilt in me. No playing with love; and I'd sworn a great oath never to meddle again. You send a handsome fellow . . . to a fine girl . . . and it's Christmas eve, and they rise above us, and the white world around us, and there isn't anybody, not a tramp on the park benches, that wouldn't wish them well—and very likely hell will come of it!' " (p. 31). This emphasis on moral consequences of human action is raised also by development in the character of Nellie. Nellie has passed into adolescence, the stage of her own life at which young women conventionally commit themselves to a romantic concept of love and marriage. For Nellie, the Henshawes represent such a concept: she is, when she visits them, " 'fair moon-struck' " (p. 26).

But again, contrast with human realities belies the myth. Throughout this section, Nellie stresses complexities. Myra's generosity with her friends is contrasted with her bitterness at her poverty. The apparent happiness of the Henshawes is contrasted with their intrigue and deceit in seemingly trivial matters. Most important, Nellie's romanticism is contrasted with her growing sensitivity to the human complexity of Myra Henshawe. Seeing Myra's unhappiness over her poverty, Nellie "glimpsed what seemed to me insane ambition," a judgment that is countered in the next scene by Nellie's appreciation of Myra's brilliance and charm with her friends: "Their talk quite took my breath away; they said such exciting, such fantastic things about people, books, music—anything; they seemed to speak together a kind of highly flavored special language" (p. 42). Finally, Nellie realizes that Myra's "chief extravagance was in caring for so many people and in caring for them so much" (p. 43).

At the end of this section, separations result from widening disparities between romantic expectations and human realities; and the transmission of the romantic myth from one generation to another is interrupted. The realities of their own lives force Myra and Oswald into petty, jealous quarrels and, eventually, into a temporary separation. Witnessing this quarrel, Nellie awakens to the human complexity in a marriage and, her romantic sensibility deeply disillusioned by her perception, she leaves the Henshawes to move into the adult phase of her own life.

At the time of their third meeting, ten years later, realism is dominant, inescapably revealed in both setting and action. The setting is "a sprawling overgrown Westcoast city which was in the throes of rapid development—it ran about the shore, stumbling all over itself and finally tumbled untidily into the sea" (p. 57). Here Nellie Birdseye finds the Henshawes, living in a "shabby, comfortless place" (p. 59). Physical changes extend to the Henshawes themselves: Oswald has "thin white hair and stooped shoulders" (p. 59) and "the tired, tired face of one who has utterly lost hope" (p. 61). But no such simple description could portray Myra Henshawe. In this last, most developed section, Myra Henshawe completely belies the simplistic, one-dimensional character of the romantic myth: when Nellie finds her, "she sat crippled but powerful in her brilliant wrappings. She looked strong and broken, generous and tyrannical, a witty and rather wicked old woman, who hated life for its defeats and loved it for its absurdities" (p. 65).[9] Myra has awakened to the personal consequences of her romantic elopement with Oswald: " 'It's been the ruin of us both. We've destroyed each other' " (p. 75).

In developing this realization of Myra's, Cather incorporates into *My Mortal Enemy* her objection to Flaubert's and Chopin's protagonists: the Henshawes' elopement and marriage represent an attempt to live according to the romantic myth that "the passion of love [may] fill and gratify every need of life, whereas nature only intended that it should meet one of many demands." As Myra explains to Nellie, " 'People can be lovers and enemies at the same time, you know. We were. . . . A man and a woman draw apart from that long embrace, and see what they have done to each other. Perhaps I can't forgive him for the harm I did him. Perhaps that's it. When there are children, that feeling goes through natural changes. But when it remains so personal . . . something gives way in one' " (pp. 88–89). It is the "individual and self-limited" nature of romantic passion that is destructive, for by definition such passion restricts one from expansive movement toward great truths. As in her review of *The Awakening*, in *My Mortal Enemy* Cather contrasts this limited passion to the greater variety of passion provided by the arts: she develops in Myra a potential for greatness, portraying her soul's yearnings for the universal values represented by music and literature. Thus, at the end of her life, Myra seeks the solace of constants: she returns to religion, nature, and literature.

With her description of Myra Henshawe's death, Cather presents an expansive movement toward metaphysical truths that reverse the commitment to an inner life of dreams seen in Emma Bovary and Edna Pontellier. Myra Henshawe realizes her soul's need for universal values, and she acts in accord with this realization. Nellie recognizes in Myra's dying actions "a yearning strong enough to lift that ailing body and drag it out into the world again" (p. 99). Removing herself from the shabby hotel room that represents the consequences of her early commitment to romantic passion, Myra uses one of her gold pieces to hire a cab to go to the cliff that reminds her of Lear. There she meets death with religion and art. Later, Nellie finds "her wrapped in her blankets, leaning against the cedar trunk, facing the sea. Her head had fallen forward; the ebony crucifix was in her hands. She must have died peacefully and painlessly. There was every reason to believe she had lived to see the dawn" (p. 101).

In the final pages, Cather continues the outward movement of her theme of awakening through Nellie Birdseye. Throughout the novel, the relation between Myra and Nellie has been that of tutor to student: the older woman initially represents to Nellie the traditional romantic myth. By the time of their second meeting, Myra emerges from the dream to act as a human tutor to Nellie. In the last pages, Myra's cry, " 'if youth but knew!' " (p. 75), calls for an extension of the theme of awakening into the future. This final movement begins with Myra, who utters the words from which the title is taken, " 'Why must I die like this, alone with my mortal enemy?' " Nellie responds with "dread," for she "had never heard a human voice utter such a terrible judgment upon all one hopes for" (p. 95). But, as she must in her growth toward personal identity, Nellie completes the process alone. After her initial revulsion, Nellie "grew calmer" and "began to understand a little what she meant" (p. 96). And later, after the death of Myra Henshawe, Nellie continues her own awakening. In these final pages, Nellie does not reject love itself, nor does she experience a "disillusionment [that] leaves her hopeless."[10] Throughout the novel, Nellie is markedly different from Myra Henshawe, for, as Nellie points out, she has youth, and "for youth there is always the hope, the certainty, of better things" (p. 58). What Nellie *does* reject is the over-idealization of love that occurs when *"a common feeling* [is] exalted into beauty by imagination, generosity, and the flaming courage of youth" (pp. 104–5; my emphasis). With this understanding, Nellie has the potential to move into the future without the self-limiting romantic illusion of the young Myra Driscoll Henshawe or of Chopin's Edna Pontellier: she has the potential to become the narrator of *My Mortal Enemy,* with the capacity to understand and appreciate the complexly human woman, Myra. It is, then, Nellie who completes the theme of the novel in her awakening to the limitations of the romantic myth—a myth that insists people fit themselves into simplistic categories that ignore the complexities of time and change. By the end of *My Mortal Enemy,* the character Nellie joins the narrator Nellie. The strength of the book lies in the growth that has resulted in this union, making possible the narrator's tone as she combines compassion and objectivity to tell of Myra Driscoll Henshawe's human complexities, her combination of meanness and greatness, worldliness and spirituality, hatred and love.[11]

Myra Driscoll Henshawe awakened to limitations accompanying romantic love and to the freedom offered by metaphysical truths; her awakening remained, however, within the confines of a marriage based on romantic love. Only through the narrator, Nellie Birdseye, is there the possibility of growth beyond such confines. With Marie Rogers, the protagonist of Agnes Smedley's *Daughter of Earth,* the awakening to limitations ensuing from conventions of romantic love occurs as an early step in a larger process. In one sense, then, *Daughter of Earth* begins where *My Mortal Enemy* leaves off, with a turning away from romantic love and toward commitment to a higher value. The adult narrator, Marie Rogers, introduces the narrative with such a commitment: "Now I stand at the end of one life and on the threshold of another. Contemplating. Weighing. About me lie the ruins of a life. Instead of blind faith,—directness, unbounded energy; and instead of unclearness, I now have the knowledge that comes from experience; work that is limitless in its scope and significance. Is not this enough to weigh against love?"[12] The rest of the novel retraces Marie Rogers's development to that point of commitment, beginning with "the first thing I remember of life" (p. 4).

A major difference between Marie Rogers and previous protagonists of novels of awakening—Emma Bovary, Edna Pontellier, and Myra Driscoll Henshawe—lies in their childhoods. Unlike the luxury in which Emma, Edna, and Myra were raised—luxury that provided time and materials for romantic fantasies—the deprivation of Marie Rogers's youth meant "there was but one thing on which I could depend—poverty and uncertainty" (p. 41). And unlike protagonists to whom female models of passivity and subservience promised happiness, to Marie such models led only to poverty and misery. Marie's mother married for love; at thirty, she was a woman worn old by endless work and disappointment. In Marie's childhood, the girls or women granted the most respect were those who followed male patterns, Marie's Aunt Mary, "a woman with the body and mind of a man"

(p. 14), and her Aunt Helen, who demonstrated that "to be a hired girl drawing your own money gave you a position of authority and influence in the community" (p. 23).

Thus for the girl Marie, the reality of everyday existence belied any romantic fiction of happiness through love. She came to believe that "the true position of the husband and wife in the marriage relationship" (p. 67) was that marriage made women subservient and men tyrannical. More basically, the "little drama of the lowly" (p. 56) in which Marie participated disproved the fundamental dream of happiness for the just: "On the one hand stretched my world of fairy tales, the song of 'The Maple Leaves Forever,' the tales of good little girls being kind to animals, of color, dancing, music, with happiness in the end even if things were not all right now. On the other hand stood— a little house with a rag pasted over a broken window-pane; a lone struggling morning-glory trying to live in the baked soil before the porch; Annie being dragged by her tousled streaming hair; my father, once so straight and handsome, now a round-shouldered man with tobacco juice showing at the corners of his mouth" (p. 72).

Initially, limitations imposed on the child Marie created both an intellectual and an emotional blindness. Intellectually, she knew nothing of the world outside the narrow confines of an illiterate family on the lowest economic rung of society; emotionally, she learned that "love and tenderness meant only pain and suffering and defeat" (p. 148). To survive, she suppressed all such emotions: "I was a savage beast and I harbored injuries and hatreds in my heart. Right or wrong, it is true. It is. The ways of life had taught me no tenderness" (p. 92).

From this early blindness, the process of awakening moves in two directions. First, commitment to outward, intellectual expansion through education and work provides the basic structure of the novel: Marie goes from a child of poverty to a grade school student, to kitchen help, to teacher in New Mexico, to traveling magazine saleswoman, to student in Arizona and California, to journalist in New York and, finally, to dedicated socialist and revolutionary of the Indian movement. Redefinition of values accompanies this outward physical progression. Marie's goals were initially conventional and materialistic: beginning her higher education, for example, she felt "before me now lay a university degree; and beyond—well, it might be position, one day money and power" (p. 250). Gradually, however, Marie turns from this early materialism until, through study with a teacher in the Indian movement, she "touched for the first time a movement of unwavering principle and beauty—the struggle of a continent to be free" (p. 269). The result represents the climax of Marie's growth toward intellectual awakening; she achieves identity and value and, with them, a basis for action: "The Indian work was the first thing I had ever suffered for out of principle, from choice. It was not just living, just reacting to life—it was expression. It gave me a sense of self-respect, of dignity, that nothing else had ever given me" (p. 327).

Simultaneously, the second direction of awakening develops Marie's emotional self. Her capacity for tenderness grows in her increasing affection for her mother, her friends, and, finally, in her ability to love a man. But as the two selves in Marie develop, tension results from their contradictory demands. Marie has learned from experience that the needs for work and for love are not only incompatible but, for a woman, mutually destructive. As Marie matures, she resists any affection she feels for members of her family, resolving "I would not let [love] ruin me as it ruined others!" (p. 148). Similarly, Marie resists affection toward men and the accompanying integration of sex with love: for her, "sex had no place in love. Sex meant violence, marriage or prostitution, and marriage meant children, weeping nagging women and complaining men; it meant unhappiness, and all the things that I feared and dreaded and intended to avoid" (p. 181). Unable to resolve the "war being waged within my own spirit, a war between my need and desire of love, and the perverted idea of love and sex that had been ground into my being from my first breath" (p. 194), Marie separates from her first husband.

This increasing tension between the needs for work and for love comes to a climax when Marie falls in love with and marries Anand, a fellow worker in the Indian movement. In this relationship she, like other women in novels of awakening, attempts to unify the private and public lives she had previously kept separate. Gradually, however, jealousy and misunderstanding occur both between Marie and Anand and among other workers in the Indian movement, and eventually the relationship threatens their work. Recognizing that "our love . . . was destroying us" (p. 386), they separate, and the book returns to its beginning, with the sacrifice of love for freedom.

The awakening of Marie Rogers is, like other awakenings of women in literature, an awakening to limitation and conflict—to the inevitable conflict between the need for personal love and the need for meaningful public action. And, like other protagonists of novels of awakening, Marie sacrifices love for freedom. But the nature of that sacrifice differs radically from that of Emma Bovary or Edna Pontellier, for Marie Rogers defines freedom in terms of worldly action and work that are liberating in their broad social and ethical implications. In this sense, she is similar to male protagonists of the *Bildungsroman.*

Behind this affirmation of freedom in work are certain other characteristics that distinguish Marie Rogers. First, she does not seek to escape time. The major awakening in *Daughter of Earth*—that to the Indian movement—is valuable precisely because Marie is so intensely aware that the basic human realities are of change and death, for "life itself is the one glorious, eternal experience, and . . . there is no place here on this spinning ball of earth and stone for anything but freedom. For we reach scarce a hundred before we take our place by the side of those whom we have directly or indirectly injured, enslaved, or killed" (pp. 269–70). For Marie, only the conviction of ideas releases one from temporal limitations. Imprisoned in The Tombs, she contrasts herself with other women prisoners: "They were physical women—as I had once been physical. But now I had some measure of thought, some measure of belief in the power of ideas; in this only did I differ from them. When the world, with its eating and sleeping, its dancing and singing, its colors and laughter, was taken from these women, they were without understanding or resistance. It was easy to make beasts of such women. They had nothing to support themselves with" (p. 317).

Second, Marie Rogers differs from the earlier protagonists of the novel by the extent to which she takes responsibility for herself: she quite simply refuses to accept the passivity and dependency so characteristic of the thinking of Emma Bovary and Edna Pontellier. And third, Marie moves outward to a far broader context than is evident in most novels of awakening: her expanding consciousness is measured by awareness of such figures as Emma Goldman and of such events as women's suffrage, miners' efforts to unionize, the IWW, WWI, and, most important, the Indian freedom movement.

Emma Bovary and Marie Rogers represent the extremes in the novel of awakening, the one imprisoned within an imagination shaped by romantic myths and the other committed to a movement for freedom on the other side of the globe. Most novels of awakening fall between the extremes, as does George Eliot's *Middlemarch*. In Dorothea Brooke, George Eliot presents a female character of great soul, searching for "something beyond the shallows of ladies'-school literature."[13] The novel begins with Dorothea's sense of disparity between her needs as a human being and the role expected of her as a woman: "What could she do, what ought she to do?—she, hardly more than a budding woman, but yet with an active conscience and a great mental need, not to be satisfied by a girlish instruction comparable to the nibblings and judgments of a discursive mouse" (pp. 20–21).

The pattern is similar to that of other novels of awakening: a young girl, denied direct experience of life, shapes her imaginative existence through literature and views marriage as the means by which the inner life of the imagination will join with the world of action.[14] In the opening pages, romantic illusion characterizes Dorothea, who, "with all her eagerness to know the truths of life, retained very childlike ideas about marriage. She felt sure that she would have accepted the judicious Hooker, if she had been born in time to save him from that wretched mistake he made in matrimony; or John Milton when his blindness had come on" (p. 7). Dorothea's romantic hero takes a different form from that of Emma Bovary or Edna Pontellier; the blindness is similar, however, as are the results. Seeking deliverance "from her girlish subjection to her own ignorance" (p. 21), Dorothea marries Edward Casaubon, an elderly scholar whom Dorothea has transformed imaginatively into "a living Bosseut . . . a modern Augustine who united the glories of doctor and saint" (p. 18).

Two major stages occur in Dorothea's awakening. In the first, Dorothea recognizes and comes to terms with the results of her own blindness. On their wedding trip, both Dorothea and Edward Casaubon experience the disparity between their illusions about marriage and its reality. For Dorothea, this experience initially involves the vague feeling "that the large vistas and wide fresh air which she had dreamed of finding in her husband's mind were replaced by anterooms and winding passages which seemed to lead nowhither" (p. 145). Finally, following a disagreement, she begins "to see that she had been under a wild illusion in expecting a response to her feeling from Mr. Casaubon, and she had felt the waking of a presentiment that there might be a sad consciousness in his life which made as great a need on his side as on her own" (p. 156). Her awakening sympathy is crucial, for with it comes outward movement, to realistic perception of the world and her place in it, and to a moral response to this world. Dorothea thus turns from "the moral stupidity [of] taking the world as an udder to feed our supreme selves" (p. 156) to the enlarged and, finally, liberating awareness that others have "an equivalent centre of self, whence the lights and shadows must always fall with a certain difference" (p. 157).

Growth occurs from this point. In her relation to Casaubon, Dorothea struggles for "resolved submission" (p. 313). In the process, she passes from her dream of herself as "a lamp-holder" assisting "the highest purposes of truth" (p. 13) to duty as a "new form of inspiration" giving "a new meaning to wifely love" (p. 202). Here Dorothea's search for what she could do and what she ought to do (p. 20) takes a typically feminine form: Dorothea is an exceptional person, fully conscious that her husband's needs necessitate her denial of all that is most vital in herself; and she experiences a "benumbing" helplessness (p. 348) at the situation. But she is simultaneously committed to her sense of a moral ideal—her greatness lies, in fact, in this commitment. Dorothea's sense of "only the ideal and not the real yoke of marriage" (p. 353) leads to her submission to Casaubon while he is alive and, finally, to his anticipated request that after his death she dedicate herself to his work.

The second stage of awakening—to personal growth in love—occurs not with Casaubon's death but with the terms of his will revoking Dorothea's inheritance if she marries his nephew, Will Ladislaw. The result for Dorothea is personal rebirth. Upon hearing of the will, she has a "vague, alarmed consciousness that her life was taking on a new form, that she was undergoing a metamorphosis in which memory would not adjust itself to the stirring of new organs" (p. 359). Dorothea's metamorphosis involves release from her illusion that her marriage with Casaubon was like an ideal relationship: she experiences "a violent shock of repulsion from her departed husband, who had had hidden thoughts, perhaps perverting everything she said and did" (p. 360). Simultaneously, she "was conscious of another change which also made her tremulous: it was a sudden strange yearning of heart towards Will Ladislaw" (p. 360) and an opening to the possibility of love between them.

From this second major awakening, movement toward the union of Dorothea and Will Ladislaw follows: Dorothea experiences "the first sense of loving and being loved" (p. 465); their relationship is thwarted by Dorothea's misunderstanding of Ladislaw's actions toward the married Rosamond Vincy and ends finally with understanding, shared commitment, and marriage. This second major phase of awakening is based, as the first was, on Dorothea's yearning "towards the perfect Right, that it might make a throne within her, and rule her errant will" (p. 577) and on her feeling "the largeness of the world" and that "she was part of that involuntary, palpitating life, and could neither look out on it from her luxurious shelter as a mere spectator, nor hide her eyes in selfish complaining" (p. 578). But Dorothea's adjustment to this large moral sense is basically one of personal will and perspective: her attempts to act, whether to plan better housing for tenants or to assist the idealistic young physician, Lydgate, remain severely restricted by her position as a woman.

In this outcome, Dorothea Brooke is representative of women in other novels of awakening—Elizabeth Bennet, Emma Woodhouse, Isabel Archer—who are capable of dual movement, both inward to self-knowledge and outward, toward awareness of social, ethical, and philosophical truths, but whose awakenings are to limitations and whose achievements are measured by their adjustments to their role as women. Many, like Dorothea, find extension to the world through marriage to a man whom they both respect and love. In the final chapter of *Middlemarch,* for example, Eliot describes the marriage of Dorothea and Will Ladislaw, a union bound by strong love in which "Will became an ardent public man" (p. 610), working for the reforms Dorothea had yearned for in her youth, and Dorothea gave him "wifely help" (p. 611). But few authors comment so directly as George Eliot on this special role of the exceptional woman in a world shaped by men: "Many who knew [Dorothea], thought it a pity that so substantive and rare a creature should have been absorbed into the life of another, and be only known in a certain circle as a wife and mother. But no one stated exactly what else that was in her power she ought rather to have done" (p. 611).

Thus, in their quite different approaches to their common subject, these five novels provide a starting place for discussion of the novel of awakening. All present protagonists who seek value in a world that expects a woman to define herself by love, marriage, and motherhood. For each, an inner, imaginative sense of personal value conflicts with her public role: an awakening occurs when she confronts the disparity between her two lives. As is illustrated by these five novels, treatments of this common theme differ dramatically. For Emma Bovary and Edna Pontellier, the primary movement of awakening is inward, to private imaginative values; for Myra Driscoll Henshawe and Marie Rogers, primary movement is outward, to metaphysical, moral, and social values. Dorothea Brooke's initial awakening of a moral sense prepares for a second awakening of love. But after noting these differences, we return to similarities among the novels. Each presents an awakening to limitations. Each presents a resolution only at great cost to the protagonist: she must deny one element of herself, whether by the extreme of Emma's and Edna's suicides or by Dorothea's turning from a direct, active public life. And, finally, each presents the dilemma of the individual who attempts to find value in a society that relegates to her only roles and values of the woman, ignoring her needs as a human being.

KAREN E. ROWE

"Fairy-born and human-bred":
Jane Eyre's Education in Romance

Among cultural functionalists and psychological folklorists, whether Freudian or Jungian, it is a well-accepted premise that fairy tales fulfill basic psychic needs for both the individual and society.[1] Moreover, the patterns for maturation that literary versions of fairly tales by Charles Perrault, Madame d'Aulnoy, Madame de Beaumont, and the Brothers Grimm disseminated throughout England during the eighteenth and nineteenth centuries differed substantially for men and women.[2] In keeping with prevailing social norms, young boys were educated to become England's parliamentary leaders, the land-endowed clergy, or captains of industry, while women were trained in the arts of domestic management and genteel accomplishments, those qualities that gave rise later to the image of a Victorian "angel in the house," a figure venerated yet isolated from the main currents of economic and political life. One paradigm for masculine development is found in the English folktale "Jack the Giant Killer," which implicitly sanctions challenges to authority (in fantasy), the overthrow of giants, and an eventual ascent to an honored position in society.[3] By contrast, popular tales for young girls, including *Cinderella, Sleeping Beauty, Beauty and the Beast,* portrayed acquiescent females who cultivated domestic virtues in dreamy anticipation of a prince's rescue by which the heroine might enter magically into marriage—her highest calling. Insofar as fairy tales reflected the status quo and transmitted accepted cultural values and behaviors, heroine tales, we may assume, perpetuated romantic paradigms that profoundly influenced women's fantasies and the subconscious scenarios for their real lives.[4]

Less explored than the impact of folktales on social conditioning are the specific implications of internalized romantic patterns for women who write and read novels. Folktale patterns exert a subtle yet pervasive influence on the structure of female *Bildungsromane* and on our expectations as readers and literary critics. *Jane Eyre* conforms in some salient respects to Jerome Buckley's definition of a "typical Bildungsroman plot," in which a "child of some sensibility" (Jane) encounters hostile forces (Mrs. Reed and Reverend Brocklehurst), receives an education (Lowood), and overcomes the limited opportunities of a repressive home by seeking independence (employment as a governess), not in a city but in the constrictive environs of a secluded gothic mansion at Thornfield. It is not education in a formal sense that facilitates Jane's growth and maturation, but rather the confrontation with male sexuality and the temptations of a transforming love that will metamorphose her from a plain, lowly Jane into a beautiful lady of the manor. Such is not the usual psychology of a male *Bildungsroman,* in which interiority, self-sacrifice, and romantic love hardly figure as primary motifs or the major crises of development. Instead, Jane Eyre's experience resembles far more the subgenre of the romantic fairy tale that sets forth a limited pattern for female maturation, a paradigm that Charlotte Brontë initially finds appealing, but later renounces because it subverts the heroine's independence and human equality.

From observing fairly-tale paradigms in this quintessential romantic fiction, I would argue that Charlotte Brontë both consciously allows these patterns to govern her narrative and tempers them with alternative models of mature love. As prominent themes, Brontë examines two problems: first, the tension between female and male processes of maturation. Jane Eyre is a heroine whose life is molded by romantic ideals drawn from childhood readings of fairy tales, often under the tutelage of the nursemaid, Bessie. Jane's choices, according to fairy tale and Victorian mores, are limited to spinsterhood (which Charlotte, her sisters, and *Villette*'s Lucy Snowe embrace) or marriage, the plausible and popular resolution for a female *Bildungsroman.* As a subtext for female growth, the fairy tale psychologically inculcates a dependent and selfless sacrifice, one designed to culminate in marriage. In Jane's struggle to achieve maturity, contrary to our expectations, she wavers between rebellious independence and a martyr's submission to fate, between the dictates of a stricter reason and the impulses of love and romance. At the structural level the book meanders between patterns adopted from *Gulliver's Travels* and other masculine stories, replete with journeys, trials, and battles, and the romantic fantasies of love and marriage based primarily upon *Cinderella, Sleeping Beauty, Beauty and the Beast, Snow-Drop,* and *The Blue Beard,* in which passivity, domesticity, and a rescuing prince are hallmarks.[5]

As a second problem, Brontë explores Jane's dilemma when fairy-tale expectations prove unreliable, indeed dangerous, as they lead Jane closer to an illicit and immoral liaison with Mr. Rochester. To what alternative models of romance or female maturation does the heroine turn when confronted with the disillusionment of an aborted marriage? Does the "Reader, I married him" of Brontë's final chapter represent a capitulation to romantic fantasy, or rather a closure derived from a more mature vision of complexities in human relationships? Indeed, in *Jane Eyre* we see how female identity emerges from solitary introspections and from within relationships, but in order to be completely self-identified, organically whole (measured by wealth, the power to make choices, and independent actions), Jane must separate from Rochester, only subsequently to reunite on a basis of human equality. The perplexity that assails literary critics and readers as they attempt to justify Brontë's conclusion may resolve itself, if we recognize that she abandons midway a romantic paradigm derived from heroine tales and supplants it with structures borrowed from Shakespeare and Milton. Miltonic and Shakespearean models for romance may offer little change from the constraints of fairy tale, but in the dialectic of Brontë's fiction, this replacement reveals her concept of human love, as it must function in the "real" world of post-lapsarian nature, not in the realm of adolescent dreams or fantasies. Charlotte Brontë thus tests the paradigm of fairy tale for her *Bildungsroman* and finds it lacking, precisely because it can give shape only to the child bride of Rochester, not to the substantial human being who is Jane Eyre.

Very early Jane testifies to the impression of oral and literary tales upon her young imagination, an influence heightened by her emotional need for fantasy escapes from her dependent but persecuted role in the Reed household. Presiding over kitchen and nursery, Bessie fulfills the role of a classic Mother Goose or Mother Bunch, gifted with a "remarkable knack of narrative; so, at least," the mature Jane judges "from the impression made on me by her nursery tales."[6] "Narrated on winter evenings, when she chanced to be in good humor" and would bring "her ironing-table to the nursery hearth," Bessie's "passages of love and adventure taken from old fairy tales and older ballads" fed Jane's "eager attention" (p. 11). In sharp contrast to Mrs. Reed's authoritarian detachment, Bessie's maternal warmth enables Jane to anticipate fulfillment of her cherished fantasies about home and family. More important, it is from Bessie as a figure of *la sage femme* and tale-teller that young Jane inherits her penchant for narrative, which she later revives by composing her autobiography (if we accept Brontë's framework).[7] The tendency to represent her life by shaping it into a narrative of romance and adventure becomes, in fact, the mode of Jane Eyre's history. Just as Brontë molds her own fiction, so too she attributes to her heroine the imagination to reformulate events into patterns borrowed initially from "old fairy tales" and from *Gulliver's Travels*. Through these readings, Jane experiences the dual aspirations of her personality, either to fulfill patterns of romance set forth in nursery chronicles or to pursue worldly adventures into mysterious geographies.

Jane Eyre outwardly resembles classic fairy-tale heroines, as critics often acknowledge by likening her progress to Cinderella's ascent from hearth to palace.[8] Orphaned by age four months, Jane is subjected to a stepmother whose "insuperable and rooted aversion" is as cruel as any portrayed in *Cinderella* or *Snow-Drop* (p. 29). Adhering to usual paradigms, this stepmother's ire stems also from maternal revulsion and jealousy of her husband's attentions, although Brontë makes clear that Jane comes under the guardianship of her Uncle Reed, not her natural father. Remanded to a "solitary and silent nursery" and employed "as a sort of under-nurserymaid, to tidy the room, dust the chairs, etc.," Jane daily hears reproaches of her dependence, physical inferiority, and poverty in comparison with her Reed cousins (pp. 30, 32). Like her folkloristic predecessor, the cinder-maiden, Jane finds herself treated as "even less than a servant," one who is excluded from the "usual festive cheer" of "Christmas and the New Year" (pp. 15, 30). Jane transforms her solitude into a positive vantage point from which to view the world without becoming tainted by it, while she cultivates patient service and cherishes fantasies of escape. As in *Cinderella*, virtue becomes identified with the suffering cinder-lass rather than with the spoiled stepsisters, Eliza and

Georgiana, whose temperaments are respectively "headstrong and selfish" or "spoiled" and "insolent" (p. 17). These childhood deprivations compel Jane to yearn for a stable family—a wish momentarily implemented through her poignant attachment to Bessie and ultimately fulfilled by the rediscovery of her "true" cousins, Diana and Mary Rivers. As a lower-class godmother, however, Bessie lacks the miraculous power to transform plain Jane into a beautiful princess or to free her from Gateshead.

As in many feminine folktales the heroine's attempted flights— whether imaginary or real—are thwarted by a stepmother's superior cunning; so too Jane's rebellious challenges to Mrs. Reed's authority result in even stricter confinements—the torture of the red room and the deathtrap of a "charity" school. A grotesque version of Sleeping Beauty's chamber or Snow-Drop's coffin, the red room functions like these archetypes as a punishment imposed by a spiteful stepmother and as a symbolic restraint on the heroine's passions. Giving rise to lurid superstitions rather than to romantic dreams as in *Sleeping Beauty,* the chamber in which Mr. Reed "breathed his last" seems to lie under a "spell, which kept it so lonely in spite of its grandeur" (p. 16). Even the "looking-glass," inspired perhaps by *Snow-Drop,* assumes a nightmarish cast, as Jane seeks comforting proof of her substantiality and finds instead a "strange little figure there gazing at me with a white face and arms specking the gloom, and glittering eyes of fear . . . like one of the tiny phantoms, half fairy, half imp, Bessie's evening stories represented as coming up out of lone, ferny dells" (p. 16). Only the first in an evolving series of self-portraits, Jane identifies herself here as a "phantom" from the "fairy" or "spirit" world, revealing her childish susceptibility to folklore as well as to literary fantasies. As a prelude to Jane's later romance with Rochester, Brontë deliberately characterizes her as a being doubly impressed: by superstitions gleaned from English folk legend and by gothically embellished tales of heroines imprisoned by evil stepmothers.

From the perspective of heroine tales, Jane's immurement in the red room is a variation on the deaths and sleeps that afflict all adolescent females in these folktales. As paradigms would predict, Jane's "fit" of "unconsciousness" heralds the arrival of a miraculous rescuer. Although apothecary Lloyd seems an unprepossessing prince, we must recall that Jane is still ten years old, not yet ready for romantic revelations. Symbolic (by virtue of his profession) of the male's curative powers to counteract Mrs. Reed's malevolent maternity, Mr. Lloyd seems both a reincarnation of the benevolent father/uncle and an emissary from the world outside Gateshead.

Moreover, Lloyd inaugurates Jane into an alternative mode of self-discovery and freedom, one associated with masculine models. Between Lloyd's first and later visit, Jane seeks solace almost instinctively in books, only this time begging Bessie "to fetch *Gulliver's Travels* from the library," a work more realistic than fantastical to Jane's untutored literary sensibility:

This book I had again and again perused with delight. I considered it a narrative of facts, and discovered in it a vein of interest deeper than what I found in fairy tales: for as to the elves, having sought them in vain. . . . I had at length made up my mind to the sad truth, that they were all gone out of England to some savage country . . . whereas Lilliput and Brobdingnag being, in my creed, solid parts of the earth's surface, I doubted not that I might one day, by taking a long voyage, see with my own eyes . . . the diminutive people . . . of the one realm: and . . . the towerlike men and women, of the other. [p. 23]

Jane's attraction to the "elves" and "imps" of England and the Lilliputians reflects her own feelings of diminution amid shadows cast by looming adult persecutors. Conditioned by literary visions, for instance, she enters Mrs. Reed's drawing room and looking up, discovers the "black pillar . . . the straight, narrow, sable-clad shape standing erect on the rug" with the "grim face at the top" (p. 33). Brobdingnagian Mr. Brocklehurst towers over "little" Jane, taking on grotesque proportions reminiscent also of the devouring wolf in *Little Red Riding Hood:* "What a face he had, now that it was almost on a level with mine! what a great nose! and what a mouth! and what large prominent teeth!" (p. 34).[9] Brontë captures a psychological truth by thus portraying Jane's distorted attributions of size, much as fairy tales and *Gulliver's Travels* do, where heroines and heroes must "grow up" before they "see" the world in its proper human dimensions.

But the appropriate paradigm for Jane's subsequent growth becomes momentarily ambiguous, precisely because *Gulliver's Travels* differs in narrative form and intent from romantic fairy tales. Whereas heroine tales encourage hearth-bred patience and expectations of a prince's rescue, *Gulliver's Travels* sends the hero forth to discover worldly realities through experiential suffering, however stumbling and often mistaken his perceptions. Feminine tales preach a gospel of everlasting happiness, as romantic yearnings give way to ideal marriages. Gulliver's experiences may (or may not) yield greater worldly knowledge and self-awareness for hero and reader alike; his tale tells us that truths are tenuous and knowledge, by virtue of the human condition, fallible. In keeping with their respective genres, the romantic tale cultivates faith in human potential by idealizing psychological and moral triumphs, while Swift's fictional satire provokes cynicism, since his seemingly rational appraisal of humankind reveals mainly baser instincts. Romanticists seek chivalric knights—the satirist sees only Yahoos. For Jane Eyre at age ten, literary models thus provide two discrete paradigms toward mature knowledge, corresponding to dual impulses within her own nature. Acquiescent in her servitudes, she can nurture feminine domestic skills and virtues, while dreamily awaiting the romantic prince and marriage as her promised reward; or, according to masculine archetypes, she can defy larger-than-life authorities and journey into foreign environments, seeking a rugged independence, but sacrificing hearth and family comforts.

Acting out both paradigms in her removal from Gateshead to Lowood, Jane mournfully relinquishes Bessie's "enchanting stories" and like a Gulliverian "desolate wanderer" ventures into an alien environment that tests her stalwart defiance of unjust mastery, while supplying her with idealized models of female endurance and industry. Barely one remove from her stepmother's spiteful imprisonments, Jane must fight tenaciously for life at Lowood, the death-riddled charitable institution, where Mr. Brocklehurst imposes an unjust servitude upon many worsted-robed orphans as cruelly as Mrs. Reed had afflicted the solitary Jane. Simultaneously, Lowood inaugurates a new phase in Jane's romantic education, as her adolescent servitude and waiting prepare her for the awakening at Thornfield and shattering disillusionments beyond. Starved for maternal guidance, she venerates Miss Temple (like a fairy godmother) as a paragon of compassion and learning, who transforms Jane into a respectable governess, if not a great beauty. Helen Burns schools her in Christian submission and makes us perceive the underlying religious imperative which preaches that women must endure suffering and control aberrant passions with rigidly exercised morals and reason. Comparable to the waiting periods during which tale heroines, such as Cinderella and little Beauty, practice domestic arts to improve their marketability and enhance their virtue, so too Jane Eyre expends "eight years" in service, which as autobiographer she passes over "almost in silence" (p. 85). The goal toward which such training leads, whether in romantic fantasies or fictions, is enacted when Miss Temple turns cleric's wife and leaves behind a legacy that Jane all too readily resurrects in her later fantasies about Rochester. Having internalized Miss Temple's teachings, Jane relinquishes this "fairy godmother," as before she had renounced Bessie, and yearns for "courage . . . to seek real knowledge of life amidst its perils" (p. 87).

It can be argued that in leaving Lowood Jane Eyre participates less in a feminine fairy tale and more in a masculine adventure, because she acts upon her own initiative. Surely Brontë prepares us from earliest childhood for Jane's double impulses toward liberty—the rescue through a *grand amoureux* or freedom to control her life gained through her own celibate adventures. If Brontë's fiction were unequivocally "romantic," then at this crucial moment of awakening from adolescence, we might predict the appearance of a prince as the direct agent, much like Mr. Lloyd earlier. But instead, we discover Jane reaffirming her independence as a wanderer who must make her own way in the world and become her own redeeming guardian. As a prefiguration of modern rebellious heroines, Jane is still largely unilluminated or unselfconscious about her motives. She certainly does not conceive of her acts (nor does Brontë) as deliberate rejections of mythic patterns or of foreordained mandates for feminine behavior. Rather, she sees herself as part of another female tradition of the homeless, orphaned, and plain, who like patient Griseldas must work their way through the world, not hoping for the blessings of the fairy princess, but laboring for mere survival: "I desired liberty; for liberty I gasped; for liberty I uttered a prayer; it seemed scattered on the wind then faintly blowing. I abandoned it and framed a humbler supplication; for change, stimulus: that petition, too, seemed swept off into vague space: 'Then,' I cried half desperate, 'grant me at least a new servitude!' " p. 88).

In *Jane Eyre* the disparity between masculine and feminine modes of psychological growth generates conflict; that is, in struggling toward mature independence, Jane must reconcile fantasies from fairy tales, as promulgated by Bessie, with the realities of a brutal world. By conjoining trial/journey motifs with patterns of patient servitude and waiting from heroine narratives, Brontë makes Jane's final reunion with Rochester much less the sentimental ending of a conventional nineteenth-century female *Bildungsroman* and more the autobiographical emergence of a "real" woman. Superficially, Jane's autobiography may seem a paean to romantic wish fulfillment, the fictional apotheosis of many an adolescent's cherished dreams. But, though tempting, it is deceptively easy to conclude that by adapting heroine tales Charlotte Brontë intends readers to accept unthinkingly the "happy-ever-after" ending of "Reader, I married him."[10] For Brontë, we should remember, focuses upon Jane's near surrender to an immoral liaison with Rochester not to approve romantic fantasies but, conversely, to expose the dangers of the psychosexual dependency they encourage. Besides *Cinderella,* Brontë also invokes *Sleeping Beauty, The Blue Beard,* and *Beauty and the Beast* as archetypes for Jane's maturation in order to heighten the psychic and moral conflicts engendered by her first confrontation with Rochester's sexuality. In Rochester and Bertha, Jane finds not simply a legal impediment to wedlock, but also the fearful threat of carnality from which she must flee to preserve her soul and sanity. While Jane's *rite de passage* recreates the sexual subtext of many romantic tales (as Bettelheim might argue), paradoxically it also illustrates (as I would suggest) the need to reject childhood dreams in order to nourish a woman's maturity, only then to achieve equality in marriage.

Although Jane herself initiates the journey from Lowood, her seeming liberation quickly metamorphoses into a deceptive imprisonment at Thornfield, a psychic enslavement more invidious because disguised as a romantic fulfillment. Jane enters literally and figuratively into a realm of "thorns," in the same way that Sleeping Beauty waits her awakening in a castle overgrown with briars. As Jane paces the galleries in half-enchanted reveries, Thornfield with its "bedsteads of a hundred years old" seems in a slumber reminiscent of the ancient tale (p. 108). Enveloped by inward visions more romantic than gothic, Jane at first treads obliviously along the passage, which "with its two rows of small black doors all shut" resembles, she says, "a corridor in some Bluebeard's castle" (p. 110).[11] Only later will Jane as autobiographer (or Brontë as author) sense the truth of this simile, when the skeletal wives in Bluebeard's locked closet assume loathsome contours in the flesh of Bertha Mason. Brontë's allusions to *Sleeping Beauty* and *The Blue Beard* stress the alternatives for either ecstatic happiness or a husband's thralldom over a disobediently curious wife. An inviting haven that may suddenly transmute into a foreboding prison with attic secrets, Thornfield also externalizes Jane's ambivalences, as in dreamy limbo between adolescence and womanhood, she wishes and waits. But will she awaken like Sleeping Beauty to embrace her prince or like Beauty to confront the Beast?

Surely Brontë had in mind visions from English folklore and fairy tale when she chose to portray Jane's meeting with Rochester as he gallops round a bend in Hay Lane to "break the spell" of Jane's romantic yearnings.[12] Yet like a demon lover, Rochester seems a prince already flawed, when his *black* horse stumbles and falls. He rejects, then begrudgingly leans upon Jane to regain his seat, while curiously she plays the angelic rescuer rather than distraught maiden. He proceeds to a sequestered manor not to liberate a princess, but to confine himself as a Beast therein. Despite Jane's overt disclaimers that "it *was* an incident of no moment, no romance," she finds Rochester's "dark face, with stern features and a heavy brow" a potent aphrodisiac (pp. 118, 116). Although Rochester's urbane cynicism seems at odds with belief in romantic legends, he too endows this encounter with fantastical qualities: "'When you came on me in Hay Lane last night, I thought unaccountably of fairy tales, and had half a mind to demand whether you had bewitched my horse: I am not sure yet'" (p. 125). Thus, Brontë's characters seek half seriously, half playfully for fairy-tale rationales for their inexplicable attraction, in part (we shall discover), to avoid painful realities that threaten their union.

Shifting away from patterns in *Cinderella, Sleeping Beauty,* and *The Blue Beard,* Brontë turns toward *Beauty and the Beast* as her exemplar for Jane's developing relationship with Rochester. Whether she knew Madame de Beaumont's tale from the elegant and widely popular nineteenth-century retelling remains uncertain.[13] But that Brontë would find Beaumont's literary folktale a suggestive analogue seems hardly surprising, since her fiction shares the same fascination with conflicts between virtue and bestiality, deceptive appearances and underlying realities, and focuses comparably on the "release" of a bewitched hero and education of an innocent maiden. Although she remains a governess, unlike Beauty, who is elevated to pampered splendor, Jane responds analogously to Rochester's luxurious drawing room, "fairy place . . . with snowy mouldings of white grapes and vine-leaves" and "crimson couches and ottomans" (p. 107). Like Beast's castle, Rochester's parlor-boudoir becomes the setting for Jane's first exposure to masculine passion, foreshadowed by the virginal white-and-crimson decor, the bacchic grapes and vine leaves. Requesting leave to see her sup, Beast in Beaumont's variant mockingly queries, "Tell me, do not you think me very ugly?" (p. 145). With candor unusual for a terrified heroine who sees a monster, Beauty replies calmly, "That is true . . . for I cannot tell a lie, but I believe you are very good-natured" (pp. 145–46). Summoned forth to the "dining-room" of Thornfield, Jane receives her master's question with equal aplomb: " 'You examine me, Miss Eyre,' said he; 'do you think me handsome?' " (p. 134). Characteristically honest, she replies, " 'No, sir,' " regretting then that she " 'was too plain' " and " 'ought to have replied that . . . tastes differ; that beauty is of little consequence, or something of that sort' " of proper banality (p. 134).

If the question of beauty and ugliness remained at the level of social intercourse, it would warrant little attention. But in both tale and fiction the motif of the male's bestial appearance points to the crux of the heroines' psychic dilemmas: having cultivated virginal virtues through adolescent self-discipline, both Beauty and Jane must now confront masculine sexuality, symbolized outwardly by their suitors' animality. According to fairy tales, young females must overcome lingering fears of male dominance in order to enter successfully into womanhood. Thus, Beauty's terror quickly modulates to tenderhearted pity, then eager longing for Beast, who lavishes upon her splendid clothes, furnishings, and hospitality. Rochester initially eschews ostentatious gifts and substitutes instead gruff cross-examinations after dinner. During such evenings by the hearth, Jane (like Beauty) discovers beneath the "preciously grim . . . granite-hewn features" a man of seemingly irrefutable morals whose "former faults," she rationalizes, "had their source in some cruel cross of fate" (pp. 134, 150). Under the guidance of a "beautiful lady," the faithful and loving Beauty succeeds in releasing the spell cast by a "wicked fairy" upon Beast (p. 150). Similarly seduced into a *mésalliance terrible* by the deceptive sorcery of Bertha, so too Rochester looks to Jane as the "cherished preserver" with magical potions: " 'Tell me, now fairy as you are,—can't you give me a charm, or a philter, or something of that sort, to make me a handsome man?' " (p. 247). Jane overtly discounts " 'the power of magic' "; yet, in her heart she believes that " 'a loving eye is all the charm needed: to such you are handsome enough,' " thereby testifying to her internalization of fairy-tale morals (p. 247). In Beaumont's folktale, Beast's sudden transformation into a prince corroborates Beauty's trust in his moral worth. But Brontë's complex fiction (and by implication human nature) does not permit an easy, magical confirmation of Jane's belief in Rochester's "higher principles, and purer tastes" (p. 150). Rochester only masquerades as a diamond in the rough, while he hides the graver sins of an immoral nature, one capable of concealing deadly secrets by immuring them in third-story rooms.

Bestiality in Brontë's novel does not equate simply with physical ugliness, nor merely signify man's baser sexual drives. Rochester's egocentric compulsion to possess Jane becomes sacrilegious when he defiantly rationalizes his nuptials as an atonement for previous crimes of passion. His need to display Jane betrays itself in schemes to drape her in " 'satin and lace' " with a " 'diamond chain round' " her neck, while Jane steadfastly refuses to disguise her status as a " 'plain, Quakerish governess' " and become an " 'ape in a harlequin's jacket,—a jay in borrowed plumes' " (p. 261). Nonetheless, lulled by her affections into misguided romantic trust, Jane not only translates Rochester's brutish visage into a beloved physiognomy, she also seems mesmerized by his willful control: "For a moment I am beyond my own mastery. What does it mean? I did not think I should tremble in this way when I saw him—or lose my voice or the power of motion in his presence"

(p. 246). As Rochester transforms from monster to seeming prince to an "idol" who stands between her and God, conversely Jane loses her autonomy. More potent than Mrs. Reed's or Brocklehurst's persecutions, this immersion in romantic fantasy threatens her integrity. Rochester subsumes Jane in his wish-fulfilling dream, one to which she is susceptible because it resembles patterns instilled by Bessie's nursery fables and reactivated in adolescence. As surely as Rochester clothes Jane in silks and gossamer veils, he just as insidiously masters her spirit by fulfilling her internalized fantasy in which a beast turns dazzling prince. Those traits of rebellious independence, outspokenness, and high moral principles that distinguished the young Jane seem gradually preempted, as she, like Cinderella and Beauty, falls under a hypnotic spell.

Were it not for a forced separation, Jane and Rochester might continue mute, both spellbound by discrete enchantments, but unable to profess their mutual adoration. In Beaumont's tale Beauty, we should recall, requests leave to tend her sick father, promising to "return in a week" lest Beast "die with grief" (p. 147). Similarly, Jane departs for Gateshead with like assurances to Rochester, not envisioning that she will be detained, as was Beauty, far longer by selfishly manipulative stepsisters. The separations become trials that test each heroine's faithfulness to her suitor: Beauty reflects on "the uneasiness she was likely to cause poor Beast" (p. 148) and Jane sketches Rochester's portrait that she might gaze upon her "friend's face" (p. 236). Both heroines hasten back to their lovers—Beast near death in his garden and Rochester languishing from melancholia at Thornfield. In a double fictional adaptation of Beauty's reunion with Beast, Jane first rediscovers Rochester meditating on the stile amid hedges of roses and briars and then accepts his Midsummer Eve's proposal in the "Edenlike" garden of Thornfield.[14] Unlike Beauty, Jane does not look literally upon the face of a dying Beast; rather, it is the anticipated loss of Rochester through marriage to Blanche Ingram and her own dismissal as governess that spurs her avowal: " 'I have known you, Mr. Rochester; and it strikes me with terror and anguish to feel I absolutely must be torn from you for ever. I see the necessity of departure; and it is like looking on the necessity of death' " (pp. 254–55). In keeping with tale conventions, Rochester's subsequent proposal, " 'But,

Jane, I summon you as my wife,'" and her ecstatic pledge, "'Then, sir, I will marry you,'" miraculously reverse these dire prophesies of death and separation—though only temporarily.

What is on trial in *Jane Eyre*, however, is not merely the heroine's self-will versus her acquiescence, but also the validity of an entire concept of romance derived from fairy tale. By involving Jane in a succession of "charades," Brontë indicates that fantasies of romantic love can delude maidens and blind them to sexual realities and male dominance. When Rochester remolds his meadow reunion with Jane into a "'Conte de fée,'" even Adèle denies the existence of fairies and nominates him "'un vrai menteur'" (p. 270). And when Rochester divests his disguise as "one of the old Mother Bunches" who tell fortunes, Jane remains rapt in a "web of mystification" so dense that she questions, "Where was I? Did I wake or sleep? Had I been dreaming? Did I dream still?" (pp. 193, 201, 203). These questions pertain not simply to this charade, but also to Jane's dilemma throughout her stay at Thornfield. Both the prophetic dialogue with Rochester as sibyl and the subsequent garden proposal should signal moments of awakening when Jane crosses the threshold from late adolescent dreams of princes to the reality of womanhood and marriage. Such would seem to be Jane's progress, as she watches Adèle in the "slumber of childhood" as if she were an "emblem of my past life," while "all my life was awake and astir" on the eve before her nuptials (p. 288). But Brontë's subversive gothic symbolisms and literary allusions imply that Jane still sleeps in an imaginary realm, like a heroine in *Beauty and the Beast* or in Shakespeare's *A Midsummer Night's Dream.* Half in jest, half in earnest, Jane contemplates her soon-to-be title as "young Mrs. Rochester," not trusting but that it may prove illusory: "'Human beings never enjoy complete happiness in this world. I was not born for a different destiny to the rest of my species; to imagine such a lot befalling me is a fairly tale—a daydream'" (pp. 260–61).

Although Richard Mason dramatically overthrows Jane's fantasy, the wedding is aborted for causes more deep-seated than Rochester's overt attempt at bigamy. For Thornfield's attic secret is not only the hidden Victorian specter of carnality, but also the sexual relationship between mother and father that the child (in Freudian theory) fears to see but ultimately must surmount in growing toward independent maturity.[15] Acting out a primal scene, Bertha and Rochester grapple in an intimate and violent embrace:

Mr. Rochester flung me behind him: the lunatic sprang and grappled his throat viciously, and laid her teeth to his cheek: they struggled. . . . He could have settled her with a well-planted blow; but he would not strike: he would only wrestle. . . . The operation was performed amidst the fiercest yells, and the most convulsive plunges. Mr. Rochester then turned to the spectators: he looked at them with a smile both acrid and desolate.

"That is *my wife*," said he: "Such is the sole conjugal embrace I am ever to know—such are the endearments which are to solace my leisure hours!" [p. 296]

This fierce battle mocks what might have been Jane's virginal initiation by substituing a loathsome vision of copulation for the romantic expectation of "happy ever after." Brontë's exaggeration together with Rochester's appeal to the spectators (including Jane and the reader) heighten the impression of a voyeuristic fantasy abruptly transformed into a psychodrama that reenacts a child's distorted vision of parental coupling. Recall the Brobdingnagian proportions of Reverend Brocklehurst and Mrs. Reed, those surrogate parents who epitomize sexual repression legitimized by a sanctimonious piety. Just as that pair thwarts ten-year-old Jane's passionate outbursts, so likewise Rochester's sordid grappling with Bertha prevents a premature sexual commitment and forces Jane to reexamine the nature of her love relationship. That she has regressed during her engagement to Rochester is made clear by this primal scene. Merely intuited before, the psychic truth now becomes compelling—the necessity of both losing Edward and of relinquishing the child within. Jane's fall from innocence is painful, yet nonetheless fortunate, because it completes her separation from parent surrogates and wakens her from romantic illusions.

Charlotte Brontë's disillusionment with fairy tale is figured also by Jane's confrontation with Bertha in the "goblin's cell," where there is no way out, except to face the psychosexual realities that romantic myth disguises.[16] Prior to the wedding, the *rite de passage* from plain Jane to a brilliant Mrs. Rochester had seemed a magical progress toward "happy love and blissful union" (p. 288). But as the charade's "pantomime of a marriage" foreshadows, Thornfield as a mansion for a "Bride" transmutes suddenly into "Bridewell," a prison for demented

past wives and future child mistresses. Brontë (through Jane) encounters what Helene Moglen terms "the creative cul-de-sac of the
romantic mode," where marriage leads back to Victorian patriarchy
rather than forward to a mature female identity.[17] While seeming to
promise women independence by creating an image of connubial
union between equals, in reality "romance" perpetuates a master/slave
relationship. Marrying Rochester, Jane would be victimized by her
sexual acquiescence and become a despised paramour, not an individual with equal "spirit,—with will and energy" (p. 320). Jane must
reject even the message of *Beauty and the Beast*—that her love can
save Rochester, transform monster into man—on Christian grounds
that each being finds redemption from God, not from earthly "angels."
Furthermore, Jane must renounce the tale's implicit plea for romantic
submission, because although fitting for the passive Beauty, it would
doom the more assertive Jane to a subjugation she abhors, as her rebellions against John Reed, Brocklehurst, and later St. John witness.
Losing her virtue and independence, even to gain the prince of her
dreams, becomes an intolerable sacrifice, as Jane proclaims: " 'I care
for myself. The more solitary, the more friendless, the more unsus-
tained I am, the more I will respect myself.' . . . Physically, I felt, at
the moment, powerless as stubble exposed to the draught and glow of
a furnace—mentally, I still possessed my soul, and with it the certainty
of ultimate safety" (pp. 319, 320).

Wakening for the last time in her Thornfield bedchamber and from
a dream in which she "lay in the red-room at Gateshead," Jane discovers not childhood's *ignis fatuus* but a "white human form" with
"glorious brow earthward," who speaks "so near, it whispered in my
heart—'My daughter, flee temptation!' " (pp. 321, 322). Whether a
reincarnation of the natural mother or a projection of the "mother
within" Jane herself, this *sage femme,* more primeval than Bessie or
Miss Temple, blesses her true advent into maturity.[18] As Jane journeys
into nature's bleak, unknown regions to search for self without romantic illusions or paternalistic guardians, she puts away childish
belief in Bessie's "old fairy tales and older ballads." Jane herself un-
locks Thornfield's garden gate and sets forth on an independent,
Gulliverian quest along "a road I had never travelled, but often noticed and wondered where it led" (p. 323). Her subsequent choice at

"Whitcross" signifies not only a psychic turning from Thornfield to strike out "into the heath" toward Marsh End, but also a structural crossroads for the novel (pp. 324, 325). Leaving behind English folklore and the fantasy realms of *Cinderella, Sleeping Beauty, The Blue Beard,* and *Beauty and the Beast,* Charlotte Brontë relocates Jane in a postlapsarian landscape where Christian suffering ultimately yields new wisdom and a new concept of romance.

Although Jane remains untainted because she flees the tempter, she has seen in Bertha and Rochester an allegory of human concupiscence. Paradisiacal gardens and idyllic marriages alike become the stuff of a Midsummer Eve's dream. To renounce a childish pursuit of perfect nuptial bliss is, however, to inaugurate simultaneously the more painful struggle toward adult self-knowledge within a fallen world—a quest for which Christian models, drawn from Shakespeare and Milton, perhaps provide more appropriate paradigms. Brontë's adaptation, for instance, from *King Lear* recalls both Cordelia's banishment and Lear's own tribulations. Outcast on the moors, with Nature her mother and God her spiritual father, Jane is "brought face to face with Necessity," with the primitive need for food, shelter, and charity, needs subsequently filled by the Rivers sisters in a house whose distant light "shining dim, but constant" guides her toward a new, gentle beneficence (pp. 328, 330).[19] Whereas earlier Brontë had heightened similarities between the Reed cousins and Cinderella's evil siblings, here she abandons fairy tales. Diana the classical huntress and Mary the Christian mother, as the names suggest, become Jane's new avatars of female strength, tenderness, and learning. Jane enters into a life more real than fantastical, where Hannah the housekeeper bakes *goose*berry pies instead of narrating sentimental folktale. Having "crossed the threshold of this house," Jane feels "no longer outcast, vagrant, and disowned by the wide world," and she can begin "once more to know myself," albeit rebaptized as Jane Elliott (p. 339). Reborn of nature and the spirit, as signified by St. John's raising her from the wet doorstep, Jane, like King Lear, grows in wisdom. Although it is neither instantaneous nor painless, her saga leads ultimately to a reconciliation with Rochester, not to death, in part because her story is a female derivative of *King Lear*—a romance, not the tragedy found later in Lucy Snowe's story in *Villette.*

Knowledge, Brontë's allusions to *King Lear* emphasize, requires a stripping away of deluding fantasies and a remolding of more realistic visions of human nature. No longer a rootless orphan, Jane rediscovers her "true" identity through a reunion with her Rivers cousins and through the wealth from Uncle John, which establishes her as a self-reliant woman, no longer compelled by need to serve any master. Although it may remind us of Cinderella's rise from rags to riches, Jane's ascent from "indigence to wealth" is "solid, an affair of the actual world, nothing ideal" like fairy-tale rewards for marriage (p. 384). The subsequent years during which Jane reconceives herself not as a heroine of an internalized fairy tale but as a mature, worldly woman serve as an essential preparation for the reunion with Rochester. Jane's new independence displaces whatever romantic ideals linger, and it also grants her a new freedom of choice, sufficiently strong to reject St. John's proposal of marriage. St. John embodies an excessively disciplined reason and Christian piety toward which Jane gravitates in a pendulum swing from Rochester's equally extreme passion. Although he may seem outwardly to be a prince charming or at least a Christian savior, St. John no longer *appears* to Jane's imagination as an ideal figure surrounded with the glow of her own romantic illusions. Instead, in this fallen realm Jane more easily challenges St. John as "an equal—one with whom I might argue—one whom, if I saw good, I might resist" (p. 409). Jane revolts against St. John's sterile proposal, which mocks her "'woman's heart'" and which would reduce her to "'a sole helpmeet'" whom St. John might "'influence efficiently in life, and retain absolutely till death'" (pp. 411, 408). Rejecting the presumption of servitudes to male masters, whether in the guise of passion or Christian duty, Jane covets instead a mature equality, domestic amenities, and shared affections—an ideal balance of nature, the intellect, and the spirit, epitomized by the humanistic sisterhood of Mary and Diana.

While Jane learns about equality, Rochester (like Gloucester in *King Lear*) undergoes a trial of fire and blindness. A condign punishment for his amorous lusts, the conflagration at Thornfield serves as a purgation and, in his heroic attempt to save Bertha, Rochester finally assumes responsibility for his self-engendered sins. Like Lear and Gloucester, who discover the blessings of pity and forgiveness, Rochester survives his travails with new humility, though with diminished vitality. Even if he forfeits the eyes with which he lusted and the hand he offered Jane in a bigamous marriage, Rochester paradoxically emerges with his pride mortified and a belief in divine, not human, agents of grace. Rochester and Jane can reunite, because both come closer to a human equality by virtue of mutual need. While proclaiming, " 'I am independent, sir, as well as rich: I am my own mistress,' " Jane, at the same time, accepts her dependent needs for home and family, desires capable of fulfillment within a marriage based on mutual feeling rather than on devouring mastery (p. 438). These lessons are not awakenings in the fairy-tale sense, where instantaneous love allows one to live happily ever after; rather they are enlightened perceptions, hard-won within a real world where fallible humans must perforce exist. Though disabused of romantic ideals and severely tested by harsh experience, neither Jane nor Rochester is irrevocably ruined, only changed and humanized. Jane Eyre's saga may begin like a fairy tale, but Brontë transforms the paradigmatic into a personal history, investing her *Bildungsroman* with a realistic understanding of female needs for assertive choices and an individuality far different from that of acquiescent romantic heroines.

Brontë's choice of Shakespearean dramas and *Paradise Lost* to underscore these psychological changes requires that readers revisualize the context and the concept of romance. Brontë's evocations of *A Midsummer Night's Dream* correspond with Jane's early fantasies of love; the motifs from *King Lear* illuminate Jane's stumbling journey across rain-pelted moors toward restored kinship, independence, and an experiential rather than fantasy knowledge of humankind; and Ferndean's pastoral rejuvenation reminds us of Leontes's poignant reconciliation with Hermione in *A Winter's Tale* where nature, too, reflects the joy of a mature love renewed. With stark amazement, Leontes presents his hand to Hermione (once thought dead), finding that "O, she's warm!" as "she embraces him" and "hangs about his neck" (5.3.109, 111, 112). Similarly, the blind Rochester gropes for Jane's " 'small fingers' " with his "muscular hand," then seizes her "shoulder—neck—waist," until Jane is "entwined and gathered to him" (p. 437). "That she is living" Paulina assures a doubting Leontes (5.3.115), just as Rochester marvels at his " 'vision' " and " 'dream' " fulfilled

" 'in truth—in the flesh? My living Jane?' " (p. 437). As in Shake-speare's later romances, Brontë's fiction incorporates a dramatic pattern that proceeds from comic promise, to tragic separation, and finally to revivifying reunion. Midsummer's happiness at Thornfield gives way to winter's alienation, but earns a springtime reconcilation wrought from Christian repentance, forgiveness, and humility.

In part Brontë assimilates Shakespeare's concept of romance, be-cause, as a product of the nineteenth century, she still defined married love within the context of a Christian universe where innately sinful beings must seek regenerative grace. Hence, as a literary model of hu-man relationships, "romance" encompasses not merely love's delights, but also the sterner recognitions of passion's excess, human follies, separation and trial, and the need for growth in self-knowledge. By forcing Jane to confront Bertha Mason and the aborted nuptials, Brontë introduces complex, psychosexual truths and thus signifies that fairy-tale idealizations simplify and delude, often glossing over hu-man sexuality, deceit and sin, male dominance and female subservience. Brontë's substitution of Shakespearean and Miltonic prototypes for fairy-tale paradigms signals her desire to portray romantic love in a postlapsarian, not a fantasy realm. Romantic fairy tales portray life as a comedy with an infinite wealth of happy endings. Shakespeare, Mil-ton, and Brontë create romances in which human love momentarily transcends life's tragedies but cannot eradicate them. Brontë makes plain the final Christian context for Jane's marriage by deliberately echoing the final lines of *Paradise Lost,* when Adam and Eve go forth into the world sustained by complementary strengths from God as a merciful provision for their human survival: "Then he stretched his hand out to be led. I took that dear hand, held it a moment to my lips, then let it pass round my shoulder: Being so much lower of stature than he, I served both for his prop and guide. We entered the wood, and wended homeward" (p. 451).[20] In Brontë's novel, as in her dra-matic and epic analogues, marriage unites equals in the sight of a benevolent God who pities men and women their frailties and gives them each other as props for this fallen life of woods and wanderings. Although she could and did deny the illusions of fairy-tale romance, Brontë turns to *A Winter's Tale* and *Paradise Lost* to reaffirm the possibility of romantic love that culminates in wedded bliss—a reassurance which perhaps Brontë herself and surely her readers still needed.

Jane Eyre's popular appeal as a female *Bildungsroman* stems largely from its classic reformulation of fairy-tale motifs to which, as readers schooled by our culture's folklore, we cannot help being drawn. As I have illustrated, the story begins with an echo of *Cinderella* and then transforms into a variant of *Beauty and the Beast,* one modified however by gothic shadows and psychological depths permitted to nineteenth-century novelists. From its opening *Jane Eyre* plays upon a collective, folkloric unconscious, engaging readers to transfer youthful romantic expectations from their own psyches into the fiction and to judge its success by the fidelity to fantasy paradigms. When Jane's dreams disintegrate in the face of Bertha Mason's grotesque incarnation and Rochester's revealed perfidy, our resulting angry disillusionment suggests how strongly we expect this narrative to end with a beatific marriage. And although the third volume with St. John and the Rivers sisters is crucial to Jane's maturation into true womanhood, it is remarkable how many readers repress or dismiss these events, clinging in memory only to the reassurances of Ferndean and "Reader, I married him."

Although Jane may seem at the end a Mother Goose tale-teller, who recasts her own history in a romantic tale, we must recall that Jane as heroine (and narrator) changes, bringing to the novel's ending a mature rather than naive self-consciousness. Jane is, after all, a " 'mocking changeling' " who Brontë tells us is " 'fairy-born and human-bred,' " precisely because human trials and wisdom temper her romantic fantasies (p. 441). Those childhood readings at Bessie's knee can mislead readers as well as Jane into expecting fairy-tale fulfillments when, in actuality, the domestic realism of the reconciliation testifies to Jane's mature concept of romance, one patterned after Shakespearean and Miltonic models. "Fairy-born" marriages recede before Brontë's vision of "human-bred" mutuality between man and woman. And Brontë's sophisticated exploration of the fantasies and truths—psychological and cultural—which are embedded in fairy tales teaches us, as readers and critics, the power of folkloric paradigms of romance and the disillusionment of accepting charades and pantomimes.

BRENDA R. SILVER

The Reflecting Reader in *Villette*

"Who *are* you, Miss Snowe?" Ginevra Fanshawe asks the narrator-protagonist of Charlotte Brontë's *Villette,* a question echoed by generations of readers and critics and encouraged by Lucy Snowe herself.[1] An orphan, an outsider, a woman without family or country, an "inoffensive shadow," and a ray so hot that at least one person shields his eyes from it—Lucy both courts and laments the roles assigned to her by others in what is rightfully read as her search for selfhood. Ultimately, however, *who* Lucy is is inseparable from *what* she is: a teller of tales unspeakable in the presence of either her comfortable and comforting godmother and the friends who surround her at La Terrasse, or the colder, more worldly, yet equally uncomprehending eavesdroppers at the pensionnat on the Rue Fossette. If, as has been argued, the "reality" of a narrative is a mutual creation of the text and its readers, and this act depends on the author's ability to stimulate the imagination in such a way as to make us think in terms different from our own,[2] then Lucy, as if aware of this relationship, has self-consciously structured her use of silence and revelation to immerse us in a world as complex and conflicted as that which she herself experienced. Knowing, however, that she cannot trust others to perceive her as she is—that even when she is not invisible she is more than likely to be misread—Lucy goes one step further: she projects her readers into the landscape of the novel, the text, and asks them to use their imaginations in a mutual act of creation which in turn validates her own emerging self. In this way her narrative both inscribes her evolving identity and establishes a community of readers whose recognition and acceptance provide the context necessary for an individual's growth to maturity—a context all too often denied to women.

Although several critics have recently explored the role of Lucy's narration in the discovery and creation of her identity, most have assumed that she is an "unreliable" narrator whose voice, according to Helene Moglen, is characterized by "indirection" and "neurotic rationalization," and whose form for the novel is "the form of [her] neuro-

sis: a representation of the novel's subject."[3] Mary Jacobus is more
direct: "Lucy lies to us. Her deliberate ruses, omissions and falsifica-
tions break the unwritten contract of first-person narrative (the confidence between reader and 'I') and unsettle our faith in the reliability
of the text."[4] Gilbert and Gubar, on the other hand, accept Lucy's narrative reticence and evasions, her apparent attempts to mislead the
reader, and attribute her "anxious and guilty" feelings about her narrative to the fact that her "life, her sense of herself, does not conform
to the literary or social stereotypes provided by her culture to define
and circumscribe female life." The result is nothing less than a "mythic
undertaking—an attempt to create an adequate fiction of her own."[5]

But it can also be argued that Lucy is less evasive and even less unreliable than most critics have assumed—that she is, in fact, a self-
consciously reliable narrator of unusual circumstances whose narrative
choices ask her "readers" to perceive her on her own terms.[6] The difficulty may be that Lucy's terms are so different from the maxims and
prejudices of the culture she inhabits and portrays that they are read
by even sympathetic readers as perverse or implausible. Here I am
borrowing the term and the concept of "implausibility" put forward
by Nancy Miller in her essay "Emphasis Added: Plots and Plausibilities in Women's Fiction."[7] In this piece, Miller defines the persistent
misreading of women's texts as extravagant, implausible, unmotivated,
or unconvincing in terms of the reader's expectations of what a narrative should be, and illustrates how these expectations are in turn determined or judged according to the dominant cultural ideology. Taking Gérard Genette's analysis of "Vraisemblance et Motivation" as her
starting point, Miller cites Genette's distinction between three different forms of narratives: the "plausible narrative," which implicitly and
silently obeys the conventions of genre and the cultural maxims on
which they rest; the "arbitrary narrative," which deliberately and silently destroys this collusion but refuses to justify itself; and the narrative with "a motivated and *artificial plausibility.'*" The last type,
"exemplified by the 'endless chatting' of a Balzacian novel, we might
call 'other-directed,' for here authorial commentary justifies its story
to society by providing the missing maxims, or by inventing them"
(pp. 38–39). As Miller points out, however, glossing Genette's analysis, what might *seem* to be silent or even absent in the arbitrary narra-

tive—that is, an alternate set of maxims—"may simply be inaudible to the dominant mode of reception" (p. 39).

Within this framework, Lucy's tale employs characteristics of both the artificially plausible narrative and the seemingly arbitrary narrative that in fact inscribes an alternative ideology, and both these narrative modes are encoded in her dialogue with the reader. Her constant shifting between self-justification and "silence" thus becomes a plausible portrayal of the conflicting needs and desires she confronts and experiences without being able to count on either the ear or the understanding of those who dictate social behavior—and plots of novels. Rather than misleading or lying to us, or to herself, Lucy is deliberately creating not only a new form of fiction for women, but a new audience—part critic, part confidante, part sounding board—whose willingness to enter her world and interpret her text will provide the recognition denied to women who do not follow traditional paths of development.

In order to test this hypothesis, we must trace Lucy's relationship to the fictionalized reader in the text, the created recipient of her tale. There are, in fact, particularly in the beginning of the novel, at least two readers to whom Lucy reveals different aspects of her experience and herself, in order to justify them to her critics or to confide them to a sympathetic listener. Later, as the narrative and Lucy's sense of herself evolve, the reader develops into an audience so accustomed to and accepting of Lucy's "strange stammerings" (chap. 36), that the different readers are merged into one.

A similar development in the nature of the audience might also explain the ambiguity that informs our perception of the reader's gender. Although most readers today, I suspect, automatically think of the fictionalized reader addressed by Lucy as female, on the rare occasions that Lucy refers to her reader by pronoun, she uses the generic "he" and "his" (chaps. 8, 29, 30). In addition to following an accepted literary convention (and despite the fact that most novel readers were women), Lucy may deliberately be positing a male audience to emphasize that the power to pass both literary and moral judgments on her story belonged, in the public sphere, predominantly to men. Lucy's narrative choice here reflects her creator's experience in one such forum—critical reviews—where she had already suffered the pain of being labeled unconventional, unchristian, unfeminine, and unsexed. That the harshest judgments came from other women, writing anonymously, highlights the force that social maxims exert on women's self-perceptions and the complexity of gender identification for unconventional women—and women writers.[8]

In her presentation of herself to others, then, Lucy is trebly constrained: as woman, as heroine, and as storyteller. From this perspective, the split between the two readers in the early part of Lucy's narrative may well signify a split between those readers who accept the cultural maxims about women in a patriarchy and want to find them mirrored in novels—an audience that speaks with a male voice and male authority and might well condemn her actions—and those readers, similar to the female personifications who populate Lucy's psychic landscape, in whom she can confide.[9] If this distinction breaks down later in the novel when the different readers begin to merge, it may be owing to Lucy's sense that she has so shaped her audience to her own ends that gender becomes insignificant.

In the beginning of her narrative, however, the entity whom Lucy addresses explicitly as "reader" stands at a distance from Lucy herself in a potentially antagonistic posture. This reader first appears in her description of the eight years that intervene between the visit to Bretton described in the early chapters and the events that leave her on her own without family or support. "I will permit the reader," she writes, "to picture me . . . as a bark slumbering through halcyon weather, in a harbour still as glass—the steersman stretched on the little deck, his face up to heaven, his eyes closed: buried if you will in a long prayer"—the situation in which "a great many women and girls are supposed to pass their lives" (chap. 4). The identification of the reader here with the way things are supposed to be—with the conventional expectations for women's lives—makes this reader the exponent of truisms about women that Lucy knows from her own experience are not valid. The irony of her "permission" to her readers to deceive themselves emphasizes society's refusal to see or to admit the actual circumstances of her—and by implication other women's—existence. The result of this refusal is to invalidate Lucy's perception of her own reality, and to make Lucy herself invisible. From society's perspective, then, Lucy has no being, and her subsequent presentation of herself as a shadow, as well as other characters' misreading of her nature and her needs, mirrors her social reality.

Lucy's insight into the disparity between social expectations and reality for women, however, clashes throughout the novel with her simultaneous awareness that she has internalized the very maxims that restrict her development by their failure to recognize her existence. Not only does she lack a blueprint for her journey to selfhood—that is, a conventional plot—but she envisions and presents herself as a divided being whose strengths and weaknesses, as well as her economic and emotional needs, are continually at odds with each other. Forced by circumstances into self-reliance and exertion, denied the luxury of remaining in the prayerful sleep assumed of women, she struggles to compromise between her necessarily unconventional actions and her need to remain within the social structure. As Lucy herself tells us, early in life she developed "a staid manner of my own which ere now had been as good to me as cloak and hood of hodden grey; since under its favour I had been enabled to achieve with impunity, and even approbation, deeds that, if attempted with an excited and unsettled air, would in some minds have stamped me as a dreamer and zealot" (chap. 5).

Coming at the moment of her decision to go to London, this statement inscribes the parameters of Lucy's social and narrative stance: her realism and her rebellion. Her cloak of staidness ensures her the acceptance and help not only of Mrs. Barrett, her old nurse, but of the old waiter at the London inn who becomes the first of her many guides. Later, it secures her the approval of Madame Beck and the Count de Bossompierre, also enabling figures, and prevents others from detecting her love for Graham or Paul. But this cloak also masks her other self: the woman who chafes at her restrictions, even while apologizing for her pleasure in walking around London by herself or being rowed through the night to the boat that will carry her over the channel. And nowhere is this conflict clearer than in her dialogue with her two readers at the onset of her journey: the conventional or socialized reader, who embodies society's maxims about women and whom she creates to ask the implied questions and make the implied criticisms she anticipates in her relation with the world; and the rebellious or unsocialized reader, in whom she confides those perceptions and feelings so far removed from the social conventions as to have little or no plausibility if uttered aloud. If, in her justification of her actions to the socialized reader, she self-consciously creates an "artificially plausible" narrative, the dialogue with the rebellious reader assumes a shared perspective—an arbitrary narrative—that gradually dominates both readers and informs the text.

Before tracing the evolution of her two readers, however, we must examine the circumstances that force Lucy to create her own life. By the time we meet her at Bretton, all the seeds of the disaster that starts her upon her journey have already been sown, and she herself has begun to develop the social and narrative stances that become more pronounced later on. The most significant factor is, of course, her solitude. Residing with unidentified kinfolk, picturing her stay at Bretton as a period of calm in a pilgrim's progress, Lucy has already acquired a sense of herself as an outsider, an observer rather than an actor, who is capable of telling Polly that she must learn to hide her feelings and not expect too much from others. This restraint is particularly necessary, she implies, in the situation that prompts her remark: the unequal power relationship that exists between young men such as Graham, her god-brother, who go to school and visit friends, and the girls who sit at home reading and sewing and waiting for them.

Although Polly's role as Lucy's psychological double is well established, Kate Millett's cultural interpretation of this doubling is worth noting here: "Brontë keeps breaking people into two parts so we can see their divided and conflicting emotions; [Polly] is the worshipful sister, Lucy the envious one. Together they represent the situation of the girl in the family"[10]—the situation, we might add, of a younger sister in a family with an adored son. Under these circumstances, the sister/girl might, like Polly, choose to serve the idol; or she might resent the privilege and desire, however unconsciously, the power for herself. Lucy, even at this age, is divided between the two responses, but she does refuse to play Polly's role, and this choice inevitably increases her isolation. Instead, she adopts the protective facade of coolness, calm, and quiet that serves both to confine her conflicting desires and mask her rebellion.

Nowhere, perhaps, are the effects of Lucy's solitude more evident than in the loss of social status that accompanies her loss of family, a clear indication of the interconnected role of class and gender in determining a person's development—and worth. Denied the material support and visibility traditionally provided by father, husband, or kin, and denied the education that men of her class usually received, she had few if any options open to her that would not further her alienation from her class or prevent her from following the acceptable routes for female development: marriage or death. We have only to contrast the course of Graham's life after his family suffers a financial setback to Lucy's to see vividly the obstacles working against her growth. Both, as Lucy unequivocally states, began life in the same social station.[11] But whereas Graham enters his father's profession, medicine, and by virtue of it moves out into the world and up the social ladder—not to mention his support of his mother—Lucy withdraws into the two hot closed rooms of Miss Marchmont's house before crossing the channel to enter the conventual environment and enclosed garden of the Rue Fossette. The perils of her friendless and solitary state are graphically illustrated upon her arrival in Villette, when she not only has to ask the now lordly Graham to speak for her and suggest an inn, but, once separated from him, becomes the victim of male pursuit and harassment.

If these "respectable" men perceive Lucy, the solitary streetwalker, as a prostitute, they are only assigning to her the role often assumed by women left in her position—a role simultaneously recognized and outlawed by society. Lucy chooses another path. In leaving England to seek work as a governess/teacher, she adopts one of the few means of support available to embarrassed gentlewomen, but this choice also forces her to "admit the realities of her status as a paid employee and resign herself to the loss of her place in English society."[12] However exhilarated Lucy may be walking around London or aboard ship, she realizes only too well that her loss of status will prevent her from achieving what women were expected to desire—marriage with an equal or superior and the protection that such a union would offer her. Denied the wealth, position, or beauty that would make her a desirable object of possession, she will be unable to overcome the inequality inherent in the relationship between supposedly passive women and successful young men such as Graham. Although Lucy is clear-sighted enough to perceive that she does not have the means to play the traditional female roles enacted by other women in the novel— Ginevra, Paulina, or Mrs. Bretton—the desires she represses haunt her still. They surface both in her poignant questions to Paul at the end of the novel: "Ah, I am not pleasant to look at——?" and "Do I displease your eyes *much?*" (chap. 41); and in her yearning to assume woman's most traditional role by becoming, in her words, one of those who "lay down the whole burden of human egotism, and gloriously take up the nobler charge of labouring and living for others" (chap. 31).

The conflict between Lucy's acknowledgment of her social position and the emotional needs that she has internalized (a conflict that is reflected in her creation of the two readers) is further complicated by her unfeminine desire to be her own person—to achieve independence— and her knowledge of her powers: an active intellect and the ability to feel strongly and act decisively. When Ginevra, observant in her own worldly way, defines Lucy during their mirror scene after the play by declaring "Nobody in the world but you cares for cleverness" (chap. 14), she simultaneously acknowledges one of Lucy's strongest attributes and reflects its lack of value in the context of cultural expectations for women. Early in the novel, Lucy measures her pride of intellect (and it is great) against the transformation into a beautiful wife and mother she observes in a less intelligent woman who had been at school with her. Intelligence, she perceives, does not lead to social visibility or acceptance: she recognizes the older woman but is not in turn recognized by her. The language of this scene captures Lucy's conflicting self-definitions and her characteristic response: "Wifehood and maternity had changed her thus, as I have since seen them change others even less promising than she. Me she had forgotten. [The "she" here is ambiguous: wifehood and motherhood, or the woman? Both, I would say.] I was changed, too, though not, I fear, for the better. I made no attempt to recall myself to her memory: why should I?" (chap. 5). Why indeed!

Lucy partly resolves the conflict between intelligence and womanhood by insisting throughout the novel that *others* perceive her as clever, or interested in learning, or quick, whereas in truth she was none of these things. In much the same way, she justifies to the reader her major decision to go forward into the classroom (rather than backward into the nursery) as a reaction to what she describes as Madame Beck's masculine challenge to her gifts. A closer look, however, reveals that through this "justification" she transforms what appears to be an arbitrary personal choice into an assertion of female selfhood broad enough to include intellectual ambition and achievement. She creates, that is, a plausible social and narrative context for her own self-development that in turn opens the way for other women to follow her. Later, goaded into intellectual activity by Paul, she declares: "Whatever my powers—feminine or the contrary—God had given them, and I felt resolute to be ashamed of no faculty of His bestowal" (chap. 30).

The power of conflicting cultural maxims revealed by Lucy's seeming denial of her own strengths manifests itself in linguistic as well as psychological evasions. Forced by her situation to speak as well as to act for herself, she adopts speech patterns that allow her simultaneously to justify her actions—both to society and to herself—and to mask their true import. The most striking of these is her well-documented presentation of herself as acted on, an object, rather than as actor, the subject or agent of the sentence or the deed. At every turning point in the novel, at every moment of decision, Lucy chooses instinctively to break free of social constraints and go forward to self-discovery and growth, even while denying that the decision or action is hers. "Fate," she writes, "took me in her strong hand" and directed her to knock at the door of the pensionnat; "a bold thought"—to go to London—"was sent to my mind; my mind was made strong to receive it" (chaps. 7, 5). Further complicating her self-presentation is her clear sense of what she is and is not, of what she will or will not do, a certainty that often masks itself in the grammatical construction, "it did not suit me." Later, however, as Lucy begins to gain confidence and a sympathetic audience, her assertions of herself as agent, "I," rather than object, "me," become more frequent; but she continues to the end to insist that other people or changed circumstances guide her and are responsible for her economic and social success.

While many critics have offered explanations for what Moglen calls Lucy's "language of passivity," they often fail to look at what I have been emphasizing: the reality of the codes that discourage women from actively pursuing their own ends except through marriage, and the limited models for development and access to material support once they are denied the protection of family and friends.[13] The problem of voice illustrated by Lucy's difficulty in saying "I" reflects her isolation within a culture that rejects her strengths for lack of a context in which to read them—the same isolation that forces her to create her own readers. In her conversation with Graham about the illness induced by her solitude, Graham's question " 'Who is in the wrong, then, Lucy?' " evokes the response. " 'Me—Dr. John—me; and a great abstraction . . . me and Fate' " (chap. 17). Fate here becomes the ironic embodiment of those circumstances that Lucy knows better than to speak aloud, even if she had the words to describe them, since they lack the social recognition or cultural context that would make her narration of them plausible. In fact, society itself is at a loss for words when describing Lucy's state, just as Dr. John is at a loss to prescribe anything to cure her. His suggestions for her future care—change of air and scene, cheerful society, exercise—may bear, as Lucy comments in one of her classic understatements, "the safe sanction of custom, and the well-worn stamp of use" (chap. 17), but they fail utterly to recognize how inimical "custom" and "use" are to women in Lucy's uncustomary situation. For custom and use are exactly those forces that move Lucy to justify her tremendous delight in walking around London alone, frown on her unaccompanied journey to Boue-Marine where she is the only woman in the hotel breakfast room, permit respectable men to pursue a solitary woman across town for their sport, and ultimately imprison her alone in the school during the vacation. Lucy's "bad grammar," then, her "me," accurately captures the way custom and use blind society to the reality of lives like Lucy's and reduce women to objects.

Yet another interpretation of Lucy's language of passivity is made possible by Miller's analysis of how psychology and fiction have supported the customary reading of women's ambitions and desires as erotic or romantic, thereby severely limiting their range of self-expression in either social discourse or daydreams. Quoting Freud's statement—" 'In young women erotic wishes dominate the phantasies almost exclusively, for their ambition is generally comprised in their erotic longings; in young men egoistic and ambitious wishes assert

themselves plainly enough alongside their erotic desires' " (p. 40) —
Miller finds in women's novels a challenge to this restrictive view,
finds another economy: "In this economy, egoistic desires would assert themselves paratactically alongside erotic ones. The repressed
content, I think, would be, not erotic impulses, but an impulse to
power: a fantasy of power that would revise the social grammar in
which women are never defined as subjects; a fantasy of power that
disdains a sexual exchange in which women can participate only as
objects of circulation" (p. 41). This power, however, will manifest
itself as what it is—the power of the weak—and " 'the most essential
form of accommodation for the weak is to conceal what power they
do have.' "[14]

Lucy, then, must conceal in her discourse her supposedly masculine
"ambitious wishes" as well as her erotic desires, both of which forcefully assert themselves on the one occasion when she is empowered
by society to adopt the role of actor on the public stage. One of the
most notable aspects of this scene, the school play, is its deliberate
confusion of sex roles and gender identification. Cast as a man in a
plot written by someone else, Lucy brilliantly enacts the initiative, the
competitiveness, the courtship, the wit, and the power that in real life
are denied her by her social status and her gender. As Graham says
after the fact, she made "a very killing fine gentleman" (chap. 16),
and her first act, once in the role, is to conquer the duplicitous Zélie
St. Pierre by asserting the weakness of the latter's female sex.

Although Lucy does not want to *be* or to *win* the beautiful and self-
confident Ginevra, the object of her desire within the fantasy/play, she
clearly relishes the freedom to exercise her hidden powers. Her consciousness of this desire emerges in her acknowledged source of inspiration: the presence of Graham in the audience, the brother/rival
who animated her to act "as if wishful and resolute to win and conquer" and in the process to "rival" and then "eclipse" him (chap. 14).
What Lucy also recognizes, however, is that the roles men such as
Graham play naturally by virtue of their gender, she can fill only by
proxy, and her rejection of her faculty and relish for dramatic expression is in part a refusal to dissipate her energy on goals that she can
achieve only by adding the tokens of manhood to her female self in
the fantastic realm of the theater. The self-respect implicit in her re-

fusal to dress completely as a man for the role—to deny her female-
ness—demands that her search for identity and fulfillment occurs on a
different stage. For her, the audience at the play did not number "personal friends and acquaintances"; "foreigners and strangers," the crowd
could not provide the recognition necessary for her growth (chaps.
15, 14).

Although Lucy rejects living by proxy (Ginevra's way) and refuses
to perform before an audience of strangers, the play does allow her to
test her powers and find her voice, an experience that informs her on-
going dialogue with her chosen audience, the reader. "Who will lend
me a tongue?" she asks near the end of her tale, knowing only too
well that she can rely on no one but herself. Her struggle to take control of her narrative (as well as of her life) is mirrored in the creation of an audience whose presence and responsiveness increasingly
provide her with the strength to be that comes from external recognition. The complexity of her relationship with her readers and the
changing roles she assigns to them as the narrative progresses reflect
in turn the difficulty of growing to selfhood amidst the contradictory
needs and desires imposed upon her by the prevailing cultural codes.

Even before she explicitly projects and names her readers, however,
while still at Bretton, Lucy's awareness of the social and emotional
forces shaping her identity colors her narrative presentation of herself.
Early in the second chapter, for example, we read, "I, Lucy Snowe,
plead guiltless of that curse, an over-heated and discursive imagination," and we wonder to whom she is speaking and why she talks of
herself in this way. The implied listener, depicted as judge and jury,
is almost certainly a precursor of the conventional socialized reader
before whom Lucy feels it necessary to disclaim the passionate expression of emotion enacted by Polly, even while implicitly admitting its
power. Lucy names herself here by emphasizing the cold aspect of her
name as well as the light, names herself as the plain, shy, dowerless
girl who already perceives that emotions as strong as those displayed
by Polly may find no outlet in the world created by her circumstances—
and might well hinder her power to survive.

Throughout the first part of the novel, Lucy continues to preserve
her self by distancing those emotions that threaten her precarious economic and psychic equilibrium, particularly her feelings for Graham.

After a night of suffering, for example, caused by her bitter knowledge that the romance Madame Beck suspects between her and Dr. John does not exist, the "Next day," she tells us, she "was Lucy Snowe again" (chap. 13). A curious cross-over of roles between Polly and Lucy, however, occurs in the one scene where Lucy does act out her love for Graham—the night she loses his letter. " 'Oh! they have taken my letter!' cried the grovelling, groping monomaniac": this is Lucy's depiction of herself (chap. 22). The phrase "monomaniac" echoes her previous description of Polly's attachment to her father as "that mono-maniac tendency I have ever thought the most unfortunate with which man or woman can be cursed" (chap. 2). The teasing response that Lucy's display of her feelings evokes in Graham makes us feel that her refusal to declare her love to him (she acknowledges it in a variety of ways to herself and her readers) is not neurotic, or evasive, or even mistaken. Graham may guide her in her explorations of her external environment from feelings of kindness or "camaraderie," but he will never perceive her inner life or fulfill her emotional needs. She ob-serves him directly; he, as in the recognition scene in the nursery, sees her in the mirror of his own egotism and therefore fails to see her at all. It is not surprising, then, that she justifies to the reader her de-cision to conceal her identity from him by saying it would have made little difference had she "come forward and [announced], 'This is Lucy Snowe!' " (chap. 16).

Lucy's public silence and private dialogue with her reader are de-liberate responses to what is perhaps the most potentially destructive aspect of her solitude: the isolation of vision that excludes her from the social discourse necessary for an ontological affirmation of self. However great her emotional self-discipline, Lucy realizes early on the need to acknowledge and share her perceptions of reality in order to continue to be. Thus, she reacts to her observation of Polly at the Bretton tea table by confiding, "Candidly speaking, I thought her a little busy body" (chap. 2). The as yet unnamed recipient of this con-fidence serves a crucial function both in the narrative and in Lucy's development, for no one actually present during that scene would have understood Lucy's rejection of Polly's exaggerated acting of the female role, just as no one at La Terrasse, including Mrs. Bretton, "could con-ceive" her suffering during the long vacation: "so the half-drowned life-boatman [Lucy] keeps his own counsel, and spins no yarns" (chap. 17). Continually a confidante herself, a mediator who interprets the infant Polly's unspoken need to say goodbye to her cherished Graham and who later smooths the way to their union by speaking for them to Mr. Home, Lucy, in her formative years, has no one to hear her un-uttered words, or to speak in her place. The one exception is perhaps Miss Marchmont, who interprets Lucy's lack of words when confronted with an unorthodox question about suffering and salvation not as silence but encouragement (chap. 4). No wonder Lucy loves her, and after her death turns increasingly to the reader to fill the gap. Speak she must, though, for to remain silent would be to become the cretin who makes mouths instead of talking, and whose silence becomes a metaphor for Lucy's own potentially arrested development. To over-come this two-fold silence, Lucy evolves another reader, a nonjudg-mental reader, a sharer of the insights that she cannot communicate to those more in tune with the accepted social codes.

When first left on her own, however, after the metaphoric ship-wreck, Lucy's recognition of society's power to render her invisible and mute leads her initially to endow her newly created "reader" with the conventional assumptions about women and novels that she must challenge and change for her own life and tale to be plausible. The irony evident in her first direct address to this reader ("I will permit the reader to picture me . . . as a bark slumbering through halcyon weather . . .") allows her simultaneously to mock those who choose to remain locked within their traditional expectations and to offer them an alternate version of reality that would reflect and validate her existence. This same ironic stance informs Lucy's care to keep the reader abreast of the chronological "story" in her narrative, even as she manipulates the sequence and imagery to reveal a deeper stratum of her psychic life and the true meaning of her tale. "Has the reader forgotten Miss Ginevra Fanshawe?" (chap. 9), she asks after she is well established as a teacher and as a prelude to the introduction of Dr. John. The tinge of sarcasm in her question indicates that the per-ceptive reader will recognize the priorities implicit in the seemingly discontinuous narrative structure: the need for economic security—the effort of learning French and mastering a strange environment—far outweighed any other considerations in those early days. Later, the question "Does the reader, remembering what was said some pages back, care to ask how I answered [Graham's] letters . . . ?" (chap. 23) reminds both the curious reader and herself of her need to keep her emotions in check in the midst of the "new creed . . . a belief in happiness" that she has just described.

Often, Lucy's mode in dealing with the reader is a form of cooptation that transforms the reader into an accomplice in whatever observation she is about to make: "I need not explain, reader," or "The reader will not be surprised," or "My reader, I know, is one who would not thank me for an elaborate reproduction of poetic first impressions; and it is well, inasmuch as I had neither time nor mood to cherish such" (chap. 5). In this last address, she is undercutting romantic expectations as deliberately as she does when she rejects metaphors of buds and sylphs in describing the substantial young women of Villette (chap. 20) or tells us that "M. Paul stooped down and proceeded—as novel-writers say, and, as was literally true in his case—to 'hiss' into my ear some poignant words" (chap. 28). By mocking fictional and thereby social conventions, by challenging her readers to share her perceptions, she creates an audience who learns to read her narrative for what it is—the nontraditional story of a woman's life and a text in which she is not an invisible outsider but the informing presence.[15]

This dialogue, however, no matter how sarcastic it may be about conventions, also serves as self-protection and stems from Lucy's conflict between rebellious self-expression and survival. In this context, the reader becomes a foil whose role is to help her keep her own emotions in check. Thus, the irony in her early addresses is often directed as much toward herself as toward the social maxims she criticizes; she uses it to curb her own imagination and desires when she feels them destructive of her precariously held security, or to define herself within the limits she recognizes as realistic for someone in her position. When, after her romantic vision of Europe, she adds the postscript, "Cancel the whole of that, if you please, reader—or rather let it stand and draw thence a moral . . . *Day-dreams are delusions of the demon*" (chap. 6), she asserts the boundaries of what is possible in the battle she is then fighting for survival. When she makes comments such as "The reader must not think too hardly of Rosine" (chap. 13) for chattering to Dr. John, or "Think not, reader, that [Ginevra] thus bloomed and sparkled for the mere sake of M. Paul" (chap. 14), the sarcasm aimed at these two women is also a way of confronting her own potentially self-destructive frustration at the fact that her position and personality prevent her from acting as freely as Rosine and Ginevra do. In the first of these examples, she is also leveling an ironic eye on her own tendency to idolize Dr. John and the dangers of that idolization. One of the most painful of these exchanges occurs at the time she is fighting her disappointment at the loss of Graham's attention: "The reader will not too gravely regard the little circumstance that about this time" Madame Beck temporarily borrowed Graham's letters (chap. 26). The irony here is a self-protective reaction meant to distance the anger and pain that she is unable to allay except by containing them.

Rather than an attempt to deny the strength of her feelings or to deceive herself about them, as some critics have maintained, these passages speak to Lucy's recognition of the need to confront and control what she cannot realistically hope to gain or fulfill. To act out her emotional needs at this time might well threaten the economic and social security she achieves by ruthless, if painful, self-control. A revealing example of this struggle, and of her conscious involvement of the reader as a foil, occurs when Graham comes to take her to the theater: "And away I flew, never once checked, reader, by the thought which perhaps at this moment checks you: namely, that to go anywhere with Graham and without Mrs. Bretton could be objectionable" (chap. 23). The fact is that "society" might well look askance at this arrangement, except that society in the form of Mrs. Bretton, as Lucy tells us immediately, sees their relationship as that of brother and sister. In the face of society's blindness to any other possibility, Lucy reacts by saying that she would feel self-contempt and shame for suggesting an intimacy that did not exist. In this exchange, the reader, as society's voice, is reassured that all is conventional and well. By now, however, Lucy has also trained her reader to hear and approve what is not stated explicitly: the consciously chosen restraint that allows her to maintain the limited relationship offered her, and to benefit from it.

The dialogue with the reader, then, is both ironic and deadly serious, for Lucy's ability to retain her sense of her own integrity in spite of her invisibility and her conflicting needs is crucial for her growth. As the narrative (and with it Lucy's sense of selfhood) progresses, we can chart the nature of her development by the number and kind of addresses to her various readers. Not surprisingly, she appeals to her reader most often during times of intense self-conflict and when, owing to the lack of recognized context or precedent for her responses, she is least able to express herself openly. These moments occur both when she is alone and in social gatherings. Thus, left on her own, Lucy responds to the weight of her isolation ("To whom could I complain?") by deliberately rationalizing and justifying to the socialized reader what are by conventional standards her unorthodox actions and feelings: "In going to London, I ran less risk and evinced less enterprise than the reader may think" (chap. 5); "Before you pronounce on the rashness of the proceeding, reader [her decision to go to Villette], look back to the point whence I started" (chap. 7). By combining irony and defensiveness, these early explanations constitute a critique of the codes she recognizes as limiting even as they define her sense of self and her discourse. Although she gives the socialized reader permission to interpret her experience along traditional lines, she suffers from the potential misreading and its ability to control her life. The second address continues, "consider the desert I had left, note how little I perilled: mine was the game where the player cannot lose and may win"—a clear indication of a conscious choice aimed at physical as well as psychic survival, and part of Lucy's challenge to the fiction that women pass their lives in a long sleep.

The nature of her addresses to the reader begins to change once Lucy is accepted into the foreign world of the pensionnat at the Rue Fossette. After her introduction to Madame Beck, she appeals to the reader four times in quick succession to share her confused reaction of admiration and shock at discovering a woman so powerful, so independent, so successful, and, in many ways, so like her! Simultaneously observed and observing, she gains the strength to offer a compelling portrait of this fascinating woman to the "sensible reader" who will recognize that she did not gain "all the knowledge here condensed for his benefit in one month, or in one half-year" (chap. 8). With Madame Beck's power—and eye—to stimulate her, she educates the reader as she herself learns of her ability to control her environment—and her tale.

Once she enters the classroom and immerses herself in teaching and learning ("My time was now well and profitably filled up. . . . It was pleasant. I felt I was getting on" [chap. 9]), her rare addresses to the reader are limited to ironic observations about Ginevra and Rosine, who play more traditional female roles, with the exception of the crucial scene when she refuses to tell Dr. John—or the reader—why she is staring so intently at him: "I was confounded, as the reader may suppose, yet not with an irrecoverable confusion; being conscious that it was from no emotion of incautious admiration. . . . I might have cleared myself on the spot, but would not. I did not speak. I was not in the habit of speaking to him" (chap. 10). He, as she has already told us, barely notices her existence. Her decision not to reveal herself where she "can never be rightly known" has, not surprisingly, led to the strongest accusations of narrative unreliability, as well as accusations of lying, neurosis, and perversity—the word she herself uses during this scene: "There is a perverse mood of the mind which is rather soothed than irritated by misconstruction." But is it not possible that by this silence Lucy is creating a script other than that in which the lost god-brother/prince reappears and rescues her from her changeling role, the romantic or erotic fantasy that Lucy finds it necessary to forgo while she makes an independent life for herself as a teacher? In terms of conventional fictions, she may be unreliable and her decision "implausible," but in terms of the subtext, her silence and refusal reflect the lack of a language or a plot by which women can communicate ambitions and desires outside of those encoded in the accepted social or literary conventions. I am reminded here of Miller's appropriation of Jakobson's observation about communication: " 'The verbal exchange, like every form of human relation, requires at least two interlocutors; an idiolect, in the final analysis, therefore can be only a *slightly perverse fiction*' " (p. 43). To transform Lucy's silence and refusal into a statement of alternative plausibility and action requires the participation of a reader willing to recognize and respond to her need for anonymity as part of her process of self-identification and growth.

Paradoxically, her silence initially gives Lucy power; under its protection she can observe and confront Graham's blindness toward Ginevra and plunge into the role of mediator in others' communications.
She has begun the process that allows her, on the night of the play, to
find her own voice. Left alone during the long vacation, however, she
faces the "dumb future" with a despair she no longer tries to hide
from even her socialized readers (the religious reader, moralist, cynic,
epicure) or to justify herself except by saying, "perhaps, circumstanced
like me, you [reader] would have been, like me, wrong" (chap. 15).
The need for companionship, the need to speak, that drives her to the
confessional at the height of her despair, becomes, once outside the
church, a "confession" to a reader whose by now sympathetic hearing
she relies on when she rejects Père Silas's tempting offer of religious
community and chooses instead to live her life as a "heretic narrative"
(chap. 15). In the scenes that follow this confession, she has ample
opportunity to test the mettle of her now transformed reader/confessor,
for her revelation to Graham that she is "Lucy Snowe" plunges her
into a deeper stratum of isolation than that she had experienced before
she was "known." During her stay at La Terrasse and the subsequent
weeks, when her self-control and clarity of vision are most sorely
tried, she turns to the reader more often than at any other time during
the narrative.[16] Most of her addresses obsessively explain what she
calls the "seeming inconsistency" of her portraits of Graham, an inconsistency that reflects her struggle to say honestly what she instinctively knows: that he is neither as perceptive nor sensitive nor selfless
as he appears to others in public. Limited by his "masculine self-love"
and conventionality, lacking the necessary sympathy, he will never replace the reader as the sharer of Lucy's inner life.

The battle against self-delusion that Lucy fights during this section
of the narrative with the explicit help of the reader reaches its climax
in the "Vashti" chapter. In fact, the five evocations of the reader
during this chapter accurately inscribe the process of Lucy's self-
recognition and growth. First, making use of an endearment that jars
us coming from her usually more satiric pen, she shares with the
"dear reader" both the initial ecstasy that Graham's letters brought
her and the mellowing effect that time and self-knowledge had on
their message. Next, she reminds the reader of her compromise in an-

swering the letters—a struggle in which reason vanquishes imagination, but at a price: the painful confession to the reader of why it was acceptable for her to go out alone with her "brother" Graham. Immediately following this admission, she sees the light in the attic, indicative of the presence of the nun, which "the reader may believe . . . or not." Graham's disbelief, however, causes Lucy to comment negatively on his "dry, materialist views," views which color his subsequent "callous" reaction to Vashti, the passionate actress who enacts Lucy's own rebellion and self-mastery. Graham's "branding judgement" impresses upon Lucy once and for ever his inability to perceive who or what she is. The final vision of Graham that she offers to the reader that night mirrors her acceptance of his separateness: "Reader, I see him yet, with his look of comely courage and cordial calm" amidst the chaos released by Vashti's desires. He has become a statue, heroic perhaps, the ideal suitor for Polly, but not for Lucy a responsive human being.

After the period of solitary confinement and silence that follows this eventful night, Lucy returns to her dialogue with the reader stronger and calmer. She is now able to be warmly ironic and even humorous about the "perverseness" that leads her to "quarrel" with M. Paul (in contrast to her decision *not* to quarrel with Graham) and continues to define her distinctive emerging self. At least part of the change of tone—and the relative sparseness of the addresses to the reader she now speaks to without justification as a true companion— can be attributed to Paul, whose belief in her "fiery and rash nature" (chap. 26) gives her a warmer image of her self and whose own perverseness badgers her into speaking to him directly. One scene deserves note: the evening at the Hotel Crécy when her open anger and forgiveness wins from M. Paul a smile that she presents to the reader as her own accomplishment ("You should have seen him smile, Reader, . . ." [chap. 27]). Emphasizing his contrast to Graham, this smile transforms Paul from a mask or a statue into a human being.

Unable, however, to trust Paul completely, Lucy continues to share with the reader the difficulties of the unfolding relationship and of the man: "the reader is advised not to be in any hurry with his kindly conclusions" (chap. 30). Most significant, perhaps, she alludes again and again to the "perverse" aspect of her character that now prevents

her from succumbing to Paul's "Est-ce là tout?" or remaining in the
classroom when he seeks her on the evening after the country outing
during which he had called her "sister" and encouraged her love
(chaps. 29, 33). This behavior suggests that Lucy is experiencing a
potentially irresolvable conflict between her long-concealed erotic desires and her supposedly masculine ambitious wishes. On the one
hand, her greatest outburst of self-assertion—"I want to tell you [Paul]
something . . . I want to tell you all" (chap. 41)—arises from erotic
jealousy and wins her a proposal of marriage. On the other hand, her
perverse silences reflect a highly developed instinct to protect the independence and power that she has achieved outside of erotic fulfillment, a power that continues to sustain her after Paul's death. Before
this occurs, however, she makes good use of her own and her reader's
accumulated strength to support her during the climactic, visionary
night in the park when she believes she has lost Paul. Drugged and
again alone, she repeatedly calls upon the reader during this scene to
share her perception of what she terms the "TRUTH." Employing the
words "we" and "us" in her appeals (chap. 39), she identifies her
readers completely with her own perspective and includes them in a
deliberate but psychologically necessary misreading of the scene.

At the end of her narrative, when Lucy asks the reader to "scout the
paradox" of her three happiest years, she appeals for the last time to
the community she herself has created to grant credence to the highly
unconventional conclusion of her tale. She has by this time given us
ample warning that "endings" for women are problematic, and traditional plots no help in assessing her own experience. She has explicitly
shared with the reader her final words on the lives of the two more
familiar fictional women after their marriages: Ginevra fails to come
to the expected bad end, and, in fact, fails to develop at all; and Polly,
she cannot help admitting to the reader, however blessed in the resolution of her tale, bears a distinct resemblance to a pampered and
adoring spaniel (chaps. 40, 36).[17] Equally unexpected, perhaps, Lucy's
life does not end with Paul's; the observant reader will have noted
that the school clearly continues to prosper and that Lucy, by the time
she begins her narrative, knows the West End of London as well as
her beloved City (chap. 6). Rewriting the traditional novel to illustrate the limited plots available to women in literature, as in life, she

has survived the destruction of the romantic fantasy and grown into another reality.

The path, however, to a maturity that is intellectually and financially fulfilling, and I would argue existentially fulfilling as well, involves more than just the telling of the tale; ultimately, Lucy's development resides in the mediation of the reader who grants her the recognition and the reality of her perceptions lacking in the external world. As readers ourselves, to the extent that we can enter into and accept Lucy's cryptic conclusion, we will join "in friendly company" with the "[p]ilgrims and brother mourners" (chap. 38) who acknowledge pain and hear, as Miss Marchmont did, the unspoken word of encouragement. Otherwise, we remain among those readers whose sunny imaginations still demand conventional endings, and who cannot conceive, as Lucy herself does, that while life for someone in her position is hard, in the reflections provided by the reader she has gained the power to grow and to speak, and with it the power to endure.

ELIZABETH LANGLAND

Female Stories of Experience:

Alcott's *Little Women* in Light of *Work*

"I want my daughters to be beautiful, accomplished, and good, to be well and wisely married, and to lead useful and pleasant lives. . . . To be loved and chosen by a good man is the best and sweetest thing which can happen to a woman, and I sincerely hope my girls may know this beautiful experience."[1]

Marmee's words in Louisa May Alcott's *Little Women* express the goal of female ambition and growth: the passive state of being chosen and becoming "good wives," which is also the title to the second part of this children's classic. But Marmee's words are subtly belied by the context in which they are spoken. She is "holding a hand of each [daughter, Meg and Jo], and watching the two young faces wistfully." The love felt by a mother and her daughters infuses the scene; and it radiates throughout the novel so that when Meg marries we tend to share Jo's frustration—"I think it's dreadful to break up families so"— rather than to celebrate Meg's arrival at "the sweetest chapter in the romance of womanhood" (LW, 281). Although the novel never formally acknowledges this tension and ambivalence, *Little Women* expresses them throughout, indirectly opposing a vision of female fulfillment in a community of women to female self-realization in marriage to a man.[2]

Little Women is Alcott's most famous novel of female development; it is not, however, her only novel charting that development. *Work: A Story of Experience,* begun in 1861 but not finished until 1873 (five years after *Little Women*), explores an alternative model for female growth and fulfillment. In *Work,* independent female exploration of the world culminates in the establishment of a female community. The fact that composition of *Work* was interrupted by Alcott's writing of *Little Women* suggests the ideas of *Work* are in the background of *Little Women.* In fact, the developmental pattern expressed in *Work* is central to understanding key tensions in *Little*

Women, and it clarifies the implicit message of Alcott's children's classic. Together *Little Women* and *Work* demark the process by which Alcott first explored and then affirmed the power of female community. The idea of female community already embedded in the values in *Little Women,* serves to counterpoint and ultimately contradict the socially expected values of female passivity and self-suppression through marriage.

Little Women is Alcott's "social romance," *Work,* her "feminist romance." *Little Women* romanticizes the process by which girls become women and good wives. The novel tells the story of four girls, Meg, Jo, Beth, and Amy March, possessed of strikingly different personalities and motivated by widely disparate desires, who sail into the happy harbor of marriage and motherhood. Only Beth, who dies on the eve of her womanhood, fails to marry. While Meg and Amy cultivate domestic and social talents that lead inevitably to marriage, Jo's personality and interests are highly at odds with her fate. Unlike her sisters, Jo seeks independence and autonomy, but her marriage to Professor Bhaer reduces the complex difficulties and ignores the problems of fulfillment that must attend a woman of her ambition in that social situation. As "social romance," *Little Women* embraces society's idealistic prescription for female happiness and self-realization.

Christie Devon, like Jo March in spirit and ambition, is the protagonist of Alcott's "feminist romance." She pursues adventure and knowledge in the world at large; and although she marries, her husband departs for the Civil War on her wedding day. This confluence of marriage and war highlights marriage as simply another stage in Christie's development, rather than as a haven and termination of her growth. Married only long enough to conceive a daughter, her husband's death and her early widowhood free Christie to consolidate her female supporters into a congenial community of women. *Work,* more than *Little Women,* romanticizes the possibility of a nurturing female community. *Work* is thus a "feminist romance" that embodies Alcott's vision of female possibility and significance, a vision implicit in *Little Women* but submerged and ultimately denied there.

This essay looks first at *Work* to clarify the submerged developmental pattern in *Little Women.* It then turns to biographical sources that fed Louisa May Alcott's two autobiographical novels. Finally, in the light of *Work* and Alcott's life, it offers an interpretation of Alcott's classic that locates greater complexity and appeal in the simple tale of women growing to adulthood than has heretofore been acknowledged. *Little Women* reveals what Sandra M. Gilbert and Susan Gubar in *The Madwoman in the Attic* have noted in other nineteenth-century novels: two plots. We are interested in the submerged plot: "the one plot that seems to be concealed in most of the nineteenth-century literature by women . . . is in some sense a story of the woman writer's quest for her own story; it is the story, in other words, of the woman's quest for self-definition."[3]

Work presents a female tale of development strikingly like that of the male novel of development, the *Bildungsroman*. Instead of keeping the girl safe within family circles and trading one male authority for another in marriage, *Work* launches the heroine from an uncongenial home and depicts her experiences and education in the wider world. Although the protagonist, Christie Devon, is denied the sexual affairs of the male *Bildungsheld* (which would surely be inappropriate given Alcott's audience), she has the equivalent debasing and exalting relationships with men, and redeems from despair an alter ego in the figure of a fallen woman.[4] This pattern of independence and experience is rare in women's fictions; it differs so dramatically from the historical reality of women's opportunities and possibilities. That Alcott adopted such a paradigm in *Work* reveals a deliberate unsettling of convention and expectation. The story of women's *possibilities,* not their real experience, needed to be told. To tell it, Alcott adopted patterns from the story of male development.

Work opens with Christie's departure from an unsympathetic home. She is an orphan whose aunt and uncle have stood in the place of parents. " 'Uncle doesn't love or understand me,' " Christie recognizes, so at twenty-one, she is prepared " 'to take care of myself; and if I'd been a boy, I should have been told to do it long ago!' " She intends to " 'travel away into the world and seek my fortune!' ", refusing to " 'sit and wait for any man to give me my independence, if I can earn it for myself.' "[5] She has a spirit "which can rise to heroism and a heart hungry . . . for love and a larger, nobler life" (W, 12). Christie understands her alternatives if she stays in the safety and seclusion of home:

Christie plainly saw that one of three things would surely happen if she lived on there with no vent for her full heart and busy mind. She would either marry Joe Butterfield in sheer desperation, and become a farmer's household drudge; settle down into a spinster, content to make butter, gossip, and lay up money all her days; or do what poor Matty Stone had done, try to crush and curb her needs and aspirations till the struggle grew too hard, and then in a fit of despair end her life, and leave a tragic story to haunt their quiet river. [W, 12]

Early marriage, narrow spinsterhood, suicide—they all come to about the same thing for a woman, self-destruction. Some wider experience of the world is as necessary to female development as it is to male growth. Like the male *Bildungsheld,* Christie thus heads for the city, where she begins her education into life.

Christie's education, too, parallels that of the male hero. She pursues several occupations (household servant, actress, governess, companion, and seamstress), and she meets and even redeems a wealthy roué, Mr. Fletcher, who proposes to her and whom she refuses. Her experiences ultimately lead her into despair and poverty and to the brink of suicide. Then begins the process of her redemption, in which two men, Reverend Powers and David Sterling, figure. But central to that redemptive process are the female bonds Christie has been forging through her experiences. Rescued from suicide by Rachel, a fallen and outcast woman, Christie can in turn befriend this woman. She is lodged, first in a home of a Dickensian washerwoman and then in the home of a Quaker lady. She discovers an exalted love with David Sterling, but is married to him only long enough to conceive; she is widowed before the birth of their daughter.

Before Christie is widowed, her life closely follows that of the male *Bildungsheld.* But while traditionally the male finally marries and finds some accommodation to society, Christie must look beyond the male *Bildungsroman* plot for her fulfillment, because for women marriage means self-suppression not self-assertion. Alcott uses the altar only as a way station to Christie's ultimate fulfillment in a female community, where Christie finds a new social order, based on identity through community. And that order, Alcott implies, must start with women.

Work is a polemical fiction that demonstrates its message clearly.

In its final scenes, Christie mediates between wealthy women, who want to help alleviate suffering, and working women, who need their help. She is herself the center of a family that includes her mother- and sister-in-law and her daughter. She extends this female community to include a fugitive slave, Hepsey, a laundress, Mrs. Wilkins, and a wealthy lady, formerly a pupil of hers. These several women join hands at the novel's end, "A loving league of sisters, old and young, black and white, rich and poor, each ready to do her part to hasten the coming of the happy end" (W, 442). Little Ruth, Christie's child, spreads "her chubby hand above the rest; a hopeful omen, seeming to promise that the coming generation of women will not only receive but deserve their liberty, by learning that the greatest of God's gifts to us is the privilege of sharing His great work" (W, 443). The novel's exultant vision of a "happy end," of the "good time that is coming," is grounded in female values and is embodied in female community. This vision comes at the close of the Civil War, a fratricidal war, a war that expresses the failure of men to be brothers. For Alcott, the Civil War showed how brothers relate; *Work* shows the relationships of sisters.

Christie Devon has the power to lead the way. She bridges and heals divisions—"old and young, black and white, rich and poor"— and, we might add, North and South, man and woman. At the end of the novel, Christie earns a supreme tribute for first reforming the roué, Mr. Fletcher, then rejecting him as husband, and finally transforming him into friend instead of lover: "for she was a woman who could change a lover to a friend, and keep him all her life" (W, 440). Women, self-defined, embody the values that will heal the breaches of the Civil War and will inform a new world.

Alcott's *Work* is significant in that it affirms what *Little Women* ultimately has to deny: the importance of women together, the possibility of growth in female community. Christie is a heroine who realizes her ambition, expressed in the novel's opening pages: " 'I'll get rich; found a home for girls like myself; or, better still, be a Mrs. Fry, a Florence Nightingale' " (W, 6). She does even better than that. Her uncle's wealth has been distributed widely. She supports her own family, and that family provides help for working women everywhere. Behind Christie's achievement stands the social alternative she rejected:

marriage and devotion to a man. Christie began the novel in antago-nism to her uncle but in sympathy to her aunt Betsey, whom, she early recognized, "made a bad bargain when she exchanged her girlish aspirations for a man whose soul was in his pocket" (W, 8). Women who marry exchange their aspirations for a man's. The best they can hope for, then, is that they meet a man whose aspirations are like their own. *Little Women* rewards Jo March with Professor Bhaer and his school for boys. In contrast to this, Alcott's *Work* gives Christie a scope of her own. Marriage is only a brief step in her education, and it is but a part of the total female experience that marks her develop-ment and increases her credibility with the working women: "wife-hood, motherhood, and widowhood brought her very near to them" (W, 429). Those women perceive "that a genuine woman stood down there among them like a sister, ready with head, heart, and hand to help them help themselves" (W, 429). Christie's personal ethic—" 'but we don't make bargains . . . we work for one another and share everything together' " (W, 419)—expresses the novel's so-cial ethic. Uncle Enos's grumbling reply to this ethic reveals its basis: " 'So like women!' " Women, the novel suggests, can affirm commu-nity; they do not measure achievement or find happiness in personal material gain, but in relationships and work. Work defines the self, while community affirms the self. Alcott's is a polemical and idealistic vision, but one which she succeeds in rendering in her fiction.

Although we risk oversimplification by seeing in *Work* the model of female development Alcott wanted to propose and in *Little Women* the model she felt she ought to propose, there is a kernel of truth to this schema. The tensions between Louisa May Alcott's life and her depiction of that life in *Little Women* testify to her anxiety over con-flicts between her vision and the ideas and values of those around her. Despite its popularity, *Little Women* was seldom a labor of love. Al-cott's biographer, Martha Saxton, tells us that,

Louisa was reluctant to write the book that was to bring her so much fame and money. The project was something of an assignment. For years her father had discussed the need for plain stories for boys and girls about childish victories over selfishness and anger. And Louisa's publisher wanted a "girl's book". . . .

Louisa had always used writing to get away from herself and her unhappiness, but *Little Women* forced her to relive the most difficult years of her life. Instead of a retreat into a heady, imaginary world Louisa sat day after day, recreating her past into shapes and pictures of what it should have been.[6]

Alcott was not entirely in sympathy with the subject matter of a "girl's book." In a letter to Sam May, Alcott complained that "publishers are very perverse & wont let authors have their way so my little women must grow up and be married off in a very stupid style."[7] Related to this artistic complaint, Alcott's experiences as an adolescent were often difficult and painful. Her life had not been the ideal she was to depict in fiction. The mother in *Little Women* is a resource of strength and encouragement for her daughters. Abba Alcott was a constant emotional and financial drain on Louisa's energies. She turned to Louisa for the "security, love, money, or comfort" that was absent in her marriage. At times Louisa May Alcott felt almost "strangulated" by the demands of her mother and sisters.

Similarly, Mr. March, depicted as a support in *Little Women*, reflects only obliquely Bronson Alcott, a self-absorbed, improvident transcendental philosopher.[8] In *Literary Women*, Ellen Moers has wryly observed that "transcendental improvidence we now know to have been a source of much literary industry on the part of American women."[9] Alcott pursued her career as a writer to support her family, a role necessitated by her father's abdication of financial responsibility, and one wonders if, in this respect at least, and perhaps too in Jo's tomboyish rebellions and angers, Alcott did not impart something of herself to the character of Jo March. These slantings of the truth of Alcott's adolescence merge into a larger evasion in *Little Women:* marriage as female fulfillment. It was not Abba Alcott's fulfillment, and it was not her daughters'. Louisa May Alcott never married, and she continued throughout her life to care for her parents financially and emotionally. She helped educate her sisters and adopted their children after the death of their mother or father.

The narrative surface of *Little Women* asserts that marriage is woman's fulfillment. Underneath this principal narrative, however, lies a possibility closer to Alcott's experience. We cannot easily chart the deep ambiguities that must have informed Alcott's responses to her family members, but the experience was surely not entirely negative. Out of the smithy of her own experience, Alcott forged an identity based on family. In her most popular novel, she was to include part of that understanding, the salutary effect of female community on women's development.

Little Women opens with the March sisters grumbling over the burdens they have to bear. It is Christmas, and each girl has a small amount of money to purchase some item she has long desired: Meg wants "pretty things"; Jo, a novel; Beth, new piano music; and Amy, a "box of Faber's drawing pencils" (LW, 11–12). This first chapter, "Playing Pilgrims," charts the girls' shift from self-absorption in their own wishes to a more selfless desire to buy special presents for the mother, "Marmee." The chapter concludes with a message to all the daughters from their father, absent as chaplain in the Civil War battlefields, to "do their duty faithfully, fight their bosom enemies bravely, and conquer themselves so beautifully that when I come back to them I may be fonder and prouder than ever of my little women" (LW, 17). Each girl acknowledges her weakness and shoulders her "burden" to begin her metaphorical journey to the Celestial City; as Christmas gift, each girl receives her own copy of *Pilgrim's Progress*. Subsequent chapter titles are, in fact, drawn from Bunyan's tale and point out the parallels between his work and Alcott's, although the bourne of little women is marriage, not Christian's Celestial City.

For Bunyan's Christian, the journey to the Celestial City (which is to say the end of development and growth) entails self-actualization, a discovery of spiritual significance in opposition to worldly values. The derived analogous journey for women entails lessons similar to Christian's, but it emphasizes self-suppression without an ultimate self-actualization. It stresses the cultivation of obedience, docility, and gentleness, the virtues of "little women": Beth finds the Palace Beautiful, Meg goes to Vanity Fair, Amy plunges into the Valley of Humiliation, Jo meets Apollyon. Stages in Christian's journey are in this way distributed among the March sisters, each of whom has a particular vice to conquer before she will have achieved that model of self-sacrificing femininity the book on the surface prescribes. The parceling out of Christian's journey in *Little Women* contributes to a sense that women cannot be fully actualized. Instead of developing a full personality, each girl conquers a vice. Growth focuses on a trial or two for each

girl, and thus maturation seems truncated. The woman's journey culminates in the passive state of being "loved and chosen" by a husband
on whom to base purpose and identity. In *Little Women,* the pilgrim's
spiritual tale provides a justification and rationale for the social development that has always been open to women. The main point of Bunyan's theological allegory thus helps enforce the expected message of
Alcott's "girl's book": a disengagement from the active world and its
strife and a retreat from self-assertion into marriage.

Jo's story, however, resists this "official" pattern. Her sisters overcome girlish faults of vanity, envy, narcissism, and pride; they reach
predictable ends. Placid, good Meg conquers her female envy, vanity,
and "false pride" (LW, 103), and settles down in her "dovecote"
with her penniless husband and her babies. Beth, the quintessential
good "little woman," "an angel in the house" (LW, 269), sacrifices
herself so cheerfully that no one notices "till the little cricket on the
hearth stops chirping, and the sweet, sunshiny presence vanishes, leaving silence and shadow behind" (LW, 52). Beth's death is an extreme
but perfectly consistent form of the extinction women face.[10] Pretty
Amy, more materialistic and selfish than the others, wants to marry a
rich man and be a "queen of society." She manages to fall in love with
wealthy Laurie and thereby acquires wealth and ease legitimately, rec-
onciling her womanliness with her narcissism.

In contrast to her sisters, Jo is "rough and wild." The burden of anger she bears is traditionally a male vice. Jo is clearly discontented
with her female role and its possibilities; she likes " 'boys' games and
work and manners' "; she has a boy's name; she " 'can't get over her
disappointment in not being a boy' "; and she forms a friendship of
equals with the boy next door, Laurie Laurence, whose grandfather
observes that Jo "seemed to understand the boy as well as if she had
been one herself" (LW, 68). Jo thinks that "keeping her temper at
home [the role of women] was a much harder task than facing a rebel
or two down South [the prerogative of men]" (LW, 13, 19). Facing
a rebel, of course, requires action and assertiveness; keeping one's
temper requires docility and self-denial. Carried further these poles of
experience represent the individual achievement proper for boys and
the suppression of individuality appropriate for girls.

Alcott never depicts Jo as dependent, passive, or timorous. Jo regrets that she can't "read, run, and ride as much as she liked" (LW, 50); she enjoys "adventures" and claims " 'I'm going to find some' " (LW, 59). She likes "to do daring things" (LW, 60), and is " 'not afraid of anything' " (LW, 65). The "gentlemanly attitudes, phrases, and feats . . . seemed more natural to her than the decorums prescribed for young ladies" (LW, 270). "Jo's ambition," the narrator tells us, is "to do something very splendid; what it was she had no idea as yet, but left it for time to tell her" (LW, 50). She reiterates that she wants to do " 'something heroic and wonderful that won't be forgotten after I'm dead.' " (LW, 164). This general ambition increasingly gathers in her desire to be a great writer, an ambition encouraged by her family: " 'I think I shall write books, and get rich and famous' " (LW, 146).

Although Jo is boyish, she is not presented as unwomanly. The distinction is important to Alcott. Jo wants the freedom and prerogatives of men; she needs this scope to develop and to fulfill her ambitions. She is antagonistic only to the limitations of womanliness: the "decorums" expected of ladies and the expectation that she will restrict her ambitions and her achievements by falling in love with a man. Not surprisingly, then, the narrator reveals that Jo "had no tender fancies as yet, and rather scorned romance, except in books" (LW, 164). Since sexual love means for women an explicit cessation of equality, Jo and Laurie cannot marry—despite the wishes of generations of readers that they do so—because they will be forever equals, joining each other for pranks and adventures, riding, racing, skating, Jo renounces Laurie as one too much like herself: " 'too fond of freedom not to mention hot tempers and strong wills' " (LW, 367). Sexual love, the novel implies, is incompatible with such frank and open friendship, such parity of spirit and energy. Laurie has to be turned over to gentlewoman Amy, who redeems the beast in man: "Women work a good many miracles, and I have a persuasion that they may perform even that of raising the standard of mankind." (LW, 466). In Alcott's novel, mature sexual love always involves one person correcting another, as when Mrs. March confesses to Jo that she too had a hot temper, but, through Mr. March's careful guidance, has learned to correct it. Jo seems to realize the dangers of sexual love: its capacity to stifle ambition and thwart identity, to trivialize friendship with men, and to disrupt the nurturing community of women. For Jo, leaving home to marry entails a sacrifice of the fruits of her maturity—personal autonomy and identity, her community of women at home, and her role as provider within that home.

Jo's struggles thus define the contradictions between theory and practice, idealism and reality for women, who are not different *sub specie aeternitatis* from men. Jo's life is informed by the understanding *Work* expresses directly: "there are substantial heartfelt interests for women of all ages, and under ordinary circumstances, quite apart from love."[11] Jo's presentation throughout *Little Women* shows that female fulfillment may not be found in the traditional roles of marriage and motherhood, and her development affirms the value of Alcott's alternative, female community.

A community of women enables friendship, and it enables identity. It furthers human development. When Professor Bhaer appears, Jo is already mature and self-defined. This development began with responsibility and support in the home. From the beginning, *Little Women* depicts Jo as "the man of the family" (LW, 15). Mr. March is serving in the Civil War, and Jo bears the responsibility of providing for the family. When her father falls ill and her mother must join him, Jo sacrifices her "one beauty," her hair, for money to cover the expenses of the journey. The episode, as represented equates Jo's cutting her hair with a masculine assertion of responsibility. Jo not only acts like the man of the family in this episode, but she now looks "boyish." Yet, she cries for the loss of her beauty, and this detail endears her to us as a woman. Jo doesn't usually give in to tears, because they are an "unmanly weakness" (LW, 92), and she often resolves to bear her difficulties "like a man." But Jo is a woman with a woman's feelings, and because she cries we recognize the enormity of her sacrifice. The episode contrasts another famous hair-cutting, that of Maggie Tulliver in George Eliot's *The Mill on the Floss*. Where Maggie's is an act of defiance, a protest against expectations of female beauty, Jo's marks a major step in her development. The act is not defiant, but represents a willingness to accept responsibility for others, and it expresses individual and familial pride. Wealthy Aunt March ultimately gives Mrs. March the money to travel, accompanying the gift. as she always does, with a lecture on the family's folly and improvidence. Although Jo need not have cut her hair simply for the money, her gesture does defy the tyranny of the old woman and frees her family from humbling obligation.

Jo's assumption of male responsibility within her community of women makes the March family a context in which she can grow. Rather than inhibiting development as it does in the *Bildungsroman*, where the protagonist must leave and where female protagonists who stay are generally thwarted, family gives scope to Jo's development. It is in effect and in conceptualization the *Little Women*'s analogy for the community of female family and friends Christie Devon heads in *Work*. It makes possible individual female growth and self-realization.

In her adolescence and young womanhood, Jo is fiercely independent. She and Meg are both early allowed to work to support the family, since their parents believe they "could not begin too early to cultivate energy, industry, and independence" (LW, 48–49). Marmee adds that "work is wholesome . . . and give[s] a sense of power and independence better than money or fashion" (LW, 137). We recognize here the explicit message of *Work*, which insists that the new era will be ushered in if each does her share faithfully "with words or work, as shall seem best" (W, 442). Although *Little Women* allows an implicit distinction between women's work and men's work, so that Meg can say, without being contradictory in this same context, " 'Men have to work and women to marry for money' " (LW, 179), Jo remains "happy to do something to support herself" (LW, 51). In Alcott's view the capacity of work to give significance to individual life exists for women as well as for men.[12]

Even after her father's return, Jo still sees herself as the man of the family. She is protective and loving toward her sisters and mother, and reminds Marmee that " 'if anything is amiss at home, I'm your man' " (LW, 358). She even feels toward Meg and Marmee as a father and husband would. She laments that she cannot " 'marry Meg myself, and keep her safe in the family' " (LW, 228). She tells Marmee that "mothers are the *best* lovers in the world." (LW, 483). Jo's responses ought not strike us as unnatural. She is all womanliness in her warmth, affection, and devotion to her family. When Beth's health begins to fail, Jo accepts the responsibility of breadwinner, and earns the money necessary to send her ailing sister to the mountains or sea.

Jo is the one who must finally accept Beth's imminent death, and it is she to whom Beth entrusts the difficult and painful task of telling other family members. Jo's impetuosity and temper lead her into scrapes as a girl, but we watch her mature within the family to conquer her weaknesses and enhance her strengths. Challenged by family responsibilities, Jo finds the stimulus she needs to reach maturity. Jo's concern for Beth and her relationship with her finally transform Jo into the successful writer she has always striven to be. Bereft after Beth's death, Jo is advised by Marmee to write a "simple tale for the family." "It [is] a great success," and Jo receives from her family the praise and encouragement to "'grow as happy as we are in your success'" (LW, 481).

What makes Jo attractive to generation after generation of women readers is that she finds scope for development within the family, and that she knows friendship and parity with boys; she achieves autonomy. She is nurtured and accepted. Her resourcefulness is met with gratitude, her strength deemed a welcome shelter for the weak. She prospers as a writer and allows herself scope to develop her talents. The secret of her fulfillment lies in her commitment to the community of women that nurtures her and not in her marriage to Professor Bhaer. Jo feels free to explore her abilities as long as she is contributing to her family's comfort, a freedom that usually is a male prerogative. Since the home is not inimical and unsympathetic to Jo's aspirations, she need not leave to grow but can thrive within it. Her emotional development is not arrested. Her ambitions take on acceptable womanly cast since Jo's ambitions, however self-actualizing, are also pursued for the benefit of others. She tells Marmee, "'That's what I tried for, and that's why I succeeded. I never get on when I think of myself alone, so it will help me to work for you'" (LW, 302). Following her ambitions in New York City, Jo discovers that "money conferred power: money and power, therefore, she resolved to have, not to be used for herself alone, but for those whom she loved more than self" (LW, 382). Jo demonstrates the traditionally female "selflessness," but without the crippling dependencies, self-suppression, and self-abnegation that usually accompany it. Selflessness, so translated, is no longer a "female" trait but a "male" assumption of responsibility for others.

For Jo, then, marrying entails a sacrifice of those things she values: personal ambition, autonomy, and identity; her community of women at home; and her role as provider within that home. Mature sexual love, including marriage and motherhood, means a loss of Jo's identity and role as family mainstay, a loss of female community in which that identity and role are played out, and a sacrifice of parity with men.

Alcott's novel cannot resolve the contradictions between its dominant narrative pattern of marriage and motherhood and the suggestion of fulfillment within a community of women that occupies the core of Jo's story. It cannot even acknowledge this contradiction directly. Jo undergoes the development of an autonomous person within a female community, and then she must leave that community and the identity she developed there to marry. The plot has taken her in one direction and then doubled back in the end. *Little Women* cannot acknowledge these conflicting texts; it must, however, circumvent them. Thus it argues that Jo is simply waiting to develop fully into womanhood. She learns to have a "heart." "For Jo," the narrator tells us, "brain had developed earlier than heart" (LW, 360). The novel means by "heart" a sexual passion, since Jo's love for sisters, mother, books, and writing illuminates the novel throughout. Jo is simply a little late in developing. That is, the novel pretends there is no discontinuity between Jo's early wishes and satisfactions and her marriage to Professor Bhaer; it never acknowledges the conflicting versions of female identity that it presents. Marmee complacently leaves Jo " 'to enjoy your liberty till you tire of it, for only then will you find that there is something sweeter' " (LW, 367). Later, Jo metamorphoses into the "little woman" and "good wife" she was all along expected to become.

Seen in this light, Jo's marriage is tacked on to the narrative; or, rather, the submerged plot of female development is ignored for the sake of a conventional happily-ever-after, what Alcott called being "married off in a very stupid style." The end of the novel presents us with Jo March Bhaer happily ensconced at Plumfield, an estate inherited from Aunt March and turned into a rollicking school for boys. She is herself the mother of two sons and remembers her past literary ambitions as "selfish, lonely, and cold." Professor Bhaer has practically ordered her to quit writing sensational romances. She adds, "I haven't

given up the hope that I may write a good book yet, but I can wait."
(LW, 540–41). But she, unlike Louisa May Alcott, will not be writing "a good book," absorbed as she is in little Rob and Teddy and the rest of her brood. She is "Mother Bhaer" to the Professor, to the children, and to the novel.[13]

Little Women denies the full significance of Jo and her development to her mother's and sisters' lives. A man and marriage are the "best and sweetest thing[s] which can happen to a woman." *Work: A Story of Experience* idealizes the role Louisa May Alcott lived, a mainstay to an extended family that affirmed the significance of her existence. This later novel asserts the discovery of such a community not as a retreat or regression, but as the culminating point of growth. The submerged text of *Little Women* emerges as the main text of *Work.*

There yet remains a story within the story within the story. If *Little Women* encloses a story of female community within a traditional story of female destiny in marriage, it also recognizes the disharmonies and tensions within female community itself. Those discords played often in Louisa May Alcott's own life; the silencing of those disharmonies in *Work* reduces the complexity of experience and makes that novel seem propagandistic, what I call a "feminist romance." The sounding of those contrapuntal strains in *Little Women* gives this novel a richness that *Work* lacks. Once we have recognized the implicit criticism of marriage or the "social romance" in *Little Women* and found the enclosed story of an enabling female community, we can also recognize the stifling effects of such symbiosis. Closeness has its dangers as well as its rewards, and Jo struggles alone with the suffocating demands of family after Beth's death: "Poor Jo, these were dark days to her, for something like despair came over her when she thought of spending all her life in that quiet house, devoted to humdrum cares, a few small pleasures, and the duty that never seemed to grow any easier" (LW, 477). This despair has haunted Jo periodically throughout the novel and has sent her as far away as New York City to find a balance between her need for separation from her family and integration with it. In acknowledging that the tie which binds can constrict, Louisa May Alcott gives *Little Women* a human complexity she denies to *Work.*

Neither novel fully acknowledges the difficulties of female development. But both are sensitive to its demands and prerogatives. Through their respective protagonists, each argues a parity of need and ability in men and women. But the fulfillment of a female's needs and abilities differs from a male's. Female growth, as Alcott sees it, takes place through integration rather than separation. When that growth is allowed its full flowering, it must shape the world, just as a man's does. For Alcott, that shape is more humane; it is our hope for the future where people, like things, are not isolated and defined, pieces of property "fixed up square," but individuals, coexistent one with another. *Little Women* draws on Christian's tale in *Pilgrim's Progress* for its dominant metaphors. But Bunyan's tale in fact tells two stories: the story of Christian's journey to the Celestial City and the story of his wife's, Christiana's, subsequent journey. Accompanied by Mercy, her children, and Mr. Greatheart, Christiana, too, travels to the Celestial City. Her journey better expresses a community of salvation; his focuses more narrowly on a single, saved individual. *Work* draws on Christiana's tale. In *Work*, Bunyan's *Pilgrim's Progress* has been re-envisioned as a model, one no longer dictating female self-suppression, but one affirming the discovery of a female ethos and identity in community. In Alcott's feminist romance, the story she wanted to tell of female development has taken precedence over her social romance, that conventional story expected of her. In *Work*, Alcott's little women have grown up and taken their place in the world.

III TWENTIETH-CENTURY REFORMULATIONS:

Claiming a Tradition

ELIZABETH R. BAER

The Sisterhood of Jane Eyre

and Antoinette Cosway

If there's one hypocrisy I loathe more
than another it's the fiction of the
"good" woman and the "bad" woman.

     Jean Rhys, "Vienne"

I want to understand the connections
—between the tower where Bertha Mason Rochester
is displayed to Jane Eyre as a warning
—with this place, this city, my doorstep
where I've learned to interfere between
the prostitute's scream and the pimp's knife
is to invite their unified disgust.

     Robin Morgan, "Battery"

Feminist critics have been engaged, during the past decade, in two
projects of reclamation: the recovery of "lost" women writers, such as
Zora Neale Hurston and Mary Wilkins Freeman, and the rereading
of women authors, such as Austen and Eliot, to discover the messages
about women inscribed in their texts. Adrienne Rich precisely pin-
points the purpose and value of the latter enterprise:

Re-vision—the act of looking back, of seeing with fresh eyes, of entering
an old text from a new critical direction—is for us more than a chapter in
cultural history: it is an act of survival. Until we can understand the assumptions in which we are drenched we cannot know ourselves. And this
drive to self-knowledge, for women, is more than a search for identity: it
is part of her refusal of the self-destructiveness of male-dominated society.
A radical critique of literature, feminist in its impulse, would take the
work first of all as a clue to how we live, how we have been living, how
our language has trapped as well as liberated us; and how we can begin
to see—and therefore live—afresh.[1]

131

One of the nineteenth-century texts that has undergone closest feminist scrutiny is Charlotte Brontë's *Jane Eyre*. Elizabeth Hardwick, Patricia Meyer Spacks, Tillie Olsen, Ellen Moers, Elaine Showalter, and, of course, Sandra M. Gilbert and Susan Gubar, have each, in turn, "re-vised" *Jane Eyre* for their readers.[2]

But well before any of these women, a West Indian writer by the name of Jean Rhys had spent ten years "re-vising" *Jane Eyre* for twentieth-century readers. Her revision is a novel, *Wide Sargasso Sea*, which is itself in need of re-vision insofar as it has been misread by so many critics.[3] *Wide Sargasso Sea*, published in 1966 and awarded the prestigious William H. Smith Award, is a *Bildungsroman* that tells the story of the woman who becomes Bertha Rochester, the madwoman in the attic in *Jane Eyre*. That Rhys envisioned the work as a novel of development is evidenced by her comment to an interviewer: "She [Bertha] seemed such a poor ghost, I thought I'd like to write her a life."[4] That Rhys herself saw her novel as a revision, indeed as an affirmation of her colonial identity, is manifest in a confidence to another interviewer:

> The mad wife in Jane Eyre has always interested me. I was convinced that Charlotte Brontë must have had something against the West Indies and I was angry about it. Otherwise, why did she take a West Indian for that horrible lunatic, for that really dreadful creature? I hadn't really formulated the idea of vindicating the mad woman in the novel but when I was rediscovered I was encouraged to do so.[5]

Rhys has not, however, written simply a sequel to *Jane Eyre*, but what might be termed a "post-dated prequel."[6] In a curious departure from literary tradition, Rhys has written a novel that exists both before (in a literary sense) and after (in reality) the novel *Jane Eyre*. Unlike other literary pairs (for example, Radcliffe's *The Mysteries of Udolpho* and Austen's *Northanger Abbey*, or Atwood's *Lady Oracle* and the Cartland gothic of your choice), Rhys has commandeered *Jane Eyre* as *her* sequel and in doing so, forever "revises" our reading of that text by the creation of hers.

If *Jane Eyre* was a revision of the Cinderella story for nineteenth-century readers, suggesting that not only marriage but also autonomy constitutes the happy ending, then *Wide Sargasso Sea* is a (p)revision of *Jane Eyre* for twentieth-century readers. Antoinette's[7] story is the inversion of all fairy tales: her prince, a stranger from an exotic land, does not rescue her but imprisons her; does not bring her back to life but kills her; is not kind and noble but self-serving, a victim himself. Rhys collapses the fairy-tale dichotomy of the good woman (usually blonde) and the bad woman (usually dark-haired); she does not allow her readers to fall into the comfortable trap of seeing Jane as the spunky survivor and Bertha as the congenitally crazy obstacle to the romance. Instead, in what is a stroke of genius, she consciously constructs a series of parallels between Antoinette and Jane—between their lives, their circumstances, their attitudes and reactions—parallels so strong that we can only conclude that they are doubles, sisters, orphans in the patriarchy.

These parallels, in addition to many beautifully sensitive echoes of Brontë's novel (which reveal Rhys as an astute reader as well as an evocative writer) lead to one undeniable conclusion: Rhys is asserting that Antoinette's madness is not so aberrant—that insanity could have been Jane's fate, too. Rhys asks for a "re-vision" of Brontë's work. She asks us to forgo our initial romantic reading of the novel, at age thirteen or fourteen, when we saw Jane as the pure, attractive virgin and "Bertha" as the repulsive, crazy witch. She forces us to examine, finally, how Jane survived, and to conclude that it is Antoinette's warning that makes Jane's marriage to Rochester possible, that the real meaning of sisterhood is the courage of one generation to empower the next. Jane, ever the good pupil, heeds the warning provided by Bertha and refuses a relationship with Rochester until it can be a relationship of equals. The lesson she learns from Bertha, and that Rhys wants us to learn from *Wide Sargasso Sea,* is, in Rich's words, "an act of survival." Rhys insists that we see afresh the stories of the patriarchy, that we re-vise patriarchal definitions of women's lives, that we recognize the importance of the female literary tradition, and finally, that we forge our own criteria for success and failure in the female novel of development.

Feminists, who have been enormously attracted during the past decade to the novels of Jean Rhys, have nevertheless struggled somewhat guiltily to explicate the bleak endings of these novels: *Quartet* (1928),

After Leaving Mr. Mackenzie (1930), *Voyage in the Dark* (1934), *Good Morning, Midnight* (1939), and *Wide Sargasso Sea* (1966). The recurrent charge (largely from male critics) is that the novels are little more than chronicles of victimology and, as such, inappropriate paradigms for the liberated women of the 1970s and beyond. "All her heroines are born victims," asserts one critic. Another claims, "All Jean Rhys's modern women are victims, sisters of that Antoinette Cosway," heroine of *Wide Sargasso Sea*.[8] Greil Marcus describes Rhys as "a writer who once seemed to offer 'a challenge to the social and moral order' [but who] can be dismissed merely as a creature of her time or, worse, as merely neurotic—a great stylist to be sure, but not much more."[9]

No critics, however, have discussed *Wide Sargasso Sea* as a *Bildungsroman,* as a quest for identity, yet like its predecessor *Jane Eyre,* it chronicles the gropings and growth of its heroine. Measured against the standards of the male *Bildungsroman,* Antoinette's development, ending as it does in madness and suicide, is an abject failure. Perhaps this is what has tempted critics to use the facile label, victim. Instead, I would like to suggest a radically different reading: when looked at in the context of the female quest, Antoinette is at least partially successful. Given the time at which she lived (1830s), her colonial background, her convent education, and the limited scope of possibilities for women, Antoinette's final torching of Thornfield Hall is an act of assertion, of defiance, of symbolic identification with her West Indian heritage. She courageously re-writes the Cinderella story, alerting subsequent generations of women to the fallacy (and the danger) of giving it credence.

Both *Jane Eyre* and *Wide Sargasso Sea* open with images appropriate for novels about development: the former with mention of chilly weather that makes a walk impracticable, the latter with mention of an old, unrepaired road which, likewise, makes travel difficult. Yet despite the obstacles to travel, both Jane and Antoinette will be impelled on arduous journeys. The signs of impediment in the early pages of these novels predict that Jane will almost always travel in dreary, misty, cold weather (the one exception being her flight from Thornfield on a warm summer's morning, which she recalls she was too saddened to notice) and that Antoinette will almost always travel under duress, in a forced evacuation from one life to another. Both women will reside in five locations before their journeys reach completion: Jane at Gateshead, Lowood, Thornfield, Marsh End, and Ferndean; Antoinette at Coulibri, Mt. Calvary, Granbois, an unnamed house in Jamaica, and finally Thornfield.

A list of further parallels between the novels and their protagonists provides strong evidence of Rhys's intent to establish Jane and Antoinette as doubles, as sharing oppression, and with a potential for madness and also for survival. Jane is an orphan when her story opens; Antoinette experiences a growing estrangement from her mother, culminating in her mother's death.[10] Both girls confront, at Gateshead and Coulibri, a family situation where a male child is strongly preferred: an early lesson in the politics of patriarchy. Both girls are raised by aunts and have strong, nurturing surrogate mothers from the servant class: Jane's Bessie and Antoinette's Christophine. Their status as orphans is suggestive, of course, of the status of all women, as Gilbert and Gubar have noted: "Jane's terrible journey across the moors suggests the essential homelessness—the nameless, placeless, and contingent status—of women in a patriarchal society."[11]

Both girls, in significant early scenes, are hit on the head with an object thrown by another child, and in both instances this aggression is unjustified; Jane and Antoinette both respond with ensuing sickness and with rage. In both cases, the incident helps them to perceive and articulate the oppression of their situations. Both girls then proceed to convent schooling; though these schools are isolated and cramped by religion, they nonetheless provide a small field for Jane and Antoinette's endeavors. After initial discomfort, the two feel secure in this environment. Later, upon leaving the convent (and totally inexperienced with men), the first man each encounters is Edward Rochester. Both women subsequently marry Rochester, marriages in which money is a significant factor. Perhaps most important for the narratives, both women are visionaries: they have dreams that tell them the future and they wisely heed these dreams.

In fact, Jane Eyre and Antoinette Cosway Mason Rochester parallel each other so closely that one can make a convincing case for a shared identity: Jane and Antoinette are doubles. In his classic study, *The Double,* Otto Rank documents case after case of double stories in literature where male characters make a bargain with the devil to sell their soul (their shadow, their mirror reflections, their double) in order to better their financial and physical situation.[12] The catastrophe in the story occurs when the man begins a relationship with a woman: the double interferes, becomes a rival of sorts. And Antoinette and Jane are unwitting rivals for Rochester's affection. Jane, about to become Rochester's wife, discovers that he already has a wife: she discovers her double. Jane sees the mad wife as a nightmarish prediction of her future should she marry Rochester. Antoinette had no such timely warning. Jane, in a break from the competitive relationship of male doubles, heeds her warning. Seeing that marriage to Rochester will rob her of her identity, she flees—and returns only when a balance of money, power, and abilities has been achieved. This balance prevents either Jane or Rochester from being the oppressor.

It is the last parallel between Jane and Antoinette—the fact that both women experience visionary dreams—upon which I wish to concentrate, for these dreams are the most dynamic locus of "re-vision" in *Wide Sargasso Sea*. Antoinette has a sequence of three dreams in the novel, roughly equivalent to the traditional three stages of the quest and the three parts of the novel itself: separation, descent/initiation, return.[13] These dreams also, of course, chronicle her development as a woman.

That "development," as I have noted above, has been labeled a failure and a chronicle of victimology by male critics. Nancy Miller, in a provocative and innovative article entitled "Emphasis Added: Plots and Plausibilities in Women's Fiction," confronts women novelists' digression from the male "norms" of plot. Using Mme. de Lafayette's *La Princesse de Clèves* and George Eliot's *The Mill on the Floss,* Miller presents a new theory about "how difference can be read":

I am arguing that the peculiar shape of a heroine's destiny in novels by women, the implausible twists of plot so common in these novels, is a form of insistence about the relation of women to writing: a comment on the stakes of difference within the theoretical indifference of literature itself.[14]

Miller further notes:

The point is, it seems to me, that the plots of women's literature are not about "life" and solutions in any therapeutic sense, nor should they be. They are about the plots of literature itself, about the constraints the maxim places on rendering a female life in fiction.[15]

Although Miller nowhere refers to Rhys, she offers a valuable argument for refuting the critics who insist on reading this novel as solely a story of victimization. In *Wide Sargasso Sea,* Rhys comments on the very plausibility of writing a female novel of development. I will call on Miller's article once again to help establish this connection.

Miller quotes from Freud's essay "The Relation of the Poet to Daydreaming" (1908), in which Freud asserts that daydreaming and writing are functions of the same impulse, and distinguishes between the fantasies of women (almost exclusively erotic) and those of men (predominantly ambitious and egotistic, but also erotic). Miller demonstrates a healthy skepticism for this "anatomy is destiny" argument, suggesting that women ought to be able to fantasize both possibilities. Nonetheless, Miller concludes that while, as Freud would have it, the hero of male literature demonstrates a certain sense of security in his perilous adventures, the heroine of female fiction (at least in France) adopts instead "a variant of Murphy's law . . . If anything can go wrong, it will. And the reader's sense of security, itself dependent on the heroine's, comes from feeling not that the heroine will triumph in some conventionally positive way but that she will transcend the perils of plot with a self-exalting dignity."[16]

The connection that both Freud and Miller make between (day)-dreaming and the act of writing is, of course, highly suggestive when examining two texts in which the protagonists themselves dream, and dream sequential, foreboding dreams. By inscribing the dreams in the text, then, Brontë and Rhys reveal the process of female creativity; each heroine imagines, writes, her life as she dreams. Both Rhys and Brontë have created novels in which there exist, in effect, two texts: the surface text, which is an archetypal fairy tale, and the submerged text, the dreams, which continually revise the fairy-tale surface. The surface text exists as a paradigm of the usual pattern of female development, or more accurately, the norm of female stagnation and manipulation in fairy tales. The dreams, however, nudge the consciousness of Jane and Antoinette and, ultimately, become the instrument of their development, their awakening. When, near the conclusion of each novel, the surface texts and dream texts merge, the dreams have successfully demonstrated to the protagonists that life is not like a fairy tale, that they must write their own plots.

Looking first at the dreams in *Wide Sargasso Sea,* we see that each of Antoinette's three dreams is triggered by an event that brings her closer to her imprisonment, and ultimate death, in Thornfield tower. The first dream occurs when she is still a young girl at Coulibri. Visitors, unusual at Coulibri, have stopped by to introduce themselves to Antoinette's mother. These new neighbors will be the vehicle of her remarriage to Mr. Mason, whose son Richard is responsible for arranging Antoinette's and Rochester's marriage. Antoinette recalls the dream:

I went to bed early and slept at once. I dreamed that I was walking in the forest. Not alone. Someone who hated me was with me, out of sight. I could hear heavy footsteps coming closer and though I struggled and screamed I could not move. I woke crying. . . . I woke next morning knowing that nothing would be the same. It would change and go on changing.[17]

This is a dream of menace, of foreboding. Antoinette finds herself in a forest, the scene of evil and vulnerability in many fairy tales. She senses a dreaded presence but is powerless to control or escape the approach of that presence. She and Rochester have begun their doomed and ineluctable journey toward each other.

If, however, we accept Miller's suggestion that "the heroine's destiny . . . is a form of insistence about the relation of women to writing," then this dream and the two that succeed it are less a formula about Antoinette's life than they are her articulation, realization that the first stage of her development, the "separation," is about to occur. She relinquishes the comfortable security of childhood. She acknowledges that the plots will "change and go on changing." Her story will not end "happily ever after."

The second dream/chapter in Antoinette's life/novel occurs during her stay at the Mt. Calvary convent; again the dream is triggered by strangers. Her stepfather has visited her and announced his intention to withdraw her from the convent and introduce her to some "English friends." He refers, of course, to Rochester. Although Antoinette cannot consciously or rationally know what her fate will be as a result of this meeting, she has a strong sense of foreboding. In this second dream, Antoinette again leaves Coulibri in the night and walks toward the forest. This time she can see the face of the man, a face "black with hatred." The man is leading her and she acknowledges a sense of helplessness: "I follow him, sick with fear but I make no effort to save myself; if anyone were to try to save me, I would refuse. This must happen" (p. 60). Antoinette wears a white dress, symbolic of her vulnerability, her virginity, her wedding. They reach the forest; Antoinette does not know where she is being taken. "'Here?'" she asks. Suddenly the forest turns into an enclosed garden: West Indian landscape becomes Thornfield. Then Antoinette is brought to a set of steps leading upward:

It is too dark to see the wall or the steps, but I know they are there and I think "It will be when I go up these steps. At the top." I stumble over my dress and cannot get up. I touch a tree and my arms hold on to it. "Here, here." But I think I will not go any further. The tree sways and jerks as if it is trying to throw me off. Still I cling and the seconds pass and each one is a thousand years. "Here, in here," a strange voice said, and the tree stopped swaying and jerking. [p. 61]

The "tree" of course is Rochester as he carries Antoinette up the stairs to the third floor of Thornfield. Here, as throughout her novel, Rhys subtly mirrors the imagery of Brontë: both Brocklehurst and Rochester are described by Jane in phallic terms, as pillars and trees. This dream, far more concrete and threatening than the first, warns of the quickening approach of Rochester. It (p)revises the fairy-tale marriage and honeymoon of Antoinette and Rochester, revealing the bride's sexual initiation to be a loss of power and control. The sudden transformation, a commonplace in fairy tales, turns the natural forest into a cultivated garden: her marriage is a trap, an imprisonment. Ultimately, it is a descent into madness. Antoinette awakens and tells the nun in the dormitory "'I dreamed I was in Hell.'" The nun advises her: "'That dream is evil. Put it from your mind'" (p. 61). But Antoinette will dream yet another dream, an evil dream, evil because the fairy-tale innocence of the surface text must be re-vised.

That incident closes Part I of *Wide Sargasso Sea*. Part II is narrated by Rochester (except for a short hiatus by Antoinette). (It is one of Rhys's innovations in *Wide Sargasso Sea* to give a voice to the voiceless in *Jane Eyre,* a novel narrated entirely by Jane. In *Wide Sargasso Sea,* in contrast, we are given the perspectives of Antoinette, of Rochester, and even of Grace Poole.) Because Part II of the novel is narrated by Rochester, we get no account of Antoinette's dreams in this section. Just as Rochester, in *Jane Eyre,* tries to "own" Jane after their engagement by coy comments and elaborate gifts, so Rochester here signals his possession of Antoinette by appropriating her voice. Part II of the quest is descent/initiation, and this section of the novel records Antoinette's "death" before her rebirth in Part III. During Part II, Antoinette herself says to Rochester, " 'There are always two deaths, the real one and the one people know about' " (p. 128).

On their first evening at Granbois, Antoinette and Rochester have a tragically sad conversation:

"Is it true," she said, "that England is like a dream? Because one of my friends who married an Englishman wrote and told me so. She said this place London is like a cold dark dream sometimes. I want to wake up."

"Well," I answered annoyed, "that is precisely how your beautiful island seems to me, quite unreal and like a dream." [p. 80]

Aside from the obvious connection of Antoinette's query with her own dreams (in which England figures as something from which she wants to wake up), this exchange between husband and wife reveals each one's inability to accept the reality of the other's world. Rochester admits this. "I did not love her. I was thirsty for her, but that is not love. I felt very little tenderness for her, she was a stranger to me, a stranger who did not think or feel as I did" (p. 93).

Shortly after their arrival at the honeymoon house, one afternoon Rochester follows a path into the forest. "It is hostile," he muses, reiterating his usual failure to be at east in nature. What he finds in the forest reverberates strangely with Antoinette's dream sequence. He stumbles first upon what was once a paved road, then upon the ruins of a stone house, and finally upon trees with bunches of flowers surrounding them. Remembering Antoinette's despair at the crumbling road on page one and the burning of Coulibri, the reader wonders if

Rochester has passed into a time warp; this sense is intensified when, as darkness comes on, he sees a little girl: "I met her eyes and to my astonishment she screamed loudly, threw up her arms, and ran" (p. 105). Rochester has somehow blundered into Antoinette's first dream: here is Antoinette as a young girl, encountering the stranger in the forest. Surface text and subtext merge briefly here. When Rochester returns home, he pulls out a book on obeah that offers the following explanation:

"A zombi is a dead person who seems to be alive or a living person who is dead. A zombi can also be the spirit of a place, usually malignant but sometimes to be propitiated with sacrifices or offerings of flowers and fruit." [p. 107]

The little girl in the forest, then, is a zombi; Antoinette, having lost her parents, her money, her identity, her autonomy, is in a sense dead already.

The name of the honeymoon house, Granbois, links it with the great woods of Antoinette's dreams. Rochester's narration tells of growing alienation between the newly married couple. Rochester, the menacing figure of the dream, refuses to call his wife by her given name and instead provides her with a stout English name, Bertha. Antoinette later recalls, "Names matter, like when he wouldn't call me Antoinette, and I saw Antoinette drifting out of the window with her scents, her pretty clothes and her looking glass" (p. 180). Antoinette's identity, her sense of herself, slips further and further from her grasp. She experiences a growing division—Antoinette/Bertha, dead/alive—which Rhys deftly mirrors in the two texts. Bertha emerges in the surface text; Antoinette keeps her identity alive only in her dreams.

Antoinette makes one final desperate effort to heal the split of herself and her marriage: she obtains an aphrodisiac from Christophine. In an inversion of many fairy-tale plots, Antoinette administers the magic potion instead of taking it herself. The magic does not work. The following morning, Rochester awakens, a feeling of cold his strongest sensation: he is calm, rational, emotionless. He goes to the bedside of the sleeping Antoinette. Instead of awakening her with a kiss, as the prince is supposed to do, "I drew the sheet over her gently *as if I covered a dead girl"* (p. 139, italics mine). Destructive rather than chivalrous, Rochester does the reverse of what men do in fairy tales. Part II is a narrative of foreboding. It is important to note that this is *Rochester's* narrative. He is the instrument of descent/initiation, of death. His forebodings become a self-fulfilling prophecy. Antoinette, as we have seen, "dies." But the very fact that she narrates Part III, that she again revives her voice, is an act of assertion, a rebirth, a return.

Antoinette's first words to us as the "madwoman in the attic" concern awakening to the chill of early morning. She waits for Grace Poole to light the fire in the fireplace: "In the end the flames shoot up and they are beautiful" (p. 179). Antoinette associates warmth and fire with the West Indies, with passion, with freedom, with the past. The final conflagration becomes then an assertion of her colonial identity and of release. She has been given a gray wrapper to wear in the attic but much prefers a red dress brought with her from the West Indies. She describes the dress as "the color of fire and sunset, the color of flamboyant flowers"; it "has meaning" (p. 185). "The scent that came from the dress was very faint at first, then it grew stronger. The smell of vetivert and frangipani, of cinnamon and dust and lime trees when they are flowering. The smell of the sun and the smell of the rain" (p. 185). Like warmth and fire, the dress represents her home, her past, her identity; now Antoinette seeks to recover these. When the dress fuses with the fire in her mind, Antoinette determines what she will do:

But I looked at the dress on the floor and it was as if the fire had spread across the room. It was beautiful and it reminded me of something I must do. I will remember I thought. I will remember quite soon now. [p. 187]

This passage is followed immediately by the third and final installment of Antoinette's recurring and prophetic dream, in which she fantasizes/foresees the end. The dream begins in the tower in which Antoinette had implicitly been confined at the end of her last dream, the tower in which she is actually imprisoned now. Her first act in this dream is to take candle and keys from the snoring Grace Poole, and let herself out of the tower: a dream of escape, of liberation. "I walked as though I were flying" (p. 187). In the ensuing four pages of the dream, Antoinette frequently describes the sensation of floating or flying. She becomes a bird, a reincarnation of Coco, the parrot of her childhood. As she proceeds along the corridors of Thornfield, Antoinette never looks behind her for, as she explains, "I do not want to see that ghost of a woman who they say haunts this place" (p. 187). The "ghost" is, of course, herself. She enters a large room decorated in red and white, suggesting the clash between herself and Rochester. Here she starts the fire. She returns to the hall. "It was then that I saw her—the ghost. The woman with the streaming hair. She was surrounded by a gilt frame but I knew her" (p. 189). In a sense, then, Antoinette has exchanged places with her alter ego: she has reentered her real self. Earlier in the novel, she saw the real Antoinette drift out of a window and she became Bertha, the identity Rochester imposed upon her. Now, she sees the ghost ("who they say haunts this place") in a mirror; by exteriorizing the image imposed on her, she reclaims herself.

Immediately following this vision, Antoinette (still in the dream) climbs to the third story and out onto the battlements. "Then I turned around and saw the sky. It was red and all my life was in it" (p. 189). Again, red is connected with her past, her real self. She goes on to recount the conclusion of the dream:

I heard the parrot call as he did when he saw a stranger, Qui est là? Qui est là? and the man who hated me was calling too, Bertha! Bertha! The wind caught my hair and it streamed out like wings. It might bear me up, I thought, if I jumped to those hard stones. But when I looked over the edge I saw the pool at Coulibri. Tia was there. She beckoned to me and when I hesitated, she laughed. I heard her say, You frightened? And I heard the man's voice, Bertha! Bertha! All this I saw and heard in a fraction of a second. Someone screamed and I thought, Why did I scream? I called 'Tia' and jumped and woke. [p. 190]

In this final passage, then, Antoinette becomes the parrot who jumped with clipped wings on fire to its death at Coulibri. Antoinette, too, jumps to her death. Just as the parrot saved Antoinette's family, Antoinette's jump saves Jane. Her presence in the tower has served as a warning to Jane to leave Rochester; now, in Jane's absence, she destroys the tools given Rochester by the patriarchy, the tools of authority and power. Although Jane and Antoinette are both orphans, their "sisterhood" becomes the means of survival.

Also in this passage, Antoinette sees Tia, her childhood friend, once again, and her name is the last word she speaks. Here, Antoinette enacts the rebellion of the oppressed; setting Rochester's house afire, she follows the model of the rebellious servants of her childhood. Antoinette's death is an act of self-destruction. But it is also clearly an act of assertion, of reconnection with the warmth, red, beauty, and passion of her West Indian identity. Her third dream is the dream of return. And it is a dream of escape. For finally, Antoinette refuses to live out her life, confined to a tower, labeled insane. She will not be Bertha.

The reader's sense of *Wide Sargasso Sea* as a "post-dated prequel" and of the sisterhood of Jane and Antoinette is strengthened enormously by juxtaposing Jane's dream sequence with the one we have just examined. Jane has five recounted dreams in *Jane Eyre* and her third dream is unmistakably the same as Antoinette's third dream. Because Jane only dreams the destruction that Antoinette actually accomplishes Jane survives to dream on; her life then revises Antoinette's life and carries to completion the needed re-vision of fairy-tale plots.

Jane describes her first dream to us after she has asserted the credence she gives to such extrasensory perceptions: "I never laughed at presentiments in my life; because I have strange ones of my own. Sympathies, I believe, exist."[18] Such a belief in sympathies is especially significant since Jane's first dream occurs directly after Bertha's attack on Mr. Mason, an attack which marks the beginning of Jane's initiation to the secret of her double. Jane's dream is about a "baby-phantom" (p. 194), which alternately wails and laughs, cuddles and runs away. Jane recalls Bessie's warning to her when she was six: "to dream of children was a sure sign of trouble, either to one's self or one's kin" (p. 193). And, just as Antoinette's first two dreams, in *Wide Sargasso Sea,* are dreams of a child, of foreboding, of journeys and transformations, so Jane is called away the following day to Mrs. Reed's deathbed.

Returning to Thornfield, several weeks later, Jane stops overnight at an inn and dreams a second vivid dream:

I dreamt of Miss Ingram all the night: in a vivid morning dream I saw her closing the gates of Thornfield against me and pointing me out another road; and Mr. Rochester looked on with his arms folded—smiling sardonically, as it seemed, at her and me. [p. 213]

Again, Jane's dream is a warning: her unconscious self strives to instruct her conscious self that there is an impediment to the marriage; the submerged text of the dream instructs the surface fairy-tale text that Cinderella doesn't really happen. The impediment in the dream takes the form of Miss Ingram, the woman Jane supposes *will be* Rochester's wife; but, of course, Miss Ingram represents Bertha, Rochester's *existing* wife. Mr. Rochester's smile suggests complicity in the deceit. Jane's dream tells her she will once again be impelled to leave.

Despite this powerful dream, Jane accepts Rochester's proposal, made in the garden a fortnight later. Her acquiescence is commented upon by a sign of nature: a sudden violent storm descends upon the garden at midnight. Lightning strikes the old chestnut tree, a common symbol in gothic novels of the patrilineal possession of a mansion, and splits the tree in half. Rhys echoes this symbol of bifurcation and bigamy by identifying Rochester as a tree in Antoinette's second dream.

Two nights prior to her marriage, during Rochester's absence from Thornfield, Jane dreams her third dream, a dream which occurs in two parts. As in Jane's second dream, this dream carries the impact of "a strange, regretful consciousness of some barrier dividing" her and Rochester (p. 247). In the dream, Jane again carries a child; this time, they follow "the windings of an unknown road" (p. 247) on a dark, gusty, rainy night trying desperately to overtake Rochester who is ahead of them on the road. In part two of this dream, Jane confronts a shocking spectacle: "Thornfield Hall was a dreary ruin, the retreat of bats and owls" (p. 248). Still carrying the burdensome child, Jane hears Rochester galloping away. Like Antoinette, she mounts the battlements of Thornfield:

I climbed the thin wall with frantic, perilous haste, eager to catch one glimpse of you from the top. . . . I saw you like a speck on a white track, lessening every moment. The blast blew so strong I could not stand. I sat down on the narrow ledge; I hushed the scared infant in my lap: you turned an angle of the road; I bent forward to take a last look; the wall crumbled; I was shaken; the child rolled from my knee, I lost my balance, fell, and woke. [pp. 248–49]

Compare with this the final line of Antoinette's third dream: "I called 'Tia' and jumped and woke." When Jane awakens from this dream of Thornfield in ruins, she discovers a stranger in her room whom she describes as "the Vampyre" (p. 250). It is Bertha. While Jane watches, horrified, from her bed, Bertha takes Jane's bridal veil, throws it upon her head, gazes in the mirror, and in a gesture of warning, defiance, and destruction, rends it, as lightning did the chestnut tree, in half.

Thus, in a sense, the two protagonists exchange dreams: Bertha, the "mystery, that broke out, now in fire and now in blood, at the deadest hours of the night" (p. 185) prompts Jane's dreams, dreams which continually rebuke Rochester's labeling of Jane as an elf and a fairy. Jane dreams of the destroyed Thornfield well before Antoinette and in that sense prompts her. Both women dream of children, children that represent their lost selves, their lost identities, what they seek to recover during the "return" of the quest cycle.

Jane's final two dreams are dreams of direction: one, the night after her aborted wedding, tells her to flee; the other, a recurring dream, in which "amidst unusual scenes, charged with adventure, with agitating risk and romantic chance, [she] still again and again met Mr. Rochester, always at some exciting crisis" (p. 323). It is, of course, another kind of sympathy, a voice, which finally brings Jane back to Thornfield in search of Rochester. There she is confronted with a blackened ruin "as I had once seen it in a dream" (p. 374).

In an eassy entitled "Jane Eyre: The Temptations of a Motherless Woman," Adrienne Rich describes Jane as resisting four temptations on her quest: first, that of victimization and hysteria at Gateshead; next, that of self-hatred and self-immolation at Lowood; third, that of romantic love and surrender at Thornfield; and, finally, that of passive suicide at Marsh End.[19] Just as Rich sees Jane resisting temptation, so Rhys's novel encourages us to see Brontë, Antoinette, and all women dreamers/writers as resisting temptation, the temptation of writing a sugary romance that ends "happily ever after." Rhys depicts Antoinette in the very throes of this struggle as she muses about England on the day she obtains the love potion from Christophine. She daydreams/writes the conclusion of her life/story:

After summer the trees are bare, then winter and snow. White feathers falling? Torn pieces of paper falling? They say frost makes flower patterns on the window panes. I must know more than I know already. For I know that house where I will be cold and not belonging, the bed I shall lie in has red curtains and I have slept there many times before, long ago. How long ago? In that bed I will dream the end of my dream. But my dream had nothing to do with England and I must not think like this. I must remember about chandeliers and dancing, about swans and roses and snow. And snow. [pp. 111–12]

Antoinette juxtaposes here two versions of England: the fairy-tale version of "swans and roses," which is the version she has been taught as a colonial child, and the version of her dreams, the England of cold and confinement.

We see Antoinette, in this passage, with both her vision and re-vision of England, the two texts of *Wide Sargasso Sea*. These two texts merge at the conclusion of the novel when Antoinette herself finally rejects the fairy-tale text and heeds the dream text. It is at that moment that she, like Jane, recovers her childhood, her identity. The dream, not the fairy tale, becomes the instrument of her awakening, her assertion, her autonomy.

Wide Sargasso Sea is a "re-vision," then, in several senses. It encourages us to be "resisting readers"[20] toward *Jane Eyre* by warning us of the dangers of *misreading* it as a romance with marriage as the solution. The point of *Jane Eyre*, according to Rhys, is that Jane's transformation is not magical, temporary, and external, as was Cinderella's, but internal and thorough. And that she gains equality with Rochester not by having the correct shoe size but by heeding the warning of Bertha and refusing marriage until it is based on equality. *Wide Sargasso Sea* also re-vises our perceptions of Antoinette/Bertha. She and Jane are not polar opposites, nor a handy dichotomy, but sisters, doubles, orphans in the patriarchy. Each woman, in her own way, resists temptations, rejects "swans and roses," and wrests her identity from the patriarchal hypocrisy of "happily ever after."

Both Rhys and Brontë have refused to adopt the male novel of development for their purposes, but instead have inscribed in their novels a series of dreams that represent the difficulty and ambivalence of writing a female novel of development. By making Antoinette the instrument of Jane's survival, by making Antoinette's story the story from which Janes learns, Rhys insists on the crucial importance of women telling their own stories and tracing their own traditions. Rhys, then, would agree with Rich: re-vision is an "act of survival."

BLANCHE H. GELFANT

Revolutionary Turnings:

The Mountain Lion Reread

Like the whirling circle of fireworks that Jean Stafford describes in *The Catherine Wheel,* her novel *The Mountain Lion* is brilliant in its revolutions. Its action turns upon an overturning of expectations: a subversion of forms, myths, and manners which it draws on only to demolish. It is social satire, comedy of manners, Western romance, hunting adventure, fairy tale, and *Bildungsroman*—all of these, and none. For it refuses the demands of each of these forms as though in deliberate revolt against them. It subverts the traditional theme of initiation by arresting the growth of the children, Ralph and Molly Fawcett, with terrible finality. It subverts the myth of the American West—of open space as freedom—by denying the future promised by a once boundless land. It subverts the myth of the East—of inviolable ideas as freedom—by creating the past and preserving it as ashes. For all its abundance—an extraordinary richness of detail as well as motif— it leaves us with a wasted sense of emptiness. This is the residue of its brilliant and destructive tour de force, an appropriate and typically clever turn, since the novel is about residue. We are reminded of this by the literal presence of ashes in a conspicuous place in the novel, in Mrs. Fawcett's parlor. This macabre and comic touch, the preservation of Grandfather Bonney's remains, shows Mrs. Fawcett's infatuation with the past, an infatuation shared by Miss Pride in *Boston Adventure* and by Katherine in *The Catherine Wheel.* All three characters wish that time could be stopped, so that the present would exist as a perpetual past. A vain wish, since time as we trace it around the clock moves intransigently through its revolutions; and Stafford's concern as novelist is with resistant characters caught in this movement and destroyed.

In *The Catherine Wheel,* the destruction is stunningly graphic: Stafford's heroine is consumed in flames, turned to ash, on a whirling

Reprinted from the *Massachusetts Review* © 1979 by kind permission of the editors.

wheel of fireworks. This flaming circle, a spectacle intended for pleasure, resembles a medieval instrument of pain, a "spinning rack" that
tortured victims by its turnings. I suggest the analogue—that we as
readers are pained as we are pleasured by the brilliant spectacle of
Stafford's art. *The Mountain Lion* hurts us not only because of the
fate of the children, but more pervasively because of the devastating
picture of America it presents. Judging with a moral absoluteness that
reminds us of the Puritan heritage it both satirizes and sustains, the
novel denies greatness to America in any form. It shows everything
diminished, like Miss Runyon's miniature houses in Covina; or everything come to an end, like the species of wonderful wild animals in
Colorado.

Showing man diminished is the satirist's stock-in-trade, as we know
from Swift's Lilliputians; and showing the end of his world, as Stafford
does in her novels, is the work of the apocalyptic writer. *The Mountain
Lion* belongs to the wasteland tradition of apocalyptic writing, but we
have failed to recognize this because it dazzles us with liveliness, only
to shock us with loss. We are left with the sense of things ended: the
West depleted and left to childish men like Uncle Claude; Covina,
California, overrun by pests, a disaster area like Los Angeles in Na-
thanael West's apocalyptic novel, *The Day of the Locust;* and the East
evaporated to a gaseous gentility belched up by Reverend Follansbee
at tea.

Everything ends—the novel ends—with Molly's death. This death
effects the most complete revolution, turning the book we have been
enjoying as comedy to pathos and melodrama. If we have not anticipated the death, then we must admit we are incorrigible American
optimists, believers in fairy tales. For we expect ugly ducklings to turn
into swans; and lost children, like Hansel and Gretel, to find safety at
home; and wise children, who see the emperor naked, to achieve acclaim. But Molly dies, ignominiously, her epitaph an insult. *The
Mountain Lion* brings its revolutions to an end with violence; while
like fireworks, for a brief and brilliant duration, it sparkles—with the
wit, satire, and startling rectitude, moral and verbal, that enliven all
of Stafford's fiction.

As a social satirist, Jean Stafford is a stern uprighteous judge whose
standards for human being and conduct no character meets. In *The*

Mountain Lion—of greater scope than either *Boston Adventure* or *The Catherine Wheel,* her other novels—she surveys the American scene, East and West, to find everyone everywhere reduced to caricature. She presents us with our familiar stereotypes, which is a way of preserving our prejudices, and her own. In Mrs. Fawcett she produces a typified suburban mother: fussy, supercilious; addicted to cleanliness, ritual, and gentility; and always apprehensive, possessing her children through her fear and her guilt. We might laugh her off, except for her implication in her father's death, an example to Ralph and Molly of how members of a family can destroy each other. The tea-drinking, discreetly belching, chinless, platitudinous Reverend Follansbee is also familiar; but he cannot be wished away, as Molly tries to do, nor can his small revengeful cruelties be circumvented. He hounds Molly, and makes Ralph vomit. Miss Runyon the postmistress, suspected of having "set her cap for Mr. Kenyon," is everyone's spinster: a respository of silly fears, silly interests (like the Sunday "funnies"), and sexual repressions. To escape her fate young girls like Leah and Rachel must keep their hair curled, their complexions pink, and their clothes frilly so that young men will want to marry them. Winifred Brotherman, for a while a stereotyped "tom-girl," turns at marriageable age into another coquette, exchanging her blue jeans for party dresses, and her horse for her boyfriend's car. She taunts Molly by a transformation that the lank, dark, slouching girl cannot effect. Molly is susceptible, however, to the prejudices that run rampant through *The Mountain Lion,* to our monumental shame. Here is the area where generosity abounds—in distrust of "others," of Japanese, Germans, blacks, Catholics (Jews are put in their place in *Boston Adventure*). Poor people show up at the ranch as migrant scarecrows, arriving, multiplying, and then disappearing into the night. Had they stayed and shed their invisibility, Molly might have found a friend such as Emily Vanderpool finds in Stafford's story "Bad Characters," a girl's account of her Colorado childhood: the friend gets Emily arrested for "lifting," but meanwhile saves her from herself. The stereotyped "bad characters" around Ralph and Molly offer no outside chance of rescue: neither the menacing Mexican gardener, a "bad man" who sings "bad songs" in Spanish; nor the wised-up little Japanese children who tell of impossibly bad things men and women do; nor the wizardly old wizened black cook Magdalene at the ranch who "botches" goats without mercy, and eats beaver tails and calf testicles with relish.

In their comic-strip outlines, and in their mindlessness, Stafford's characters are cartoon figures: flattened, glossy, gross. But they represent the adult world where eventually the children must find their grown-up roles. Insofar as Ralph and Molly understand this, we can understand their reluctance to assume these roles, and their desperate eagerness to find others. Ralph wants "to go out West," to run away from civilization, like Huckleberry Finn; and Molly starts "to go crazy," like Holden Caulfield in *The Catcher in the Rye,* a novel that *The Mountain Lion* in various ways anticipates. Like Holden and his sister Phoebe, Ralph and Molly band together against the adult world; but unlike them, they lose their coherence, a devastating, irreversible loss, as they approach this world through an inevitable journey from childhood to adolescence.

Stafford portrays this journey in images derived from Freudian dream psychology and from Puritan brimstone sermons, sex and sin being synonymous in Ralph's mind and, perhaps, in hers. Her novel rings with Calvinistic overtones, sounded by the motif of poisoned blood. Is it coincidence that Grandfather Bonney died of blood poisoning, and that Ralph and Molly, "half poisoned," suffer profuse nosebleeds? The novel implies that evil is an inherited contamination that streams through human history and catches the young in its dirty course. "Molly, tell me all the dirty words you know," Ralph cries in the dark tunnel of adolescence where he feels sexual desire as his soul's damnation. Stafford supports this moral judgment by corroborative language—"corruption," "vileness," "black, sinful mind"; and by evocations of hell. Throughout the journey scene she conjures up vile fogs and crepuscular darkness; bats and snakes and corpse-like humans; sulphur and suffering and the devil himself. This melodramatic vision of hell merges with sexual nightmare as Ralph dreams of a precipitous fall amid swarming snakes, and as Stafford exploits conventional Freudian symbols of train and tunnel, one entering the other in darkness. All this is clever and contrived, and dates the novel, but also makes it the permanent impression of a sensibility of the times. It reminds us of a naive era when some people grew up thinking that corruption was simply sex, while some people never grew up because they died of such naiveté. Ralph seeks innocence and manhood, perhaps an impossible coalescence. Molly is implicated in his quest because she is the only one he finds untainted by sex (he does not understand repression): "Molly, alone . . . did not urge him to corruption."[1] His older sisters threaten his innocence by arousing incestuous fantasies—from which Molly alone can save him by a fanatical purity. In desiring both innocence and manhood, Ralph faces a dilemma that seems indigenous to American fiction and, perhaps, to American life. How he tries to deal with this dilemma is his story in *The Mountain Lion.*

When early in the novel Ralph cries, "Golly *Moses,* I'd like to go out west" (p. 8), he expresses the pristine wish of the mythic figure of American culture—the roving young hero who leaves civilization for the still uncontaminated places in the continent—wilderness, prairie, or mountain—where he can enact the timeless ritual of initiation to manhood. As in myth, Ralph is summoned to his journey by a mysterious messenger: Grandfather Kenyon, a "half legendary" visitor, a "sort of god of September" (p. 55). Kenyon resembles at times an Indian, at times a "massive, slow-footed bear" (p. 33), both fabulous creatures of the West. When Ralph enters Colorado he comes upon the landscape of fable: of immeasurable mountains, forests, glaciers, glades, streams, valleys, and pastures; and of animals—coyotes, elk, deer, bighorn, beavers, cattle, and horses; and of rangy strong men, and hunting rituals; and of golden light that transfigures everything, including a mountain lion, into dream. Here he too is transfigured from a puny frightened inept child to hunter. Equipped with his gun he prepares to join the male tribe by fulfilling its ritual. Alone and unafraid he will find a sacred spot in the wilderness where he will confront a legendary animal, one personified by a name. In the mystically charged encounter that brings together hunter and prey, the boy will acquire courage and skill and pride—and become a man. The greatest account of this myth in American fiction—one that embodies the tension of merging innocence with manhood—is William Faulkner's "The Bear." Ike McCaslin, the boy who hunts Old Ben in a southern wilderness, casts his indelible shadow over Ralph hunting Goldilocks in a Colorado mountain (and more recently, over Norman Mailer's character D.J. hunting Grizzer, old "Mr. Bear," in an Alaska frontier in

Why Are We in Vietnam?). Like Ike, womanless and childless, and
like Uncle Claude, the same, when Ralph enters the hunt he commits
himself to a ritual that excludes women. For the West is the symbolic
country where boys become men; and where girls, even the closest of
sisters, become not only extraneous or intrusive, but also threatening.
As a female, Molly encumbers Ralph in his obsessive stalking of the
mountain lion and the masculinity that is its trophy. Her constant
presence reminds him of a part of himself he can no longer endure,
and indeed, must annihilate, if he is to grow up—the feminine part of
his nature.

Thus *The Mountain Lion* presents us with a study of childhood ambivalence and social intolerance. For the society Ralph will enter does
not tolerate shared or ambivalent sex roles: it demands clear-cut identity. This demand destroys both Ralph and Molly as it divides them
from each other and involutes their love with hate. It destroys them
because they have been too integrally a part of each other—almost as
one in thought and feeling, and even with simultaneous nosebleeds—
to be separated by the unequivocal sex roles society prescribes. Ralph
is too sensitive to become like Claude—the strong solitary male defined in the great masculine myth of the West; and Molly is too
"ugly"—and too smart, quirky, cantankerous, and critical—to become
a coquette, like Rachel and Leah. Molly dies—in what I take to be a
sacrificial ceremony disguised in the novel as accident. She is sacrificed
so that Ralph can live, and live up to the myth of the West, to an
image of manhood that makes violence and destruction its consummation. "Learning the ways of a man," "proving his worth or manliness,"
Ralph inherits the confused values transmitted through the hunt. Killing, he learns, is an art. Through killing, as through art, one enters the
world of ritual where time is stopped and the past kept intact. Thus
killing may turn into an act of love, for as one stops time, he stops
change and keeps the object of his love forever fixed in its perfection,
like the figures on Keats's grecian urn. If Ralph's is the logic of madness, it nevertheless informs romantic literature. Ralph becomes a romantic hero when he determines to kill the mountain lion, an animal
whose beauty arouses his erotic fantasy, because he loves her: "Goldilocks . . . would be killed . . . out of his own love for her golden
hide" (p. 220). Once he has her dead, he can possess her forever:

"have her stuffed and keep her . . . all his life" (p. 218). Ralph also wants Molly immutable; and his love and his desire for possession are implicated in the accident that assures him that Molly will never change. Perhaps mistakenly, Ralph loves Molly for the "innocence" in which he seeks his own salvation. But he sees innocence despoiled by time and change which have already tainted him. If Molly grows up she too may fall into the pit of snakes, which already she fears with phobic terror; if she grows up she may lose her virginal purity—she may become a woman. Ralph's dilemma dooms his sister. Wedged between a cult of violence and a cult of virginity, she is crushed to death. And she collaborates in this fate. She too does not want to grow up and have to cope "with all the tommyrot with which people were constantly trying to ruin her life" (p. 182). To deny this "tommyrot," she willfully deludes herself that a girl can marry her brother, or barring that, her horse. She refuses the knowledge into which we all must fall; her innocence is indistinguishable from ignorance and fear. Rather than face life, Molly wishes to die, and she reveals this wish by her negation of her body. She tries consciously never to be conscious of her body, and she speaks of it ominously as "a long wooden box with a mind inside." We can guess that Ralph in his oneness with his sister intuits her death wish; and we know he shares it. When his initiation rite demands violence, he finds a way to fulfill this wish with apparent impunity, because the hunt sanctifies killing. Through a ritual that sublimates murderous instincts, Ralph tries to save his sister—from life, from violation, from herself. At the same time, by making her the scapegoat in his rite, he tries to save himself. So both children are sacrificed, and the myth of the West, which separates boys from men, and men from women, prevails. Seeing Ralph step into this myth and rigidly enact its ritual, we cannot believe he kills Molly without unconscious design or without cultural sanction. We have become too highly sophisticated in our reading of the intentions of a person or a society to think that accident, even one so obviously contingent as Ralph's, strikes gratuitously, without motive or purpose, as a purely freak occurrence. Within the novel, Molly is seen as a freak, and chosen for her destiny.

Why does Molly *want* to die? She knows and tells: "I know I'm ugly. I know everybody hates me. I wish I were dead" (p. 139). I

need not elaborate here on the involuted meanings that revolve about
a woman's physical appearance, nor figure the price any American
woman must pay for being ugly—for being *defined* as ugly, that is, by
her culture. At the end of Katherine Anne Porter's famous novella
"Old Mortality," an elderly maiden aunt reveals to the young heroine
the persecution she has suffered because of her protruding teeth and
receding chin: "All my life the whole family bedeviled me about my
chin. My entire girlhood was spoiled by it. Can you imagine . . . people who call themselves civilized spoiling life for a young girl because
she had one unlucky feature?"[2] All of Molly's features are unlucky:
height, "heavy eyebrows," dark skin, "prominent nose," lank black
hair, weak eyes. In Ralph, her double, these features turn to advantage
as he grows tall, dark, and handsome; and, by a miracle reserved only
for him, no longer needs eyeglasses. Molly's pretty older sisters, smugly
on their way to marriage, serve as foil and reprimand to the quirky,
awkward, critical, contentious little girl who strikes everyone as a "discord," being opposed to all "in temperament, in capacity, in propensi-
ties." These last are not Jean Stafford's words but Charlotte Brontë's
describing Jane Eyre, another child misfit. Jane Eyre develops inner
strength by becoming contemptuous of all those she could "never
please" because she was not by nature a "sanguine, brilliant, careless,
exacting, handsome, romping child."[3] She grows up to take a respected
place alongside a grateful Rochester, now blind, crippled, and dependent upon her love. Like Jane, little Maggie Tulliver in *The Mill on
the Floss* is also quick-witted and satiric; like Molly, dark in com-
plexion and moods; and like both a "discord" because she is smart
and does not hide her brains or her pride in having them. Maggie
grows up to be beautiful and desired, triply desired by two lovers and
her brother. Her fate—to die locked in her brother's arms—would
have been a consummation for Molly, separated abruptly and irrevocably from Ralph as he conforms to a myth of masculinity. An American girl, caught between the culture of a superannuated East, as depicted in the novel, and a boisterous, male West, Molly can find no
place for herself, no vindication. Unlike Jane, she never learns to assert an identity by making moral choices that would allow her to live
and eventually prevail. Unlike Maggie she never turns from ugly
duckling into swan. Perhaps beauty, or mere prettiness, might have

saved her from death, though not from the inanity that seems in the novel inseparable from female survival. Molly's sisters can grow up because they remain fairy-tale creatures, two pretty Goldilockses who will trip through life without ever getting lost or encountering menace, or ever threatening the suburban Disneyland world in which they live. They pay for their immunity to danger and disapproval with insipidity; they grow up by never really growing up, and their rites of passage are spurious though presented in the novel as common to girls. They do not suffer as Molly does, but in their own way, they are as blighted by prettiness as Molly is by her intelligence—her "handicap," her mother calls it—and her appearance. That women are judged by appearance, whether beautiful or ugly, Stafford sees as their misfortune. In her Jamesian story "The End of a Career," Stafford's heroine discovers that being blessed with rare and exquisite beauty is a form of curse. All her life she has cared for her beauty as though it were a sacred jewel whose brilliance must not be allowed to dim; that has been her career and the waste of her life. For at the end she learns what we should have known all along, that appearance is superficial, though it may be all in a woman that society values. The young woman in another story, "The Echo and the Nemesis," finds beauty and intellectual brilliance burdens too heavy for her to carry. So she splits her personality in two, bestowing beauty on one self, and brains on the other: a solution of insanity, painful and full of diabolical self-punishment: she eats herself into obesity—a fate worse than death for the American woman. In *The Mountain Lion*, Molly's brains cannot save her from the blight of her looks; and her character is demoralized by her acceptance of society's judgment that her looks are ugly. The ugly looks she gives to others—making gross faces at them—reflect what she has seen mirrored to her as an identity and a judgment. Molly collaborates in her own destruction when she accepts this image as her own. She is Stafford's brilliant study in introjection. Finally hating herself for the same reasons others hate her, because she assaults their sense of female beauty, she wants to erase herself from view, to disappear, to die. Though she is precocious, ambitious, critical, and discerning, her talents go to waste; her epitaph is "trash." Conventional beauty and simpering ways would save her, she thinks: "If only she had yellow hair, she thought, she would be an entirely different kind of person" (p. 214). But the image in the mirror does not reflect Shirley Temple. She comes to hate the image so much that shortly before she dies she adds her own name to her "list of unforgivables" (p. 217). Then she breaks down and cries, "and all the time she cried she watched herself in the mirror, getting uglier and uglier until she looked like an Airedale" (p. 217). In death she resembles "a monkey." Her limp body evokes the judgment with which the book ends: "The pore little old piece of white trash" (p. 231).

Although *The Mountain Lion* is Ralph's story, it tests us by our judgment of Molly. We sympathize with Ralph's desire for autonomy, and we see he has been betrayed by the male tribe that he thinks will grant it. In time the stereotyped "gosh darn" weekend whooping cowhands at the ranch deprive him of his dream of the West. In time Uncle Claude, his only possible model for manhood, reveals "a ponderous stupidity, a sort of virile opacity" (p. 168) that masks indifference to suffering, and malice to those who suffer or allow themselves, like Molly, to be "unhealthy"—that is, introspective, thoughtful, "bookish," critical, and smart (like Jean Stafford).[4] But though he is alone, Ralph can enter and be entertained in the world closed to Molly—because he is male, and handsome, and willing to accommodate to the "fat merchants" against whom he and Molly were once allied. But Molly remains intransigent; perhaps that is what we mean when we call her neurotic. And even if she would accommodate to the world as shown in the novel, she could not be accepted because her looks are hopeless. She tries. Even at the last, grown tall, her latest misfortune as a girl, she is still trying to cope, by stooping and sidling through the schoolhall like a crab. But such maneuvers make her more of a freak: more eccentric, more isolated, more unhappy, and finally, hopeless.

Can we imagine for Molly a life that does not end in futility, madness, or death? In 1947, reviewers of *The Mountain Lion* did not trouble themselves over this question, though they admitted being shocked by the "unexpected horror" with which the book ended. They were troubled, however, by the possibility that readers might miss the "terrible" "underlying truth" concealed almost entirely, they feared, beneath a brilliant surface—that of Stafford's witty and subtle and highly sophisticated style. In his *New York Times* review, Howard Mumford Jones expressed the worry that "naive readers may miss the deeper psychological developments of the tale." This was a shared apprehension. As another reviewer wrote: " 'The Mountain Lion' is likely to beguile many a reader into thinking that he has hold of merely a shrewdly perspective and amusing novel of children, when what he really has in his hand is a charge of psychological dynamite." Such doubts about the common reader's ability to understand *The Mountain Lion* show the critics responding to an uncertain tension within the novel between form and theme, or between expectation and fulfillment. This is the tension I ascribe to *The Mountain Lion*'s revolutionary turnings, its radical movements away from the expectations that its traditional forms arouse. That this tension produces in the reader both pleasure and pain—pleasure at the expectation of the familiar, and shock at "unexpected horror"—still another reviewer clearly discerned: "though you read it [*The Mountain Lion*] with amusement, you will feel it aching in you like a tooth for days." All these responses suggest that *The Mountain Lion* creates confusion in the reader: she thinks she is reading one kind of book, a traditionally amusing one, but she feels and reacts to another. No doubt Jean Stafford imagined herself writing one kind of book, a humorous satire well within the tradition of the American Western; but she could not imagine within that tradition a life for an odd young adolescent girl, since, traditionally, none existed. Thus *The Mountain Lion* describes a critical impasse in consciousness—of a character who cannot grow up in the West, and of a writer who cannot imagine for this character any destiny other than early death. That we do not entirely accept Molly's death as an inexplicable and intrusive accident, and that unlike early reviewers, we wonder about ways to circumvent this accident seem to me cause for celebration. For beyond the revolutions in its chosen literary traditions that *The Mountain Lion* shows us when we approach it formalistically, it reveals as a social document a revolution—or the possibility of a revolution—in consciousness. Today we can imagine what thirty-five years ago Jean Stafford could not—a future for Molly. That future requires another literary form, one in process of being shaped. I mean the novel that will present a portrait of the artist as a young woman; a novel of initiation that will describe female rites of passage. Molly Fawcett had dreamt of becoming a poet, but she lacked not only a typewriter (for which she wrote letters of solicitation comic to us and futile to her); she lacked a sense of the reality of this possibility, examples for a way of life she could barely imagine, let alone live. She belonged like the mountain lion to an endangered species, for which at the time there were no plans for preservation. In hunting Goldilocks, Ralph imagined that death would preserve this graceful, rare golden creature. Art, Jean Stafford's art as novelist, has preserved Molly, an awkward adolescent misfit. But life itself—and the revolutions it brings in understanding, manners, taste, social vision, and sympathy—makes it possible for us to preserve the life we see wasted by death in art. The possibility of a life for Molly that we can now imagine into the novel gives it its most radical and hopeful turning upon itself, and revitalizes as it revolutionizes us as readers.

ELIZABETH ABEL

Narrative Structure(s) and Female Development: The Case of *Mrs. Dalloway*

I wish you were a Kangaroo and had a pouch for small
Kangaroos to creep to.
  —Virginia Stephen to Violet Dickinson, June 4(?), 1903

Our insight into this early, pre-Oedipus, phase comes to us as a
surprise, like the discovery, in another field, of the Minoan-
Mycenean civilization behind the civilization of Greece.
  —Sigmund Freud, "Female Sexuality," (1931)

We all know Virginia Woolf disliked the fixity of plot: "This appalling narrative business of the realist," she called it.[1] Yet like all
writers of fiction, she inevitably invoked narrative patterns in her
work, if only to disrupt them or reveal their insignificance. In *Mrs.
Dalloway,* a transitional work between the straightforward narrative
of an early novel like *The Voyage Out* and the experimental structure
of a late work like *The Waves,* Woolf superimposes the outlines of
multiple, familiar yet altered plots that dispel the constraints of a unitary plan, diffuse the chronological framework of the single day in
June, and enable an iconoclastic plot to weave its course covertly
through the narrative grid. In this palimpsestic layering of plots, *Mrs.
Dalloway* conforms to Gilbert and Gubar's characterization of the
typically female text as one which both inscribes and hides its subversive impulses.[2]

The story of female development in *Mrs. Dalloway,* a novel planned
such that "every scene would build up the idea of C[larissa]'s character,"[3] is a clandestine story that remains almost untold, that resists direct narration and coherent narrative shape. Both intrinsically disjointed and textually dispersed and disguised, it is the novel's buried
story. The fractured developmental plot reflects the encounter of gender with narrative form and adumbrates the psychoanalytic story of

female development, a story Freud and Woolf devised concurrently and separately, and published simultaneously in 1925. The structure of Woolf's developmental story and its status in the novel illustrate distinctive features of female experience and female plots.

Woolf repeatedly acknowledged differences between male and female writing, detecting the influence of gender in fictional voice and plot. While insisting that the creative mind must be androgynous, incandescent, and unimpeded by personal grievance, she nevertheless affirmed that differences between male and female experience would naturally emerge in distinctive fictional shapes. She claims,

> No one will admit that he can possibly mistake a novel written by a man for a novel written by a woman. There is the obvious and enormous difference of experience in the first place. . . . And finally . . . there rises for consideration the very difficult question of the difference between the man's and the woman's view of what constitutes the importance of any subject. From this spring not only marked differences of plot and incident, but infinite differences in selection, method and style.[4]

The experience that shapes the female plot skews the woman novelist's relationship to narrative tradition; this oblique relationship may further mold the female text. In a remarkable passage in *A Room of One's Own,* Woolf describes one way in which the difference in experience can affect the logic of the female text:

> And since a novel has this correspondence to real life, its values are to some extent those of real life. But it is obvious that the values of women differ very often from the values which have been made by the other sex; naturally, this is so. Yet it is the masculine values that prevail. . . . And these values are inevitably transferred from life to fiction. This is an important book, the critic assumes, because it deals with war. This is an insignificant book because it deals with the feelings of women in a drawing-room. A scene in a battlefield is more important than a scene in a shop—everywhere and much more subtly the difference of value persists. The whole structure, therefore, of the early nineteenth-century novel was raised, if one was a woman, by a mind which was slightly pulled from the straight, and made to alter its clear vision in deference to external authority. . . . the writer was meeting criticism. . . . She met that criticism as her temperament dictated, with docility and diffidence, or with anger and emphasis. It does not matter which it was; she was thinking of something

other than the thing itself. . . . She had altered her values in deference to the opinions of others.[5]

Woolf explicitly parallels the dominance of male over female values in literature and life, while implying a different hierarchy that further complicates the woman novelist's task. By contrasting the "values of women" with those which "have been made by the other sex," Woolf suggests the primacy of female values as products of nature rather than culture, and of the named sex rather than the "other" one. No longer the conventionally "second" sex, women here appear the source of intrinsic and primary values. In the realm of culture, however, masculine values prevail and deflect the vision of the woman novelist, inserting a duality into the female narrative, turned Janus-like toward the responses of both self and other. This schizoid perspective can fracture the female text. The space between emphasis and undertone, a space that is apparent in Woolf's own text, may also be manifested in the gap between a plot that is shaped to confirm expectations and a subplot at odds with this accommodation. If the early nineteenth-century woman novelist betrayed her discomfort with male evaluation by overt protestation or compliance, the early twentieth-century woman novelist, more aware of this dilemma, may encode as a subtext the stories she wishes yet fears to tell.

Feminist literary criticism, Elaine Showalter states, presents us with "a radical alteration of our vision, a demand that we see meaning in what has previously been empty space. The orthodox plot recedes, and another plot, hitherto submerged in the anonymity of the background, stands out in bold relief like a thumbprint."[6] The excavation of buried plots in women's texts has revealed an enduring, if recessive, narrative concern with the story of mothers and daughters—with the "lost tradition," as the title of one anthology names it, or, in psychoanalytic terminology, with the "pre-Oedipal" relationship, the early symbiotic female bond that both predates and coexists with the heterosexual orientation toward the father and his substitutes. Frequently, the subtleties of mother-daughter alignments, for which few narrative conventions have been formulated, are relegated to the background of a dominant romantic or courtship plot. As women novelists increasingly exhaust or dismiss the possibilities of the romantic plot, however, they have tended to inscribe the maternal subplot more emphatically. In contemporary women's fiction, this subplot is often dominant; but in the fiction of the 1920s, a particularly fruitful decade for women and women's writing, the plot of female bonding began to vie repeatedly with the plot of heterosexual love. Woolf, Colette, and Cather high-lighted aspects of the mother-daughter narrative in works such as *My Mother's House* (1922), *To the Lighthouse* (1927), *Break of Day* (1928), *Sido* (1929), and "Old Mrs. Harris" (1932).[7] In *Mrs. Dalloway,* written two years before *To the Lighthouse,* Woolf struc-tures her heroine's development, the recessive narrative of her novel, as a story of pre-Oedipal attachment and loss.

In his essay "Female Sexuality," Freud parallels the pre-Oedipal phase of female development to the allegedly matriarchal civilization lying behind that of classical Greece, presumably associated here with its most famous drama; his analogy offers a trope for the psychological and textual strata of *Mrs. Dalloway.*[8] For Freud conflates, through the spatial and temporal meanings of the word "behind" (*hinter*), no-tions of evolution with those of static position. Clarissa Dalloway's rec-ollected development proceeds from an emotionally pre-Oedipal fe-male-centered natural world to the heterosexual male-dominated social world, a movement, Woolf implies, that recapitulates the broader sweep of history from matriarchal to patriarchal orientation. But the textual locus of this development, to revert to the archaeological im-plications of Freud's image, is a buried *sub*text that endures through-out the domestic and romantic plots in the foreground: the metaphors of palimpsest and cultural strata coincide here. The interconnections of female development, historical progress, and narrative structure are captured in Freud's image of a pre-Oedipal world underlying the in-dividual and cultural origins we conventionally assign the names Oe-dipus and Athens.

Woolf embeds her radical developmental plot in a narrative matrix pervaded by gentler acts of revision; defining the place of this reces-sive plot requires some awareness of the larger structure. The narrative present, patterned as the sequence of a day, both recalls the structure of *Ulysses,* which Woolf completed reading as she began *Mrs. Dallo-way,* and offers a female counterpart to Joyce's adaptation of an epic form.[9] *Mrs. Dalloway* inverts the hierarchy Woolf laments in *A Room of One's Own.* Her foregrounded domestic plot unfolds precisely in shops and drawing rooms rather than on battlefields, and substitutes for epic quest and conquest the traditionally feminine project of giving a party, of constructing social harmony through affiliation rather than conflict; the potentially epic plot of the soldier returned from war is demoted to the tragic subplot centering on Septimus Warren Smith. By echoing the structure of *Ulysses* in the narrative foreground of her text, Woolf revises a revision of the epic to accommodate the values and experience of women while cloaking the more subversive priorities explored in the covert developmental tale.

A romantic plot, which provides the dominant structure for the past in *Mrs. Dalloway,* also obscures the story of Clarissa's development. Here again, Woolf revises a traditional narrative pattern, the courtship plot perfected by Woolf's elected "foremother," Jane Austen. Woolf simultaneously invokes and dismisses Austen's narrative model through Clarissa's mistaken impression that her future husband is named Wickham. This slight, if self-conscious, clue to a precursor assumes greater import in the light of Woolf's lifelong admiration for Austen and Woolf's efforts to reconstruct this "most perfect artist among women" in her literary daughter's image; these efforts structure Woolf's essay on Austen, written shortly after *Mrs. Dalloway.*[10] Woolf's treatment of the romantic plot in *Mrs. Dalloway* reveals the temporal boundaries of Austen's narratives, which cover primarily the courtship period and inevitably culminate in happy marriages. Woolf condenses the expanded moment that constitutes an Austen novel and locates it in a remembered scene thirty years prior to the present of her narrative, decentering and unraveling Austen's plot. Marriage in *Mrs. Dalloway* provides impetus rather than closure to the courtship plot, dissolved into a retrospective oscillation between two alluring possibilities as Clarissa continues to replay the choice she made thirty years before. The courtship plot in this novel is both evoked through memories of the past and indefinitely suspended in the present, completed when the narrative begins and incomplete when the narrative ends, sustained as a narrative thread by Clarissa's enduring uncertainty. The novel provides no resolution to this internalized version of the plot; the final scene presents Clarissa through Peter Walsh's amorous eyes and allies Richard Dalloway with his daughter. The elongated courtship plot, the imperfectly resolved emotional triangle, becomes a

screen for the developmental story that unfolds in fragments of memory, unexplained interstices between events, and narrative asides and
interludes.

When Woolf discovered how to enrich her characterization by digging "beautiful caves" into her characters' pasts,[11] her own geological
image for the temporal strata of *Mrs. Dalloway,* she chose with preci-
sion the consciousness through which to reveal specific segments of
the past. Although Clarissa vacillates emotionally between the allure
of Peter and that of Richard, she remembers Peter's courtship only
glancingly; the burden of that plot is carried by Peter, through whose
memories Woolf relates the slow and tortured end of the relation
with Clarissa. Clarissa's memories, by contrast, focus more exclusively
on the general ambience of Bourton, her childhood home, and her
love for Sally Seton. Significantly absent from these memories is Richard Dalloway, whose courtship of Clarissa is presented exclusively
through Peter's painful recollections. Clarissa thinks of Richard only
in the present, not at the peak of a romantic relationship. Through
this narrative distribution, Woolf constructs two diversified poles structuring the flux of Clarissa's consciousness. Bourton is to Clarissa a pastoral female world spatially and temporally disjunct from marriage
and the sociopolitical world of (Richard's) London. The fluid passage
of consciousness between these poles conceals a radical schism.

Though the Bourton scenes Clarissa remembers span a period of
several years, they are absorbed by a single emotional climate that creates a constant backdrop to the foregrounded day in June. Woolf ex-
cises all narrative connections between these contrasting extended moments. She provides no account of intervening events: Clarissa's marriage, childbirth, the move and adjustment to London. And she indicates the disjunction in Clarissa's experience by noting that the London
hostess never returns to Bourton, which now significantly belongs
to a male relative, and almost never sees Sally Seton, now the unfa-
miliar Lady Rosseter. Clarissa's life in London is devoid of intimate
female bonds: she is excluded from lunch at Lady Bruton's and she
vies with Miss Kilman for her own daughter's allegiance. Woolf
structures Clarissa's development as a stark binary opposition between
past and present, nature and culture, feminine and masculine dispen-
sations—the split implicit in Woolf's later claim that "the values of

women differ very often from the values which have been made by the other sex." Versions of this opposition reverberate throughout the novel in rhetorical and narrative juxtapositions. The developmental plot, which slides beneath the more familiar romantic plot through the gap between Peter's and Clarissa's memories, exists as two contrasting moments and the silence adjoining and dividing them.

Woolf endows these moments with symbolic resonance by a meticulous strategy of narrative exclusions that juxtaposes eras split by thirty years and omits Clarissa's childhood from the novel's temporal frame. There is no past in *Mrs. Dalloway* anterior to Clarissa's adolescence at Bourton. Within this selective scheme, the earliest remembered scenes become homologous to a conventional narrative point of departure: the description of formative childhood years. The emotional tenor of these scenes, moreover, suggests their representation of deferred childhood desire. Clarissa's earliest narrated memories focus on Sally's arrival at Bourton, an arrival that infuses the formal, repressive atmosphere with a vibrant female energy. The only picture of Clarissa's early childhood sketched in the novel suggests a tableau of female loss: a dead mother, a dead sister, a distant father, and a stern maiden aunt, the father's sister, whose hobby of pressing flowers beneath Littré's dictionary suggests to Peter Walsh the social oppression of women, an emblem of nature ossified by language/culture. In this barren atmosphere, Sally's uninhibited warmth and sensuality immediately spark love in the eighteen-year-old Clarissa.[12] Sally replaces Clarissa's dead mother and sister, her name even echoing the sister's name, Sylvia. She nurtures Clarissa's passions and intellect, inspiring a love equal to Othello's in intensity and equivalent in absoluteness to a daughter's earliest bond with her mother, a bond too early ruptured for Clarissa as for Woolf, a bond which Woolf herself perpetually sought to recreate through intimate attachments to mother surrogates, such as Violet Dickinson: "I wish you were a Kangaroo and had a pouch for small Kangaroos to creep to."[13] For Clarissa, kissing Sally creates the most exquisite moment of her life, a moment of unparalleled radiance and intensity: "The whole world might have turned upside down! The others disappeared; there she was alone with Sally. And she felt she had been given a present, wrapped up, and told just to keep it, not to look at it—a diamond, something infinitely precious, wrapped up, which, as they walked (up and down, up and down), she uncovered, or the radiance burnt through, the revelation, the religious feeling!—when old Joseph and Peter faced them."[14] This kind of passionate attachment between women, orthodox psychoanalysts and feminists uncharacteristically agree, recaptures some aspect of the fractured mother-daughter bond.[15] Within the sequence established by the novel, this adolescent love assumes the power of the early female bond excluded from the narrative.

The moment Woolf selects to represent Clarissa's past carries the full weight of the pre-Oedipal experience that Freud discovered with such a shock substantially predates and shapes the female version of the Oedipus complex, the traumatic turn from mother to father. As French psychoanalytic theory has clarified, the Oedipus complex is less a biologically ordained event than a symbolic moment of acculturation, the moment, in Freud's words, that "may be regarded as a victory of the race over the individual," that "initiates all the processes that are designed to make the individual find a place in the cultural community."[16] For both women and men, this socialization exacts renunciation, but for women this is a process of poorly compensated loss, for the boy's rewards for renouncing his mother will include a woman like the mother and full paternal privileges, while the girl's renunciation of her mother will at best be requited with a future child, but no renewed access to the lost maternal body, the first love object for girls as well as boys, and no acquisition of paternal power. In *Mrs. Dalloway*, Woolf encapsulates an image of the brusque and painful turn that, whenever it occurs, abruptly terminates the earliest stage of female development and defines the moment of acculturation as a moment of obstruction.

Woolf organizes the developmental plot such that Clarissa's love for Sally precedes her allegiances to men; the two women "spoke of marriage always as a catastrophe" (p. 50). Clarissa perceives Peter in this period primarily as an irritating intruder. The scene that Clarissa most vividly remembers, the scene of Sally Seton's kiss, is rudely interrupted by Peter's appearance.[17] Both the action and the language of this scene hint at psychological allegory. The moment of exclusive female connection is shattered by masculine intervention, a rupture signaled typographically by Woolf's characteristic dash. Clarissa's response to this intrusion images an absolute and arbitrary termination: "It was like running one's face against a granite wall in the darkness! It was shocking; it was horrible!" (p. 53). Clarissa's perception of Peter's motives—"she felt his hostility; his jealousy; his determination to break into their comradeship"—suggests an Oedipal configuration: the jealous male attempting to rupture the exclusive female bond, insisting on the transference of attachment to the man, demanding heterosexuality. For women this configuration institutes a break as decisive and unyielding as a granite wall. Clarissa's revenge is to refuse to marry Peter and to select instead the less demanding Richard Dalloway in order to guard a portion of her psyche for the memory of Sally. Woolf herself exacts poetic justice by subjecting Peter Walsh to a transposed, inverted replay of this crucial scene when Elizabeth, thirty years later, interrupts his emotional reunion with her mother by unexpectedly opening a door (in the granite wall?), asserting by her presence the primacy of female bonds. "Here is my Elizabeth," (p. 71) Clarissa announces to the disconcerted Peter, the possessive pronoun he finds so extraneous accentuating the intimacy of the mother-daughter tie.

Clarissa resists the wrenching, requisite shift from pre-Oedipal to Oedipal orientation, yet she submits in practice if not totally in feeling. The extent of the disjunction she undergoes is only apparent in the bifurcated settings of her history, the images reiterating radical divides, the gaps slyly inserted in the narrative. The most striking of these images and gaps concern Clarissa's sister Sylvia, a shadowy and seemingly gratuitous character, apparently created just to be destroyed. Her death, her only action in the novel, is recalled by Peter rather than by Clarissa and is related in two sentences. This offhand presentation both implants and conceals an exaggerated echo of Clarissa's split experience. A young woman "on the verge of life" (p. 118), Sylvia is abruptly killed by a falling tree that dramatically imposes a barrier to life in a gesture of destruction mysteriously associated with her father: "(all Justin Parry's fault—all his carelessness)" (pp. 118–19). The shocking attribution of blame is only ostensibly discounted by parentheses: recall Woolf's parenthetical accounts of human tragedy in the "Time Passes" section of *To the Lighthouse*. The deliberate decision to indict the father contrasts with the earlier story, "Mrs. Dalloway in Bond Street," where Sylvia's death is depicted as a tranquil, vague event absorbed by nature's cyclical benevolence: "It used, thought Clarissa, to be so simple. . . . When Sylvia died, hundreds of years ago, the yew hedges looked so lovely with the diamond webs in the mist before early church."[18] The violence of Sylvia's death in the novel and the very incongruity between the magnitude of the charge against her father and its parenthetical presentation suggest a story intentionally withheld, forcibly deprived of its legitimate proportions, deliberately excised from the narrative yet provocatively implied in it, written both into and out of the text. This self-consciously inscribed narrative gap echoes the gap in Clarissa's own narrative, as the dramatic severance of Sylvia's life at the moment of maturity echoes the split in her sister's development. The pastoral resonance of Sylvia's name also implies a larger female story of natural existence abruptly curtailed.[19] A related narrative exclusion suggests a crucial untold tale about Clarissa's relation to her mother, remarkably unremembered and unmentioned in the novel except by a casual party guest whose brief comparison of Clarissa to her mother brings sudden tears to Clarissa's eyes. The story of the pain entailed in this loss is signaled by but placed outside the narrative in the double gesture of inclusion and exclusion that structures Woolf's narration of her heroine's development. By locating the clues to this discontinuous narrative in the marginal moments of her text, Woolf creates an inconspicuous subtext perceptible only to an altered vision.

Woolf's discrete suggestion of an intermittent plot is politically astute and aesthetically adept. Her insight into the trauma of female development does subvert the notion of organic, even growth culminating for women in marriage and motherhood, and she prudently conceals her implications of a violent adaptation. The narrative gaps also challenge the conventions of linear plot and suggest its distorted regimentation of experience, particularly the subjective experience of women. These gaps, moreover, are mimetically precise: juxtapositions represent sudden shifts, silence indicates absence and loss. Perhaps Woolf's most striking achievement, however, is her intuition of the "plot" Freud detected in female development. Despite Woolf's obvious familiarity with the popularized aspects of Freudian theory, and despite the close association of the Hogarth Press with the Freudian oeuvre, there can be no question of influence here, for Freud first expounded his view of a distinctively female development the year of *Mrs. Dalloway*'s publication.[20] Rather than influence, *Mrs. Dalloway* demonstrates the common literary prefiguration of psychoanalytic doctrine, which can retroactively articulate patterns implicit in the literary text. The similarities between these fictional and psychoanalytic narratives clarify the structure of Woolf's submerged developmental plot and the power of Freud's submerged demonstration of the loss implicit in female development.

Only late in life did Freud acknowledge the fundamentally different courses of male and female development. Prior to the 1925 essay entitled "Some Psychical Consequences of the Anatomical Distinction Between the Sexes," Freud clung, though with increasing reservations, to a view of sexual symmetry in which male and female versions of the Oedipal experience were fundamentally parallel. His growing appreciation of the pre-Oedipal stage in girls, however, finally toppled his view of parallel male and female tracks, inspiring a new formulation of the distinctively female developmental tasks. Female identity is acquired, according to this new theory, by a series of costly repressions from which the male child is exempt. The girl's developmental path is more arduous and bumpy than the boy's smoother linear route. For though the male child must repress his erotic attachment to his mother, he must undergo no change in orientation, since the mother will eventually be replaced by other women with whom he will achieve the status of the father; he suffers an arrest rather than a dislocation. The girl, in contrast, must reverse her course. Like the boy, she begins life erotically bonded with her mother in the symbiotic pre-Oedipal stage, but unlike him she must replace this orientation with a heterosexual attraction to her father. She must change the nature of her desire before renouncing it.

How, Freud repeatedly asks, does the girl accomplish this monumental shift from mother to father? Though the answers he proposes may be dubious, the persistent question indicates the magnitude of the event. The girl's entire sexuality is defined in this transition. She switches not only the object of her erotic interest, but also her erotic zone and mode, relinquishing the active, "masculine," clitoridal sexuality focused on her mother for the passive, receptive, "feminine," vaginal sexuality focused on her father. Freud goes so far as to call this change a "change in her own sex," for prior to this crucial shift, "the little girl is a little man."[21] This comprehensive change in sexual object, organ, and attitude, the shift from pre-Oedipal to Oedipal orientation, inserts a profound discontinuity into female development, which contrasts with that of "the more fortunate man [who] has only to continue at the time of his sexual maturity the activity that he has previously carried out at the period of the early efflorescence of his sexuality."[22] The psychosexual shift that occurs in early childhood, moreover, is often reenacted in early adulthood, for marriage typically reinstates a disruption in women's experience, confined until recently to a largely female sphere prior to the heterosexual contract of marriage.[23]

The circuitous route to female identity, Freud acknowledged, is uniquely demanding and debilitating: "a comparison with what happens with boys tells us that the development of a little girl into a normal woman is more difficult and more complicated, since it includes two extra tasks [the change of sexual object and organ], to which there is nothing corresponding in the development of a man."[24] No woman completes this difficult process unscathed. Freud outlines three developmental paths for women; all exact a substantial toll. If she follows the first, the girl negotiates the shift from mother to father by accepting the unwelcome "fact" of her castration, detected in comparisons between herself and little boys. Mortified by this discovery of inferiority, aware she can no longer compete for her mother with her better endowed brother, she renounces her active sexual orientation toward her mother, deprived like herself of the valued sexual organ, and accepts a passive orientation toward the superior father. Unfortunately, the girl's renunciation of active sexuality normally entails repressing "a good part of her sexual trends in general," and this route leads to sexual inhibition or neurosis, to "a general revulsion from sexuality."[25] If she chooses the second path, the girl simply refuses this renunciation, clings to her "threatened masculinity," struggles to preserve her active orientation toward her mother, and develops what Freud calls a "masculinity complex," which often finds expression in homosexuality.[26] Only the third "very circuitous" path leads to the "normal female attitude" in which the girl takes her father as the object of her passive eroticism and enters the female Oedipus complex. Curiously, however, Freud never describes this route, which turns out to be only a less damaging version of the first path toward inhibition and neurosis.[27] To the extent that her sexuality survives her "catastrophic" repression of her "masculine" desire for her mother, the girl will be able to complete her turn to her father and seal her femininity by desiring his baby. "Normal" femininity is thus a fragile, tenuous proposition; no unique course is prescribed for its achievement. Freud's most optimistic prognosis assumes a doubly hypothetical, negative form: "If too much is not lost in the course of it [development] through repression, this femininity may turn out to be normal."[28] The achievement of this femininity, moreover, is only the first stage, for the female Oedipus complex, like the male, must itself be overcome, and the hard-won desire for the father renounced and transferred to other men. Female development thus entails a double disappointment in contrast with the single renunciation required of men. No wonder Freud concludes the last of his essays on femininity by contrasting the youthful flexibility of a thirty-year-old male with the psychical rigidity of a woman the same age: "Her libido has taken up final positions and seems incapable of exchanging them for others. There are no paths open to further development; it is as though the whole process had already run its course and remains thenceforward insusceptible to influence—as though, indeed, the difficult development to femininity had exhausted the possibilities of the person concerned."[29]

In *Mrs. Dalloway,* Woolf suggests the developmental turn that Freud accentuates in his studies of femininity. The narratives they sketch share a radically foreshortened notion of development, condensed for Freud into a few childhood years, focused for Woolf in a single emotional shift. Both narratives eschew the developmental scope traditionally assumed by fiction and psychology, committed to detailing the unfolding of a life, and both stress the discontinuities specific to female development. Woolf, moreover, portrays the sexual and emotional calcification that Freud suggests is the toll of "normal" development. Clarissa is explicit about her unimpassioned response to men, a response she perceives as a failure and a lack, a guarding of virginity through motherhood and marriage. Her emotional and physical self-containment is represented by her narrow attic bed, where she reads Baron Marbot's memoirs of the retreat from Moscow, a victory achieved by icy withdrawal.[30] The association of her bed with a grave—"Narrower and narrower would her bed be" (pp. 45–46)—links her adult sexuality with death. Yet, in a passage of extraordinary erotic writing, Woolf contrasts the description of the narrow bed with Clarissa's passionate responses to women, implying through this jux- taposition the cost of the pivotal developmental choice:

Yet she could not resist sometimes yielding to the charm of a woman, not a girl, of a woman confessing, as to her they often did, some scrape, some folly . . . she did undoubtedly then feel what men felt. Only for a mo- ment; but it was enough. It was a sudden revelation, a tinge like a blush which one tried to check and then, as it spread, one yielded to its expan- sion, and rushed to the farthest verge and there quivered and felt the world come closer, swollen with some astonishing significance, some pres- sure of rapture, which split its thin skin and gushed and poured with an extraordinary alleviation over the cracks and sores! Then, for that moment, she had seen an illumination; a match burning in a crocus; an inner mean- ing almost expressed. But the close withdrew; the hard softened. It was over—the moment. Against such moments (with women too) there con- trasted (as she laid her hat down) the bed and Baron Marbot and the candle half-burnt. [pp. 46–47]

Woolf's language renders a passion that is actively directed toward women, and implicitly "masculine" in attitude and character, yet also receptive and "feminine," epitomized in the image of the match in the crocus, an emblem of active female desire that conflates Freud's sexual dichotomies. The power of the passage derives in part from the inter- meshed male and female imagery, and the interwoven languages of sex and mysticism, a mélange that recurs in Clarissa's memory of Sally Seton's kiss. Fusion—of male and female, active and passive, sacred and profane—is at the heart of this erotic experience. Freud's opposi- tion of active, "masculine," pre-Oedipal sexuality to the passive, "feminine," Oedipal norm denies the basis for this integration. Claris- sa's momentary illumination is enabled only by the sexual orientation Freud devalues as (initially) immature and (subsequently) deviant. Woolf's passage suggests the potential completeness Freud denies the pre-Oedipal realm and calls into question the differentiation of normal from aberrant sexuality. The stark contrast between the passionate moment and the narrow bed, another juxtaposition that conceals a schism between two radically different sexual worlds, subverts the opposition normal/abnormal. Woolf here elevates Freud's second developmental path over the costly route toward "normal femininity," as she valorizes a spontaneous homosexual love over the inhibitions of imposed heterosexuality.

As the passage continues, the gap between the sexual options emblematized by the moment and the bed evolves into the familiar split between Sally Seton and Richard Dalloway, the split that structures the developmental plot. The allegorical image of the bed leads to a more concrete description of Clarissa's reaction to her husband's return: "if she raised her head she could just hear the click of the handle released as gently as possible by Richard, who slipped upstairs in his socks and then, as often as not, dropped his hot-water bottle and swore! How she laughed!" (p. 47). The contrast between the passionate moment with women and the narrow marital bed becomes a leap from the sublime to the (affectionately) ridiculous. Opening with the conjunction "But," the next paragraph signals a turn away from mundanity back to "this question of love . . . this falling in love with women" (p. 48), inaugurating Clarissa's lengthy and lyrical reminiscence of Sally Seton. The opposition between Clarissa's relationships with men and women modulates to the split between her present and her past, her orientation and emotional capacities on both sides of the Oedipal divide. Woolf, like Freud, reveals the cost of female development, but she inscribes a far more graphic image of the loss entailed, questions its necessity, and indicates the price of equating female development with acculturation through the rites of passage established by the Oedipus complex.

These are radical claims, and Woolf suggests them indirectly. In addition to her use of juxtaposition as a narrative and rhetorical strategy, Woolf encodes her developmental plot through characters who subtly reflect Clarissa's experience.[31] Perhaps most interesting of these is the infrequently noticed Rezia Warren Smith, wife of Clarissa's acknowledged double who has drawn critical attention away from the mirroring function of his wife. Rezia's life, like her name, is abbreviated in the novel, yet the course of her "development" suggestively echoes that of the heroine. Like Clarissa, Rezia finds herself plucked by marriage from an Edenic female world with which she preserves no contact. Her memories highlight the exclusively female community of sisters collaboratively making hats in an Italian setting that is pastoral despite the surrounding urban context: "For you should see the Milan gardens!" she later exclaims, when confronted with London's "few ugly flowers stuck in pots!" (p. 34). The cultural shift from Italy to England, like the shift from Bourton to London, locates this idyllic female life in a distant, prelapsarian era—before the war, before industrialization, before marriage. Marriage and war explicitly coalesce for Rezia as agents of expulsion from this female paradise: Septimus comes to Milan as a British soldier and proposes to Rezia to alleviate his war-induced emotional anesthesia. Rezia's memories of Italy, a radiant temporal backdrop to her painful alienation in marriage and a foreign culture, provide a pointed parallel to Clarissa's memories of Bourton. And Rezia's final pastoral vision, inspired by the drug administered after Septimus's suicide, significantly begins with her sense of "opening long windows, stepping out into some garden" (p. 227), thus echoing Clarissa's first recollection of Bourton, where she had "burst open the French windows and plunged . . . into the open air" (p. 3). The death of her husband releases Rezia to return imaginatively to a past she implicitly shares with Clarissa: the female-centered world anterior to heterosexual bonds. After this moment of imaginative release and return, Rezia disappears from the novel, having accomplished the function of delicately echoing the bifurcated structure of the heroine's development.

The relation of Clarissa and Rezia exists only for the reader; the two women know nothing of each other.[32] Woolf employs a different strategy for connecting Clarissa with Septimus, whose death severs the link between these female characters, releasing each to a new developmental stage, Rezia to return imaginatively to the past, Clarissa at last to transcend that past. Septimus's suicide enables Clarissa to resolve the developmental impasse that appears to be one cause of her weakened heart, her constricted vitality. Critics have amply explored Septimus's role as Clarissa's double. As important as this psychological doubling, however, is Woolf's revision of developmental plots, her decision to transfer to Septimus the death she originally imagined for Clarissa,[33] to sacrifice male to female development, to preserve her heroine from fictional tradition by substituting a hero for a heroine in the plot of violently thwarted development, a plot that has claimed such heroines as Catharine Linton, Maggie Tulliver, Emma Bovary, Anna Karenina, Tess Durbeyfield, Edna Pontellier, Lily Bart, and Antoinette Cosway Rochester. By making Septimus the hero of a sacrificial plot that enables the heroine's development, Woolf reverses narrative tradition.

It is a critical commonplace that Clarissa receives from Septimus a cathartic, vicarious experience of death that releases her to experience life's pleasures more deeply. Woolf's terms, however, are more precise. The passage describing Clarissa's reaction to Septimus's suicide suggests that he plays a specific role in Clarissa's emotional development. Woolf composes this passage as a subtle but extended parallel to Clarissa's earlier reminiscence of her love for Sally and Bourton.[34] The interplay between the language and structure of these two meditative interludes, the two major sites of the developmental plot, encodes Clarissa's exploration of a conflict more suppressed than resolved. By interpreting Septimus's suicide in her private language of passion and integrity, Clarissa uses the shock of death to probe her unresolved relation to her past. The suicide triggers Clarissa's recurrent preoccupation with this past, providing a perspective that enables her belatedly both to admit and to renounce its hold. On the day in June that encloses the action of *Mrs. Dalloway,* Clarissa completes the developmental turn initiated thirty years before.

Woolf prepares the parallels between the two passages by inaugurating both with Clarissa's withdrawal from her customary social milieu. The emotions prompting Clarissa's first meditation on Sally and the past are initially triggered by her exclusion from Lady Bruton's lunch. Woolf then describes Clarissa's noontime retreat to her solitary attic room as a metaphorical departure from a party: "She began to go slowly upstairs . . . as if she had left a party . . . had shut the door and gone out and stood alone, a single figure against the appalling night"; Clarissa is "like a nun withdrawing" (p. 45). Later that night, when Clarissa hears the news of Septimus's suicide, she does leave her party and retreats to an empty little room where "the party's splendor fell to the floor" (pp. 279–80). The first passage concludes with her preparations for the party, the second with her deliberate return to that party. Within these enclosed narrative and domestic spaces, Clarissa relives through memory the passionate scene with Sally on the terrace at Bourton. The second passage replays in its bifurcated structure the male intervention that curtails the original scene. In this final version of the female/male juxtaposition, however, the emotional valences are reversed.

Clarissa's meditation on Septimus's death modulates, through her association of passion with death, to a meditation on her relation to her past. Woolf orchestrates the verbal echoes of this passage to evoke with increasing clarity the scene with Sally Seton. Septimus's choice of a violent, early death elicits in Clarissa the notion of a central self preserved: "A thing there was that mattered; a thing, wreathed about with chatter, defaced, obscured in her own life. . . . This he had preserved" (p. 280). The visual image of a vital, central "thing" initiates the link with the earlier description of passion as "something central which permeated" (p. 46). The echoes between these passages develop through their similar representations of passion's ebb: "closeness drew apart; rapture faded, one was alone" (p. 281); "But the close withdrew; the hard softened. It was over—the moment" (p. 47). As Clarissa implies that only death preserves the fading moment of passion, she prepares for her repetition of the *Othello* line that has signified her love for Sally Seton: "If it were now to die, 'twere now to be most happy" (pp. 51, 281). The metaphor of treasure which precedes this explicit allusion to the scene with Sally further connects Clarissa's response to Septimus ("had he plunged holding his treasure?" she wonders) with her memory of Sally's kiss as "a present . . . a diamond, something infinitely precious" (pp. 52–53). Septimus's death evokes in Clarissa the knowledge of what death saves and what she has lost; her grief is not for Septimus, but for herself. Woolf weaves the verbal web between the two passages to summon once again the crucial scene with Sally on the terrace at Bourton, to enable Clarissa to confront her loss. Clarissa's appreciation of this loss, at last fully present to her consciousness, crystallizes in the contrast that concludes this segment of the passage: "She had schemed; she had pilfered. She was never wholly admirable. . . . And once she had walked on the terrace at Bourton" (p. 282).

With this naming of the original scene, Woolf abruptly terminates

Clarissa's recollection, replaying with a brilliant stroke Peter Walsh's interruption, the sudden imposition of the granite wall. The masculine intervention this time, though, is enacted not by Peter but by Richard, and not as external imposition but as choice. Clarissa's unexpected thought of Richard abruptly and definitively terminates the memory of Sally, pivoting the scene from past to present, the mood from grief to joy: "It was due to Richard; she had never been so happy" (p. 282). The dramatic and unexplained juxtaposition encapsulates the developmental plot and the dynamics of its central scenes. This final replay of the developmental turn, and final microcosm of Woolf's narrative method, however, represent the abrupt transition positively. The joy inspired by Clarissa's thought of Richard persists as she celebrates "this having done with the triumphs of youth" (p. 282). Woolf does not fill in the gap splitting past from present, grief from joy. We can only speculate that Septimus's sacrificial gift includes a demonstration of Clarissa's alternatives: to preserve the intensity of passion through death, or to accept the changing offerings of life. By recalling to Clarissa the power of her past *and* the only method of eternalizing it, he enables her fully to acknowledge and renounce its hold, to embrace the imperfect pleasures of adulthood more completely. Through Septimus, Woolf recasts the developmental impasse in the general terms of progression or death. In the final act of the developmental plot, she qualifies her challenge to the notion of linear, forward growth.

Woolf signals the shift in Clarissa's orientation by concluding the interlude with Clarissa's reaction to the old lady across the way, an unnamed character who only functions in the novel as an object of Clarissa's awareness. The earlier meditative passage concludes with Clarissa's reflection in the looking glass; this one with an analogous reflection of a future identity. After Clarissa's thoughts shift from Sally and the past to Richard and the present, Woolf turns the angle of vision one notch further to open a perspective on the future. The old lady solemnly prepares for bed, but this intimation of a final repose, recalling Clarissa's earlier ruminations on her narrowing bed, carries no onus for the heroine, excited by the unexpected animation of the sky, the news of Septimus's suicide, the noise from the party in the adjacent room. Release, anticipation, pleasure in change, regardless

of its consequences—these are Clarissa's dominant emotions. Her identification with Septimus and pleasure in his suicide indicate her own
relief in turning from her past. The gulf between Clarissa and the
unknown lady discloses the female intimacy forfeited to growth, yet
Clarissa's willingness to contemplate an emblem of age instead of
savoring a memory of youth suggests a positive commitment to development—not to any particular course, but to the process of change
itself. The vision of the old lady simultaneously concludes the developmental plot and the depiction of Clarissa's consciousness; the rest of
the narrative turns to Peter and Sally. The developmental theme resides in the interplay between two interludes in the sequence of the day.

Freud's comparison of the pre-Oedipal stage in women to the
Minoan-Mycenean civilization behind that of classical Greece provides
a metaphor for the course and textual status of Clarissa's development.
It also suggests a broader historical analogue to female development,
though not an analogue Freud himself pursues. Freud's psychoanalytic
version of ontogeny recapitulating philogeny assumes a genderless
(that is, implicitly masculine) norm: personal development repeats
the historical progression from "savage" to civilized races.[35] In *Mrs.
Dalloway*, Woolf intimates more specifically that *female* development
condenses one strand of human history, the progression from matriarchal to patriarchal culture implicit in Freud's archeological trope.
Woolf's fascination during the years she was composing *Mrs. Dalloway* with the works of Jane Harrison and the *Oresteia*, which traces
precisely the evolution from Mycenean to Athenian culture, may have
fostered this concern with the relation of gender to cultural evolution.[36] The developmental plot embedded in *Mrs. Dalloway* traces the
outline of a larger historical plot, detached in the novel from its
chronological roots and endowed with an uncustomary moral charge.

Woolf assigns the action of *Mrs. Dalloway* a precise date: 1923,
shortly after the war that casts its shadow through the novel. Through
the experience of Septimus Warren Smith and the descriptions of soldiers marching "as if one will worked legs and arms uniformly, and
life, with its varieties, its irreticences, had been laid under a pavement
of monuments and wreaths and drugged into a stiff yet staring corpse
by discipline" (pp. 76–77), she suggests that the military discipline
intended both to manifest and cultivate manliness in fact instills rigor

mortis in the living as well as the dead. For women, the masculine war is disruptive in a different way. Woolf's imagery and plot portray the world war as a vast historical counterpart to male intervention in female lives. In one pointed metaphor, the "fingers" of the European war are so "prying and insidious" that they smash a "plaster cast of Ceres" (p. 129), goddess of fertility and mother love, reminder of the force and fragility of the primary female bond. Rezia's female world is shattered by the conjunction of marriage and war. The symbolic association of war with the developmental turn from feminine to masculine orientation will be more clearly marked in *To the Lighthouse*, bisected by the joint ravages of nature and war in the divisive central section. By conflating Mrs. Ramsay's death with the violence of world war, Woolf splits the novel into disjunct portions presided over separately by the mother and the father.

In *Mrs. Dalloway*, Woolf more subtly indicates the masculine tenor of postwar society. The youngest generation in this novel is almost exclusively, and boastfully, male: Sally Seton repeatedly declares her pride in her "five great boys"; the Bradshaws have a son at Eton; "Everyone in the room has six sons at Eton" (p. 289), Peter Walsh observes at Clarissa's party; Rezia Warren Smith mourns the loss of closeness with her sisters but craves a son who would resemble his father. Elizabeth Dalloway is the sole daughter, and she identifies more closely with her father than her mother (the plaster cast of Ceres has been shattered in the war). Male authority, partially incarnate in the relentless chiming of Big Ben, is more ominously embodied in the Doctors Holmes and Bradshaw, the modern officers of coercion. Septimus is the dramatic victim of this authority, but Lady Bradshaw's feminine concession is equally significant: "Fifteen years ago she had gone under . . . there had been no scene, no snap; only the slow sinking, water-logged, of her will into his. Sweet was her smile, swift her submission" (p. 152). The loose connections Woolf suggests between World War I and a bolstered male authority lack all historical validity, but within the mythology created by the novel the war assumes a symbolic function dividing a pervasively masculine present from a mythically female past.

Critics frequently note the elegiac tone permeating *Mrs. Dalloway*, a tone which allies the novel with the modernist preoccupation with the contrast between the present and the past.[37] Nostalgia in *Mrs. Dalloway,* however, is for a specifically female presence and nurturance, drastically diminished in contemporary life. Woolf suggests this loss primarily in interludes that puncture the narrative, pointing to a loss inadequately recognized by the conventions of developmental tales. The most obvious of these interruptions, the solitary traveler's archetypal vision, loosely attached to Peter Walsh's dream, but transcending through its generic formulation the limits of private consciousness, is not, as Reuben Brower asserts, a "beautiful passage . . . which could be detached with little loss," and which "does not increase or enrich our knowledge of Peter or of anyone else in the book."[38] Through its vivid representation of a transpersonal longing for a cosmic female/maternal/natural presence that might "shower down from her magnificent hands compassion, comprehension, absolution" (p. 86), the dream/vision names the absence that haunts *Mrs. Dalloway.* In the mundane present of the novel, the ancient image of the Goddess, source of life and death, dwindles to the elderly nurse sleeping next to Peter Walsh, as in another self-contained narrative interlude, the mythic figure of woman voicing nature's eternal, wordless rhythms contracts, in urban London, to a battered old beggar woman singing for coppers. The comprehensive, seductive, generative, female powers of the Goddess split, in the contemporary world, into the purely nurturant energy of Sally Seton and the social graces of the unmaternal Clarissa, clad as a hostess in a "silver-green mermaid's dress" (p. 264). The loss of female integration and power, another echo of the smashed cast of Ceres, is finally suggested in the contrast between the sequence envisaged by the solitary traveler and the most intrusive narrative interlude, the lecture on Proportion and Conversion, where Woolf appears to denounce in her own voice the twin evils of contemporary civilization. Rather than a sign of artistic failure, this interruption calls attention to itself as a rhetorical as well as ideological antithesis to the solitary traveler's vision. Sir Bradshaw's goddesses of Proportion and Conversion, who serve the ideals of imperialism and patriarchy, renouncing their status as creative female powers, are the contemporary counterpart to the ancient maternal deity, now accessible only in vision and dream. The historical vista intermittently inserted in *Mrs.*

Dalloway echoes the developmental progress of the heroine from a nurturing, pastoral, female world to an urban culture governed by men.

One last reverberation of the developmental plot takes as its subject female development in the altered contemporary world. Through the enigmatic figure of Elizabeth, Woolf examines the impact of the new historical context on the course of women's development. Almost the same age as her mother in the earliest recollected scenes at Bourton, Elizabeth has always lived in London; the country to her is an occasional treat she associates specifically with her father. Elizabeth feels a special closeness to her father, a noticeable alienation from her mother. The transition so implicitly traumatic for Clarissa has already been accomplished by her daughter. By structuring the adolescence of mother and daughter as inverse emotional configurations, Woolf reveals the shift that has occurred between these generations. As Clarissa vacillates between two men, while tacitly guarding her special bond with Sally, Elizabeth vacillates between two women, her mother and Miss Kilman, while preserving her special connection with her father. Elizabeth's presence at the final party manifests her independence from Miss Kilman; her impatience for the party to end reveals her differences from her mother. The last scene of the novel highlights Elizabeth's closeness with her father, whose sudden response to his daughter's beauty has drawn her instinctively to his side.

The opposing allegiances of daughter and mother reflect in part the kinds of female nurturance available to each. Elizabeth's relation with the grasping Miss Kilman is the modern counterpart to Clarissa's love for Sally Seton. Specific parallels mark the generational differences. Miss Kilman's possessive desire for Elizabeth parodies the lines that emblazon Clarissa's love for Sally: "If it were now to die, 'twere now to be most happy" becomes, for Elizabeth's hungry tutor, "If she could grasp her, if she could clasp her, if she could make her hers absolutely and forever and then die; that was all she wanted" (pp. 199–200). Sally walks with Clarissa on the terrace at Bourton; Miss Kilman takes Elizabeth to the Army and Navy Stores, a commercial setting that exemplifies the web of social and military ties. Miss Kilman, as her name implies, provides no asylum from this framework. Losing the female sanctuary, however, brings proportionate compensations: Elizabeth assumes she will have a profession, will play some active role in masculine society. Woolf does not evaluate this new developmental course, does not tally losses and gains. If she surrounds the past with an aureole, she points to the future in silence. She offers little access to Elizabeth's consciousness, insisting instead on her status as enigma—her Chinese eyes, "blank, bright, with the staring incredible innocence of sculpture" (p. 206), her Oriental bearing, her "inscrutable mystery" (p. 199). Undecipherable, Elizabeth is "like a hyacinth, sheathed in glossy green, with buds just tinted, a hyacinth which has had no sun" (p. 186); her unfolding is unknown, unknowable. Through the figure of Elizabeth as unopened bud, Woolf encloses in her text the unwritten text of the next developmental narrative.

The silences that punctuate *Mrs. Dalloway* reflect the interruptions and enigmas of female experience and ally the novel with a recent trend in feminist aesthetics. The paradoxical goal of representing women's absence from culture has fostered an emphasis on "blank pages, gaps, borders, spaces and silence, holes in discourse" as the distinctive features of a self-consciously female writing.[39] Since narrative forms normally sanction the patterns of male experience, the woman novelist might signal her exclusion most succinctly by disrupting continuity, accentuating gaps between sequences. "Can the female self be expressed through plot or must it be conceived in resistance to plot? Must it lodge 'between the acts'?" asks Gillian Beer, the allusion to Woolf suggesting the persistence of this issue for a novelist concerned with the links of gender and genre.[40] In her next novel Woolf expands her discrete silence to a gaping hole at the center of her narrative, a hole that divides the action dramatically between two disjunct days. *To the Lighthouse* makes explicit many of the issues latent in *Mrs. Dalloway*. The plot of female bonding, reshaped as the story of a woman's attempts to realize in art her love for an older woman, rises to the surface of the narrative; yet Lily's relationship with Mrs. Ramsay is unrepresented in the emblem Lily fashions for the novel, the painting that manifests a daughter's love for her surrogate mother as a portrait of the mother with her son. Absence is pervasive in *To the Lighthouse*. The gaps in *Mrs. Dalloway* are less conspicuous, yet they make vital and disturbing points about female experience and female plots. The fragmentary form of the developmental plot, where the patterns of experience and art intersect, conceals as insignificance a radical significance. The intervals between events, the stories untold, can remain invisible in *Mrs. Dalloway*—or they can emerge through a sudden shift of vision as the most absorbing features of Woolf's narrative.[41]

CATHARINE R. STIMPSON

Doris Lessing and the Parables of Growth

From 1952 to 1969, Doris Lessing published the five novels that were to make up the series entitled *Children of Violence*. Taking on the largest possible obligations that a novel of development might impose upon an author, she wished to dramatize "the individual conscience in its relations with the collective."[1] Her example of the individual conscience, Martha Quest, has become a character whom readers mentally lift from the page and incorporate into their own lives as a reference point. She is a Wilhelm Meister, an Isabel Archer, a Paul Morel, for the last decades of a monstrous century and millennium. Martha is also a woman, a possible descendant of Isabel Archer rather than Wilhelm Meister or Paul Morel. However, Lessing would resist, rather than celebrate, the placing of *Children of Violence* in a tradition of a female novel of development.

Naming Martha, Lessing pointed to qualities that all her readers might need during this century. "Martha" refers to one of the two sisters of Lazarus. She leaves home to ask Christ to raise her brother from the dead. Explicitly she states a belief in His divinity and powers. "Yes, Lord: I believe that thou art the Christ, the Son of God, which should come into the world" (John 11:27). Martha personifies the principles of activity and faith, and the conviction that history might be redeemed and changed. Christ can both raise Lazarus and raze our sins. "Quest" is, of course, that significant journey in which the process of the journey may matter as much as its end. To endure that process, to achieve that end, the quester will need magister figures who may teach benignly, but, in the twentieth century, may prove to be goblins or *idiots savants* as well.

As told by *Children of Violence,* Martha's own story is one of possible redemption and change. She begins as an estranged adolescent of fifteen on a farm in Zambesia, Lessing's composite landscape of the Africa that England colonized, with Dutch aid. She is ostentatiously reading Havelock Ellis. Her father is a failure, an attractive man whom World War I has ruined. Her mother is frustrated and bitter, an energetic woman also scarred by the war. Martha has one sibling, a younger brother whom her mother prefers. Having left school at fourteen, Martha is largely self-educated. She gets a job as a legal secretary in the colony's provincial, segregated capital. Because she thinks too much in a culture that dislikes thought, she must repress herself. To do that, she drinks too much, and plays too hard.

At eighteen, she marries Douglas Knowell, a civil servant running to pomposity and fat. Their wedding takes place in March 1939: Hitler, seizing Bohemia and Moravia, marches toward the war that will help to destroy British colonialism. Four years later, the proper Knowell marriage is a disaster. As Douggie wallows in self-pity, and threatens to rape Martha or to kill her and their little daughter, Martha leaves. Her friends and family turn against her; her mother, a betrayer, disowns her, for a while.

Martha, in her own place, has an affair with a Royal Air Force sergeant. She helps to start the Communist party of Zambesia. As an activist to whom the party is an equivalent of self and part of a vanguard group that is a central and centering presence, she is both "Red" and "kaffir-loving," characteristics equally abhorrent to colonial society. She marries again: Anton Hesse, a German Communist interned in Zambesia, whose first wife and family are dying in European concentration camps and who needs a more secure immigration status. The marriage is a sexual fiasco. Anton suffers from premature ejaculation, and, ironically, bourgeois domestic values. Both have affairs, Martha with Thomas Stern, a Polish Jew in exile. She embarks upon a Laurentian discovery of the power, joy, and compulsions of sexuality. However, Thomas will leave for Palestine, to fight for Israeli nationhood, and then for a remote African village, in which he dies.

In 1945, with peace, the patterns of Martha's life fall apart. Her father drifts, half-drugged, into death. The party flounders, as its founders move away and postwar politics rush over it. Martha and Anton have a proper divorce. Life has tamed him. Symbolically, he has learned tennis and will doubtless marry the daughter of a rich colonial businessman. Finally realizing an adolescent dream, Martha sails to England and to the London that World War II has devastated, but not destroyed. Her move is much more than a reenactment of the progress to the city by the young provincial man, or woman. For the morally ambitious white, leaving the colonies is a survival act. The women who want to go, but who do not, become what they feared they might become: anxious, emotional, self-conscious conformists who wear masks of bright cheer.

Martha finds a job as live-in secretary to a writer: Mark Coldridge, one of four sons of an elite British family. A brother, Colin, flees to Russia when he is accused of being a Communist spy. Eventually, Martha becomes Mark's lover; a surrogate mother to his son and Colin's son; and a friend of Mark's wife, Lynda, who stays in the basement with female companions when she is not in mental hospitals. At once chivalrous and obsessive, Mark loves her hopelessly. In her basement apartment, Lynda is an obvious sign of buried and ignored psychic energies.

Located in Bloomsbury, the house entertains all of postwar English politics and culture. In the late 1970s, the local government buys it. Martha lives alone, and then goes to a commune in the country to help with the children. However, for years, the inhabitants of the house have prepared for a Catastrophe. Mark has mapped the increase of atomic, biological, and chemical weapons; of fallout and pollution; of war, famine, riots, poverty, and prisons. As Lessing believes it will, the world acts out a logic of homicide and suicide. The Catastrophe does happen. Because authorities lie, and because catastrophes are such chaos, no one knows precisely what has occurred. It may have been a chemical accident, or the crash of a plane with nuclear bombs. Whatever the cause, the effects are clear.

In the brave new shattered world, Mark runs a refugee camp—before his death. He has married again: Rita, the illegitimate daughter of Zambesians whom Martha had once known. Lynda may be dead. Martha has escaped to an island off the coast of Ireland or Scotland. Her last words are in a letter of 1997 to Francis, Mark and Lynda's son. She tells him about a black child, Joseph, who has been with her on the island. In a world in which many children are deformed mutants, he may be a genuinely evolutionary one. He may have paranormal powers, even more effective than those that Lynda, Martha, and Francis have developed. Martha explains:

He says more like them are being born now in hidden places in the world, and one day all the human race will be like them. People like you and me are a sort of experimental model and Nature has had enough of us. [FGC, p. 648]

Reconstituting itself after the Catastrophe, the world may be breeding a new child, a savior. However, it may also be generating new governments, huge, quarreling, stratified bureaucracies. Joseph is to be a gardener, as Thomas was. Lessing cannot say if he will tend vegetables, or guard our dreams of paradise; if he is to be a serf, or a sage who will, as Marx promised, dissolve divisions between labor of the mind and of the hands.

Such a summary but hints at Lessing's narrative immensities, at the hugeness of her plots and subplots. She asks us to take them seriously, a request at once bolder and less truistic than it seems. Lessing acknowledges that other media—movies, television—are influential. She also assumes that speaking can mean more than writing; that logos may be livelier off than on the page. "Everywhere, if you keep your mind open, you will find the truth in words *not* written down. So never let the printed page be your master" (italics hers).[2] However, she believes, as perhaps only a self-educated farm child can, in the moral and cognitive strength of texts. She does not revel in the postmodern theory that all verbal acts are fictions, language performances, language at play. She pays tribute to the nineteenth-century novel and to the rare book—a *Moby Dick,* a *Wuthering Heights,* a *The Story of an African Farm*—that is on "a frontier of the human mind."[3] Martha may thread her way through literature to revalidate its authority and to reinterpret it, but Lessing also asserts that a writer must be responsible. In essays and in *Children of Violence,* she accosts an "ivory-tower" literature and critics who acclaim it.

The writer must speak *for,* as well as *to,* others. So doing, the writer both serves as a voice for the voiceless, as a witness for the inarticulate, and helps to form a community of the like-minded. Because the writer can reveal that what we thought to be a private hallucination is actually a collective thought, literature can grant us our sanity.

In brief, despite the science fiction she now publishes, Lessing is marvelously old-fashioned, a great traditionalist. *Children of Violence* is an urgent, urging cultural achievement, a composition meant as explanation and guide. Between *A Ripple from the Storm* (1958) and *Landlocked* (1965), Lessing became a public student of Sufi, of Islamic mysticism. A scholar whom she praises has said, "The Sufi teacher is a conductor, and an instructor—not a god."[4] With secular modesty, she seeks to conduct us to and instruct us in truths greater than ourselves. *Children of Violence* is, then, a parable—of epic proportions.

Lessing's primary lesson demonstrates the necessity of growth, particularly of consciousness. Like many moderns, she finds consciousness the precondition of conscience. Understanding must inform our will, perception, judgment. She fears repetition, the active reproduction of social and psychic conditions, and nostalgia, a mental reproduction of the past that longing infiltrates. Martha is frantically wary of "the great bourgeois monster, the nightmare *repetition*" (APM, p. 77). One of the saddest ironies of *Children of Violence* is that Martha, who refuses to be like *her* mother, tells her daughter that she is setting her free. Being left, Caroline will have nothing to imitate. Yet Caroline apparently becomes a well-behaved junior member of Zambesia's elite: what Martha's mother wanted Martha to become and the antithesis of what Martha would have praised, the replication of her fears.

To picture her theory of growth, Lessing consistently employs natural imagery: a tree, a blade of grass. To conceptualize it, she calls on evolutionary theory, not of the Victorians, but of the Sufis. In *Children of Violence,* Lessing uses epigraphs to inform us of her intentions. They are annotations and shorthand exegeses. Significantly, she begins Part IV of *The Four-Gated City*, the last pillar in her blueprint of the architecture of Martha's soul, with passages about Sufi thought:

Sufis believe that, expressed in one way, humanity is evolving towards a certain destiny. We are all taking part in that evolution. Organs come into being as a result of a need for specific organs. The human being's organism is producing a new complex of organs in response to such a need. In this age of the transcending of time and space, the complex of organs is concerned with the transcending of time and space. What ordinary people regard as sporadic and occasional bursts of telepathic and prophetic power are seen by the Sufi as nothing less than the first stirrings of these same organs. The difference between all evolution up to date and the present need for evolution is that for the past ten thousand years or so we have been given the possibility of a conscious evolution. So essential is this more rarefied evolution that our future depends on it. [p. 448]

Both tropes and theory reinforce the sense that growth has the force of natural law. It transcends individual choice. We may choose to obey or to neglect that law, to dwell within its imperatives or to deny them, but we cannot decide whether or not it exists.

Lessing's commitment to the expansion of consciousness tempts one to call *Children of Violence* an example of Lukács's theory of the novel: "the adventure of interiority; the story of the soul that goes to find itself, that seeks adventures in order to be proved and tested by them, and by proving itself, to find its own essence."[5] She herself has named *The Four-Gated City* a *Bildungsroman:*

This book is what the Germans call a *Bildungsroman*. We don't have a word for it. This kind of novel has been out of fashion for some time. This does not mean that there is anything wrong with this kind of novel. [FGC, p. 655]

If the genre groups together tales of "the formation of a character up to the moment when he ceases to be self-centered and becomes society-centered, thus beginning to shape his true self";[6] and if one thinks of Martha as entering into, and then discarding, several societies, then Lessing's label for the last novel holds for her series as a whole. An admirer of Mann, she has produced another twentieth-century *Bildungsroman* in which people and groups are maladjusted and ill. Images of physical, mental, and psychosomatic sickness abound in *Children of Violence:* Martha's pinkeye; Captain Quest's medicine chests; Mr. Anderson's infirmity (he is a retired civil servant who reads government reports and sci-fi pornography); Douggie's ulcers; Lynda's hands, nails bitten until they bleed; babies, after the Catastrophe, born with two heads and fifty fingers. Martha is Lessing's Hans Castorp; Africa and England her sanitorium, her *Berghof.*

Because of the nature and intensity of her sense of social illness, Lessing has grafted the Western apocalyptic tradition to the *Bildungsroman.* For her, we inhabit a period of terrors and decadence. At its best, our age demands a stifling conformity; at its worst, it provokes fear, exploitation, oppression, violence. The End is both imminent and immanent.[7] Like most prophets of the apocalypse since 1945, Lessing is profoundly aware of the splitting of the atom and the origins of atomic warfare. A madman, a fool, a committee—each might bring this dread upon us. In *Ecce Homo,* Nietzsche predicted the rebirth of tragedy when mankind became conscious, without any feeling of suffering, that it had behind it the hardest, but most necessary, of wars. Lessing believes that mankind has before it the hardest, but most unnecessary, of wars, and the suffering of that vision overwhelms *Children of Violence.* The apocalypse we are manufacturing may not permit anyone to survive, let alone a society to enter a reconstituted history.

In the nineteenth-century female *Bildungsroman,* the young woman protagonist often dies—physically or spiritually. Maggie Tulliver drowns, she and her brother clasped in each other's arms.[8] In Olive Schreiner's *The Story of an African Farm,* Lyndall "chooses to die alone rather than marry a man she cannot respect."[9] Martha avoids such a fate. She survives the Catastrophe, and endures until she is an old woman in her mid-seventies. As a *Bildungsroman, The Four-Gated City* differs from many of the genre in that Lessing describes far more than her protagonist's maturing years.[10] The novel of development has become the novel of an encyclopedic life, as if the relations between conscience and its collectives were a part of a complex, lengthy process. Yet, Lessing hardly ignores death. Rather, our Cassandra, she broadens the drama of the death of the female protagonist until it becomes that of her culture. She rewrites the female *Bildungsroman* to enlarge the sufferings of a young woman until they become the doom of the collective. The struggle between the woman who would be freer than her society permits her to be also changes to become a struggle between an enlightened group, a saving remnant, that would free society from its self-destruction and the larger group that is in love with its own diseaseful death.

Lessing must obviously reconcile the comic promise of the *Bildungsroman,* that we can within history pass from youth to a semblance of maturity, with the tragic promise of the apocalypse, that history as we know it will explode. She does so through the Sufi belief in "the possibility of a conscious evolution . . . this more rarefied evolution that our future depends on." If each of us nurtures consciousness as we pass from youth to a semblance of maturity, if we join with others who are doing the same thing, then we may either avert the apocalypse, or live through it and protect those children whose minds are even more potent than our own. Lessing adapts, from apocalyptic historiography, the myth of individual and collective rebirth. Such myths have consistently attracted her. In 1957, she exulted: "I am convinced that we all stand at an open door, and that there is a new man about to be born, who has never been twisted by drudgery."[11] *Children of Violence* tests and re-tests these myths, to retain them in a grimmer, more shadowed form. In *Landlocked,* Thomas, naked, in bed with Martha, says:

Perhaps there'll be a new mutation though. Perhaps that's why we are all so sick. Something new is trying to get born through our sick skins. I tell you, Martha, if I see a sane person, then I know he's mad. You know, the householders. It's we who are nearest to being—what's needed. [p. 116]

Since the evolution of consciousness matters so much, Lessing devotes a great part of *Children of Violence* to Martha's own. The narrative is a detailed, subtle account of the methodology of growth, in which Martha is a case study, an exemplary figure, and our potential representative.[12] The fact that she is a woman is less important than the fact that she can give the lie to official lies and ultimately exercise the paranormal psychic powers that Lessing believes are the birthright of us all. As an excellent critic says, "Ultimately, the deepest task of [Lessing's] characters is to achieve a personal wholeness that subsumes sexual identity or gender under a larger principle of growth."[13]

Such statements embody a complication about Lessing. She is among our most brilliant, persuasive anatomists of contemporary women's lives. She writes compellingly about their friendships: that of Martha and Alice; of Martha and Jasmine, a revolutionary who stays in Africa; of Martha and Lynda; of Lynda and her flatmate Dorothy. She dramatizes the pressures on them to perform and conform. She knows about their disabilities, the need to please, the complicities, the denials and self-denials. Though Martha is incorrigibly heterosexual, Lessing has no illusions about men or male chauvinism, in conservative sets or in the radical sects more dedicated to ideologies of equality. Men exploit, patronize, and ignore women. They demand attention, nurturance, sexual gratification, and service. They seek compliant daughters, willing bodies, or mothers they can possess without complication. They use, abuse, exhaust, and bore women.

Despite all this, Lessing separates herself from the "feminine" and from feminism.[14] She has, I suggest, several motives. Perhaps she has internalized an evaluation of women's activities, especially those of the middle class, as trivial, time-wasting, and private. If so, it might spill over onto her sense of women's politics. Certainly her fear of the apocalypse distances her from them. She has written:

I don't think that Women's Liberation will change much though—not because there is anything wrong with their aims, but because it is already clear that the whole world is being shaken by the cataclysms we are living through: probably by the time we are through, if we get through at all, the aims of Women's Liberation will look very small and quaint.[15]

In part because of her political history in general, Lessing also distrusts any doctrine, ideology, party, or group that holds a fragment of reality and offers it up as if it were the whole. Consistently, she deplores compartmentalizing the world, separating off those parts, and then fearing the differences we have ourselves created. In her first days in London, Martha lunches with Phoebe, a left-wing Labourite who will become a noxious combination of Mrs. Quest and bureaucrat. In one of the many scenes in which Lessing insists that privileged moments of vision occur in our daily life, in our walks down an ordinary street, Martha broods:

There was something in the human mind that separated, and divided. She sat, looking at the soup in front of her, thinking. . . . For the insight of knowledge she now held, of the nature of separation, of division, was clear and keen—she understood, sitting there, while the soup sent a fine steam of appetite up her nostrils, understood *really* . . . how beings could be separated so absolutely by a light difference in the texture of their living that they could not talk to each other, must be wary, or enemies. [FGC, p. 82]

Finally, Lessing writes out of a colonial experience. She has said that to be an African, growing up in that vast land, is to be freer than an Englishwoman, a Virginia Woolf, enwebbed in custom and the city.[16] However, being an African also entails participation in a rigid, hierarchal social structure. Within it white men may dominate white women, but white women dominate all blacks. They have the privileges of class and color. White women subject blacks to their needs, whims, neurotic fantasies, and orders. A Myra Maynard, the wife of a

powerful judge, exercises covert political power over colonial affairs
and overt domestic power over her "kaffirs." In such a place the progressive conscience must first confront the presence of the "colored" or
"native" problem. The treatment of the blacks is the primary structuring agent of a sense of injustice and of public guilt. For Martha,
black women have a double symbolic function. Neither entails a sustained mutuality between black women and white. Icons of both a
greater imprisonment and a greater spontaneity, they remind her of
the injustices against which she must rebel, of the manacles she must
unlock, and of a life less arid than her own. In labor in the town's
"best" maternity hospital, Martha reveals that duality:

[Martha] heard the sound of a wet brush on a floor. It was a native
woman, on her knees with a scrubbing brush. . . . Martha tensed and
groaned, and the native woman raised her head, looked over, and smiled
encouragement. . . . [She] gave a quick look into the passage, and then
came over to Martha. . . . "Bad," she said, in her rich voice. "Bad. Bad."
As a fresh pain came, she said, "Let the baby come, let the baby come, let
the baby come." It was a croon, a nurse's song. . . . Martha let the cold
knot of determination loosen, she let herself go, she let her mind go dark
into the pain. . . . Suddenly . . . Martha looked, and saw that the native
woman was on her knees with the scrubbing brush, and the young pink
nurse stood beside her, looking suspiciously at the scrubbing woman. The
brush was going slosh, slosh, wetly and regularly over the floor. [APM,
p. 146]

White men and women share more than black subordination: an
ambivalent response to the "mother country," a feminized metropoli-
tan center to which a colonial country is tied. It, too, helps to obliter-
ate the resentments gender inequalities breed. Colonials feel physically superior, tougher, stronger. They are also the romantics, the
black sheep, the eccentrics who refused to accept the manners of the
mother country. Yet they feel blunt, envious, even crude, a sense of
dependency and inferiority that Australians call "the cultural cringe."
Men and women alike are the stalwart, but crass, younger children in
a global family whose power they at once disdain and revere.

As Martha grows, then, she acts out a feminist analysis that Lessing
will not extend to an endorsement of a feminist program. Instead,
Martha discovers other truths, other principles. They enable her to

survive, to continue the process of discovery, and to learn which collectives impede, and which enhance, the self; which citizenships destroy, and which burnish, being. Among her primary tools is a cognitive alter ego, a diligent self-consciousness, the Watcher, a capacity for apperception and self-criticism in her experiments with roles. Even during her first marriage, as she takes "every step into bondage with affectionate applause for Douglas," (APM, p. 250), she is still "secretly and uneasily curious." At its worst, the Watcher devolves into mocking, derisive self-hatred. At its best, it guards against self-deception, wool-gathering, and bad faith. The origins of the Watcher are as obscure as the genes that carry instructions for the child's optic nerves once were, but they include Martha's parents' nagging reminders that she was unwanted and the presence of multiple discrepancies in her life: between reality and what people say about it; between reality and what books say about it; between reality and what her dreams say about it. Each discrepancy stimulates a sense, at once intellectual and emotional, of alienation. Any reasonable child regards gaps between the self, the self-in-the-world, and the world warily—if the child is to stay reasonable.

When consciousness is too watchful to accept the going interpretations of reality, but too fragile to examine its own examinations fully; when consciousness is too vital to permit the will to lapse and collapse into acceptance of the false and the ordinary, but the will is too weak to dictate ruptures from them, then a person, a Martha, learns the value of negation. Saying no, saying I will not, is halfway between submission to the life she despises and one she might actively build for herself; halfway between conformity and authenticity. Negation is inseparable from de-education, from unlearning the formal and informal instructions of a colonial society and of its leaders, a Mr. and Mrs. Maynard.

Martha's most critical act of negation is to leave her first marriage. It proves that she can push her rejections beyond thought and speech. Abandoning Douglas, she walks out on social acceptability; on access to power; on money, comfort, and security; on the pretty, perky, willful daughter to whom she is intricately attached. A particular unfairness of a generally unfair society is the refusal of its petty elite to see Martha's pain over Caroline, which never heals, and its eagerness to rally around Douglas, who so cheerfully plays by their rules. To walk away, Martha must overcome a talent for negating her negations, for repressing her dislike of Douglas, particularly in bed. Only a few weeks before she ends the marriage, he tells her he is going away on business.

> It was a moment when the hatred between them shocked and dismayed them both.
>
> "Well, perhaps it's just as well we'll—have a break for a few weeks, eh, Matty?" He came over and stood a few inches from her, smiling in appeal.
>
> She at once responded by rising and kissing him—but on the cheek, for her lips, which had intended to meet his, instinctively moved past in revulsion. This revulsion frightened her so much that she flung her arms about him and warmly embraced him.
>
> The act of love immediately followed. [APM, p. 279]

Because of the nature of the dominant society, Martha's need for negation will be persistent. A middle-aged woman in London, she will have to say no to Dr. Lamb, the sardonically named psychiatrist, and to the institutional power he conveys; to Jack, once her lover, and to the temptations of masochism he now holds out.

Negation demands something beyond the self to repudiate. Realizing that ego ideal of the modern period, the free and autonomous ego, Martha must also learn that the most stringent self-explorations, the most exacting and fertile meditations, begin in solitude. Her childhood in the awesome African landscape has prepared her for this. She copes with her fear of an empty historical landscape in which she has no patterns to follow. Before she leaves Douglas, she thinks, realistically: "there was no woman she had ever met she could model herself on" (APM, p. 274). She also unravels her dependency on the cold comforts of narcissism. If having a role model means shaping identity through gazing at another's image, being narcissistic means doing so through having another's gaze. Martha has stared at her image in a mirror, or she has waited passively while men watch her. Unhappily, narcissism is as encrusted with guilt as a white dress in a field wet with mud. Guilt oozes from the belief that the recipient of a look has disappointed the onlooker. To have been seen is to be found wanting. Finally, at a Communist party meeting, in a dingy office, Martha regards a new member:

She's what I used to be; she looks at herself in the looking glass, and she sees how her face and body form a sort of painted shell, and she adores herself, but she is waiting for a pair of eyes to melt the paint and shoot through into the dark inside. [RS, p. 114]

In isolation, however, the naked self is not alone. Through self-analysis, Martha confronts hidden ranges of repressed material: memories, fantasies, terrors, anger, violence—the worst of which the devil personifies. Lessing accepts George Eliot's dictum that no private life has not been determined by a wider public life, a maxim compatible with her early Marxism. That public life means the French and Russian revolutions, World Wars I and II, colonialism, the Spanish Civil War, the cold war, wars of national independence. Breaking down her defenses, breaking into the unconscious, Martha understands that she wants to break up the world as well. This child of violence has internalized the thanatotic rage of global war and the looming apocalypse. Like Freud, Lessing believes we can never wholly purge the past, but seeing the experiences we have battened down helps to shake their spell.

Despite her liberal belief in the individual and freedom, Lessing, writing a *Bildungsroman,* goes beyond the picture of the atomistic self spinning alone atop social space. If Martha rejects the nuclear family, she enters an extended family in which cords of choice replace those of blood and law. If she refuses biological mothering, she becomes a surrogate parent. Lessing is too flexible to feminize wholly the nurturing role and evoke the spirit of a Great Mother to rationalize women as mothers. Mark's son Francis is a paternal/maternal figure.

However, within *Children of Violence* is a sense of the intractability of nuclear family bonds that makes a flight toward a modern extended family necessary. The ties between mothers and daughters, particularly between Martha and May Quest, are especially taut.[17] Martha cannot forgive May her inability to love without demands, complaints, and possessiveness. May cannot forgive Martha her unconventionality, her sexuality, her difference. Yet, because May did bear Martha, and because their disappointments in each other are intense, they cannot forget each other. Their mutual consciousness is so acute that in each other's company, they get sick. They see each other for the last time in London; May is old, Martha middle-aged. Both want to cry:

As she vanished from her daughter's life forever, Mrs. Quest gave a small tight smile, and said, "Well, I wonder what all that was about really?"
"Yes," said Martha. "So do I."
They kissed politely, exchanged looks of ironic desperation, smiled and parted. [FGC, pp. 286–87]

In *Children of Violence,* irony is a useful tool for digging out sham and cant, but it is treacherous. For the disappointed, it becomes an iron rod, a staff of punishment, a mark of waste.

For Martha, the political party, like the extended family, becomes a community of choice. Deftly, incisively, dryly, Lessing dramatizes the mechanics of the small progressive party: the lobbying, maneuvering of agendas, interplay between insiders and outsiders, the desire for a charismatic leader, the gratifying sense of busyness, the feeding on ideology and hope because of the absence of real power. However, Martha is unable to find a party that fuses a radical ideology and power; vision and efficiency; prophetic zeal and historical wisdom; humanitarian ideals and humane behavior. Though brilliant organizer and analyst, Anton has neither heat, nor heart, nor humor. Martha is too modern, too mobile, too psychological to be like Charlotte Brontë's Shirley Keeldar, but Shirley's cry against a cold sectarianism is the precursor of Martha's progress beyond organized politics:

Must I listen coolly to downright nonsense . . . ? No. . . . all that *cant* about soldiers and parsons is most offensive. . . . All ridiculous, irrational crying up of one class, whether the same be aristocrat or democrat—all howling down of another class, whether clerical or military—all exacting injustice to individuals, whether monarch or mendicant—is really sickening to me: all arraying of ranks against ranks, all party hatreds, all tyrannies disguised as liberties, I reject and wash my hands of.[18]

Significantly, Martha's deepest discoveries about eros—that bond, at once simple and mysterious, that generates a little community—take place outside of the nuclear family and the party. Within them, she has picked up warning signals about repression; about evasive silence about sexual realities; about the sublimation of eros, not into culture, but into violence. She has also succumbed to sexual myths. Science has reassured Martha and Douggie that the rational practice of certain positions will guarantee ecstasy. Romantic poetry has whispered that "love lay like a mirage through the golden gates of sex" (APM, p. 26). The patriarchy has praised her for being deferential, compliant, a Galatea before the Pygmalion of the phallus. A reaction against Victorianism has instructed her to find self-esteem in being good in bed, no matter when, or with what man. Martha begins as a modern to whom sexual competence has the gravity of grace.

Sex with Thomas, a married man, pulls down all such illusions. He is warm, direct, generous. As Martha educates herself in sheer orgasmic pleasure, she experiences both a new simplicity of will, a clarity of action, and a dissolution of the ego that serves, paradoxically, to strengthen that very simplicity of will. As the boundaries of the self blur into the other, Thomas and Martha become each other's histories. Later, with Mark and Jack, Martha will find in sex an even more expansive fusion between self and world, an access to "an impersonal current . . . the impersonal sea" (FGC, p. 496). Sadly, Martha's most vital sexual experiences are with men who are flawed prophets: Thomas cannot pass beyond violence and chaos; Jack transmogrifies his knowledge of the body into sadistic domination; Mark, despite his brains and strength and kindliness, cannot transcend Western rationalism. In his camp, after the Catastrophe, he writes: "I can't stand that nasty mixture of irony and St. John of the Cross and the *Arabian Nights* that they all (Lynda, Martha, Francis) went in for" (FGC, p. 652). Martha's most educational prophetic experiences, with a woman, are asexual.

Laying bare Martha's sexual growth, Lessing balances delicate insight and problematic theory. Both maternal and erotic sexuality can threaten freedom. Often cheerfully, the pregnant woman becomes her body. She relaxes into natural time, into the blind impersonal urges of creation. The woman in love is unappeasable, hungry, restless, dependent upon her man. For Martha, such lapses from liberation are characteristic of a "female self," a simplistic genderizing of identity that Lessing is most guilty of when she talks about female sexuality. To avoid the constrictions of the "female self," and to sharpen her capacity for insights, Martha begins to practice a willed repression of and indifference to sexual claims. She has only one biological child. Later, in London, she decides:

When a woman has reached that point when she allies part of herself with the man who will feed that poor craving bitch in *every* woman (italics mine), then enough it's time to move on.

When it's a question of survival, sex the uncontrollable can be controlled. [FGC, p. 301]

Lessing has shown that same mingling of persuasive perception and puzzling theory in an earlier, more poignant picture of repression: the character of Mrs. Van. Highly intelligent, sensitive, tough, she has tutored Martha in the limits and courage of the reformist conscience in Zambesia. She has refused to rebel against her proper marriage and a maternal role. So doing, she has deliberately, if secretly, traded passion for autonomy within the system and political stature. She is a good wife to the husband who does not gratify her and a good mother—to him, her children, grandchildren, servants, clients, and friends. In return, she is an active liberal. In a quick, sad scene, she remembers her wedding night. Lessing wants us to admire her resolve, mourn for her innocence, and dislike a society in which a woman of Mrs. Van's talents must make such compromises. At the same time, she gives Mrs. Van dabs of a sexual rhetoric of swords and soft spots that Norman Mailer, Lessing's lesser and contemporary, also deploys, if far more raucously:

Cold tears had run down over her cheeks all night . . . (an) image . . . filled the girl's mind through those long hours while she lay awake by a man who also lay awake, waiting for her to turn to him. The image was of something deep, soft, dark and vulnerable, and of a very sharp sword stabbing into it, again and again. She had not moved . . . and so the sword had not stabbed into her never again, the soft dark painful place which she felt to be somewhere under her heart had remained untouched. She had remained herself. [RS, pp. 204–5]

Behind Martha's emerging ego, behind her relations with several communities, are her discoveries of the powers of consciousness. To become a pioneer of the mind, Martha must often crawl through swamps of primordial fear. She first learns to read her dreams. They are both hieroglyphic psychological texts and prophecies. Martha often dreams of:

"That country" . . . pale, misted, flat; gulls cried like children around violet-coloured shores. She stood on coloured chalky rocks with a bitter sea washing around her feet and the smell of salt was strong in her nostrils. [RS, p. 84]

The meaning of the dream will deepen as she grows. The sea is her passage out of Africa to England, but it will become a metaphor for the universal mind and energy in which she will learn to travel, too. Consistently, in Lessing's vocabulary, "shell" is a synecdoche for the mechanisms that protect the self from threatening pain and psychic depths. It evokes armor—of sea creatures and war. "That country" of the dream foreshadows the island on which Martha will die. Although Lessing persistently uses sleep as a metaphor for mindless oblivion, for loss of consciousness, and awakening as a metaphor for new powers of vision, sleep is the site of the dreams that minister to us and that we must monitor. Significantly, Anton refuses to admit that he has nightmares. He tries to banish memory and live glibly in the day.

Martha goes on to listen to, to hear, other people's emotions. Because of her need to know what he is going to do first if she is to react in ways that serve her best interests, and because of their intimacy, she trains herself with Douglas. She does not add new skills, but nurtures an ability that is there. During a bizarre conversation with Douggie about their divorce, she responds: "For a moment she was frightened; then she understood she was not frightened, her heart was beating out of anger. She had become skilled in listening to her *instinctive* responses to Douglas." (RS, p. 24, italics mine) Such a refined empathy tells Martha what is special about other people, but she can also go beyond differences to appreciate a common ground of being. Psychic auditing, in league with the imagination, the ability to see worlds other than our own, can be a basis of a human ecology. Lessing can, then, speak of "colour prejudice" as "only one aspect of the atrophy of the imagination that prevents us from seeing ourselves in every creature that breathes under the sun."[19]

Finally, Martha accepts and explores her paranormal powers, her capacities for ESP, mental telepathy, and sending and receiving messages through the mind. She first hears niggling words, phrases, and bits of music. A feature of *Children of Violence* is the coherence with which Lessing describes shards of consciousness—as if her own style reflected the sense that might lie beyond fragmentation. When Martha stops resisting such signals, she discovers that they are only apparently random: they, in fact, have meaning. Her first guide is her own adventurous spirit, but eventually she finds the "mad" Lynda. In a friendship beyond friendliness, the two "work" together. The word signifies how hard a discipline the expansion of consciousness can be, and how chary Lessing is about ordinary toil, in the home or public labor force, as a field of growth. Martha is not one of the new women whose *Bildungsroman* includes the narrative of a career.

Lynda is Lessing's vehicle for a radical criticism of psychiatry. Rigid, officious, less sure of themselves than they pretend to be, psychiatrists are the policemen of the contemporary mind. Out of several motives, they control our prophets, like Lynda, through calling them schizoid. Though she does not go mad, Martha must experience the sensations of insanity in her rites of passage toward a greater comprehension of the mind. So doing, she lives out a statement of her father, that most defeated of her teachers, who, when he speaks, says too little, too late. As far as he can see, "everyone is mad" (APM, p. 270). For Captain Quest, madness only explains the world. For his more resilient daughter, "the climax of education is insanity," and her *Bildungsroman* is a text in which "madness is moralized into a condition of responsible consciousness."[20]

As Martha's powers enable her to lose the ego but not the world; to shatter barriers but not to slump into violence, nihilism, or infantile regression, she becomes a member of another community: that of her fellow sensitives. She first enters it with Lynda:

One night, going down to see if Lynda was all right, before she herself went to bed, she asked: "Lynda, do you ever overhear what people are thinking?"

Lynda turned, swift, delighted: "Oh," she exclaimed, "you do? I was waiting for you to . . ." [FGC, p. 371]

Such a society, far more than an esoteric cult, is the basis for a politics of mind. As a party, it transcends hardened theories and harsh practices. As an organization, it abolishes tricks, maneuvers, bureaucracies, and tyranny. It merges the virtues of anarchy and community. Learning to become a sensitive, oscillating between optimism and rage, Francis exults:

The old right of the individual human conscience which must know better than any authority, secular or religious, had been restored, but on a higher level, and in a new form which was untouchable by any legal formulas. We quoted to each other Blake's "What now exists was once only imagined"—and did not, for once, choose to remember the dark side of the human imagination. [FGC, p. 623]

Before, during, and after the Catastrophe, the group serves as a survival mechanism, for its members and for the mutants whose evolving consciousness may govern the future.

Lessing's politics of mind are controversial. Critics who otherwise admire her accuse her of bad faith, of sidestepping reality, of a bleak acceptance of the irreconcilability of self and society.[21] *Children of Violence* implicitly answers that we must reread the realities of conscience and the collective. If we do, we will cultivate consciousness and accept certain laws of its evolution. Then, we will grasp what a Sufi master once said:

For him who has perception, a mere sign is enough.
For him who does not really heed, a thousand explanations are not enough.[22]

If we ignore Martha's reminders, we may be heedless, groggily writing out chapters in an inadequate *Bildungsroman,* sleepwalking toward the apocalypse.

In Western culture, beliefs in the apocalypse have been entwined with utopian impulses. Both wish to wipe out time as we have clocked it. For some, the apocalypse is a prelude to a utopian world, to a New Jerusalem. Lessing, despite her belief in the apocalypse, is wary of utopian dreams, of attempts to impose them through violence and of mechanical allusions to them. In *Children of Violence,* Solly Cohen, a childish revolutionary, lives for a while in a commune named "Utopia."

Nevertheless, Martha can summon up a utopian vision, among her other powers. Throughout *Children of Violence,* her picture of the four-gated city has embodied harmony, reconciliation, integration. Her answer to Babel, it speaks against a history that has alternated centrifugal desires to separate with centripetal desires to dominate. It has been her new utopia, "rooted in the body as well as in the mind, in the unconscious as well as the conscious, in forests and deserts as well as in highways and buildings, in bed as well as the symposium."[23] It is a collective of the future toward which the individual conscience might aspire.

Whether or not one likes Lessing's epistemology and her politics of mind in *Children of Violence,* one must respond to the appeal of her stubborn belief in an active, hopeful consciousness; to Martha's returns to a picture of a four-gated city. Lessing, dramatizing the self and society in the twentieth century, tells us what they ought to mean, as well as what they do mean. Martha's visionary rehearsals are goads to growth, that old and aching promise of the *Bildungsroman.*

IV CONTEMPORARY TRANSFORMATIONS:

Creating New Traditions

ELLEN CRONAN ROSE

Through the Looking Glass:

When Women Tell Fairy Tales

> Strange, but this castle is not foreign to me.
> I somehow know the place. I know these halls,
> however grand, are where a creature prowls
> in search, he claims, of beauty. I can spy
> beneath his velvet cloak to where he
> wears beast-hide, wherein a blond prince dwells
> in turn; within the prince, whose fairness peels
> away like wax, a monster, who can free
> a new prince, smiling through new monster-jaws.
> I shall settle my gown, arrange my lace,
> and rest my ringed white hand between his paws.
> Although I fear his eyes upon my face
> may yet release in me fur, fangs, and claws,
> I sense my saving death in such a place.
>
> —"Eight Games of Strategy," Robin Morgan

"Fairy tales," Bruno Bettelheim told us in 1976, "depict in imaginary and symbolic form the essential steps in growing up and achieving an independent existence."[1] Bettelheim's convincing argument that fairy tales "represent in imaginative form" the "process" of human development (p. 12) permits us to discuss them as tales of *Bildung,* narratives of growth and development. And his reminder that they depict this process in "symbolic form" suggests that, as Sandra M. Gilbert and Susan Gubar put it, fairy tales "state . . . culture's sentences with greater accuracy than more sophisticated literary texts," because they reduce a complicated process of socialization to its essential paradigm.[2]

When we turn to the fairy tales we are most familiar with, preserved and transmitted by Perrault and the Grimm brothers, what we see is that in our culture there are different developmental paradigms for boys and girls. In fairy tales, boys are clever, resourceful, and brave. They leave home to slay giants, outwit ogres, solve riddles, find fortunes. Girls, on the other hand, stay home and sweep hearths, are patient, enduring, self-sacrificing. They are picked on by wicked stepmothers, enchanted by evil fairies. If they go out, they get lost in the woods. They are rescued from their plights by kind woodsmen, good fairies, and handsome princes. They marry and live happily ever after.

In their essays "toward a feminist poetic," Gilbert and Gubar read "Snow White" as the paradigm of women's development in a specifically patriarchal culture. Their concern is primarily with the transition to adult womanhood represented in the story by the replacement of the good queen by the wicked stepmother. For as they see it, the wicked queen is in fact the good queen at a later stage of development. We first see the queen sitting by a window, sewing. When she pricks her finger, she bleeds and is thus "assumed into the cycle of sexuality." From that moment she no longer has any prospects in the outside world. So her window is replaced by a mirror, her passive goodness by a wicked rage at the discovery of life's limitations upon her.

Not only is a woman's quest for identity deflected from engagement with the outside world (an engagement essential to the classic "male" *Bildungsroman* as formulated by Dilthey and written by Goethe and innumerable others) and "doomed to that inward search" called narcissism, but that inward quest seems itself doomed to frustration, if not failure. For when the queen questions her mirror, it answers with the voice of the king:

His, surely, is the voice of the looking glass, the patriarchal voice of judgment that rules the Queen's—and every woman's—self-evaluation. He it is who decides, first, that his consort is "the fairest of all," and then, as she becomes maddened, rebellious, witchlike, that she must be replaced by his angelically innocent and dutiful daughter, a girl who is therefore defined as "more beautiful still" than the Queen.

Gilbert and Gubar conclude that "having assimilated the meaning of her own sexuality (and having, thus, become the second Queen) the woman has internalized the King's rules: his voice resides now in her own mirror, her own mind" (p. 38).

Of course, as Gilbert and Gubar are at some pains to point out, the looking glass is not only "her own mind" but every text a woman reads. And they are not the first to have noted that "most Western literary genres [including fairy tales] are . . . essentially male—devised by male authors to tell male stories about the world" (p. 76). "Of course," Carol P. Christ adds, "women appear in the stories of men, but only in roles defined by men."[3] What a woman reads in her mirror is the tales men tell about women—madonnas and whores, saints and witches, good little girls and wicked queens.

Christ asserts that "stories give shape to lives," and I think fairy tales, like *Bildungsroman, may* have shaped lives. If college men of my generation were modeling themselves on Stephen Dedalus, college "girls" were still trying to enact the fairy tale of "falling in love and living happily ever after."[4] But perhaps stories only "give shape" to life when they reflect the shapes we sense our lives have. Women have come to recognize that neither in fairy tales nor in other patriarchal texts can we find true images of ourselves. And "as women become more aware of how much of their own experience they must suppress in order to fit themselves into the stories of men, their yearning for a literature of their own, in which women's stories are told from women's perspectives, grows."[5] This yearning can be satisfied only when women writers "shatter the mirror that has so long reflected what every woman was supposed to be" (Gilbert and Gubar, p. 76).

How this might be done is suggested by Gilbert and Gubar when they note that "some of the best-known recent poetry by women openly uses . . . parody in the cause of feminism: traditional figures of patriarchal mythology like Circe, Leda, Cassandra, Medusa, Helen, and Persephone have all lately been reinvented in the images of their female creators, and each poem devoted to one of these figures is a reading that reinvents her original story" (p. 80). In much the same way, several contemporary women writers have turned to traditional fairy tales to re-view, revise, and reinvent them "in the service of women."[6]

I am particularly interested in seeing what happens when a woman writer turns to the male cultural myths embedded in fairy tales. If they are, as one must conclude from reading Bettelheim and others, embryonic tales of *Bildung,* related to "primitive *rites de passage* and initiation rituals,"[7] what can a woman learn about her own socialization if she rewrites a fairy tale "so as to clarify its meaning"? (Gilbert and Gubar, p. 220). And what might she discover about her natural, innate pattern of development when she rewrites a fairy tale "so as to make it a more accurate mirror of female experience"? (Gilbert and Gubar, p. 220).

The texts I have chosen—Anne Sexton's *Transformations* (1971), Olga Broumas's *Beginning with O* (1977), and Angela Carter's *The Bloody Chamber* (1979)—exemplify a spectrum of female responses to patriarchal fairy tales ranging from the critical at one extreme to the creative, even visionary, at the other.[8] The most consistently critical and bitter attack on the male cultural myths embedded in fairy tales comes from Anne Sexton. *Transformations* is much more than a naughty spoof of the Brothers Grimm. "Anne Sexton was not and never claimed to be a feminist," Jane McCabe admits. "But like so much poetry by contemporary women, Sexton's poems . . . often point to larger issues; although she does not necessarily offer any solutions, many of her poems isolate and describe the difficulties of being a woman in our society. . . . [Her] feelings are the product of a society that oppresses women."[9]

A number of the poems in *Transformations* comment sardonically on the conventional fairy-tale happy ending, in which the princess is united with Prince Charming:

> Cinderella and the prince
> lived, they say, happily ever after,
> like two dolls in a museum case
> never bothered by diapers or dust,
> never arguing over the timing of an egg,
> never telling the same story twice,
> never getting a middle-aged spread,
> their darling smiles pasted on for eternity.
> Regular Bobbsey Twins.
> That story.

The anger here is directed at "that story" of romantic fulfillment belied by the suburban realities Betty Friedan had documented a scant decade before Sexton wrote this poem. But who tells us these tales? Who are "they" who "say"? In "Snow White and the Seven Dwarfs" Sexton names the culprit.

As is usual in *Transformations,* "Snow White and the Seven Dwarfs" is preceded by a prologue which provides both context and interpretive clues for the ensuing tale. This poem begins with an essay on virginity:

> No matter what life you lead
> the virgin is a lovely number:
> cheeks as fragile as cigarette paper,
> arms and legs made of Limoges,
> lips like Vin Du Rhône,
> rolling her china-blue doll eyes
> open and shut.
> Open to say,
> Good Day Mama,
> and shut for the thrust
> of the unicorn.
> She is unsoiled.
> She is as white as a bonefish.

Here "virgin" has not the "great primal sense of the word" it has for Adrienne Rich, denoting "the woman who belongs to herself."[10] "The virgin" is, rather, a commodity prized by men, whose voices blend to create the persona of the speaker of the prologue. We meet the huckster who calls her a "lovely number," the connoisseur who itemizes her features in terms of fine tobacco, porcelain, and wine, the pimp who points out that she is "unsoiled," and the sportsman who observes that "she is as white as a bonefish" (the latter a marine game fish also called a lady fish).

Like Cinderella, Snow White is described as an artifact, a doll whose eyes "Open to say, / Good Day Mama, / and shut for the thrust / of the unicorn." "Mama" is what baby dolls and good little girls who are raised by nurses and governesses call their mothers; "Good Day Mama" is a ritual formula, connoting no close, loving, knowing relationship between mother and daughter. Deprived of maternal guidance and protection, "the virgin" is fair game. In a shocking image, Sexton reveals that the male culture that defines and prizes her is in fact a rape culture. Here the unicorn, friend and companion of virgins, turns into the rapist's prick.

As Sexton's story begins, Snow White's character is unformed; she is simply "a lovely virgin." What Sexton's narrative reveals is how patriarchy molds the development of such a creature, turning her into a replica of her (step)mother, an "acceptable" adult woman.

When her unmotherly stepmother casts her out of her home, Snow White finds herself in a wilderness filled with sexual menace:

> Snow White walked in the wildwood
> for weeks and weeks.
> At each turn there were twenty doorways
> and at each stood a hungry wolf,
> his tongue lolling out like a worm.
> The birds called out lewdly,
> talking like pink parrots,
> and the snakes hung down in loops,
> each a noose for her sweet white neck.

Unprotected by a strong and loving mother, Snow White does not emerge unscathed from this ordeal in the wilderness. When she finally discovers the dwarfs' house, it seems to her "as droll as a honeymoon cottage." And while the Grimms' little girl tasted a little of each dwarf's bread, Sexton's virgin eats seven chicken livers, which reminds us that the wicked queen ordered the huntsman to bring her Snow White's heart and suggests, thus, that she is in some sense "becoming" her (step)mother; like her, she consumes organ meats. She is beginning, at least, to accept her status as a male-defined "beauty" who is ready to play house.

Enter the dwarfs, those phallic "little hot dogs,"[11] who are "wise / and wattled like small czars." Playing on the traditional and the contemporary connotations of czardom, Sexton underscores the cash nexus of capitalist patriarchy. Sizing up "the sleeping virgin," the dwarfs decide "*it's* a good omen" (emphasis mine). This precious thing "will bring us luck." And as if to bear out Andrea Dworkin's cynical observation about fairy tales, that in them "the only good woman is a dead woman,"[12] they later look upon the apparently dead Snow White "as a gold piece."

In the Grimms' version of the tale, the dwarfs put the "dead" Snow White in a glass coffin so that they can see her. In Sexton's retelling, they enclose her in glass and put her on a mountain "so that all who passed by / could peek in upon her beauty." They are waiting for their "good luck" to materialize. Their patience is rewarded when the prince arrives and covets "the glass Snow White," which the dwarfs give him—no doubt for a suitable compensation—"to keep in his far-off castle."

At the conclusion of the deal—and the story—Snow White the virgin has been successfully metamorphosed into the wicked queen, who thus becomes expendable and is put to death:

> Meanwhile Snow White held court,
> rolling her china-blue doll eyes open and shut
> and sometimes referring to her mirror
> as women do.

The cool mockery of Sexton's tone might seem to be directed against women, were it not for the evidence in the prologue and throughout the poem that the cause of female narcissism is a male-dominated culture that perceives women as objects and conditions them to become objects. Snow White is a doll, a "plucked daisy," a "dumb bunny," an Orphan Annie (making the dwarfs not only czars but Daddy Warbuckses) because, as Sexton tells the tale, she's never had a real woman to mother her into valuing herself as a person.

Sexton's Rapunzel is luckier. She has the witch, whom Sexton names "Mother Gothel."[13] In "Snow White and the Seven Dwarfs," the mirror represents the alienation of women from each other in patriarchal culture. There is a mirror in Sexton's "Rapunzel" too, but what it reflects is love between women.

The prologue to "Rapunzel" is spoken by an older woman to a younger. Declaring that "a woman / who loves a woman / is forever young," she invites her "young dear" to "hold [her]." In return, she will "hold [her] heart like a flower" and "give [her] angel fire":

> We are two clouds
> glistening in the bottle glass.
> We are two birds
> washing in the same mirror.
> We were fair game[14]
> but we have kept out of the cesspool.
> We are strong.
> We are the good ones.
> Do not discover us

for we lie together all in green
like pond weeds.
Hold me, my young dear, hold me.

Here is that loving maternal protection Snow White lacked, here
that image of the virgin as woman-unto-herself which Adrienne Rich
believes a strong mother can give her daughter. It is not incest Sexton
is advocating, but this mutually affirming bond between women, when
she names the erotic game Mother Gothel and Rapunzel play "mother-
me-do."

In retelling the Grimms' fairy tales, Sexton does not change their
endings; she merely reevaluates them. As in the original, her Rapunzel
renounces Mother Gothel for Prince Charming. But Sexton's point of
view is that of the older woman, whose voice speaks the prologue. Just
as in "Snow White and the Seven Dwarfs," her bitterness against
patriarchy—here for thwarting the natural love of women for each
other—dominates the poem. The lyrical tone with which the poem begins changes when Rapunzel is seduced by the prince,[15] as Sexton's language mocks the conventions of heterosexual romantic love. Rapunzel's
song pierces the prince's heart "like a Valentine" and her tears later
restore his sight "in the manner of such cure-alls." The delicate love
play between Rapunzel and Mother Gothel gives way to the prince's
"dancing stick" that "dazzles" Rapunzel into what Adrienne Rich has
called the "institution" of heterosexuality, which "demand[s] that the
girl-child transfer those first feelings of dependency, eroticism, mutuality, from her first woman to a man, if she is to become what is defined as a 'normal' woman—that is, a woman whose most intense psychic
and physical energies are directed towards men" (Rich, p. 219).

Rapunzel's name, Bettelheim assures us, "is the clue for understanding what happens," the key to the story's meaning (p. 148). But because he is so thoroughly convinced that the story concerns the "typical" problem of the "pubertal girl, and of a jealous mother who tries
to prevent her from gaining independence . . . which finds a happy
solution when Rapunzel becomes united with her prince" (pp. 16–17),
he doesn't pursue this insight. As a Freudian analyst, Bettelheim sees
heterosexuality as the "natural" outcome of a successfully negotiated
Oedipal phase, for women as well as men. But in his later papers,

Freud himself recognized that a girl's first affective and erotic bond, like a boy's, is with her mother.[16] And feminist scholars have recently begun to explore the implications of Freud's recognition that, as Nancy Chodorow puts it, "children of both sexes are originally matrisexual."[17] Both Chodorow and Gayle Rubin[18] take to be descriptively accurate the psychoanalytic account of how women acquire a heterosexual orientation. But Chodorow denies that such heterosexual orientation is "natural, self-evident, and unintended." On the contrary, she maintains, "it seems to be both consciously and unconsciously intended, socially, psychologically, and ideologically constructed" (p. 113). And Rubin's "exegetical" reading of Lévi-Strauss and Freud is a brilliant exposé of "a systematic social apparatus which takes up females as raw materials and fashions domesticated women as products" (p. 158) and which transforms a biological fact (sex) into a cultural role (gender). Liberated from the assumption that it is "natural" for a girl to transfer her erotic allegiance from her mother to a man, we may be more able than Bettelheim to read the clue that Rapunzel's name gives us for interpreting her story.

For Sexton, as for Bettelheim, rampion (rapunzel) is a salad vegetable. More important, it is "life-giving," perhaps because it grows in "a witch's garden / more beautiful than Eve's." If the sexual wilderness through which Snow White wanders on her way to the dwarfs' honeymoon cottage is aggressively phallic, the witch's garden is luxuriantly fecund and arguably female. Strange things grow in it. There are "carrots growing like little fish," "tomatoes rich as frogs," "onions as ingrown as hearts," and "squash singing like a dolphin." The strangest—and most mysterious—of all is:

> rampion, a kind of salad root,
> a kind of harebell more potent than penicillin,
> growing leaf by leaf, skin by skin,
> as rapt and as fluid as Isadora Duncan.

Olga Broumas, a Yale Younger Poet and lesbian feminist, has a version of "Rapunzel" which rewrites not only Grimm but Sexton, from Rapunzel's point of view. Taking as her epigraph Sexton's lines, "A woman / who loves a woman / is forever young," Broumas makes explicit what Sexton is hinting that "rapunzel" means. In her poem, the "woman who was with child / looked upon the rampion wildly, / fancying that she would die / if she could not have it." And Rapunzel wonders:

> How many women
> have yearned
> for our lush perennial, found
>
> themselves pregnant, and had
> to subdue their heat, drown out their appetite
> with pickles and harsh weeds.

Rampion, our lush perennial, our—the witch's, Eve's, Isadora's—female sexuality. How many women, Broumas asks, denied rampion, have "learned to grow thin on the bitter / root, the mandrake, on their sills."

But in the fairy tale, the pregnant woman gets her wish and her rampion. In gratitude, she gives her rampion—Rapunzel—to the witch, bequeathing her not only her child, but her wish, which is for love between women. And the daughter of the woman who has tasted rampion inherits her "relentless" hunger for the love of women:

> Climb
> through my hair, climb in
> to me, love
>
> hovers here like a mother's wish.
> You might have been, though you're not
> my mother. You let loose like hair, like static
> her stilled wish, relentless
> in me and constant as
> tropical growth.

Such a daughter will not be dazzled by the prince's dancing stick, will not accede to the patriarchal precept that lesbian love is deviant. *"Old / bitch, young / darling.* May those who speak them / choke on their words."

The last lines of Broumas's poem are spoken by Rapunzel to the witch, and by inference by the younger, overtly lesbian poet to the "middle-aged witch" who is Sexton's persona throughout *Transformations:*

> Less innocent
> in my public youth
> than you, less forbearing, I'll break the hush
> of our cloistered garden, our harvest continuous
> as a moan, the tilled bed luminous
> with the future
> yield. Red
> vows like tulips. Rows
> upon rows of kisses from all lips.

The middle-aged witch claims that her "book of odd tales" will "transform the Brothers Grimm," but Broumas's fairy tales are more literally and radically transformations of their originals. Her "Snow White," for instance, is a sequel to the Grimms' tale, in which Snow White wakens from her married trance to discover not only that her love for her mother preceded her love for Prince Charming but that it continues to take precedence over it.

Once upon a time, when Snow White was a little girl, there was a kind of matriarchy. Daddy was off fighting a war, and there were

> Three women
> on a marriage bed, two
> mothers and two daughters.
> All through the war we slept
> like this, grand-
> mother, mother, daughter. Each night
> between you, you pushed and pulled
> me, willing
> from warmth to warmth.

And then Daddy returned and merely by his presence sundered the bond among the women so that they "fought like mad- / women." The circle of women loving women and the cycle of generations— grandmother, mother, daughter—is broken when the man intrudes:

> A woman
> who loves a woman

> who loves a woman
> who loves a man.

So Snow White grows up "normal" and marries her prince. Three years later, she wakes with this fragment of a dream: *"If the circle / be unbroken . . ."* Suddenly she is revolted by her husband:

> Blond, clean
> miraculous, this alien
> instrument I had learned to hone,
> to prize, to pride myself on, instrument
> for a music I couldn't dance,
> cry or lose
> anything to.

Although it is "a curious / music, or un- / catalogued rhyme," she reverberates to the "mother / daughter" chord:

> Defenseless
> and naked as the day
> I slid from you
> twin voices keening and the cord
> pulsing our common protest, I'm coming back
> back to you
> woman, flesh
> of your woman's flesh, your fairest, most
> faithful mirror,
>   my love
> transversing me like a filament
> wired to the noonday sun.
>
> Receive
> me, Mother.

It is men who alienate women from each other, who foster rivalry, who create polar images like madonna and whore, good mother and wicked stepmother. Broumas would heal these divisions, atone the daughter with her mother, discover that the wicked stepmother with her fatal apple is really the fairy godmother, who brings Snow White the knowledge of her own female identity.

The relationship between acknowledging the primacy of the mother / daughter bond and discovering one's own sexual identity is asserted even more strongly by Broumas in "Little Red Riding Hood," where the hood is both the "mantle of blood" which the infant wears as she emerges from the birth canal and the hood of her clitoris. And while in "Snow White," men were seen as threats chiefly to the natural love between mother and daughter, in this poem they also are perceived as threatening in some way to the enjoyment by a woman of her own sexuality. When she sends her off to her grandmother's house, Little Red Riding Hood's mother warns her:

> "Stick to the road and forget the flowers, there's
> wolves in those bushes, mind
> where you got to go, mind
> you get there," I
> minded. I kept
> to the road, kept
> the hood secret, kept what it sheathed more
> secret still. I opened
> it only at night, and with other women
> who might be walking the same road to their own
> grandma's house, each with her basket of gifts, her small hood
> safe in the same part.

If Sexton's rewriting of the Grimms' fairy tales suggest that the socialization of women in patriarchy distorts our natural development, Broumas's force us to consider the possibility that lesbianism is not deviant but a natural consequence of the undeniable fact that a woman's first love object, like a man's, is her mother. At the least, we need to consider what Gayle Rubin calls the "logical extreme" of the psychoanalytic theory of female development, namely, Charlotte Wolff's proposal "that lesbianism is a *healthy* response to female socialization" (Rubin, p. 202n.; emphasis mine).

What Adrienne Rich calls "the great unwritten story" of the "cathexis between mother and daughter" (p. 226) can be written many ways. As a lesbian, Broumas understandably wants to explore the erotic ramifications of the mother/daughter bond. But a mother is not only her daughter's first love object. She is also her first and therefore most impressive image of adult womanhood. It is this aspect of the mother/daughter relationship that Angela Carter emphasizes in her retelling of "Bluebeard," the first and title story of *The Bloody Cham-*

ber. Here the strong bond between mother and daughter figures as a kind of "maternal telepathy" that sends not her brothers (as in the original) but her mother to the curious bride's rescue. As Bluebeard's sword ascends for the fatal blow, his young bride's mother bursts through the gate like a Valkyrie—or an Amazon—and fires "a single, irreproachable bullet" through his head.

It is significant that this fighting mother appears in the first story of *The Bloody Chamber.* "What do we mean by the nurture of daughters?" Adrienne Rich asks. Since "women growing into a world so hostile to us need a very profound kind of loving in order to learn to love ourselves," she concludes that "the most important thing one woman [a mother] can do for another [her daughter] is to illuminate and expand her sense of actual possibilities" (p. 250). A mother "who is a fighter" gives her daughter a sense of life's possibilities. Following her example, Bluebeard's widow and her "sisters" in the stories that follow are enabled to explore life's possibilities, to develop into adult women by learning to love themselves.

Judging from her fairy tales, Angela Carter's sense of the possibilities for a woman's growth toward healthy adult identity is more optimistic than Sexton's and more complicated than Broumas's. Sexton, we have seen, is a pessimist, angry with the status quo but apparently resigned to it. Broumas is an optimist, but a shortsighted one; if the only option to the status quo is lesbian separatism, not all women will see Broumas's as a viable alternative. In technical terms, Sexton is an analyst of fairy tales and their cultural implications, while Broumas is an improviser, using the tales as a base for imaginative speculation. Carter is both.

The Bloody Chamber contains two versions of "Beauty and the Beast," the first a fairly straightforward retelling of the original version by Mme. Le Prince de Beaumont, the second a fanciful improvisation on it. Together they constitute a critique of the ideal of adult womanhood sanctioned by patriarchy and a suggested alternative to it.

Bettleheim concludes *The Uses of Enchantment* with a lengthy discussion of "Beauty and the Beast" because for him it represents the apex of the development to adult womanhood: the successful transfer of a girl's Oedipal attachment to her father to an appropriate partner of the opposite sex (p. 308). But what seems to Bettelheim "all gentleness and loving devotion" in "Beauty and the Beast"—the attachment of Beauty to her father, the Beast's supplication of her love—is perceived differently by Angela Carter. In her first retelling of the tale, "The Courtship of Mr. Lyon," Carter—like Sexton—keeps intact the plot of the original. But again like Sexton, she highlights and subtly modifies certain of its features. Beauty's father, for instance, thinks of his daughter as "his girl-child, his pet." Unlike the timid father in the original story, he is not frightened when he discovers an apparently empty mansion in the snow storm; he seems to recognize in its masculine provision for his needs (a decanter of whiskey and a rare roast beef sandwich) something of the comfort of a men's club. And when the beast materializes, he addresses him accordingly—"My good fellow."

Beauty remains with the Beast as long as she does "because her father wanted her to do so." "Do not think she had no will of her own," the narrator cautions. And yet one must wonder whether she does. Or if she does, whether the conditions of her life will allow it to have efficacy. She seems a mere pawn, tugged in one direction by her father's call to join him in his recovered prosperity and in another by the Beast's appeal to her pity. Self-sacrifice wins out over hedonism, proving that Beauty is a truly feminine woman. In effect, the Beast blackmails Beauty into marrying him by going on a hunger strike:

"I'm dying, Beauty," he said in a cracked whisper of his former purr. "Since you left me, I have been sick. I could not go hunting. I had not the stomach to kill the gentle beasts. I could not eat. I am sick and I must die; but I shall die happy because you have come to say goodbye to me."

She flung herself upon him, so that the iron bedstead groaned, and covered his poor paws with her kisses.

"Don't die, Beast! If you'll have me, I'll never leave you."

You can almost hear his contented purr as the Beast-turned-Prince says, "Do you know, I think I might be able to manage a little breakfast today, Beauty, if you would eat something with me." In retelling "Beauty and the Beast," Carter has indicated that, in patriarchal cultural myths, women do not grow up. They simply change masters—from a beastly father to a fatherly beast. Having discovered this, she is free to invent a tale in which Beauty breaks free from paternal domination.

The patriarchal bonding implicit in "The Courtship of Mr. Lyon" is made explicit in "The Tiger's Bride," where Beauty's "profligate" father gambles with the Beast, who beggars him. He is left with nothing. "Except the girl," the Beast reminds him and persuades the father to gamble further. "My father said he loved me yet he staked his daughter on a hand of cards." He loses. Beauty wins, because in "The Tiger's Bride," the Beast is not an enchanted prince, a father-in-the-making. He is an animal, "a great, feline, tawny shape," who wears the mask and clothing of a man awkwardly and with discomfort. Moreover, he does not assume the prerogatives of patriarchy, does not ask Beauty to marry him. He asks only that Beauty strip off her clothes and stand before him naked.

What is naked is the metaphor. Earlier during her stay with the Beast, attended by a clockwork maid, Beauty had discovered her identity, as patriarchy has decreed it:

I was a young girl, a virgin, and therefore men denied me rationality just as they denied it to all those who were not exactly like themselves. . . . I meditated on the nature of my own state, how I had been bought and sold, passed from hand to hand. That clockwork girl who powdered my cheeks for me; had I not been allotted only the same kind of imitative life amongst men that the doll-maker had given her?[19]

So, although it is not easy for her to obey the Beast's command, Beauty has nothing to lose and everything to gain by stripping herself of her clothes and her socialized identity. Abandoned by men, she turns to the Beast and discovers herself. The tale ends with the Beast licking Beauty: "And each stroke of his tongue ripped off skin after successive skin, all the skins of a life in the world, and left behind a nascent patina of shining hairs."

According to Bettelheim, animals in fairy tales represent our animal nature—in general terms our "untamed id," more specifically our sexual impulses. The significance, for him, of "Beauty and the Beast" is that it suggests "that eventually there comes a time when we must learn what we have not known before—or, to put it psychoanalytically, to undo the repression of sex. What we had experienced as dangerous, loathsome, something to be shunned, must change its appearance so that it is experienced as truly beautiful" (p. 279). Carter's tale is just as much about "undoing the repression of sex" as is the original. But it is also about undoing the oppression of gender. Beauty discovers the animal in herself—her sexuality—only by stripping herself of the veneer of civilization which has socialized her as a woman.

Carter's retelling of "Beauty and the Beast" also questions the Freudian account of female development, in which a woman achieves sexual maturity by shifting her attachment from a father to a male lover. In her two versions of "Little Red Riding Hood" she offers a (nonlesbian) alternative, suggesting that a woman achieves (hetero)-sexual maturity by affirming her own sexuality through identifying with her (grand)mother. The process, as it unfolds in "The Werewolf" and "The Company of Wolves," is complex. First, as the title should suggest, in "The Werewolf" Little Red Riding Hood discovers that her grandmother and the wolf are one and the same. In so doing, she is making a very important discovery: that to be a mature woman means to be sexual, animal. Understandably, this horrifies the young girl. So she calls out to the neighbors, who drive her werewolf grandmother out of the house and stone her to death. But although the little girl kills her grandmother, she does not then go home to mother and safety. Instead "the child lived in her grandmother's house; she prospered." Little Red Riding Hood may have been initially repulsed by the knowledge that becoming an adult woman will involve acknowledging the animal in herself. But the second step in her negotiation of that developmental process is signaled by her decision to remain in her grandmother's house. She is symbolically declaring her readiness to grow up.

That process of growth is completed in "The Company of Wolves," where Little Red Riding Hood ends up "sweet and sound . . . in granny's bed, between the paws of the tender wolf." Inhabiting not only granny's house but her bed, Red Riding Hood has in a sense become her grandmother. Making love with the wolf, in a "savage marriage ceremony," she is also embracing her grandmother and thus acknowledging and affirming her adult female sexuality. Bettelheim says that it is love which transforms adult sexuality into something beautiful. Carter seems to be saying that love is not possible until one has come to accept and enjoy her sexuality, an accomplishment she associates in these stories with the mother/daughter relationship.

We began this survey of fairy tales with the mirror, symbolizing woman's quest for identity, and we have ended with the wolf, representing her ineluctable carnality. "Wolf-Alice," the last story in *The Bloody Chamber,* is full of wolves and mirrors. Not a retelling of any fairy tale I know,[20] it is nonetheless an appropriate text for concluding remarks about women writers' radical revision of traditional fairy tales.

Alice is a child raised by wolves, "not a wolf herself, although suckled by wolves. . . . Nothing about her is human except that she is *not* a wolf; it is as if the fur she thought she wore had melted into her skin and become part of it, although it does not exist." The hunters who kill her "foster mother" deliver her to some nuns, but they do not succeed in "civilizing" her. So they send her as a servant to the local Duke, who "lives in a gloomy mansion, all alone but for this child who has as little in common with the rest of us as he does." What he and Alice have in common is their dual nature; she is both wolf and human and so is he. He is a werewolf, who casts no image in the mirror. Some time after becoming the Duke's servant, Alice has her first menstrual period. As in "Snow White," the onset of her menses sends the woman in quest of her identity to a mirror. Prowling through the Duke's bedroom in search of some rags to stanch her bleeding, Alice bumps into his mirror. At first she thinks her reflection is another creature and tries to play with it. But "she bruised her muzzle on the cold glass and broke her claws trying to tussle with this stranger. . . . She felt a cool, solid, immovable surface between herself and she— some kind, possibly, of invisible cage?" Like the Queen's looking glass, this is "the rational glass, the master of the visible." As it denies the existence of the wolf-man, so it frustrates the wolf-woman's desire to know herself.

Earlier in the story, the narrator—one of the "rest of us"—says of Alice, "we secluded her in animal privacy out of fear of her imperfection because it showed us what we might have been." Her imperfection—she thinks of it as "her wound"—is her female sexuality, represented by her monthly bleeding. But unlike the rest of us—certainly unlike Adrienne Rich's Marie Curie, who died "denying / her wounds / denying / her wounds came from the same source as her power"[21]— Wolf-Alice affirms her wound, her womanhood, as she had earlier refused to renounce her animal (foster) mother. She "learn[s] to expect these bleedings . . . so that you might say she discovered the very action of time by means of this returning cycle." With this acceptance comes a power the Queen in "Snow White" lacked, the power to look behind the mirror and discover there no patriarchal dictator, but "only dust, a spider stuck in his web, a heap of rags." Consequently, Wolf-Alice's "relation with the mirror was now far more intimate since she knew she saw herself within it."

The haunting conclusion of Carter's original fairy tale suggests that women would not be the only beneficiaries of liberation from the patriarchal dictates of the Queen's looking glass. The Duke, on one of his forays through the graveyard in search of food, is ambushed and shot. Wounded, he limps home where Alice later finds him, bleeding and in pain. Although puzzled, because "his wound . . . does not smell like her wound," Alice proceeds, "without hesitation, without disgust, with a quick, tender gravity," to lick the blood and dirt from his face. The story ends with these brief paragraphs:

The lucidity of the moonlight lit the mirror propped against the red wall; the rational glass, the master of the visible, impartially recorded the crooning girl.

As she continued her ministrations, this glass, with infinite slowness, yielded to the reflexive strength of its own material construction. Little by little, there appeared within it, like the image on photographic paper that emerges, first, a formless web of tracery, the prey caught in its own fishing net, then in firmer yet still shadowed outline until at last as vivid as real life itself, as if brought into being by her soft, moist, gentle tongue, finally, the face of the Duke.

What can fairly tales, retold by women, tell us about female development? That it has been distorted by patriarchy; that it is and must be grounded in the mother-daughter matrix; that it involves not only the discovery but the glad acceptance of our sexuality. That a woman who loves the woman who is herself has the power of loving another person. And perhaps someday even patriarchy will "yield" to that power.

MARY ANNE FERGUSON

The Female Novel of Development
and the Myth of Psyche

The male novel of development or *Bildungsroman* usually ends when the hero reaches adult self-awareness after having tested his inner sense of self against reality by a series of adventures in the world. There is a mythical prototype of this form in the journeys of both father and son in the *Odyssey;* the young man sets out to find his father, to learn his patronymic, as a means of finding his own identity. Both he and his father, whose journey affirms his adult roles of father and husband, return home: the individual's success in discovering his own identity brings about his reintegration into society and the healing of the wounds society has incurred through losing him. Thus male development is essentially comic; the circular journey is spiral, the ending a new beginning on a higher plane. For the young man the journey has been an initiation. Although he has suffered in the *rite de passage,* he is ready to begin again. Although, as a learner, he may have often appeared foolish, he keeps his integrity and his dignity. Modern versions of this myth reject the possibility of individual autonomy and portray the antihero as alienated from society; he is, nonetheless, endowed with the ability to perceive ironically the absurdity of his journey. Like the ancient comic hero, he is superior to his society, and his alienation may lead to a cure for social ills.[1]

The pattern for the female novel of development has been largely circular, rather than spiral: women in fiction remain at home. Instead of testing their self-image through adventures in the outside world, they are initiated at home through learning the rituals of human relationships, so that they may replicate the lives of their mothers. Since they must assume their husband's name, learning their patronymic is not significant; for women, identification with the father can only interfere with development. Women who rebel against the female role are perceived as unnatural and pay the price of unhappiness, if not madness or death.[2] This "natural" female development is viewed as inferior to the male's. Perceived as part of nature, women in most novels are presented as incapable of autonomy and integrity. They simply *are,* their existence a part of the world that men test in their own search. The view of women as passive has been integral to the male novel of development. Most women authors have shared this view of women and have represented female characters either as finding satisfaction within their limited development in the domestic sphere or as expressing their dissatisfaction through various self-destructive means. Not until very recently have there been novels that show women successfully developing, learning, growing in the world at large. It is not surprising that such works should appear in the 1970s as women have more and more left their "place" to enter a "man's world." Literature reflects reality; the works I intend to discuss will, I hope, also help to create a new reality.

The groundwork for expanding the notion of female development beyond purely sexual maturity was paved by such novels as Erica Jong's *Fear of Flying* and Francine du Plessix Gray's *Lovers and Tyrants,* which claimed for women the right to sexual adventures as part of their development. But in their newfound sexual freedom, the characters did not find true personal freedom; their need for intellectual and spiritual growth, for a recognized function in "man's world," was not met. In a myth comparable in cultural significance to the *Odyssey,* some authors have found a pattern for showing that for women sexual maturity and human adulthood are not synonymous. In the myth of Psyche and Cupid (Eros), first written down, apparently, in the second century A.D., Eudora Welty, Lisa Alther, and Erica Jong have found a rich paradigm for representing the adventures of a sexually mature female who profits from her often painful encounters with reality to become a self-confident adult in control of her own destiny. The Psyche myth, as Lee Edwards has shown, furnishes a model of human maturation and individuation through love; it furnishes a basis for perceiving the war between the sexes as unnecessarily limiting for both and for seeing women's contemporary struggle as a source of liberation for all.[3] I shall consider here three works which to varying extents parallel and draw on the Psyche myth in their characteriza-

230   *Mary Anne Ferguson*

tion, plot, and theme: Welty's "At the Landing" (1943), Alther's *Kinflicks* (1975), and Jong's *Fanny: Being the True History of the Adventures of Fanny Hackabout-Jones* (1980).[4]

The first written version of the Psyche myth has a frame: Psyche's story is told by an old woman to console a young bride who has been kidnapped. Psyche, a beautiful mortal, is so worshiped that the goddess Aphrodite is neglected; vengeful Aphrodite sends her son Eros to punish Psyche. Instead he falls in love with her and secretly makes her his mistress; he comes to her only at night and warns her that she must not attempt to find out who he is, or even to see him. Goaded by jealous sisters Psyche disobeys her lover's command. When she takes a lamp so that she can see him and disprove their claims that he is a monster, a drop of hot oil wakens him and he leaves. So far the story could be seen as one of petty female rivalries. Furthermore, it seems to say that for a god or a male, love involves seeing and knowing but that for a woman the satisfaction of curiosity is destructive of love for both lovers. Her unknowing consent, her passive acquiescence, is tantamount to accepting rape, to denying her human need for knowledge. Sexual union is viewed as a repetitive pattern of gratification rather than a means of human development through delight. Although he sees Psyche and knows who she is, Eros, concerned with his own gratification, does not really know Psyche. As long as she and he equate her identity with her role as sex object, there is no real individual for him to know.

This truncated version of the myth has many analogues in fairy stories, such as "Sleeping Beauty" and "Beauty and the Beast," in which a happy ending ensues when the female fully accepts the male, without questions.[5] But Apuleius' story continues, to show Psyche recovering Eros after accomplishing a series of tasks in the real world. Psyche gladly accepts the four labors assigned to her by the angry Aphrodite, who holds her son captive and wants to destroy the pregnant Psyche. Although always tempted by suicide when she understands the difficulty of each task, Psyche, in undertaking the adventures, symbolically encounters the full reality of the world—earth, both vegetable and mineral, water, and underworld. Testing herself, she grows toward maturity. Her journey outward is also a psychic journey inward. In the first three adventures, she graciously accepts the cooperation of natural forces. After gaining competence and confidence both in the world and in herself, she is ready to venture alone to the underworld to seek a beauty aid from Persephone, goddess of the underworld. Psyche follows all directions, but contrary to Aphrodite's prohibition, she looks into the casket. True to herself, Psyche looks in order to obtain the beauty she feels she needs in order to win Eros back. Opening the casket causes her to fall into a deathlike sleep, from which, like Sleeping Beauty, she must be rescued by her lover. In response to her need, Eros escapes from his mother's captivity: symbolically he grows up. Aphrodite acknowledges the maturity Psyche gained in accomplishing the labors, approves the lovers' marriage, and persuades Zeus to make Psyche a goddess.

According to Apuleius, then, it is Psyche's accomplishment of the four tasks—only the last of which has any gender connectedness—which leads to the reunion of the lovers as mature individuals; their maturity is symbolized by the birth of their child. Psyche becomes competent to deal with reality through the first three adventures; the fourth leads her to a self-concept as a female human being. Aphrodite perceives Psyche's desire to have beauty for the sake of love as an affirmation of the feminine nature they share and abandons the jealousy and possessiveness that had made her into the Terrible Mother for both Psyche and Eros. In a sense, Psyche's self-acceptance of her femininity allows Aphrodite to grow up, to perceive herself happily as the grandmother of Pleasure. Even in the role of Terrible Mother, Aphrodite fulfilled the function of the Good Mother by prescribing a path that enabled Psyche to achieve full development.[6] Psyche's own mother, though a queen, was powerless to save her from her fate of exposure to a monster, as Persephone's mother was likewise unable to save her from rape by the god of the underworld. As a result of her own initiative and persistence Psyche's search is a spiral one, but she is aided by a strong mother figure whose motivation and essential nature she comes to share.

The three works I want to consider all embody the essential elements of the Psyche myth: they show a young woman's difficulty in differentiating between sex and love, the loss of love when she attempts to grow emotionally and intellectually, and her discovery of self through experience in the world, which, like Psyche's labors, symbolizes an encyclopedic knowledge. These works show the need for a powerful mother figure who provides an either positive or negative impetus and guidance for the psychic journey. And they imply at least a strong possibility that love can be recovered. In each narrative allusions to some aspect of the Psyche myth corroborate my interpretation of plot and character within the framework of the myth. Explicit references are made to the association of Psyche's name with the human soul, symbolized by a winged woman, a bird, or a butterfly, and to the fairy-tale versions of the myth. Other references link time-specific experiences to the timeless milieu of myth—death, the womb, wilderness, water. Although the works vary in setting, structure, and characterization, in each, the Psyche elements represent an initiation process that portends successful adulthood; thus they are all versions of a comic story for women paralleling the classic comic epic for men. To varying degrees, they represent the heroine's experience as encyclopedic, covering culture as well as the natural world in which Psyche labored. Knowledge acquired in a small Mississippi town is as all-inclusive as that gained from roaming up and down the East Coast in the 1960s or on the road to London and beyond in the 1720s. Unlike the antiheroes of recent dark comedic novels, the female adventurers find themselves competent to deal with their worlds; amid absurdity and brutality they maintain their sanity and also their love for humanity. Emphasizing the difference between male and female development, the stories nonetheless show female development as a paradigm by which both sexes can rejoin society and help to cure its ills.

Welty's "At the Landing" has a fairy-tale atmosphere from the beginning. A young girl, Jenny, is a captive of her grandfather who guards her against the fate of her mother, who after eloping to the city, suffered rape, abandonment, and death. The motherless girl is aware of her mother's fate and of her as a person; admiring her mother's paintings and the prisms she loved, she refuses to touch them, fearing that loving as her mother did will lead her too to disaster. Significantly, on a permitted visit to her mother's grave Jenny sees and falls in love with Billy Floyd, a fisherman who represents an ancient fertility figure, a river god. When Jenny is freed by her grandfather's death and forced from her house by a flood, Billy rescues her and casually rapes her. Jenny equates this rape with love; Welty underlines the connection to the Psyche myth by showing her interaction with Billy Floyd as the dance of two butterflies, the mythic symbol for Psyche, the soul. Billy's disappearance is the donnée for Jenny's journey, a search to find him. She must go beyond the little town, "The Landing," to the river formerly beside the town but now separated from it by accumulated silt. When she reaches the new landing, she meets a shocking fate: without receiving any help from three old women at the scene (the three fates), Jenny is gang-raped by the old fishermen at the river. Her cry of surprise and anger merges with their noises to sound like rejoicing.

It is difficult, at first reading, to interpret this ending as more than confirmation of women's limited fate and of their worst fears: venturing into the world results in rape. But the rape can be seen as a symbol of the harsh reality of the world in which one's sense of self and of autonomy will always be threatened, if not lost; it can be seen as a grim but preferable alternative to the arrested development Jenny would have faced if she had stayed on at The Landing in her grandfather's house. In giving Jenny a choice between rape and captivity, Welty weighs the tone of her tale toward tragedy; but she also promotes Jenny to the stature of a tragic protagonist who must always face such grim alternatives. Jenny's freedom to choose is not the "happily ever after" of the fairy tale but the acceptance of mature responsibility. Although she has repeated her mother's fate of being raped and abandoned, she has chosen to go beyond her mother's subsequent captivity and death. The necessary knowledge of how to escape comes to her through the mysterious albino, Meg Lockhart, her mother's relative and surrogate, who knows Billy Floyd well.[7] After observing Meg playfully wrestling with Billy, Jenny intuitively grasps Meg's knowledge of the real world and her power to "play" with the male on equal terms and to civilize him: Billy gladly fetches water for Meg after their game. Musing on this experience, Jenny comes to realize that she can become Billy's partner only through becoming an adult, so that she will have something to exchange with him: "communication would be telling something that is all new, so as to have more of the new told back" (p. 200).

Jenny learns more of the world when she goes into the town seeking Billy. In this environment she perceives Billy as a real, imperfect person, not as a godlike rescuer. This new knowledge equips her to leave the town. Her journey takes her through a wilderness: her emergence is a rebirth that affirms her mother's gift of life to her. The tone of the story deepens from fairy tale to myth as Welty emphasizes the mystical journey into life, to the river. The town through which Jenny passes "stretched and swooned" (p. 210), the natural world is ripe in summer heat, Jenny is sheltered by "an old mimosa . . . as old as life . . . that shrank from the touch, grotesque in its tenderness" (p. 211). She proceeds dreamily through a path of green branches, vines, passion flowers, through the "steaming hot shade of the wilderness," until, when she comes to the river, "the whole open sky could be seen. . . . All things, river, sky, fire, and air, seemed the same color" (p. 212). Now vision and despair seem the same. Yet Jenny's decision to leave The Landing allows us to invest Jenny's future with hope. Terrible as her experience in the world is, we can surmise that Jenny is armed with self-confidence and can survive, can even rejoice in her life. She can differentiate between the rapers' value of her only as a sexual object and her own sense of self-worth as a woman seeking love. She goes beyond the traditional expectations for women implied in the old women's indifferent question " 'Is she asleep? Is she in a spell? Or is she dead?' " (p. 214). Our knowledge of Jenny allows us to see that in refusing death, Jenny is prepared to deal with the world on its own terms; she intends to become a person whom her lover can love, when she finds him.

Writing in 1943, Welty could win credibility for such a heroine best by overtly invoking myth, as was her custom for all writing, she tells us.[8] The mythic allusions underline the tragic price of love and growth; a fairy-tale aura lends assurance that the price is worthwhile, that there will be a happy outcome after even terrible adventures. Thirty years later, authors can use the techniques of the realistic novel to achieve suspension of disbelief for the joyful survival of their heroines. Comic plots are supported by comic tone. Using first-person narrators, Alther and Jong show their heroines as ironically self-aware of their own failings and realistically aware of the absurdities of the people and events they encounter. These authors write with a self-awareness untainted by the self-deprecation characteristic of earlier women comic writers such as Dorothy Parker and Sally Benson. Alther and

Jong do not hold their heroines up to ridicule. Like male heroes, they have dignity and integrity; unlike male antiheroes they can achieve distance from themselves and from their society without alienation. Female development leads to a maturity appropriate to the realities of the modern world.

In *Kinflicks,* Alther parallels the heroine's worldly experience with the permutations of her relationship to her mother. The structure of the novel, with seven chapters of adventure alternating with seven chapters of reconciliation with a mother whose role the heroine has rejected, stresses the processes for the heroine's development. Like Psyche, Alther's heroine Ginny is self-conscious; the irony with which she views herself is expressed by a verbal wit that cuts through all pretense. Several chapters are flashbacks told by a twenty-seven-year-old woman of the world. Ginny's experiences, although sexual and apparently random like the episodes of the picaresque novel, tell the story of her development as a person. We learn of Ginny's first seduction, of her early identification with her father. We see her going to college and struggling with philosophy, earning a living, trying life in a lesbian community, getting entangled in marriage to a square male chauvinist, having a child—experiences she views as resembling the Stations of the Cross and which can be seen as versions of Psyche's three labors. She develops physically, emotionally, intellectually, socially; but all these experiences in the world—which like Psyche's first three labors represent knowledge of reality—have not brought her to a sense of integrated selfhood. Like Psyche, she must encounter death before she can accept herself.

In the seven chapters that depict Ginny's return home to be with her dying mother, Alther reveals the consciousness of both mother and daughter as they face the mother's impending death. Until her return home, Ginny had been motivated primarily by her negative image of her mother's life as one she must flee from; her development in the world has like Psyche's been propelled by her image of the Terrible Mother. Ginny comes to see that she had assumed that her mother lacked selfhood because of her role-playing as mother and had not perceived her as a self-knowing person aware of the role-playing; she is now able to separate her mother's autonomy from the limitations of her role. Although, like Psyche's real mother, Mrs. Babcock lacks the power to protect her daughter from repeating her role, she furnishes a model of a mature person capable of finding meaning in life. Perceiving as heroic her mother's acceptance of mortality, Ginny is able to help her come to a sense of conclusion, symbolized by their reading through the letter Z in the encyclopedia. Sharing the knowledge of mortality, Ginny comes to share her mother's self-acceptance as a human being, with all the limitations of being female. Although Mrs. Babcock cannot give Ginny the kind of divine imperative Psyche received from Aphrodite, she can, by freeing her from the emotional necessity of role-repetition, give her the ultimate human gift, the freedom to choose her own path. Mrs. Babcock refuses to force her daughter into repeating her pattern by passing on the advice she herself had received and acknowledges her own inability to find answers. Like the heroes of Greek tragedy, she recognizes the flaw that has led to her own tragic end, her meek dutifulness. Like the audience of Greek tragedy, Ginny is purged of her own fear of becoming like her mother. Her mother's final words, "Look after yourself, Ginny," liberate Ginny from guilt; she is free to become an autonomous adult. Ginny transcends her fear of death and seems prepared to solve the problem of being a mother without being defined exclusively by that role.

Ginny's journey to her mother and her self is a journey through the kingdom of death. The first sentence of the book declares, "My family has always been into death." Ginny's father died an accidental, violent death; her mother is now dying a lingering death from an inexorable disease. Ginny observes her and the other dying patients in the hospital and rejects both religious and atheistic rationales in favor of recognition of the uniqueness and loneliness of death for each person. Ironically, it is only in dying that Mrs. Babcock perceives her own unique selfhood.

Ginny comes to understand her mother as an individual only because she too is growing throughout her visit. As she struggles at her family's summer cottage to cut down the ubiquitous kudzu vine that is overtaking the place and to save four deserted baby birds, she begins to understand both the difficulty of life and the ambiguous demands of motherhood. She resents but cannot reject the baby birds' claim on her; she realizes that her anger at the parent birds' desertion is a projection of her anger at her own parents for dying, thus failing to guard her against mortality. This realization is a symbol of adult self-awareness; acceptance of one's mortality accompanied by a determination to fight it—her persistence with the birds—affirms life. Her labors, like Psyche's, bring her to a new threshold.

Ginny experiences her mother's renunciation of control over her daughter's life as a gift, "as though she were Sleeping Beauty just kissed by the prince" (p. 431). Her mother smiles, realizing that her gift has been received, but for both mother and daughter "delight is mixed with distress." It is better to realize that they can be free of the "generational spell" only with the mother's death. Like Jenny's mother in "At the Landing," Mrs. Babcock has been a prisoner; like Psyche's real mother, she had been powerless to help her daughter. But her negative image—she deliberately provoked her children's defiance in order to help them grow—impelled Ginny's search for other models; just as Aphrodite in her anger forced Psyche's labors, Mrs. Babcock is instrumental in her daughter's development. In reaction to her mother's death, Ginny attempts suicide. Having returned home to face death, she feels her experience in the world has been merely circular, that she has returned to the home she rebelled against without profiting from her journey. Her suicide fails—she lands in the boat when she attempts to throw herself out of it. Ginny survives, that fact in itself a validation of her mother's original gift of life and grounds for hope that she will make good use of her mother's final gift, freedom to be herself. Like Jenny, Ginny experiences her mother's death vicariously, and as a result, chooses to live. Her suicide attempt can be seen as what it so often is, a cry for help. Like Jenny, Ginny may be able to rejoice over what happens next. Now mature, she may perceive her husband differently; she may find a way to keep her daughter. Despite the dominant theme of death, Alther's book is a comic novel of development. It even becomes an artifact of its own theme: to make death comic is a triumph of art equivalent to the feat of making a fallible woman—everywoman—a true hero.

Focusing on the second part of the myth, Psyche's labors, Erica Jong transforms the myth in two major ways: she presents the heroine's experience totally from her own perspective, and she emphasizes the support received from other women. In the novel *Fanny: Being the*

True History of the Adventures of Fanny Hackabout-Jones, Jong shows us Fanny's inner development, her moral growth in response to her experience in the world. *Fanny* counters Freud's claim that women never achieve moral autonomy because they never fully separate from their mothers. Jong reverses this view by showing Fanny, originally a motherless foundling thrust into the world alone, as surviving because of her mother's aid and because of her own identification with her mother. The Psyche myth shows the human need for help in overcoming obstacles; without the ants, the reeds, the eagle—beneficent nature personified—Psyche would not have succeeded in her tasks. Whereas Psyche, Jenny, and Ginny profit from their negative mother images, Fanny identifies with a good mother powerful enough to give her crucial aid. Thereby, Jong adds a feminist dimension to the Psyche myth and makes her pattern of female development into a pattern for all human beings.

Unlike the other works we have considered, *Fanny* focuses on the mother in the mother-daughter relationship. Writing her memoirs for the enlightenment of her daughter Belinda, now seventeen, the same age Fanny had been when forced into the world, Fanny vows to tell the whole truth. Much of her lore involves the traditional mother-daughter communication about sexuality. Fanny neither abhors sex nor is reticent about it. From her earliest sexual experience—rape by her foster-father—she is able to distinguish between violence and true sexuality, between her love for her rapist in his fatherly role and her despair at his brutality. Thus Fanny starts with knowledge that separates her from the stereotype of sexual woman as masochistic and insatiable, an image emphasized in the famous eighteenth-century pornographic novel *Fanny Hill,* which Jong's *Fanny* parodies.[9] Unlike Fanny Hill, Fanny endures brutality and sadism only because she must in order to survive and to rescue her infant daughter who has been kidnapped. Unlike Fanny Hill, Fanny does more than repeat experience: she learns from it. Although Fanny's sexual adventures are as wild as any in picaresque novels, they are not told for their own sake; *Fanny* is a novel of development, like *Tom Jones.* Fanny learns about and rejects the eighteenth-century philosophies of optimism and rationalism as male views that would accept human brutality as part of "the best of all possible worlds." At the end of the novel, having like Tom

Jones come into her patrimony, Fanny has also profited from specifically female wisdom in learning her mother's story. Because of this
wisdom, she is ready to change the world; Jong's novel implies that if
Tom Jones had been female, the world of our time would have been
different. *Fanny* is truly comic, in the novelistic tradition of belief in
individual development as a means of integrating and improving society; its heroine is saved from twentieth-century cynicism only because of her female development.

The tone and pace of *Fanny* are appropriate to its epic fullness.
Brisk and cheerful under the most appalling circumstances, Fanny
approaches each new adventure with determination to learn. She is
irrepressible and capable of disliking aspects of her sexual experience
without denying her own sexuality. Fanny's escape from home, complicated by the specifically female vulnerability to rape, is more haz-
ardous than Tom's; she rightly perceives it as the only alternative to
passive acceptance of absolute patriarchal power: her foster-father,
having raped her, is willing to give her to his guests for their sexual
amusement, and her foster-mother is totally powerless. Like Psyche,
Fanny receives help from natural sources. Her horse, named for the
mythical Pegasus, carries her to safety in the home of some witches,
motherly women wise in the arts of healing, surviving, bringing into
life. They give Fanny a red garter as a talisman, and a riddlelike
prophecy for her life. Internalizing her faith in the protective power
of the garter, Fanny gradually comes to understand the horoscope,
which becomes a self-fulfilling prophecy because of her belief in it.
Although the witches' power is not enough to protect them against
murderous males who fear them, it is sufficient to help Fanny survive
and to bring her child alive into the world. The witches' power comes
from a sense of sisterhood, of female commonality of experience and
mutual helpfulness. It is her assumption of female identity during
the witches' sabbath that enables Fanny to endure, with joy, the
world's cruelties. Like the old woman who tells Psyche's story to a
frightened bride in Apuleius' frame-story, the witches give Fanny the
courage she needs.[10] As readers, we can hope that Fanny will be
equally effective in guiding her own daughter by writing her memoirs.
Jong's fictive frame is in itself an aspect of the novel as comic.

Like Psyche, Fanny achieves mature love; for both, female erotic maturity is represented by motherhood. Once her union with Eros has been accepted by the gods and she herself has become immortal, Psyche gives birth to her daughter Pleasure, or Bliss. Fanny gives birth to Belinda before finding her true love, but she does not let the bitterness of rape and incest deter her from loving and protecting her daughter. Unlike Psyche, but in keeping with the ironic tone of the comic novel, Fanny does not find her true love by seeking him. Her reunion with her Robin Hood-like friend Lancelot Robinson and their mutual recognition of their love occur by serendipity when she is seeking her daughter. Already a mother—symbolically mature—Fanny is capable of giving and receiving love.

Jong uses all the traditional devices of the male comic novel to win acceptance for the radical feminist perspective the book reveals. Heavily plotted, the story is full of the improbable "discoveries" typical of the adventure story. The witch Alice whom Fanny had left for dead reappears as the midwife who saves Fanny from the destructive male medical establishment by performing the Caesarean they forbid. Only much later do we learn that Alice is Fanny's real mother, herself the victim of rape by Fanny's foster-father. Fanny's encounter with Alice as midwife reassures her about the effectiveness of the witches' protection; she recalls her sense of empowerment at the witches' sabbath when she had said, "I felt myself—or truly that Part of myself which is most myself, my Soul—fly out of my Body and hover o'er the stone Circle and Barrows, as if I were a Bird, not a Woman" (p. 94).[11]

Recovering her sense of power enables Fanny to embark on the search for her kidnapped daughter which leads not only to rescuing her, unharmed, but to rediscovering Lancelot, who by now has overcome his former fear of women that had led him to homosexuality. Fanny learns that her foster-father is her real father and that her rape by him had been incest. He feels remorse at the discovery of this truth and makes Fanny his heir. With his fortune, Fanny establishes a home for the Newgate criminals Lancelot has rescued and made into pirates. In this way, "the adventures of Fanny Hackabout-Jones" also form a *Bildungsroman* for Lancelot. Her development and enabling discoveries save him from ineffectuality and cynicism. The absurd idealism and superhuman acts of the hero—Lancelot has twice survived being hanged—are balanced by the heroine's pragmatism. Jong's comic conclusion depends upon male-female sharing of experience.

The improbabilities of the traditional picaresque plot, carried to an extreme in *Fanny,* are an appropriate frame for the subplot about mother-daughter relationships, which is totally at odds with conventional wisdom. In such a context, the reader can accept the anti-stereotype of Fanny's harmonious relationship with Alice, her witch-mother.[12] Though both have been raped—by the same man—and have been abandoned as mothers, neither has been defined by a narrow female role. Neither has ever been the jealous possessive Terrible Mother, the Aphrodite of Psyche's experience. Neither has ever remained a captive like Jenny's mother, nor a traditional role-player like Mrs. Babcock. Nor has either been limited as was the mythical Demeter, who could not save her daughter Persephone from rape by the king of the underworld but could only mitigate her fate by winning for her the right to return periodically to earth and her mother, thereby bringing spring and agriculture to humanity. Jong has gone beyond myth to a new image of human possibility in which men and women autonomously and uniquely achieve full development and freely join in mature love. Jong goes beyond androgyny—the merging of sexual traits—to a new vision of mutuality and reciprocity based on acceptance of gender differences freed from hierarchical values.

In returning to the plot conventions of the eighteenth-century novel, Jong departs from nineteenth-century conventions that placed women in the domestic world and denied female sexuality. She also returns to a time when witchcraft was still half believed in; she needs this suspension of disbelief in order to create a myth of female power separate from the prevailing male dominance. Fanny's daughter receives the gift of life because of her grandmother's female lore and her mother's persistence and skill in surviving, with no help from the fathers. Jong manages to win our belief not only in Fanny's and Alice's rejection of the roles of rape victims and abandoned mothers but in their rational ability to separate the love they can feel for the seducer from their anger at his violence and the system that has made it effective. Jong shows the seducer as the true victim of his own lust. His victims triumph because even violation becomes an aspect of their true mission as bringers of life: they are women.

The witches themselves fulfill female roles while transcending them.[13] The two old witches are good cooks and housekeepers; they are healers, and they make it a practice to help the helpless, especially other women. In the world of women, they live without the jealousy and cattiness attributed to them by male traditions. Their "intuition" and ability to hear voices come not from supernatural sources but as the result of training their minds by "Extream Concentration, by Meditation in Solitude, and by many other Mental Rigors" (p. 76). Above all, they study to be wise and "to gain Pow'r o'er their own Minds and Bodies" (p. 77). And though tortured and almost destroyed by the men who fear them, they survive through passing on their "motherlore." Jong emphasizes that the powerlessness of other mothers to help their daughters directly is because of their own exclusion from matriarchal powers. In becoming wives and submitting to patriarchy, they have lost their birthright.

Jong's book with its unequivocally happy ending—a heterosexual woman happily married and with a child, able to initiate a life of usefulness in accordance with her own ideals—differs from the other books whose happy ending is at best implied. This difference stems from Jong's emphasis that women will succeed as women only in a world that values female wisdom. Her vision sees a new society achieved through the opportunity for full female development. Although Fanny, like male heroes, achieves wealth and position, what she learns through her adventures is not how to achieve wealth and position; she learns the truth about human motivation and relationships, about the inextricable mixture of good and evil in the world. Fanny grows in moral perception as do the best of heroes; freed from the Oedipal struggle which Freud thought of as leaving women too weak for true moral development, Fanny has the energy to achieve ethical adulthood. She learns *because* of being female, not in spite of it. Fanny's specifically female perception of the need for harmony along with her pragmatism represent traditionally female traits.[14] The world's need for such characteristics is discussed by psychiatrist Jean Baker Miller, who suggests that women today undervalue their traits because they share male values.[15] Two important recent books suggest that only through greatly increased sharing in parenting can men come to appreciate female values; in freeing women to make greater contributions to the general welfare, men will also free themselves from their crippling fear of women, a fear inculcated by the traditional relegation of all power to mothers.[16] Jong's fictive vision suggests the possibility of such a changed world; the comic tone and ending elicit our hope.

One can perceive the patterns of myth as archetypal, as "root paradigms" of the relationship of the individual to society, or even as part of the structure of the human mind. Finding these patterns in modern realistic fiction that also ends happily links hope for the contemporary world to age-old views of human nature.[17] These three writers have added psychological depth to our understanding of the pain women suffer from traditional role limitations. They explode the stereotypical view that women enjoy their pain and the more recent notion that women will deny both their sexuality and motherhood if allowed to assume traditionally male powers. Their new images are a basis for women to resist internalizing the traditional view of women as powerless. In her recent book, *Powers of the Weak,* Elizabeth Janeway describes the necessity for women to "disbelieve" cultural images as the first step toward changing the concept of power as an attribute of the powerful, toward seeing power as a relationship. The second step is bonding together as women to assert their new self-perception as partners in the work of the world.[18]

BONNIE ZIMMERMAN

Exiting from Patriarchy:

The Lesbian Novel of Development

When lesbians meet—as friends, lovers, or community—we create bonds and trust among ourselves by telling our coming out stories. Coming out is the rite of passage through which the lesbian establishes and affirms her self. Coming out is also a developmental issue, for, to paraphrase Simon de Beauvoir, one is not born but becomes a lesbian (despite popular ideology), and even if a woman recognizes her attraction for other women at the age of two, she must still name that feeling, act upon it, and choose to affirm her identity to the outside world. Coming out is process: "We spend our lives coming out, and the reality is that none of us is completely 'out' or 'in.' "[1] The coming out story is the lesbian myth of origins, the explanation of how we came to be as lesbians, how our consciousness formed and our identity developed.[2] A feminist literature of development, therefore, must address the issue of coming out because of its significance in a lesbian's life and because an increasing number of feminists now choose a lesbian life-style. In fact, coming out, even if only implied, is the next step in many more traditional female novels of development. In the novel of awakening, as analyzed by Susan J. Rosowski, the heterosexual protagonist awakens to the limitations of her role, particularly as wife and mother, escaping through death, passivity, or dreams of childhood or passion.[3] Bonnie Hoover Braendlin questions how the feminist heroine is to grow into freedom: shall this newly awakened and integrated personality merely return to her husband?[4] Increasingly, feminist heroines, as feminists in everyday life, are choosing an obvious alternative: relationships with other women. Thus, the heroines of a number of recent novels—such as Verena Stefan's *Shedding,* Kate Stimpson's *Class Notes,* Doris Grumbach's *Chamber Music,* and Marge Piercy's *Small Changes*—find a new liberation in lesbianism.

Lesbianism, therefore, can be one reasonable outcome of the refusal

244

to accept limitations posed by some female novels of development or awakening.[5] But many twentieth-century novels have focused on the development of the lesbian personality in itself. As Marianne Hirsch points out, the novel of development in the twentieth century is "the most salient genre for the literature of social outsiders, primarily women or minority groups."[6] The novel of development thus has proven very popular with lesbians, extreme outsiders among outsiders. Lesbian writers have used all modes of developmental literature: the confessional (Kate Millett's *Flying* and *Sita*), the picaresque (Rita Mae Brown's *Rubyfruit Jungle* and Sharon Isabell's *Yesterday's Lessons*), the "portrait of the artist" (Radclyffe Hall's *The Well of Loneliness* and Virginia Woolf's *Orlando*), the novel of awakening (June Arnold's *Sister Gin* and Verena Stefan's *Shedding*), and a unique version of the apprenticeship novel, the girls' school novel (Colette's *Claudine at School,* Christa Winsloe's *The Child Manuela,* Dorothy Bussy's *Olivia,* Monique Wittig's *The Opoponax,* Violette Leduc's *Thérèse et Isabelle,* and [with variations] Elana Nachman's *Riverfinger Women,* Bertha Harris's *Confessions of Cherubino,* and Rosa Guy's *Ruby*). Although differences exist among these novels and autobiographies, most dramatize a similar awakening or coming out process: the recognition of emotional and/or sexual feelings for another woman, the realization that that love is condemned by society, the acceptance of a lesbian identity either physically (through sexual initiation) or psychologically, and, in the contemporary feminist novels, the affirmation of one's lesbianism to the outside world. Because of their similarities, these works will all be considered under the general rubric of developmental literature, or the coming out novel.[7]

The paradigmatic lesbian novel of development, in many ways, is closer to the classic *Bildungsroman* than is the heterosexual feminist novel of awakening.[8] The geographic journey of the "young [wo]man from the provinces" takes place instead on symbolic or emotional terrain. The provinces in the lesbian novel of development can be interpreted as the territory of patriarchy, and the journey/quest undertaken by the lesbian protagonist is toward the new world of lesbianism. Coming out, then, provides "a point of exit from mainstream heterosexist culture."[9] The lesbian finds herself in uncharted territory, "in empty space."[10] The lesbian pilgrim progresses through this dangerous territory of heterosexuality, loosening, shedding, or finally succumbing to the constraints placed upon her free imagination (her lesbianism) by a hostile society (most often her parents, teachers, and employers, although every member of society is the lesbian's potential enemy). Along her path she is educated socially, sexually, and emotionally, often within the environs of an all-female world where the young girl awakens to her true identity, her powers, and her sexuality. In this essay I examine each stage of this developmental pattern.

Like the married heroine of the novel of awakening, the lesbian frees herself from prescribed female roles (often, in the pre-feminist literature, by identifying her authentic self with innately masculine traits),[11] but she must also free herself from loneliness and isolation. Furthermore, since the lesbian protagonist awakens into a world that is not only sexist and misogynistic, but also heterosexist and homophobic, her awakening may also bring with it guilt, shame, and self-hatred. As a girl, her love for her own sex is perceived to be innocent and harmless, but as a newly awakened sexual woman, it is severely condemned. Her new self-hatred may be exacerbated by her beloved's inability to return her feelings or to remain true to their love. Crushed between the forces of an antagonistic world (usually successfully internalized by the heroine) and the inadequacy of her first love, the lesbian protagonist may either accommodate to the outside world by rejecting her lesbianism (a rare choice) or escape from it through death or exile. While the married protagonist of the heterosexual novel of female development awakens to the limitations inherent in the male-female relationship and in woman's prescribed role, the lesbian is not limited by her lesbianism itself since relationships between women contain within themselves an ideal of infinite possibility. She may, however, be defeated and destroyed by society's rejection of her identity. Thus, the endings of many heterosexual novels of awakening seem bittersweet and resigned while, on the contrary, the endings of many lesbian coming out novels are tragic and violent. In the feminist lesbian novel, however, the end of the coming out process is freedom, not defeat. Rejecting the outside world of heterosexuality, the lesbian recreates herself in a different mode. If she is able to understand that coming out "connects us with power," then she can travel through the patriarchal landscape to the point of exit into lesbian nation.[12] The ultimate goal of the feminist lesbian novel of development, or coming out novel, is the creation of lesbian community, established through shared experience, visions, and stories that overcome "our geographical and social isolation."[13]

The developmental intentions of the lesbian novel are often clearly stated in its first paragraphs. "No one," says Molly Bolt on the first page of *Rubyfruit Jungle,* "remembers her beginnings," but most lesbian characters do their best to remedy this deficiency. "There in a back house on a small street, I was born," writes Sharon Isabell in *Yesterday's Lessons* (p. 1). *The Well of Loneliness* begins with the conception of Stephen Gordon, which is significant because Radclyffe Hall attributes lesbianism to psychobiological factors, including the desire of Stephen's parents to conceive a son. Dorothy Bussy, author of the autobiographical novel *Olivia,* forms "the history of a whole year when life was, if not at its fullest, at any rate at its most poignant" into "the shape of a story" (pp. 8, 7). Similarly, Inez (*Riverfinger Women*), writing "the pornographic novel of my life," evokes "the language of our getting older, the time of our being no longer children but young women, that is to say, forming into identifiable shapes" (pp. 3, 7). The process of the lesbian novel of development, then, is the growth into adulthood, the "forming into identifiable shapes."[14]

The lesbian novel of development thus generally focuses on the heroine's adolescence, much like the traditional *Bildungsroman.*[15] Her growth from adolescence into adulthood is an educational process often set in a girls' school or college, where the protagonist's general education is inextricably linked to the discovery of love and sexuality. In *The Child Manuela,* for example, Fraulein von Bernberg teaches Manuela about menstruation, a process that signals the beginning of a woman's heterosexual availability as sexual partner and childbearer. Manuela, however, insists that she will not marry and does not like men; instead, her budding crush on her teacher flowers after this incident, and "the child Manuela" grows not into heterosexual adulthood but into lesbianism. In *Olivia,* Mlle. Julie is responsible not only for her student's sexual awakening, but also for teaching her about literature, food, wine, theater, culture, talk, and life itself. When a journalist interviewing the adult Flavia (*A Compass Error*) asks her, "where were you educated?" she replies, ironically, "I had the luck to have some bright friends" (p. 2). In fact, Flavia had been studying for her entrance into the university during the summer of her "compass error" (her lesbian awakening), and her "bright friends" are the two older women who function in her "novitiate," her "apprenticeship," her "rehearsal" for life.[16]

Contemporary lesbian novels also incorporate the educational motif. Sharon Isabell's educational theme is evident even in the title of her novel: yesterday's *lessons*. Her lessons are in poverty, violence, racism, and survival, as well as in love and sexuality. On the one hand, her mother warns her that "you are going to have to learn that this is a hard life"; on the other, Sharon "learned about the real sweetness and feelings of every part of the body" (pp. 16, 129). For many lesbian writers, the lessons of the flesh provide a welcome respite from the harsh lessons of the outside world. For example, after exhausting the patriarchal topic of "Asoka, king of India in 273 B.C.," Inez and Abby Riverfinger move on to the education of sexual exploration: "we took our fingers out of dancing school and started them in on finger-painting lessons of the skin. . . . [we were] too uncertain even then about how to send our fingers to graduate school" and "each new closeness, each new chance, made us happier than we had ever imagined from all the books and classes we had studied" (pp. 70–74).[17]

The body and the emotions are the schools and laboratories for these young students and, in turn, their academic teachers become their teachers in love and passion. The schoolgirl crush is central to the lesbian novel of development.[18] As Flavia's "teacher," Andrée, says: "You are having the kind of crush that is natural in a girl of your age, and if you hadn't been seduced by a certain person . . . that would be that" (p. 158). Manuela's crush on Fraulein von Bernberg, Olivia's on Mlle. Julie, Claudine's on Aimée (Colette's *Claudine at School*), the collective crushes on Miss Jean Brodie, and Ellen's sexual experience with Janet Sanctissima (*Confessions of Cherubino*) are all crucial to the young women's development, despite the attempts of adults to minimize the significance of adolescent lesbian feelings. When there is no teacher for these young women, a schoolmate may serve in her stead (as in *The Opoponax, Thérèse et Isabelle, Ruby, Rubyfruit Jungle,* and *Riverfinger Women*).

The lesbian protagonist experiences her sexual awakening as a transformation. Though none is as dramatic as Orlando's transformation
from male into female, from heterosexuality into literal bisexuality,
the first experience of love or sex is nonetheless remarkable. After
Valerie Borge acknowledges Catherine's love note (*The Opoponax*),
the author writes: "When Catherine Legrand opens her eyes she
decides she must have been asleep because the light has changed"
(p. 227). The light changes dramatically in *Olivia,* whose heroine recalls that Mlle. Julie's face as she reads Racine to her students "awakened [me] to something for the first time—physical beauty" (p. 29).
Later Julie "awakens" Olivia to the beauty of Paris. But more important, Olivia awakens to life and her own potentialities:

> I went to bed that night in a kind of daze, slept as if I had been drugged
> and in the morning awoke to a new world—a world of excitement—a world
> in which everything was fierce and piercing, everything charged with
> strange emotions, clothed with extraordinary mysteries, and in which I
> myself seemed to exist only as an inner core of palpitating fire. [p. 32][19]

As the protagonist assumes her lesbian identity through her first
realization of love or sexuality, she also changes from an outsider into
one who belongs; she has "come home." In *Riverfinger Women,* Inez
begins as the *"odd person out"*—"a fat crazy queer"—but through the
process of the novel she transforms her position on the boundaries of
society from one of pitiful weakness to one of strength (pp. 5, 48).
Riverfinger women are outside the law: "tough street women" who
offer "the first promise of an armed women's nation" (pp. 4, 6).[20]

Before the young woman is completely transformed into her lesbian
self, however, she must come to a full realization of the significance
of her love and its difference from the "ordinary" crushes of young
women on teachers, older women, or schoolmates. Often this realization—her true "coming out"—involves her development from innocence to experience; usually it precipitates a confrontation with the
hostile outside world ready to label her with its strongest epithet for
women who step outside the boundaries of appropriate female behavior. While the realization of love for another woman is an awakening and a miraculous expansion of possibilities, the naming of this
love as lesbian can be inhibiting or destructive. The "ladies" Purity,

Chastity, and Modesty that hover over Orlando's transformation from man into woman also shroud the coming out process with guilt and shame (pp. 134–37). This is a step in the developmental process that is unique to the lesbian; although society reminds the heterosexual woman of her "duties" and curtails her attempt at self-expression, no equivalent exists for the violent attack of the homophobic social order on the emerging lesbian.

The climax of *The Child Manuela* is a case in point. Although all the girls at her school have crushes on the sympathetic and popular teacher von Bernberg, Manuela's feelings are unique. Christa Winsloe, writing in the age of Freud, attributes the crucial difference to Manuela's loss of her mother and her consequent need for nurturance. But, as we have seen, Manuela's "boyishness" also explains her intense, almost feverish love for the schoolmistress. After her great success as a knight in the school play, she inadvertently gets drunk and declares her passion to her schoolmates, only to be overheard by the headmistress, a harsh Prussian military woman. Isolated and disgraced, the bewildered girl still believes that "all was now well. To lie like that, to touch *her* and to be held by *her* hands—to see *her* eyes looking down—that was good and should endure for ever" (p. 303). But love for another woman cannot endure forever, as long as society discourages the pilgrim's journey into the free space of lesbianism. That society is incarnated in the headmistress who calls Manuela a pest and an infection and labels her crush "a hysterical devotion . . . an unhealthy business" (p. 283). To von Bernberg the headmistress insists, "Manuela is sexually abnormal. . . . And perhaps you know what the world—our world—thinks of such women, Fraulein von Bernberg?" (p. 285). Having spent many years repressing such feelings herself, the teacher knows well what "our world" thinks of lesbianism; thus, her final task is to teach Manuela about reality and the sickness of lesbian love:

"You must do as you are told. You have to be cured."
"Cured? Of what?"
Heavy, deliberate, one by one the words came ringing out:
"You must not love me so much, Manuela, that is not right. That's what one has to fight, what one has to conquer, what one has to kill." [p. 306]

After this final piece of instruction, Manuela is "no longer a child. She had become uncannily calm—calmer than the woman before her" (p. 306). Manuela is now a woman, unable to return to her innocent crush, but denied by her beloved's weakness the opportunity to transform it into a sustaining and nourishing mature love. Suddenly awakened to the full oppression of the lesbian, without the possibility of lesbian community at this point in history and unwilling to accommodate to her society, Manuela chooses suicide.

The awakening in *Olivia* is similar to that in *The Child Manuela* although its outcome is different. Crushes on teachers are expected and even encouraged at Les Avons.[21] However, Olivia gradually connects her passionate feelings to lesbian sexuality. First she identifies her love as the kind a man feels for a woman, but, she says, in "that way lay madness" (p. 77). Then, Julie's seductive appreciation of Olivia's body awakens the girl to her own eroticism: "And then I slowly passed my hands down this queer creature's body from neck to waist. Ah, that was more than I could bear—that excruciating thrill I had never felt before" (p. 85). But Olivia's budding lesbianism, like Manuela's, is clipped first by Julie's betrayal and then by the hostility of society, incarnate in Cara, Julie's partner and estranged lover, who finds Olivia asleep alone in Julie's study, a symbolic substitute for Julie's bed. Although Cara's invectives clearly arise from personal jealousy and anger, they also awaken Olivia to the guilt and shame of her sexual fall: "What would your mother say if she knew? If she knew how you were being led astray, demoralized, depraved? How idle you have become, and for all I know, vicious. . . . Look at you now, your hair down, your dress so untidy and rumpled, your eyes wild. Shame on you, Olivia. Shame! Shame!" (p. 90). Although the text refrains from naming Olivia's love "lesbian," the narrator then turns to conventional religious imagery to describe her transformation from innocent to guilty love: "In so short a time to be cast from the glories of Paradise into this direful region! It was the first time I learnt how near, how contiguous are the gates of Heaven and Hell" (p. 91). Cast into the hell of guilty sexual knowledge, yet unwilling to wear Stephen Gordon's "mark of Cain," Olivia retreats to the innocence of her girlish love: "Kneeling before her, I took her hand religiously in mine and kissed it, with nothing now in my heart but the very purity of pity" (p. 121). Julie leaves Olivia with nothing but memories and the gift of a paper cutter that, like the sword of chastity that separates Tristan and Isolde, symbolizes the severence of their impure love.[22] Cured of her lesbianism, Olivia adjusts to her heterosexual future, recalling her interlude at Les Avons with nostalgia and longing. *Olivia* is one of the rare lesbian novels of development that ends with the capitulation and accommodation of the protagonist to the dictates of heterosexual society.[23]

The patterns discerned in *The Child Manuela* and in *Olivia*—the realization of an atypical love, the association of difference with guilty sexuality, the inadequacy of the first lover, and the attack of the outside world—characterize most lesbian novels of development. This "sin against creation," as Stephen Gordon's mother calls lesbianism, casts Stephen, as it has countless women, out of the paradise of her ancestral home and onto the path to her true destiny. Lesbianism is also shrouded by guilt and shame in contemporary lesbian novels, with the exception of *Rubyfruit Jungle,* in which Molly Bolt is born apparently without original sin. When Sharon (*Yesterday's Lessons*), for example, is introduced to lesbianism through *True Story* magazine, she knows that "if anyone ever found out about the way I felt, my mom and dad and whole family would disown me. I just had to forget everything" (pp. 51–52). Each step along the path to lesbianism brings with it guilt and silence. When Sharon finally experiences sex with a woman, she becomes physically ill: "Her hands were gental [*sic*] and soft and her mouth was on my chest. All of a sudden I wanted to jump up and run. My body was cold and I didn't want anyone to touch me" (p. 108). Sharon's shame and her difficulty at discovering her lesbian self are disturbingly familiar to most lesbians, and her fear of exposure is justified: when her lesbianism is made known to her coworkers, their harassment forces her to quit her job. So frightening is lesbianism that it is, in fact, unspeakable.[24] Su, in *Sister Gin,* in a dialogue with the suppressed, angry, lesbian side of herself, writes, *"Lesbianism. I hope I never hear that word again"* (pp. 102–3). But words have so much power that Su must score out the dreaded word before she can throw the piece of paper away. Inez Riverfinger is also aware of the power of that word: "Think what it would mean to be a queer. Hey, lezzie, come over here" (p. 19). In a society in which lesbian sexuality is "at best a joke . . . at worst, a weapon," Inez and her friends learn how "inhibiting" it is to be a homosexual in America: "To know inside yourself at seventeen is not the same as saying it out loud" (pp. 33, 66).

Whether or not these protagonists name their feelings out loud, their interactions with lovers and the outside world follow similar patterns. In almost every lesbian novel of development, as in the conventional *Bildungsroman*, the protagonist's first lover is inadequate or inhibiting. She either betrays the young lesbian, usually leaving her for a man, or fails to protect her from the vindictive outside world. The path of true love seldom runs smooth for the protagonist of the lesbian novel. Nor does society nurture the lesbian heroine. We have seen how the attacks of the headmistress and of Mlle. Cara precipitate the destruction or accommodation of Manuela and Olivia. Stephen Gordon's "queerness" subjects her to the derision and contempt of her neighbors against which she has few weapons. Only her lesbian tutor foresees how much strength Stephen will require to survive in a homophobic world: "She'll have to tackle life more forcibly than this, if she's not going to let herself go under!" (p. 75). In *Ruby,* the violence of society is incarnated in her father, who beats and confines his daughter. Molly Bolt, in a classic lesbian experience, is thrown out of college for her lesbianism. Inez Riverfinger manages not to be expelled, but she carries within her the image of powerful naysaying men who are sometimes seen as "Daddy," sometimes as her psychiatrist, and sometimes as the "Committee," a fantasy composite of the police, the CIA, and the FBI. It is no wonder that, so often, the lesbian searches out the safety of the closet.

In the lesbian novel of development, then, the protagonist experiences an innocent and unnamed love for a teacher or schoolmate, and eventually identifies that love as distinct from that which is felt by other women. Transformed by this love into her true self, she awakens to her sexuality and passion; as a result she is betrayed or abandoned by her lover, condemned by society, and forced to choose between accommodation or escape into exile. When a lesbian chooses accommodation (which invariably suggests defeat rather than the mature adjustment of the conventional *Bildungsroman* protagonist), she returns to heterosexuality, the stereotypical conclusion to the lesbian pulp novel of the 1950s and 1960s. Among protagonists of the lesbian novels of development, Olivia and Flavia take this road to heterosexuality, although Flavia's marriage, which concludes *A Compass Error,* may be interpreted as an excruciating defeat by the existing order rather than an accommodation to it. *Ruby* is the only contemporary novel in which the protagonist chooses, or is forced into, heterosexuality. When her lesbian affair ends, Ruby remains tied to her father—the patriarchal world—and passively accepts his offer of a gentleman caller, signaling that she will eventually succumbs to the heterosexual order.

Pre-feminist lesbian novels of development offer a variety of destructive or compromised alternatives for the heroine, though at times she can surmount her oppression. Manuela escapes through death, and Margaret (in *Confessions of Cherubino*) finds another traditional form of escape for the lesbian in pre-feminist literature: madness. Stephen Gordon's exile from the heaven of her ancestral home and from her father's influence is a more positive form of escape. Through exile, she finds herself as a man/woman (she is finally able to dress as she pleases and cut her hair), as a lover (Mary Llewellyn waits along her path), and, most important, as a writer. Through her suffering and oppression, Stephen finally writes the novel that is in reality *The Well of Loneliness.* Escape for the lesbian, therefore, can be a sign of defeat, or it can be the final step in the journey to freedom.

Escape for Sharon Isabell and Molly Bolt, for example, is the continuation of their picaresque journeys. Rita Mae Brown's heroine is most reminiscent of the traditional *Bildungsheld* who returns to conquer and join the social order s/he has rebelled against. Brown does not truly challenge the standards of a sexist, classist, racist, and heterosexiest society; rather, we are encouraged to believe that Molly will someday make her movie—that is, conquer her world (which may explain the book's phenomenal popularity with both lesbian and heterosexual readers). Her accommodation, however, never includes the sacrifice of her lesbianism. If Molly becomes a powerful citizen of the heterosexual fatherland, she still will leave one foot in lesbian nation. Sharon literally rides off the pages at the end of *Yesterday's Lessons,* and if we feel that she is still "confused" and mired in the oppression that has plagued her throughout her pilgrimage, the last image of the book is, nevertheless, one of defiance: "I was flying and I was free and when I was on that bike I was happy. I begin to feel as long as I had that bike I had hope. No matter how many people laughed at me or no matter what anyone said they couldn't take that away from me. My freedom!" (p. 206).

The lesbian traveler in patriarchy, then, exits from the mainland through suicide, through madness, or, more positively, through riding away. But where does she ride to? What lies beyond the boundaries? That vision is currently being articulated, often in speculative feminist fiction, but some lesbian novels of development also suggest an answer: beyond the patriarchy lies women's community and lesbian culture. For example, in Wittig's girls' school novel, *The Opoponax*, Catherine Legrand and her companions journey away from childhood toward an adult world that exists "at the end of the park" into the battleground of women warriors imagined in Wittig's later work, *Les Guérillères:*

You say to Valerie Borge, come, that you go into the garden in the rain, you say that Valerie Borge isn't crying, you say that Catherine Legrand doesn't give her her handkerchief because she doesn't have one. You say that Valerie Borge puts three carbine five bullets into Catherine Legrand's hand and tells her to keep them. You say that you see the rain touching the trees, falling in front of the trunks, running off the leaves, that you make holes in the dirt of the paths when you walk, that your hair is getting wet and sticking to your face, that you are going to the end of the park. [*The Opoponax*, pp. 243–44]

The vision of women's community clouded over by the symbolic atmosphere of *The Opoponax* becomes clear and sharp in *Sister Gin* and *Riverfinger Women*. The developmental process in *Sister Gin* is particularly distinguished by the protagonist's growth into political awareness. Su is not a traditional *Bildungsroman* hero; instead, she develops "backward" from a fifty-year-old closeted middle-class lady to a ten-year-old angry activist. Her growth is charted by the integration of the two parts of her personality: Su, who is "correct" in health, weight, hairstyle, writing, and emotion, and Sister Gin, the madwoman, the crazy lady, the alcoholic angry political alter ego. At first Sister Gin only emerges when Su is drunk, but as Su's complacency is shaken up by menopause, she sheds her old skin to be born anew as Sister Gin and then as a newly integrated, evolved Su. The "change of life" serves as a biological metaphor for psychological and political change. It is not only the young who go on developmental journeys, discovering the point of exit from patriarchy. In fact, for a lesbian (or any woman), the development of an integrated personality may be stopped at the very point at which a male hero comes into his full powers. Patriarchal society defines women as childlike, restricts our powers and growth, and particularly limits lesbian growth with judgments of "adolescent sexuality" or "infantile disorders." The woman, like Su, who listens too closely to society's messages may find it difficult to grow up.

The part of Su that "grows up" is the angry, lesbian, radical child that had been repressed by her socialization as a "good girl." Thus, it is not only Su who is described in developmental language, but also the repressed part of her personality, her anger: Su "claimed she would not work again until her anger was twenty-one. 'I'm dedicating my life to her, whatever the trends of the times. No more anger-sitters. No more camps or schools. No more lollipops. She's going to get all the advantages my expanse of years can provide, every oppor-tunity to become whatever she wants to become, even if she just wants to get married and have lots of little angers'" (p. 200). Grown up, integrated, and angry, Su joins with other old women in righting the wrongs of women's oppression and accepts her identity as a southern woman fighting battles for southern women. She can then separate from Sister Gin—"Sister, you've done your work for now"—so that in the epilogue, Su and Sister Gin coexist in mutual love and respect. Su can finally write her play or novel, offering an invitation to all women trapped in a prolonged adolescence or hiding in the closet of neatness, calm, and dispassion: "All out come in free" (pp. 169, 205). Come *in,* she cries; join in the creation of a new world, a new women's com-munity, a "safe sea of women" (p. 92).

This new women's community—or lesbian nation—also lies at the end of the journey taken by the Riverfinger women. As outlaws, as tough, strong, free witch women, they exit through a point where male cultures, male law, and male power can no longer touch them. At this point their individual lives and individual coming out stories connect, reflect, and interact: "There are all the places where these stories touch each other and make the start of a common life, the beginning of an idea about community" (p. 14). The common life, the community alone prevents the individual from drowning in "isolation and terror" (p. 14). Alone, the lesbian traveler is vulnerable and violated; together with her sisters, she is powerful and free. Manuela, Olivia, Ruby, Stephen Gordon, Ellen, and Margaret all capitulate or are destroyed because no dream of community and solidarity sustains them. Inez Riverfinger offers them an alternative: "the dream of my women, the world where all women are strong and beautiful, even me. . . . The vision of who we are and who we can be, a race of intact human beings unafraid to give to each other, one to one, in specific ways, and more than one to one, in groups, in the new ways we are learning. To give, each time, the vision of each woman" (p. 60).

The lesbian vision of the individual in community, the growth of one into many, expands the developmental motif from that of the formation of individual identity to the formation of communal identity. Women in community—perhaps the girls' school, the consciousness-raising group, or the lesbian bar—grow up, awaken, to a new world, apart from patriarchy, in which female powers can be integrated, in which there are no limitations or compromises, in which the patriarchal, heterosexist world exacts no price. In this vision of lesbian community, "tough, strong, proud: free women" ride away through the vanishing point to a nation that might be a commune in Canada, a cell of angry old women, a feminist center or organization, or a tribe of armed warriors. Lesbian nation exists primarily in imaginative space, but it is also being created through the telling of coming out stories, through the formation of alternative images of lesbians, through the search for lesbian herstory and "heras," through the individual assertion of "I am my true self, as I really am." Lesbian nation is the cumulative product of each lesbian journey toward selfhood:

We each have our reasons for wanting to know everything there is to know about women. She who has been mystery for centuries is coming out. We who have not made common cause since the fall of the great matriarchies, we are coming together (watch out).[25]

MARGO KASDAN

"Why are you afraid to have me at your side?":

From Passivity to Power in *Salt of the Earth*

Women who develop experientially are virtually absent from American film. Female characters *are,* male characters *do.* What Molly Haskell says about the forties may be extended to film in any period:

> The preoccupation of most movies of the forties, particularly the "masculine" genres, is with man's soul and salvation, rather than with woman's. It is man's prerogative to follow the path from blindness to discovery, which is the principal movement of fiction. . . . Women are not fit to be the battleground for Lucifer and the angels; they are something already decided, simple, of a piece.[1]

Haskell explains that "women are the vehicle of men's fantasies, the 'anima' of the collective male unconscious, and the scapegoat of men's fears." She then goes on to suggest general categories of stereotypes that dominate American films (and also the novels, melodrama, operas, and popular literature from which they are derived): woman "as the 'feminine principle incarnate,'" woman "worshipped as 'mother,'" "venerated . . . as an 'earth goddess' . . . or as 'enigma.'"[2] These are only a few of the possible stereotypes; every decade has had its favorites that have catered to and gratified the social fantasies of audiences.

Yet despite differences in tone and style that characterize female types from decade to decade, the Hollywood product functions uniformly in at least one respect: the major concern of the female protagonist, whatever other issues may also be treated, is the quest for a man. The problems of pursuit, capture, and retention of a man, with marriage as a solution, a resolution, a "happy ending," provide the content of most films from 1910 to 1970. In the set of films known as "golddigger" movies, women characters played by actresses like Doris Day and Marilyn Monroe blatantly pursue marriage and husbands in "how to" films like *Pillow Talk* and *How to Marry a Mil-*

lionaire. As characters, they are as single-faceted as they are single-minded in their pursuit.

Even in "career-girl" films, like *His Girl Friday,* where the heroine has already achieved an important position, the pursuit of career does not lead to personal development. Hildy Johnson (played by Rosalind Russell) suffers from the conflict between her true calling as reporter and her desire to leave her job for marriage and babies—a normal life for a woman. Although the plot revolves around her return to her career, she never sees her change of heart as a political decision or even a choice. Manipulated by the strong male character, played by Cary Grant, she is never allowed illumination or comprehension of her situation.

Only in the area of romance is a female character permitted to progress through what might be called developmental stages. But all learning focuses on the romance. Even Katherine Hepburn, consistently considered a model of strength and assertion, goes through personal change only in the area of sexual awakening in *The African Queen* and *Summertime,* for example. The totality of her films does show progress, from the screwball comedies—*Holiday, Bringing up Baby, Philadelphia Story*—in which her goal is to catch a man, to the comedies with Spencer Tracy in which, as was the case with many forties films, she has a full-fledged career. In these last, however, she is presented as an already strong character (exactly as Hildy Johnson), having achieved her high position. For example, *Adam's Rib,* does not show her process of gaining self-confidence and the competence of an attorney. And at the end of *Woman of the Year,* where she portrays a thoroughly egocentric and single-minded reporter, she is willing to renounce her job to make a "proper home" for Spencer Tracy as her husband and fellow reporter. These films center not on female *Bildung* but on conflicts between a strong, successful woman and her male counterpart.

During the fifties, Hollywood succumbed to the combined effects of increased sales of television sets and the blacklist. A pervasive fear of producing either a financial or a political disaster led to films of bland or stridently anticommunist content. In such an atmosphere the subject of marriage was a particularly safe and sure area to develop. Against this current, in the midst of a temper so fearfully anticommunist that the merest suggestion or rumor of leftist affiliation was enough to cost jobs, a blacklisted director, Herbert Biberman, together with several other film artists, also blacklisted, set out to make a film outside Hollywood studio restrictions. The making of *Salt of the Earth* is a saga in itself.[3] The film stands as a testimony to the courage and tenacity of the filmmakers who completed the project in the face of persecution from all quarters. The film is pro-feminist, pro-union, and pro-minority. It is not surprising that pressures were brought to bear on distributors so that the film was never released commercially. Perhaps just because it was not subject to the limitations and control commonly exerted by Hollywood studios, *Salt of the Earth* stands almost alone among American films in treating a woman character as an individual who consciously changes.

Salt of the Earth presents a group of Mexican-American miners in New Mexico who vote to strike for the same safety measures white miners have. Their wives are more concerned with the inequality in plumbing. The women have to chop wood five times a day to heat water, while the "Anglos" have hot running water and indoor bathrooms. Initially, the men are deaf to the women's request that plumbing be made a union demand. However, when the company brings a Taft-Hartley injunction against the strikers, the women, who are technically exempt from the injunction, take over the strike, while the men have to take over the homes. And once the men "get a taste of what it's like to be a woman," as one of the characters says, they agree that plumbing is of prime importance. Through the women's activity as picketers, both the women and the men come to a new understanding of mutual goals and needs.

The film traces the transformation of the group through one of its members, Esperanza Quintero. It is through her eyes and her voice that the viewer apprehends the events of the story. Esperanza is a true protagonist, actually a female hero. Like male characters in fiction, she discovers her own strength as a part of the strength of the community. At the outset, triply oppressed as a woman, Mexican-American, and worker's wife, Esperanza becomes by the end, strong, active, and dignified.

Salt of the Earth begins years after most Hollywood films end: Esperanza is thirty-five years old, mother of two, expecting a third child, and ground down by the daily labor of her life. Under the credits we already see her plight—she chops wood, builds a fire, scrubs the laundry, hangs it out, watched and aided by her five-year-old daughter, Estellita. By virtue of their place as prologue, without dialogue, with only music as support, these images suggest endless repetition. This is Esperanza's life and perhaps Estellita's future. Esperanza's voice in the retrospective narration that begins moments later is already the voice of experience; the difference between the strength and assertiveness of that voice and the pictures we see of "the old way" she remembers, marks the distance she has traveled. Her ability to structure and relate the narrative is in itself a sign of her newfound place of mature retrospection.

In the beginning of the film, Esperanza is timid with her husband and oppressed by him. She is unable even to tell him that it is her saint's day and that she would like to celebrate. She tells him timidly about the installment payments due on the radio. She does not sit at the table at the evening meal but serves, and later apologizes for his washing water getting cold. After diffidently proposing that sanitation and hot running water are important issues for the union to take up, she cries because Ramon rejects the issue (and her needs). His retort defines the way women are seen: "You're a woman, you don't know what it's like up there [in the mines]." According to Ramon, the safety of men is a demand more important than sanitation. Leave it to the men, he tells her. She is unable to make the point forcefully that women's labor, chopping wood for the fire, goes unnoticed and unconsidered. Later we see that she is fearful of joining the delegation of women who want to make the sanitation issue a union demand. She says, "If Ramon ever found me on a picket line . . ." and trails off. And again, her voice-over tells that she didn't want to go to the union meeting but that "the others said one go, all go," and so she did. In this one remark lies the story of the women's mutual support.

We see that the daily life of the couple is inextricably tied up with that of the community and that Esperanza's evolution reflects the joint activity of the women. Over and over again, the women look to each other for sympathy and support: at the Mananita, the dances, and the community parties, and in the problems facing them as wives, all the women are involved. Esperanza is happy when Ramon dances with other women at her birthday celebration, and the film emphasizes the strength of the female community by cutting to Esperanza's meeting of the female delegation on sanitation demands. This emphasis reverses the ideological presentation of the dominant cinema. In traditional Hollywood films, the woman's story would now become one of infidelity, marital conflict, and pursuit of her man: that is, the political issues would become a mere backdrop for the "real" issue: romance. Here the suggestion of sexual strain in the marriage moves immediately to the real issue that is its cause: the politics of their lives. The narrative posits that social inequalities and injustices produce the marital strains and that the solution to these larger problems will provide personal and marital solutions as well.

The women's first actual confrontation with the men, their first public political action, occurs when four of them enter the strike meeting to present their request for sanitation. The image of the four at the edge of the frame among a mass of men is a concrete visual presentation of their marginal position. Esperanza's fear of going inside is mirrored by Consuelo, whose shy and halting request that plumbing be added to the list of demands is greeted in a patronizing, if kindly, way as an "announcement" that is immediately tabled. The men will simply not accept the idea that the women's needs are as important as their own. Ruth, Consuelo, and Teresa accept the public defeat, but privately we see Ruth and Teresa verbally attack their husbands. Not so Esperanza. She is quiet and defeated when Ramon grudgingly says, "At least you didn't make a fool of yourself—like Consuelo." The women have no recourse. Left in the hands of the men, the essentials of daily life would never be provided.[4]

For Esperanza, development depends on communal obligation, first in traditional women's roles as part of the newly formed Ladies' Auxiliary, and later in roles that expand in importance during the strike and prepare for their significant action in the Taft-Hartley crisis. The strike by the men occasions the women's first steps to equality. The Ladies' Auxiliary is set up and accepted, and while the women are still in their traditional roles of nurturing and nourishing, preparing food and coffee for the picketing men, it provides an opportunity for the women to work together. Esperanza does not at first come to the lines because Ramon, she says, does not approve. Her desire to be among the women, among the supporters, brings her there and she manages to slip in one day because she makes the only coffee Ramon will drink.

As the strike becomes publicized and contributions begin to come in and information requires dissemination, the women begin to help in the office, collecting the money, replying to mail, cutting stencils, filing papers, sealing envelopes, running the mimeograph machine. As Esperanza says, "We women were helping. And not just as cooks and coffee makers. . . . No one knew how great a change it was, until the day of the crisis." In other words, she recognizes that the departure from the traditional housebound duties and wifely roles has enabled the women to conceive of taking an active role in dealing with the Taft-Hartley crisis.

Now when a meeting is called to decide whether or not to obey the Taft-Hartley injunction, there are almost as many women as men. Their work as supporters has already created a bond among the women. Esperanza, identifying strongly with her female peers and friends, is now able to act for the first time. She is shy, hesitant, and self-effacing, but her involvement with the strike activities has given her enough self-confidence to raise a point about Teresa's proposal that the women take over the picket line. The directions in the screenplay underline her feelings: "She rises shyly." It seems that Esperanza's stage fright will leave her mute—but at last she finds her voice:

I don't know anything . . . about these questions of parliament. But you men are voting on something the women are to do, or not to do. So I think it's only fair the women be allowed to vote, especially if they have to do the job.[5]

We see her intervention's effect on Ramon. We can imagine the courage required to make it in the face of his objections, voiced just moments before, to the women's activity. In spite of Ramon's glare, she averts her eyes, defies him, and votes in favor of the women's action.

Women come from all over to join the picketers. The men come too, afraid the women would not stand—or in Esperanza's sarcastic interpretation, afraid they will. Ramon has forbidden Esperanza to join the picket line, but when a convoy of deputies attacks the picketers, her identification with the women, her loyalty to the community, and her growing sense of responsibility give her the strength to take action. She hands the baby to Ramon, runs down to the picket line, and disarms a deputy by striking his hand with her shoe while Ramon watches helplessly from the sidelines.

A dissolve then takes us to the Quintero home, where the effects of such action are to be felt. Esperanza has gained a new sense of herself through action and victory. She returns home that day elated, a new light in her eyes. She is more animated, more self-assured than ever before and determined to return to the picket line the next day.

The women work together on the picket line, deployed like an army to handle both the deputies and the striking men who would try to interfere. The extent of their solidarity is tested when the female leadership (in itself inconceivable until this point) is arrested. In jail, the women produce concrete evidence of their power as a group. Their chant for food, beds, and baths eventually annoys the sheriff enough to effect their release. Once Ramon takes their children out of the jail, it is Esperanza who, face set and stubborn, rises and leads the chant anew: "Queremos comidas, queremos camas, queremos baños."

While the women are in jail, life must go on, and the men must contribute to its continuation. In an important scene, Ramon and Antonio hang up the laundry and chat over the backyard fence repeating an earlier scene in which Esperanza and Luz were doing these chores. Without perceiving their own change of mind, they suddenly find themselves recognizing the validity of the women's demands. Ramon says:

Three hours! Just to heat enough water to wash this stuff! I tell you something. If this strike is ever settled—which I doubt—I don't go back to work unless the company installs hot running water for us. . . . It should have been a union demand from the beginning.[6]

In a complex and ironic turn, the men's strike has led to the women's departure from their traditional roles, causing the men to experience and understand something of the women's daily lives. Antonio compares what he calls "wage slavery" and "domestic slavery," unconsciously drawing a parallel between the men's oppression by the white owners and that of the women by the men. He suggests that the men must "give 'em [the women] equality. Equality in jobs, equality in the home." But he and Ramon are unable to internalize the comparison, threatened by the women's potential freedom. Like the women, the men are oppressed by the bosses; both are treated as children. The superintendent openly states: "Well, they're like children in many ways. Sometimes you have to humor them, sometimes you have to spank them—and sometimes you have to take their food away."[7] The men actually treat their wives this way, humoring them, forbidding them action, keeping them out of the struggle. This treatment prevents progress both for women and children. Esperanza's achievement is that she "grows up," becomes autonomous, and refuses to be restricted by Ramon. And she does so largely through her association with other women.

By standing firmly together, the women have defeated the sheriff. This triumph transforms Esperanza. She comes home from jail, bursts in, her face aglow. She looks younger, heartier, and happier. She embraces Ramon, laughs, moves lightly. The women have won—at least against the sheriff—but what remains to be settled is the quarrel with their husbands. Because of a strategy meeting with the women, Esperanza postpones a talk Ramon wants, and he walks out, furiously slamming the door. Her friends are sympathetic to her difficulty with him, and Consuelo suggests that a delegation of women talk to him. She is offering the solution she has learned works in a political situation, but Esperanza establishes the personal nature of their quarrel: "I have to work it out with him myself." Ramon cannot bear her emerging autonomy, especially in the face of his own frustration and helplessness. The threat to his male ego is enormous, and so it is completely comprehensible that Ramon should at this point decide to go on a hunting trip.

From subservience, Esperanza has moved to a philosophical and political awareness of the issues that beset the community and the couple. Impatient with the restraints placed upon her by Ramon, she is now ready to confront him. The climax of the conflict between the couple is acted out while Ramon is oiling his gun, preparing for the hunting trip. In spite of the gun, Esperanza dominates the confrontation, not with traditional symbols of power, but with her mind, her eloquence, and her political understanding of the strategies of the strike.[8]

For Esperanza, the private and the public spheres have become integrated. For Ramon, to be in the union meeting is to be a strike leader only; Esperanza can never shed her identity as mother and wife. She attends the first meeting pregnant and with Estellita in her arms. The women's demands—hot running water, indoor plumbing, sanitation— become political. When Ramon refuses to care for the children, Esperanza takes them with her, including the newborn baby, to the picket lines. There again, the domestic realm intertwines with political activism. In jail, the women chant for their domestic needs—beds, baths, and food. Esperanza's understanding that marriage is part of a political reality enables her to articulate the parallels among the oppression of women, the oppression of the workers, and the oppression of minorities. She understands that the bosses would do anything to reopen the mine and that the strikers are stronger than ever because the company has not been able to break the strike. And then she draws the parallel between racism and sexism, accusing Ramon:

Why are you afraid to have me as your friend? . . . Have you learned nothing from this strike? Why are you afraid to have me at your side? Do you still think you can have dignity only if I have none? . . . The Anglo bosses look down on you, and you hate them for it. "Stay in your place, you dirty Mexican"—that's what they tell you. But why must you say to me, "Stay in *your* place?" Do you feel better having someone lower than you? . . . Whose neck shall I stand on, to make me feel superior? And what will I get out of it? I don't want anything lower than I am. I'm low enough already. I want to rise. And push everything up with me as I go. . .. . And if you can't understand this you're a fool—because you can't win this strike without me! You can't win anything without me![9]

This moment completes Esperanza's evolution. She has gained the clarity of vision to articulate coherently the mechanism of male domination. She has gained, too, the strength to confront Ramon, as great an achievement for her alone as the confrontation with the sheriff and his deputies is for the women as a group. When Ramon would strike her, she stands up to him, defiant and unflinching, and outstares him until he drops his hand. She refuses the "old way": "Never try it on me again—never," she says, and exercises her right to sleep alone.

Esperanza's words return to Ramon on the hunting trip.[10] He suddenly understands what she has been trying to explain, and he calls to the men to return home, thus making it possible to defy the company's trump card of eviction. He finally understands that they are indeed all sisters and brothers working together.

In the course of this narrative, Ramon and the men of Zinc Town painfully reach a new understanding of their personal and political situation. As Teresa says: "Anything worth learning is a hurt. These changes come with pain . . . for other husbands too . . . not just Ramon." A visual presentation of this lesson occurs in the cross-cuts between two sequences: Esperanza giving birth, asking God's mercy, and calling to Ramon; and Ramon being beaten by deputies, asking God's mercy and calling Esperanza. The parallel between the two sequences shows the shared bond between the couple as well as the necessity for both of them to suffer in order to give birth to a new way of life.

But important as this lesson is for Ramon, there is nothing unique about a male character's movement from blindness to insight. The special quality of *Salt of the Earth* lies in Esperanza's development and the change in the community of women. If women in film are normally isolated, rarely seen in intimate and honest contact with other women as peers and friends, in *Salt of the Earth* the women enjoy and gather strength from one another, communicate, work, and help one another, not only in the usual female situations, such as the birth, but also in political revolt. In this film, identification with the community precedes individual identity; action, not reaction or reflection, is the vehicle for female development. What Ellen Morgan says in the essay on the neo-feminist novel captures the essence of *Salt of the Earth*. This film, like

the novel of apprenticeship[,] is admirably suited to express the emergence of women from cultural conditioning into struggle with institutional forces, their progress toward the goal of full personhood, and the effort to restructure their lives and society according to their own vision of meaning and right living.[11]

When Esperanza tells Ramon, "I want to rise. And push everything up with me as I go," she is at least twenty years ahead of her time.

Recent feminist film criticism (in particular, the work of Claire Johnston and Laura Mulvey) has underlined the fact that in the great majority of films made in Hollywood, "the main controlling figure with whom the spectator can identify" is male. Mulvey points out that even a female protagonist, such as the eponymous heroine of *The Revolt of Mamie Stover* (Raoul Walsh, 1956), lacks the strength and activities associated with male protagonists.[12] Indeed, Mulvey says, woman characters in films traditionally have "functioned on two levels: as erotic object for the characters within the screen story, and as erotic object for the spectator within the auditorium."[13] She points out that films often begin with the women presented to the gaze of both kinds of spectators:

both in *Only Angels Have Wings* . . . and in *To Have and Have Not* the film opens with the woman as the object of the combined gaze of spectator and all the male protagonists in the film. She is isolated, glamorous, on display, sexualized.[14]

This way of situating the female character, not only in openings but often throughout films, is achieved through technical devices that enhance the image of the actress. The use of back lighting, diffuse lighting, low-key lighting, close-ups, often in soft focus, all perfect and fetishize the image of the woman, turning her into a "scopophilic object," or an object which provides sexual stimulation through vision. Both the physical passivity of female characters (the actresses' characteristic pose) and their narrative passivity (the need to be rescued from danger) contribute to this effect. Representing women as unchanging characters deprives them of individuality. Unlike male characters, they are not to be understood, respected, and viewed in their complexity as human beings. Fixed, they are art objects displayed for a consumer or sex objects paraded for the erotic pleasure of a (male) viewer. Female viewers have access to female characters only through this male perspective.

Salt of the Earth contrasts technically and ideologically with the dominant cinema. Flat lighting, bleak locations, authentic interiors, working clothing, old cars, and unglamorous people (in most cases the strikers themselves and not professional actors) predominate, and most important, there are virtually no close-ups in the film. Significantly, one of the few close shots of Esperanza comes at the moment when, at the climax of her confrontation with Ramon, she stands up to him and moves into a close shot, saying, "You can't win anything without me!" This close-up accentuates her strength; because she moves forward into the shot, it becomes an active, rather than a carefully posed and thus objectifying, image. Esperanza, furthermore, is very rarely seen alone; most often she is within a group of women consulting, planning, working, talking, striking together. While the opening shots of the film do in fact isolate and "display" Esperanza, they differ from typical cinematic presentation because Esperanza is pregnant and engaged in unglamorous daily domestic labor. Through this unglamorous presentation, the off-screen voice that conducts the narrative, through her progress toward enlightenment that forms the narrative, the film effaces the passivity associated with women characters. Esperanza is not available on any level for the delectation of a (male) viewer. In Esperanza Quintero we see the creation of a truly complex and evolving female character who, in her activity and strength, becomes an unusual and worthy model for the female viewer.

MARY HELEN WASHINGTON

Plain, Black, and Decently Wild:
The Heroic Possibilities of *Maud Martha*

Anna Julia Cooper spoke prophetically in 1892 when she described the black woman's ascendant role in addressing the twin evils affecting the race:

The colored woman of today occupies, one may say, a unique position in this country. . . . *She is confronted by both a woman question and a race problem,* and is yet an unknown or an unacknowledged factor in both. [italics mine][1]

Cooper was even more prophetic in her metaphorical portrayal of the black woman as the "one mute and voiceless note" from the black world, a witness not yet heard from because she has *no language—but a cry.* Men can assuage their pain, Cooper writes in her powerful essay "Womanhood: A Vital Element in the Regeneration and Progress of a Race,"[2] and to some extent relieve it by the busy activity of their lives; it is women who suffer most the absence of a language because often it is their only means to power. In the twenty-seven years after slavery, Cooper saw black women being denied the word in a very specific way: they were being excluded from the ministry, the very means by which poor black men were becoming powerful users of the written and spoken word.

The silencing of the black woman within her own historical, cultural, and literary traditions has been documented by many scholars.[3] As Ann Jones writes in her essay on Zora Hurston's novel *Their Eyes Were Watching God,* this exclusion from the ministry effectively barred women from a deeper participation in the life of their culture:

Black women did not as a norm preach. That "big voice" was not hers; and in a culture in which the church plays so central a part, that was and is a crucial type of silencing. For it meant that black women were excluded from speaking and interpreting the unifying myth of the people.[4]

Alice Walker has spoken eloquently of this silencing of the black woman within *her own* tradition in her essay "In Search of Our Mothers' Gardens," in which she observes that only in music have black women been permitted some artistic freedom.[5] Novelist Paule Marshall says that although Barbadian-American women like her mother learned oratory in Barbados where they were required to recite long passages of the classics by heart, they were not expected to speak at the great communal gatherings like funerals and weddings even though they were often as skilled orators as the men. In every area of black written and oral expression, black women have been "conspicuous by their silence."[6] The passionate and articulate words of Anna Cooper, Maria Stewart, and Jarena Lee have not been included in our canons, and so are not a part of our historical and collective memories. The militant slave, the eloquent politician, the fiery preacher—all these are known as the voices of black men.

But these silences do not keep still. The evasions, concealments, and absences, the dramas of enclosure and escape, the fear of articulating one's true self, "these broken utterances" (as Anna Cooper called them), so pervasive in women's writings, are primary evidence of women's exclusion from the power of the word.[7] In Hurston's novel, the main character Janie conceals her own dreams by taking on the dreams of men until she claims the voice the community has denied her. Gwendolyn Brooks's *Maud Martha* is another example of the women's struggle for language, but Maud's struggle is even more fundamental than Janie's.[8] Janie is immersed in the folk culture and knows the language; Maud must first find the words of liberation and then she must find the courage to speak.

The silencing of Maud Martha occurs both within and without the text. Despite Gwendolyn Brooks's status as a Pulitzer Prize winning poet, no one in 1953 had more than six hundred words to say about the novel. The reviewers of Ellison's *Invisible Man* (published just the year before when Ellison was relatively unknown) suffered no such taciturnity and devoted up to 2,100 words to Ellison's novel. The *New Republic, Nation,* the *New Yorker,* and *Atlantic* magazine contained lengthy and signed reviews of *Invisible Man.* Wright Morris and Irving Howe were called upon to write serious critical assessments of Ellison's book for the *New York Times* and the *Nation.* In contrast, the *New Yorker* review of *Maud Martha* was included in their "Books in Brief" section—unsigned—suggesting that the real "invisible man" of the 1950s was the black woman. Critics called the main character "a spunky and sophisticated Negro girl"; Ellison's character was called a hero or a pilgrim. Brooks's character was never held up for comparison to any other literary character. Ellison's nameless hero was not only considered "the embodiment of the Negro race" but the "conscience of all races": the titles of the reviews—"Black & Blue," "Underground Notes," "A Brother Betrayed," "Black Man's Burden"— indicate the universality of the invisible man's struggles. The title of Brooks's reviews—"Young Girl Growing Up" and "Daydreams in Flight"—completely deny any relationship between the protagonist's personal experiences and the historical experiences of her people. Ellison himself was compared to Richard Wright, Dostoevsky, and Faulkner; Brooks, only to the unspecified "Imagists." Questions about narrative strategy, voice, and methods of characterization asked of *Invisible Man* were obviously considered irrelevant to an understanding of *Maud Martha* since they were not posed. Most critical, Ellison's work was placed in a tradition; it was repeatedly described by reviewers as an example of the "Picaresque" tradition and the pilgrim/journey tradition. *Maud Martha,* the reviewers said, "stood alone."[9] Not one of these reviewers could place *Maud Martha* in the tradition of Zora Neale Hurston's *Their Eyes Were Watching God* (1937) or Dorothy West's *The Living Is Easy* (1948), or Nella Larsen's *Quicksand* (1928). Is it because no one in 1953 could picture the questing figure, the hero with a thousand faces, the powerful, articulate voice, as a plain, dark-skinned woman living in a kitchenette building on the south side of Chicago?[10]

If Brooks's novel seems fragmentary and incomplete it is no doubt because the knowledge of one's self as a black woman was fragmented by a society that could not imagine her. With no college degrees, no social standing, lacking the militant or articulate voice, denied the supports black men could claim from black institutions, Maud Martha is the "invisible woman" of the 1950s. Shouldering the twin weights of racism and sexism, Maud showed with unsparing and brutal honesty, the self-doubt, the sense of inadequacy, the fears that black women lived with—and sometimes triumphed over. Brooks takes Maud to the edge of consciousness and out there to those edges of psychic extremity which most of us are afraid of. Maud takes the risks that allow her a rare self-awareness. "The poetry of extreme states," writes Adrienne Rich, "can allow its readers to go further in our awareness, take risks we might not have dared. It says, 'Someone has been here before.' "[11] The vulnerability Brooks allows Maud Martha as she exposes the inferiority she feels before the white world is an act of courage which necessarily precedes growth. Brooks makes us follow Maud through the subterranean passages of her life, makes us attend to her interior life: the sense of being devalued at an early age, the uncovering of rage, the disillusionment of marriage, the discovery of vitality in black traditions, and finally, that brave search for a voice to express these feelings are the real autobiographical "facts" of the life of Maud Martha.

The thirty-four vignettes that make up the novel present the life of Maud Martha from the age of seven until she is grown and married with one daughter and pregnant with a second child. Maud grows up in the urban North—on the south side of Chicago to be exact—in the 1930s and 1940s. These vignettes, ranging from one and a half to seventeen pages in length might be described as a psychological portrait of Maud. The quite unremarkable and ordinary incidents in her life are used to reveal a profound inner reality. But Maud's quiet reflections and mute reactions, while they are the rich resources of a sensitive spirit, are also inadequate responses to sexism and racism; and no one is more aware of this powerlessness than Maud: "There were these scraps of baffled hate in her, hate with no eyes, no smile and—this she especially regretted—not much voice" (p. 176).

The strange experimental style and the relentless interiority of the novel place heavy demands on the reader. There is no sustained narrative connecting events, nor is there any attempt to establish cause and effect, to supply motivation, nor to develop complex characterizations of the people in Maud's life. Brooks does not lead us by plot, conflict, and resolution to her appointed conclusions. A chapter ends and a new one begins with no connecting devices, as though Brooks stripped away all externals in order to distill the essence of Maud's interior development. Maud does not "explain her explanations"; she simply admits us into the chambers of her psyche and lets us explore and experience her anger, her vulnerability, her pride, and powerlessness, and because we are so tightly locked in with her, there is no escape into action; we must suffer with her the weight of her accumulated pain, not as observers but as fellow analysands. The meaning of Maud's life derives from the absolute fearlessness with which she confronts her own psyche. The inner reality Brooks faithfully crafts through tone, image, and gesture constantly challenges the explicit assumptions of a world outside her—a world so deeply racist and sexist that we must marvel at the sense of wholeness Maud finally achieves at the end of the novel.

Despite the powerful oppositions to her freedom, Maud Martha establishes early in life her own private metaphor for herself. In chapter one, "description of Maud Martha," she pictures herself as a dandelion, an everyday jewel, demure, common, pretty—not a thing of the heart-catching beauty like her nine-year-old sister Helen—but beautiful in her ordinariness. If she can appreciate the allurement of so common a flower, perhaps she, too, will one day be similarly cherished, and "To be cherished was the dearest wish of the heart of Maud Martha Brown." The imagery and tone of this first chapter suggest the direction of Maud's emotional and psychological growth. Even as a child, she is painfully aware of herself as a not entirely desirable object, one whose worth is there but which cannot be seen by eyes accustomed to dismissing the commonplace. She speaks of herself passively, wanting to be desired, somewhat mystified by the standards of long hair and light skin that make her one of the "lesser Blacks." She describes herself in the third person in a way that seems complicitous in her objectification. But Maud is also intended to be the detached observer whose distance and lesser status make her sensitive to the subtle insults, the violence done to simple folks, the hidden reserved meanings in the lives of the unheroic. Like them, Maud will experience violations to herself on nearly every level, and from the age of seven she is engaged in the struggle to find her real "allurements" and to see something in the lives of these ordinary people to empower her own.

From age nine to sixteen Maud is a creative, intelligent, ambitious and daring girl, participating in a wide spectrum of activities, always the sensitive and aware observer. It is she who understands the icy anger in her parents' marriage and her father's anguish when he thinks they may lose their house. In fact while her mother and Helen are ready to abandon the old house for a modern new apartment, Maud identifies with her father's love of the old. Though the chairs cry when sat on and the tables make grieving sounds, this house contains her whole seventeen-year-old history. Her family must preserve the simple, unobtrusive, hidden meanings of the house: "the talking softly on this porch," "the emphatic iron of the fence," "those shafts and pools of light, the tree, the graceful iron." The house, she understands, is like her.

But what do qualities like courage and loyalty and intelligence matter when a girl reaches the age of seventeen? In the chapter called "Helen," when Maud is seventeen and working and is the "mistress of her fate," the momentum of her life gradually lessens and the panorama constricts as Maud begins to see her life in the claustrophobic ways women have been taught—by the lens of a male world. In this chapter, when she has almost reached womanhood, she thinks back to an incident that occurred when she was eleven. She was being daring, calling out to a boy riding by in his wagon, "'Hi handsome,'" while he scowls back, "'I don't mean you, you old black gal,'" instantly reminding her of her status in his eyes, as he proffers the ride to her sister, Helen. In the inevitable comparisons between Maud and the sleek Helen it does not matter that Maud once saved her brother from five boys armed with bats and rocks, or that she stood by her father in his desperate attempts to save their house, she is still the unlovely one, the "daughter of the dusk," not the sun-lit lode of cream-yellow shining.[12] Boys hold doors open for the dainty Helen; they slam them calmly in the face of Maud Martha. To Maud's great credit she is not only mystified by but disdainful of their failure to see that she is smarter than Helen, that she reads more, that old folks like to talk to her, that she washes as much as Helen and has longer and thicker (if nappier) hair. But after the age of seventeen until she has her first child (the next ten chapters of the novel) her own self-perception is dismissed so that she can abandon herself to that obligatory quest for a man. When she is finally chosen by one of "them," or, in her words, when she "hooks" Paul, her language and attitude shift so that she now sees herself entirely through Paul's eyes. In the chapter called "low yellow," Maud engages in a grotesque act of double consciousness in which she fantasizes Paul's negative view of her, insisting on her own inferiority:

He wonders as we walk in the street, about the thoughts of the people who look at us. Are they thinking that he could do no better than—me? Then he thinks, Well, hmp! All the little good-lookin' dolls that have wanted *him*—all the little sweet high yellows that have ambled slowly past *his* front door—What he would like to tell those secretly snickering ones!— That any day out of the week he can do better than this black gal. [p. 53]

Calling herself "a black gal," Maud echoes the insult of the little boy Emmanuel, indicating that she is stuck with that eleven-year-old perception of herself.

Rewarded for her pains with marriage, Maud settles down to "being wife to *him,* salving him, in every way considering and replenishing him." In the chapter "the young couple at home," we begin to see how in myriad subtle ways it is Maud who's been "hooked," who feels hemmed in, cramped, and unexpressed in this marriage. The couple attends a musicale and afterward Paul clowns while she hopes for some interesting conversation about the event. They retire, each with a book for nighttime reading; he's reading *Sex in the Married Life* and she, *Of Human Bondage.* He is ready for sex and she for the more ethereal world of the novel and for more conversation over cocoa and toasted sandwiches. Her lack of voice and indirection become more apparent and more troublesome, for now, as a grown woman confined to a small kitchenette apartment and to being Mrs. Paul Phillips, Maud's life is even more constricted than it was at seventeen. Paul advises her, as though she were a child, to study the ideas in *Sex in the Married Life:* " 'I want you to read this book,' he said—'but at the right time: one chapter each night before retiring.' " Then he pinches her on the buttock, an overture she considers quite unpleasant at this point but to which she replies "pleasantly": " 'Shall I make some cocoa? . . . And toast some sandwiches?' " She continues to be oblique, to remain in her own thoughts instead of confronting Paul with what she wants. Self-effacement and concealment become the hallmarks of Maud's behavior toward her husband. Though she too is disappointed in their life together, her feelings are always expressed evasively. At times she even denies her own disappointment in their marriage, and once, in a classic example of self-abnegation, she worries that *he* is tired of *her:*

She knew that he was tired of his wife, tired of his living quarters, tired of working at Sam's, tired of his two suits. . . . He had no money, no car, no clothes, and he had not been put up for membership in the Foxy Cats Club. . . . He was not on show. . . . Something should happen. . . . She knew that he believed he had been born to invade, to occur, to confront, to inspire the flapping of flags, to panic people. [p. 147]

All this muted rage, this determination to achieve housewifely eminence, this noble desire to be like the women of pioneer times—toiling interminably to sustain their men (the feminine mystique of the 1950s)—masks so much of Maud's real feelings that we are compelled to consider what is missing in *Maud Martha.* Are there places in the novel where the real meaning of the character's quest is disquised, " 'hollows, centers, caverns within the work—places where activity that one might expect is missing . . . or deceptively coded.' "[13]

Something *is* missing in *Maud Martha,* something we have the right to expect in Maud's life because Maud herself expects it. She has already—in the first chapters—begun to chafe at this domestic role, and yet Brooks presents no aspiration for Maud beyond the domestic sphere. When Maud asks in the last chapter " 'What, *what,* am I to do with all this life?' " she expresses the same sense of perplexity her readers have been feeling throughout the novel. How is this extraordinary woman going to express herself? She claims not to want to be a star because she once saw a singer named Howie Joe Jones parade himself before an audience foolishly "exhibiting his precious private identity" for a thousand eyes; she vows that she will never be like that: "she was going to keep herself to herself." Creativity, she says, is not for her. But even the fact that she has considered and dismissed the possibility is revealing:

To create—a role, a poem, picture, music, a rapture in stone: great. But not for her.
  What she wanted was to donate to the world a good Maud Martha. That was the offering, the bit of art, that could not come from any other. She would polish and hone that. [p. 22]

Everywhere in the novel, however, Maud's artistic intentions are unintentionally revealed. She sees things in color and texture; she thinks of the complexity of beauty. But she questions this bent in herself as though some imaginary force had expressed disapproval of her plans: "What she wanted to dream, and dreamed, was her affair. It pleased her to dwell upon color and soft bready textures and light, on a complex beauty, on gem-like surfaces. *What was the matter with that?*" (italics mine, p. 51). Using the language of the artist, Maud surrenders her claim to be an artist, and yet the language betrays her. She is too involved in the description of the process to be uninvolved. And how is one to make an artwork of oneself except by utilizing one's gifts? Maud's gifts are words, insight, imagination. She has the artist's eye, the writer's memory, that unsparing honesty of experience which does not put a light gauze across little miseries and monotonies but exposes them, leaving the audience as ungauzed as the creator.

I wonder why Brooks in her "autobiographical novel," did not allow Maud the same kind of control over her life and her creative expression that she herself had as a writer.[14] After all, Brooks was her own model of a black woman artist in the 1950s. In her autobiography, *Report From Part One,* she describes the exuberance she felt as she waited for books she would review to arrive in the mail, the "sassy brass" that enabled her to chide Richard Wright for his clumsy prose, and her eager sense of taking on the responsibility of a writer. Brooks's description of seeing her first book in print is shot through with the wonder and pride of authorship: "Finally there came the little Harper-stamped package: ten 'author's copies' of *A Street In Bronzeville.* I took out the first copy. I turned the pages of the thin little thing, over and over. My Book."[15] During the forties, Brooks thrived as an artist in a rich and fascinating circle of writers, painters, dancers, actresses, and photographers that was active in Chicago. But Maud, who *craves* something "elaborate, immutable, and sacred," who wants to express herself in "shimmering form," "warm, but hard as stone and as difficult to break" (aren't these the compulsions of the artist?) is never allowed to fulfill these cravings.

Novelist Paule Marshall told me that she thinks women writers often make their first woman protagonist a homebody as if to expiate for their own "deviance" in succeeding out there in the world of men.

There is, she says, some need to satisfy the domestic role, and so they let their characters live it. *Maud Martha* ends in pregnancy and not a poem even though Maud is still hungry for more life and more of a "voice," for form, for something constant and immutable.

In one way the pregnancy becomes a form of rebellion against the feminine mystique because once Maud has a daughter she begins to free herself from the dominance of both her mother and her husband. She screams at Paul in the midst of her labor pains, "DON'T YOU GO OUT OF HERE AND LEAVE ME ALONE! Damn! Damn!" When her mother, who is prone to faint over blood, comes in the door, Maud sets her straight about who's important in this drama: " 'Listen, if you're going to make a fuss, go on out. I'm having enough trouble without you making a fuss over everything.' " In that one vital moment of pulling life out of herself, Maud experiences her own birth and she hears in the cries of her daughter Paulette something of her own voice: "a bright delight had flooded through her upon first hearing that part of Maud Martha Brown Phillips expressing herself *with a voice of its own*" (italics mine, p. 99). Shortly after the birth of her child, Maud speaks aloud the longest set of consecutive sentences she has uttered in the entire novel. For a woman who has hardly said more than a dozen words at one time, this is quite a speech:

"Hello, Mrs. Barksdale!" she hailed. "Did you hear the news? I just had a baby, and I feel strong enough to go out and shovel coal! Having a baby is *nothing,* Mrs. Barksdale. Nothing at all." [p. 82]

However powerful the reproductive act is, it is not the same as the creative process; a child is a separate, independent, individualized human being, not a sample of one's creative work.[16] Without work, Maud's life remains painfully ambiguous. Brooks must have felt this ambiguity in Maud's life, for when she imagined a sequel to *Maud Martha,* she immediately secured some important work for Maud and dispensed with the role of housewife. In a 1975 interview by Gloria Hull and Posey Gallagher, Brooks was asked to bring *Maud Martha* up to the present day. With obvious relish, Brooks eliminates Maud's husband:

Well, she has that child, and she has another child and then her husband dies in the bus fire that happened in Chicago in the fifties. One of those flammable trucks with a load of oil ran into a street car and about thirty-six people burned right out on Sixty-third and State Streets. *So I put her husband in that fire.* [italics mine] Wasn't that nice of me? I had taken him as far as I could. He certainly wasn't going to change. I could see that.[17]

Brooks insists that Maud has some feelings of regret at the loss of her husband, but on the way back from the funeral Maud is "thinking passionately about the cake that's going to be at the wake and how good it's going to be." Having safely put Paul in the ground, Brooks proceeds to explain how Maud Martha will get on with her own adventures. She will be chosen as a guide to accompany some children on a trip to Africa, and she will use her slender resources to help these children. She will live her life with herself at the center of it, not on the periphery of someone else's. With a different political vocabulary available in the 1970s Brooks comes close to allowing Maud to take on that weight and power she has been pressing toward for so long.

Brooks's tone as she describes the sequel to *Maud Martha*—so freewheeling, humorous, self-assured, a little rough—reveals the uncertainties and the tensions of the 1953 version. Maud needs a language that is powerful enough to confront the abuses of her life—a usable language she can fight back with, something "decently wild." Maud has a politie, precious, and prim little rhetoric that is no match for the uncouth realities of her life as a poor black woman. Rhetoric and setting seem to be at odds with each other just as they are in Brooks's 1949 poem "The Anniad," in which she tries to tell the tragic love story of a poor black woman named Annie Allen using the language of the tradition of courtly love. There is something powerful about yoking together the diction of chivalric, religious, and classical traditions and the life of a woman born into a world of "old peach cans and old jelly jars," but the power of the poem derives from the poet's ironic perspective. Maud's life is told in her own words and thoughts and so the poet's perspective is not available. Maud needs to use the vernacular.[18]

When Maud and Paul are invited to the Foxy Cats Club where sophisticated behavior and good looks are required for acceptance, she thinks about how she will handle the occasion to forestall her old feelings of inferiority. She prepares for the event in language that we know will defeat her:

"I'll settle," decided Maud Martha, "on a plain white princess-style thing and some blue and black satin ribbon. I'll go to my mother's. I'll work miracles at the sewing machine.

"On that night, I'll wave my hair. I'll smell faintly of lily of the valley." [p. 95]

These designs do not work at all. At the Club Paul goes off with the beautiful, "white-looking," curvy Maella, leaving Maud on a bench by the wall. Maud considers the language and behavior she thinks might be adequate for handling this interloper who is a threat to her peace of mind: "I could . . . go over there and scratch her upsweep down. I could spit on her back. I could scream. 'Listen,' I could scream, 'I'm making a baby for this man and I mean to do it in peace'" (p. 88). Instead of this quite strong, brassy assertiveness, Maud chooses to say nothing. The scraps of rage and baffled hate accumulate while she resists the words of power as though she has subjected her language to the same perverted standards by which she judges her physical beauty. In one of the early chapters she describes the "graceful" life as one where people glide over floors in softly glowing rooms, smile correctly over trays of silver, cinnamon, and cream, and retire in quiet elegance. By comparison the world she lives in is ugly, loud, smelly, crowded, and gray; and far from caressing her, it batters her around until she retreats into her imagination for refuge, refusing to speak in it because it does not match the world of her fantasies.

Toward the end of the novel Maud moves away from the domestic sphere, out of her little kitchenette apartment into a larger social and political world where husband and marriage no longer figure importantly. When she leaves the house, Maud Martha is subjected to subtle yet nonetheless brutal kinds of racism. Once she comprehends the extent of that abuse, she assumes a control over her experiences that leads her closer to real autonomy.

There are four important racial encounters leading up to Maud's self-affirmation. The first of these, entitled "the self-solace," occurs in that specifically female ritual place—a "beauty" shop where Maud hears a pushy, white saleswoman, selling "colored" brands of cosmetics, say that she works like a "nigger" to make the few pennies she earns. Maud pretends she is not sure she has heard the word "nigger," but she is sufficiently disturbed to close the *Vogue* magazine she is reading (reading *Vogue* could certainly separate a black woman from her own cultural vocabulary) and imagines how genteelly she would handle the woman if she had indeed said that word:

"I wouldn't curse. I wouldn't holler. I'll bet Mrs. Johnson would do both those things. And I could understand her wanting to all right. I would be gentle in a cold way. I would give her, not a return insult—directly, at any rate!—but information. I would get it across to her that ——" Maud Martha stretched. "But I wouldn't insult her." [pp. 139–40]

Both Maud and the hairdresser, Sonia Johnson, refuse to sully themselves by getting all hot and bothered over this offense. They are determined not to act like loud, uncouth women, not to behave like the word "nigger" implies black people do behave, and in their effort to keep back all their honest responses, to maintain the gracious pose, they deny their own strength. Yet even this rehearsal of what she *might* say shows some growth for Maud, for she has at least admitted the possibility of an insult and is preparing to deal with the anxiety.

In the millinery shop another condescending white saleswoman tries to manipulate Maud into buying a hat. Maud senses the woman's condescension and veiled disdain and walks toward the door. Quite desperate for this sale, the woman lowers the price, appealing "chummily" to Maud to take the hat, but with no further explanation, Maud says she does not want the hat and walks out. This time Maud asserts herself; she says aloud in a firm, direct, declarative statement: " 'I've decided against the hat,' " and she feels victorious enough to close the door with tenderness. But Maud has sniffed this woman's weaknesses—the woman needs this sale badly—and so the victory seems small and a little paltry.

The third racial encounter is in the suburban home of Mrs. Burns-Cooper where Maud goes to work as a domestic when her husband is laid off from his job. With no food at home, Maud takes the job (one of the few open to non-professional black women in the forties) out of desperation. In one day she is subjected to the civilized abuse of this thirty-four-year-old white housewife. She is told to use the back entrance, is gently admonished like a child, and is forced to listen to the woman rattle on about her life—her college days, her debut, her travels, her relatives—without the least acknowledgment of Maud's own small triumphs: "Shall I mention, considered Maud Martha . . . my own education, my travels to Gary and Milwaukee and Columbus, Ohio? Shall I mention my collection of fancy pink satin bras? She decided against it. She went on listening, in silence" (p. 161).

Though she says nothing to Mrs. Burns-Cooper, Maud's reaction in this chapter shows an important change. For the first time she identifies with Paul's daily humiliations from a dominating white boss, with the supercilious treatment he suffers from whites who think of black men and women as children. Maud decides to protest by leaving this job she so badly needs without any explanation to this woman. Her final words, not spoken aloud unfortunately, are neither retaliatory nor angry. In a moment of insight, Maud is slightly astonished by the utter simplicity of the discovery that she is, after all, a human being. Maud says to herself the words she intends to buttress her decision to walk out on Mrs. Burns-Cooper: "Why one was a human being. One wore clean nightgowns. One loved one's baby. One drank cocoa by the fire—or the gas range—come the evening, in the wintertime" (p. 163). Maud is still thinking in terms that must ultimately defeat her. The clean nightgowns, the fancy pink satin bras, and the cocoa drinking by the fireplace (or the gas range) as definitions of humanity suggest that she is still measuring her life by the superficial social standards of Mrs. Burns-Cooper's world. The tone is cold and ironic and perhaps even contemptuous, but Maud's efforts to maintain this air of icy gentility and aloofness only camouflage her real feelings. Her attempts at irony are another form of concealment.

In her reticence to confront these feelings of powerlessness and anger, Maud says fewer than fifty words aloud to white people, and yet when she finally does speak it is in a place where she must have felt more powerless than in any other place in her life. In the 1940s, a downtown department store where black women were generally only allowed to work as "stock girls" or in the kitchens of the cafeterias was fundamentally alien territory, but yet it is on these hostile grounds that Maud asserts herself. Furthermore, she articulates the meaning of the rage she has denied throughout the novel—even to herself. Perhaps the most important thing about this scene is that Maud does not speak in her own behalf but for her little girl, Paulette. Making the traditional Christmas visit to see Santa Claus with Paulette, Maud notices that Santa is merry and affectionate with the white children, but with Paulette he is distant and unresponsive, looking vaguely away from her as though she were not there. As Maud sees her own child learning the lessons of inferiority and invisibility, she breaks her silence of nearly thirty years, speaking in a clear and uncompromising statement that demands a response: " 'Mister,' said Maud Martha, 'my little girl is talking to you' " (p. 173). She forces this Santa Claus to recognize Paulette, to at least make the gestures of acceptance and concern, though Paulette, unconvinced, wants to know why Santa did not like her.

Inwardly Maud still suffers a tremendous sense of anger and impotence; she yearns to "jerk trimming scissors from her purse and jab jab jab that evading eye." She cannot resolve these feelings but she admits them, she recognizes these scraps of baffled hate, hate with no eyes, no smile. She regrets her lack of voice because she thinks if she had that voice she could let out the fires that burn and damage her from within. But she has spoken, she has summoned her anger in order to protect her child from the soul-damaging effects of racist insensitivity and stupidity.

The longest speech Maud Martha makes in the novel is her attempt to explain to Paulette that she is as much loved by Santa as any other child—as any white child. She wants to keep for her child "that land of blue," "those fairies, with witches killed at the end, and Santa every winter's lord." If the task of the analyst is to "convert repeating into remembering," to make the subject aware of traumatic memories in the effort to heal, then Maud's self-analysis is successful. She has broken that destructive cycle of mute rage and impotence that made her unable to speak. This gentle spirit raises her voice to protect her child.

These four encounters take us to the end of the novel, to a final chapter, "back from the wars," which refers to Maud's brother Harry returning from World War II and Maud's return from the wars she has been waging. In my initial reaction to this chapter I was quite critical of Brooks for allowing so vital a person as Maud to be left in a passive stance. There she is, poised on the edge of self-creation, and at the moment we expect the "illumination of her gold," she announces that she is pregnant again—and happy. But I think this critical disappointment ignores the novel's insistence that we read Maud's life in tone, in images, in gestures. Almost, we might say, in whispers. As she is raising the shade in her bedroom to look out at the dawning sunshine, she actually does whisper, "What, *what*, am I to do with all this life?" Brooks then reintroduces the raised arm image of the first chapter when Maud at seven longed to fling her arms rapturously up to the sky. In the last chapter the raised arms are like "wings cutting away all the higher layers of air." There is the suggestion of flight, her arms directing her up out of a dark valley. The movement of the arms in this instance is purposeful and powerful. With her daughter in tow Maud steps outside into the sun, feeling a sharp exhilaration and no need of "information, or solace or a guidebook or a sermon." In sharp contrast to the child whose dearest wish was "to be cherished" as a yellow-jeweled, demurely pretty dandelion, this Maud thinks of the common flower as an image of survival and self-possession: "for would its kind [like her] come up again in the spring? come, up, if necessary, among, between, or out of—the smashed corpses lying in strict composures, in that hush infallible and sincere" (p. 178).

In this last chapter Maud is out of doors on a glorious day, out of all the spaces that have enclosed her—the bedrooms, the kitchens, the male clubs, the doctors' offices, the movie theaters, the white women's houses, the dress shops, the beauty parlors. She is out of the psychic confines that made her preoccupied with her "allurements" and presumed deficiencies. Freed from this destructive self-involvement Maud thinks of the people around her, of the gloriousness and bravery in their ability to continue life "through divorce, through evictions and jiltings and taxes." There are no meadows here, only the reality of city streets, of lynchings in Mississippi and Georgia, and the grim reminder of death as the soldiers back from war, with arms, legs, and parts of faces missing, march by. Maud says she is ready for anything, and so this catalog of evils (include in that list the Negro press's preoccupation with pale and pompadoured beauties) has to be seen as Maud's growing sense of involvement with the social and political problems of her world. Even Maud's pregnancy, an inner event, not even noticeable at this point, can be seen as a powerful way-of-being in the world. For, in the midst of destruction and death, she, with the same basic equanimity of that common flower, will bring forth life.

And yet in spite of all the victorious imagery in this last chapter, there is still a sense of incompleteness about Maud's quest, some exploration not undertaken, some stoppage of the blood. Part of the problem is the privateness of Maud's story. Her constant self-analysis and self-involvement emphasize her solitariness instead of communal bonds.[19] She is alienated from the two important women in her life— her fussy, domineering mother and her vain sister. She has no women friends. In most of the events of her life, Maud is alone, and though she succeeds through heroic individual effort in rejecting society's definitions of her, she is still unable to express the full meaning of her growth. Hurston's Janie has the important advantage of telling her story to an eager, loving listener—her friend Pheoby whose life is changed by hearing her friend's life story. I am not insisting on radical changes in Maud's story. I only wish there were some way for her to know that someone in the community had grown ten feet higher from listening to it.

MARTA PEIXOTO

Family Ties: Female Development

in Clarice Lispector

Since the publication of her first novel *Perto do Coração Selvagem*
(Close to the Savage Heart) in 1944, when she was only nineteen
years old, Lispector has been recognized as one of the small number
of true innovators in Brazilian modernism, the only woman to attain
a place within that canon.[1] Critics agree that her distinctive contribu-
tion lies in her original, often strange language, dense with paradoxes,
unusual metaphors, and abstract formulations that at times elude the
rational intelligence. João Guimarães Rosa, an acknowledged master
of twentieth-century Brazilian fiction and a Joycean innovator in language himself, told an interviewer that "every time he read one of her
novels he learned many new words and rediscovered new uses for the
ones he already knew."[2] As a woman writer, Lispector did not have
the benefit of a tradition in Brazil of important female authors. One
could say that Lispector, along with her older and far less innovative
contemporary, the poet Cecília Meireles (1901–1964), are the founding members of that tradition, writers whom all younger women writers somehow take into account. Although Lispector mentions her early
discovery of Katherine Mansfield and several critics have found in her
fiction a kinship to Virginia Woolf's, Lispector preferred to think of
herself as a writer unmodified by the adjective "female."[3] Yet her numerous female protagonists testify to her fascination with the experience of women and the shape of female lives.

In Lispector's eight novels, seven of the protagonists are female, as
are most of the main characters in her five collections of short stories.
Yet criticism on her work has neglected to inquire into the specifically
female dimension of her characters. Lispector's critics, frequently concerned with tracing the affinities between the philosophical ideas present in her fiction and those of Heidegger, Kierkegaard, Camus, and
Sartre, discuss repeatedly "man's" nature and existence, and "his"
plight in a world doomed to absurdity. Other critics have analyzed her

style: her use of the epiphany, internal monologue, and certain rhetorical devices. Beyond an occasional reference to her "feminine sensibility," no mention is made of the fact that the author is a woman and her fictive world preponderantly female. Those critics' blindness to the male/female opposition in her work leads to a blurring of meaningful differences. One critic, for instance, in an otherwise valuable analysis of her short stories, discusses *father* as an important recurring motif, adding that "many times it is referred to as *father,* at others as *mother.*"[4] Even if *father/mother* in Lispector's fiction stood for an identical role, *mother* would still be the most frequent term of the pair. Revisionist readings of Lispector, which include Hélène Cixous's enthusiastic presentation of the Brazilian author as a practitioner of "écriture féminine," have begun to appear in France and in the United States.[5] Further critical readings from a feminist perspective will no doubt enrich Lispector's work with the discovery of previously unrecognized dimensions.

Family Ties (*Laços de Família,* 1960), Lispector's most studied and anthologized collection of short stories and the only one available in English, offers a good starting point for investigating symbolic functions assigned to women in her fiction and for examining her models of female development. Appearing at the beginning of her third and perhaps most fertile decade of publication (Lispector died in 1977), *Family Ties* contains well-made stories, less idiosyncratic and difficult than most of her later work. In addition to the accessibility of these stories, it is perhaps its critical evaluation of family relationships and female life from youth to old age that has gained for this collection its readership.

In only three of the thirteen stories of *Family Ties* are the central characters male. The female protagonists, middle-class women in an urban setting, range in age from fifteen to eighty-nine. The stories in which they appear can be read as versions of a single developmental tale that provides patterns of female possibilities, vulnerability, and power in Lispector's world. The author assigns traditional female roles to her protagonists: adolescents confronting the fantasy or reality of sex, mature women relating to men and children, and a great-grandmother presiding over her birthday party. Through the plots of the stories and the inner conflicts of the heroines, Lispector challenges conventional roles, showing that the allegiances to others those roles demand lead to a loss of selfhood. The protagonists' efforts toward recuperating the self emerge as dissatisfaction, rage, or even madness. The stories present the dark side of family ties, where bonds of affection become cages and prison bars.

All the stories in the collection turn on an epiphany, a moment of crucial self-awareness.[6] In the midst of trivial events, or in response to a chance encounter, Lispector's characters suddenly become conscious of repressed desires or unsuspected dimensions of their psyches. These women experience the reverse of their accepted selves and social roles as mother, daughter, wife, as gentle pardoning, giving females. In their moments of changed awareness, they may realize not only their imprisonment but also their own function as jailers of women and men. Their epiphanies, mysterious and transgressive, bring to consciousness repressed material with potentially subversive power. The negative terms which often describe these moments—"crisis," "nausea," "hell," "murder," "anger," "crime,"—convey the guilt and fear that accompany the questioning of conventional roles.[7] Internal monologues shaped by antithesis, paradox, and hyperbole display a wealth of opposing moral and emotional forces. After these characters' crises, when by recognizing their restrictions they glimpse the possibility of a freer self, they more or less ambiguously pull back, returning to a confinement they can't or won't change. The intensity of their conflicts may be enlightening for the reader, but the protagonists return to their previous situations after questioning them for only a moment.

Of the three tales of adolescent initiation in *Family Ties,* two have women protagonists. It is instructive to compare the male and female patterns. In "The Beginnings of a Fortune," a young boy suddenly fascinated with money grasps its connection with power and its usefulness in attracting girls. Yet he also sees the vulnerability to the greed of others that the possession of "a fortune" would entail. "Preciousness" and "Mystery in São Cristovão" have parallel plots on a symbolic level. Both hinge on the intrusion by several young men into a young woman's private domain. In "Preciousness," the protagonist on her way to school undergoes a violent sexual initiation when two young men, strangers passing by, reach out and briefly touch her body. She accepts and turns to advantage this negative experience, darkly intuiting it as a lesson about her fragile individuality in a world of powerful men. Unlike the young boy, who realizes that acquiring his fortune requires purposeful activity, the young girl feels within herself "something precious." Something which "did not compromise itself, nor contaminate itself. Which was intense like a jewel. Herself" (p. 102).[8] But she is "precious" also in her new status as a coveted object, able to arouse men's lust. And this second kind of preciousness undercuts, compromises, contaminates her preciousness to herself. Immediately after the attack she retreats into a profound passivity:

Until this moment she had kept quiet, standing in the middle of the sidewalk. Then, as if there were several phases of this same immobility, she remained still. . . . She then slowly retreated back toward a wall, hunched up, moving very slowly as if she had a broken arm, until she was leaning against the wall, where she remained inscribed. And there she remained quite still. [p. 111]

As a lesson drawn from this incident, she keeps repeating to herself that she is all alone in the world. Sex and its concomitants, intrusion and violence, lead her to isolation instead of relationship. Yet she also learns the necessity of protecting herself. She confronts her parents with a request for new shoes: "Mine make a lot of noise, a woman can't walk on wooden heels, it attracts too much attention! No one gives me anything! No one gives me anything!" (p. 113). She demands to be given things, possessions to compensate for her deeper dispossession, for her broken confidence in herself and in her relationship to others. And her assertiveness in demanding new shoes serves, paradoxically, her need for self-effacement, for camouflage, as a way of protecting herself.

"Mystery in São Cristovão" reworks in parable form a similar version of female sexual initiation. At the epiphanic moment, three young men on their way to a party, dressed up as Rooster, Bull, and Devil, trespass to steal hyacinths in "the forbidden ground of the garden" (p. 135) at a young girl's house, as she looks on from her window. The moment when the four participants stare at each other seems to touch "deep recesses" (p. 136) in all of them. The young men guiltily slip away leaving behind a "hyacinth—still alive but with its stalk broken" (p. 138); the young girl screams, waking up her family. Like the protagonist of "Preciousness," she too becomes passive and cannot explain anything beyond her scream. She suddenly seems to age: "to the horror of her family, a white strand had appeared among the hairs of her forehead" (p. 137).

The male and female initiation tales offer, then, a number of contrasts: activity versus passivity; a young boy who seeks wealth and power versus young girls who are "precious" themselves, metaphorically identified with jewels and flowers; preoccupation with acquisition versus concern with self-protection; entrance into the world of economic and social exchange versus retreat in fear into oneself. Development, for the young girls, clearly will not proceed according to the male model.

It is in a context of attachment and affiliation with others that the women characters develop.[9] After initiation into the vulnerability to which their female sexuality exposes them, they find protection and a measure of satisfaction in family ties. We see in other stories several of Lispector's women safely ensconced in a domestic life. The stories reflect the matrifocal organization of Brazilian society where the extended family still prevails, so much so that the word *família* usually refers not only to the small nuclear family but to a numerous network of relatives. The title story shows most clearly the ambivalent function of the family in the whole collection. In "Family Ties," the power a woman wields within the family has a negative, constricting side: deprived of the chance to develop herself beyond the scope of the family, she attempts to control those close to her.

"Family Ties" opens as Catherine says goodby to her elderly mother at the train station, feeling an awkward tenderness and relief. With this scene between the two women, as well as with flashbacks and the narration of the emotional consequences of the mother's visit, the story touches on several types of family relationships: mother-daughter, mother-in-law-son-in-law, grandmother-grandson, husband-wife, and mother-son, all presented as subtle or not so subtle struggles for power. Catherine's memories of childhood include a friendly alliance with her father against her mother's domestic rule: "When her mother used to fill their plates, forcing them to eat too much, the two of them used to wink at each other in complicity without her mother even noticing" (p. 116–17). As she looks at her mother through the train window,

Catherine becomes aware of the strong though ambivalent bonds they share:

"No one else can love you except me," thought the woman, smiling with her eyes, and the weight of this responsibility put the taste of blood in her mouth. As if "mother and daughter" meant life and repugnance. [p. 117]

Relieved of her mother's company, the daughter recovered "her steady manner of walking—alone, it was much easier" (p. 119). But that tie to her mother also facilitates in her an emotional availability: "she seemed ready to take advantage of the largesse of the whole world—a path her mother had opened and that was burning in her breast" (p. 120). This very openness to others leads Catherine, it seems, to attempt to bind her son to her in the same way she was bound to her mother. The last third or so of the story is told from the point of view of the husband who feels left out and jealous as he watches Catherine and their small son from a window, perceiving an intense interaction between them:

At what moment is it that a mother, hugging her child, gave him this prison of love that would descend forever upon the future man. Later, her child, already a man, alone, would stand before this same window, drumming his fingers on the windowpane: imprisoned. . . . Who would ever know at what moment the mother transferred her inheritance to her child. And with what dark pleasure. [p. 122]

Here, the metaphorical prison entraps all members of the family: the father, who also speaks about his own predicament, sees the male as victim of the imprisoned and imprisoning female, the mother, who transmits this family tie to the next generation. The male power, deriving from his role in the world outside the home, does not prevail in the domestic world of intimate relationships, where his wife has a power at least equal to his own:

This is what he had given her. The apartment of an engineer. And he knew that if his wife took advantage of his situation as a young husband with a promising future, she also looked down on the situation, with those sly eyes, running off with her thin, nervous child. The man became uneasy. Because he could only go on giving her more success. And because he knew that she would help him to achieve it and would hate whatever they achieved. [p. 122]

He takes revenge for her disdain by subjecting her to small humiliations: "he had gotten used to making her feminine in this way" (p. 123). Despite these dissatisfactions, it seems clear that at least the husband wishes to preserve the status quo: "When Catherine returned they would have dinner, shooing away the moths. . . . 'After dinner we'll go to the movies,' the man decided. Because after the movies it would be night at last, and this day would break up like the waves on the rocks of Arpoador" (p. 124). For the husband, then, the events of the day, like waves breaking on the rocks, seem to be minor, if recurrent, crises within the sustaining institution of the family.

The family as context for female development in Lispector's stories is, then, both positive and negative. It allows women the satisfaction of affirming ties to others but confines them to the subordinate role of ministering to other's needs, depriving them of themselves. The narrator of "Love" measures the rewards of a domestic life for the protagonist Anna, and hints at her sacrifices:

Through indirect paths, she had happened upon a woman's destiny, with the surprise of fitting into it as if she had invented that destiny herself. The man whom she had married was a real man, the children she mothered were real children. Her previous youth now seemed strange, like an illness of life. She had gradually emerged to discover that one could also live without happiness: by abolishing it she had found a legion of persons, previously invisible to her, who lived their lives as if they were working—with persistence, continuity, and cheerfulness. [p. 38]

From perspectives similar to this one, several protagonists face their crises. Women devoted to love, marriage, and children discover within themselves allegiances subversive to those roles. These stories follow the generic model that Susan J. Rosowski proposes in her article "The Novel of Awakening." Lispector's characters also attempt to find value "in a world that expects a woman to define herself by love, marriage, and motherhood."[10] For each protagonist, "an inner imaginative sense of personal value conflicts with her public role: an awakening occurs when she confronts the disparity between her two lives."[11] Lispector's protagonists also follow Rosowski's model in awakening to conflict and limitations.[12] Their social world and even their own selves cannot accommodate new allegiances. They discover that their loyalty to others excluded possibilities for themselves. As Lispector puts it in a story from another collection, "To be loyal is not a clean thing. To be loyal is to be disloyal to everything else."[13] Four stories from *Family Ties*— "Love," "The Imitation of the Rose," "The Buffalo," and "Happy Birthday"—are Lispector's versions of this kind of awakening.

In "Love," plant imagery conveys Anna's everyday awareness of herself in her thriving domesticity: "Like a farmer. She had planted the seeds she held in her hand, no others, but only those. And they were growing into trees" (p. 38). Although "at a certain hour of the afternoon the trees she had planted laughed at her" (p. 38), Anna feels steady in her chosen course. A casual encounter upsets her equilibrium. From a tram, she sees a blind man standing on the street, calmly chewing gum. His mechanical, indifferent acceptance of his fate perhaps mirrors for Anna her own blindness and restriction. The blind man is also a victim of the brutality of nature, which maims some of its creatures, a threat Anna usually forgets. When Anna continues her meditation in the botanical garden—a place that confines natural growth, making it follow a prearranged plan—a nausea analogous to Sartre's *nausée* overtakes her: "a vague feeling of revulsion which the approach of truth provoked" (p. 44). The initial tranquillity she perceives in this enclosed garden gives way to a disquieting vision of a secret activity taking place in the plants, as decay encroaches upon ripeness:

On the trees the fruits were black and sweet as honey. On the ground there lay dry fruit stones full of circumvolutions like small rotted cerebrums. The bench was stained purple with sap. . . . The rawness of the world was peaceful. The murder was deep. And death was not what one had imagined. [p. 43]

The lesson she learns in the garden unsettles Anna's sureness about her immanent family world, the seeds she had planted and which grow into trees. At home, guilt-ridden for her transgressive thoughts, Anna feels both threatened and dangerous: "the slightest movement on her part and she would trample one of her children" (p. 47). In her final considerations about the afternoon, Anna sees the blind man "hanging among the fruits in the botanical garden" (p. 47). The blind man as Anna's double provides a frightening vision of her own destiny: death among the rotting fruit as the consequence of her stunted capacity for transcendence and of the lack of personal freedom in the life she has chosen. Yet after a reassuringly ordinary evening at home, Anna seems content to forget her disturbing afternoon: "Before getting into bed, as if she were snuffing a candle, she blew out the day's small flame" (p. 48). Anna puts out the light of her confused enlightenment, a flame that could threaten her domestic life if it were allowed to burn.

"The Imitation of the Rose" contains a similar configuration of opposing forces: a familiar, domestic world threatened and undercut by the laws of another realm. For Laura, who has just returned from a mental hospital, images of light represent her powerful attraction to madness, suggesting that in madness she finds insights otherwise unavailable to her. Laura's dutiful relief at being "well" again, her drab descriptions of herself and her activities, contrast with her luminous, lively account of her mad self. Sleepiness, fatigue, obsession with method, cleanliness, and detail, a certain slowness of body and mind, boring to others as to herself—all signal that Laura is "well." An alert lack of fatigue, clarity of mind, a sense of independence, of possessing extraordinary powers, accompany her returning madness. In the encounter that sets off the struggle between sanity and madness, Laura admires the wild roses in her living room. The conflict between the impulse to send the roses to a friend and the desire to keep them for herself reflects Laura's life-long struggle between selflessness and self-hood. She can only satisfy herself and what she perceives as society's demands by an exaggerated rendition of the role of a giving, submissive woman. When "sane," she succeeds in keeping down any impulse toward clear self-definition. "Chestnut-haired as she obscurely felt a wife ought to be. To have black or blond hair was an exaggeration which, in her desire to make the right choice, she had never wanted" (pp. 60–61). The roses, in their beauty, exemplify a distinct, glorious selfhood that Laura denies herself: "something nice was either for giving or receiving, not only for possessing. And, above all, never for one to *be*. . . . A lovely thing lacked the gesture of giving" (p. 66). Yet as soon as Laura decides to give away the roses, her madness begins to return: "With parched lips she tried for an instant to imitate the roses inside herself. It was not even difficult" (pp. 68–69). Tranquillity, self-sufficiency, and clarity signal Laura's changed state; she sits "with the serenity of the firefly that has its light" (p. 71). The story ends with the husband's view of Laura, whom he watches with a fear and respect that only her madness can elicit: "From the open door he saw his wife sitting upright on the couch, once more alert and tranquil as if on a train. A train that had already departed" (p. 72). This final image implies that only in madness can Laura give herself permission to have an independent self. She departs in the metaphorical train of madness, since other departures are beyond her capability.

The role of woman in love limits severely the protagonist of "The Buffalo." She only senses her deficiencies when her husband or lover abandons her and she is deprived of her source of identity. She then feels mutilated, incomplete, because she cannot experience anger and hatred toward him. She visits a zoo in a conscious search:

But where, where could she find the animal that might teach her to have her own hatred? That hatred which belonged to her by right but which she could not attain in grief? . . . To imagine that perhaps she would never experience the hatred her forgiving had always been made of. [pp. 152–3]

She senses that she is the one who is caged, "a female in captivity" (p. 153), while a free animal watches her from the other side. She focuses on the buffalo in her effort to free herself from her own compulsion to be the loving and pardoning female. She looks to the buffalo, with its narrow haunches and hard muscles, as a masculine presence, the embodiment of her hatred and her strength "still imprisoned behind bars" (pp. 155–56). The buffalo seems to overwhelm her. She becomes terrified by the hatred which she projects upon the animal and which he in turn releases in her. As the encounter between the woman and the animal continues, it is couched in terms of a deadly struggle:

Innocent, curious, entering deeper and deeper into those eyes that stared at her slowly, . . . without wanting or being able to escape, she was caught in a mutual murder. Caught as if her hand were stuck forever to the dagger she herself had thrust. [p. 156]

Perhaps not ready to allow herself to hate, the woman faints in the final scene: "before her body thudded gently on the ground, the woman saw the whole sky and a buffalo" (p. 156). Fainting signals, no doubt, her failure of nerve: a traditionally feminine strategy of withdrawal, it obliterates from consciousness her involvement and insights. Yet the open spaces of the sky, ambiguous as this image becomes in conjunction with the fainting, seems to offer, in a story cluttered with cages, the possibility of release.

In "Happy Birthday," the protagonist belatedly rejects her family, implicitly questioning her own role as a prototypical matriarch. On her eighty-ninth birthday, when her power and the bonds of love have already been eroded, her family gathers to mimic the appearances of closeness. The narrative method—a mosaic of internal monologues interspersed with dialogues and the narrator's remote, at times ironic commentary—shows the resentment and hostility among members of the family and presents the protagonist from the outside as well as from the inside, what she is to others and what she is to herself. In a Kafkaesque progression reminiscent of "The Judgment," the old woman at first appears decrepit and later demonstrates a surprising, malevolent vigor. At the start, she is propped up, ready for the party:

The muscles of the old woman's face no longer betrayed any expression, so that no one could tell if she was feeling happy. There she was, stationed at the head of the table—an imposing old woman, large, gaunt, and dark. She looked hollow. [p. 75]

She remains aloof and passive until urged to cut the cake: "And unexpectedly, the old lady grabbed the knife. And without hesitation, as if by hesitating for a second she might fall on her face, she dealt the first stroke with the grip of a murderess" (p. 78). Cutting the cake rouses the old woman from passivity; she goes on to shatter her image as dignified and respected mother. The metaphoric association cutting/killing continues, linking the birthday gestures with those of a funeral: "The first cut having been made, as if the first shovel of earth had been thrown. . . ." (p. 78). As the matriarch surveys her family "with her old woman's rage" (p. 80), Lispector resorts again to the recurring images of female imprisonment and powerlessness:

She was the mother of them all. And, as her collar was choking her, she was the mother of them all, and powerless in her chair, she despised them. She looked at them, blinking. . . . How could she, who had been so strong, have given birth to those drab creatures with their limp arms and anxious faces? . . . The tree had been good. Yet it had rendered those bitter and unhappy fruits." [pp. 79–80]

Her scorn and anger mount, and the old woman spits on the floor. At a solicitous remark from a granddaughter, she curses them all and demands a glass of wine. The imagery and elements of the plot with sources in primitive and contemporary ritual—birthday party, funeral, spitting, cursing, wine—seem to assimilate the old woman's revolt into the very institutions she challenges, suggesting that her anger and its ritual-like expression can be encompassed within their framework.

The old woman rails against the loss of her power; in a sense she is a victim of old age. Her dominance stemmed from her personal capacity to play the most powerful role traditional Brazilian society allows women, that of mother in a mother-dominated extended family. Her ability to command attention is eerily revived when she cuts the cake, spits, and curses. These actions serve as a crude demonstration of the willfulness which in her prime she would have manifested in more subtle and socially sanctioned ways. Yet this old woman, like Lispector's other protagonists, is also ultimately a victim of her social role. Her power issued from a control of others that is neither healthy nor enduring. One of her sons, observing that "she had not forgotten that same steady and direct gaze with which she had always looked at her . . . children, forcing them to look away," thinks that "a mother's love was difficult to bear" (p. 85). Since she cannot rule the life of her progeny, she despises them. By showing the lovelessness and will-to-power of this mother's love, Lispector suggests that the role of matriarch affords a false power that entraps women as well as their families.

After the old woman's outburst, the narrative method shifts back to external presentation. She relapses into an enigmatic passivity, clutching the ghost of her power: "seated at the head of that messy table, with one hand clenched on the tablecloth as if holding a scepter, and with that silence which was her final word. . . ." (p. 83). Like so many of Lispector's female protagonists, she returns at the end to her initial situation. As they move from youth to old age, the protagonists of *Family Ties* also trace a circular path, beginning and ending in passivity—from the withdrawal of a frightened young girl to the abstraction of an old woman, her power over her family, repressive in itself, all spent.

Through the plots and internal monologues of her characters, Lispector questions, as we have seen, the conventional roles she assigns to her protagonists. A tendency similar to the subversion of stereotypes in characters and plot recurs on the level of language. Lispector destroys and recreates the meanings of certain ordinary words, redefining them through paradoxical formulations. In "Love," the title word acquires multiple and contradictory meanings as the protagonist attempts to align her confused yearnings with the *eros* and *caritas* she had always believed gave direction to her life. In "The Imitation of the Rose," madness takes on a positive value, signifying the expansion of Laura's independence and self-esteem—at the end of the story Laura is "serene and in full bloom" (p. 71)—without of course losing its acceptance of illness, the delusion of power. Anger in "The Buffalo" becomes the elusive object of a quest, while pardon is defined as covert hatred. A reversal of values also occurs in the imagery: the thriving plants, metaphorical analogues of Anna's domesticity, reappear on the literal level as the lush and rotting vegetation in the botanical garden; the birthday party is described in terms of a funeral; family ties appear as chains and cages. The tendency to redefine words and concepts, to reverse traditional metaphoric associations or draw images from negative and antithetical realms supports and furthers Lispector's questioning of "a woman's destiny."

Lispector's protagonists, as they shift from one set of specific circumstances to another, repeatedly find themselves in metaphoric prisons, formed by their eager compliance with confining social roles. Their potential development—the ability to integrate into their everyday selves the greater autonomy they desire in their moments of insight—again and again falters and stops short. For the youngest protagonists, the prison is their own fearful passivity in a society that accepts as normal intrusions by men such as the ones they experience. Anna's attachment to domestic routines blocks her from participating in a wider social and moral world, both frightening and exhilarating to her, the outlines of which she only obscurely intuits. For Laura, living according to others' expectations and suppressing her own desires leads to madness, an illusory escape into another prison. The woman in "The Buffalo" is caged in by her inability to recover emotions she had long repressed, and in "Happy Birthday" and "Family Ties," mother-love itself imprisons. These women start out and remain in spiritual isolation. Locked in desired yet limiting relationships to husbands and children, they find no allies in other women—mothers, friends, or daughters—who appear if at all as rivals and antagonists. Their only power lies in passing on an imprisoning motherly love to their children.

Carolyn G. Heilbrun and other feminist critics have pointed out that with few exceptions women writers have "failed to imagine autonomous characters," denying them even the autonomy they as authors have achieved, reserving for male characters their more assertive roles.[14] This holds true for Lispector in *Family Ties*. In "A Chicken," the limitations of the female role take on the sharpness of caricature. This story repeats the plot of failed escape from the confining roles of nurturing and submission. The protagonist, a chicken about to be killed for Sunday dinner, escapes her fate by setting off on a mad flight across the rooftops. Pursued and brought back by the man of the house, the flustered chicken lays an egg. The little girl who witnesses this surprising outcome persuades her mother to spare the chicken's life and adopts her as a pet. She seems to intuit a similarity between the chicken's predicament and the possibilities her own future may hold. (Another girl has the same understanding of chickens in a story from another collection which begins: "Once upon a time there was a little girl who observed chickens so closely that she knew their soul and their intimate desires.")[15] Gender determines the meaning of the chicken's adventure. During her escape the chicken is described as "stupid, timid, and free. Not victorious as a cock would be in flight" (p. 50). In her attempt to cast off the passivity expected of her and to assert her independence, the chicken echoes the central action of several other stories. Acquiring a "family tie" ends the chicken's adventure. It literally saves her life, but does not provide her with enduring dignity or even safety. Her reprieve lasts many years but not forever: "Until one day they killed her and ate her, and the years rolled on" (p. 52). Like the women she represents, the chicken's dilemma takes the form of an opposition between independence and nurturing: women may choose one role but not both and Lispector's women end up settling for the latter. After her "epiphany" the chicken returns to a timid life. Occasionally she recalls her "great escape":

Once in a while, but ever more infrequently, she again remembered how she had stood out against the sky on the roof edge ready to cry out. At such moments, she filled her lungs with the stuffy air of the kitchen and, had females been given the power to crow, she would not have crowed but would have felt much happier. [p. 52]

Ellen Moers analyzes ways in which women authors use birds "to stand in, metaphorically, for their own sex."[16] The chicken in this and other stories written later is Lispector's comically distorted image of the selfless, nurturing female incapable of sustained self-determination. The perspective implicit in this choice of metaphor includes compassion but also condescension, an attitude that carries over to Lispector's presentation of women in other stories of *Family Ties*. Most of the stories end with the female protagonist silent and described from an external vantage point, perhaps another sign of the author's desire for distance between herself and her characters. It is tempting to suppose that for her these stories may have functioned as a kind of exorcism. She presents in excruciating detail protagonists bound in "women's destinies" and measures the extent of their disadvantage. Through this repeated exercise, Lispector could perhaps free herself—and her future characters—for richer, more varied roles. Indeed, Lispector's imagination seems to require repeated incursions into the same themes. As one of her narrators puts it, "How many times will I have to live the same things in different situations."[17] Lispector allows her later female protagonists greater independence. Among them are several writers, a painter, and women engaged in spiritual quests that are not invariably cut short by their return to confining feminine roles.

Within the predominantly bleak view of female possibilities in *Family Ties*, there is a curious exception, represented by the grotesque, almost fantastic protagonist of "The Smallest Woman in the World." This story elaborates on a supposedly documentary anecdote: a bewildered explorer meets the smallest member of the smallest tribe of

African pygmies—a tiny pregnant woman, measuring a foot and a half—and names her Little Flower. Readers of the Sunday newspaper react to her story and see her life-size picture. She herself does not experience an epiphany but instead causes moments of insight in other characters. Women of all ages seem fascinated by this hyperbolic representative of the fragility and powerlessness associated with their sex. One woman fights against an involuntary identification with Little Flower: "looking into the bathroom mirror, the mother smiled, intentionally refined and polite, placing between her own face of abstract lines and the primitive face of Little Flower, the insuperable distance of millennia" (p. 92). While those considering Little Flower turn to her amazing smallness and supposed vulnerability with a greedy interest, wanting to possess the miracle and even use her as a pet, the small creature herself feels powerful and contented. Living constantly with the danger of being devoured by animals and members of other tribes, she experiences the triumph of having so far endured:

And suddenly she was smiling. . . . A smile that the uncomfortable explorer did not succeed in classifying. And she went on enjoying her own gentle smile, she who was not being devoured. Not to be devoured was the most perfect feeling. [p. 94]

Even her incipient motherhood will not lead her to confining bonds, for among the Likoualas a dubious practice prevails: "when a child is born, he is given his freedom almost at once" (p. 89). In answer to a question put to her by the explorer, Little Flower says that it is "very nice to have a tree to live in that was hers, really hers. Because—and this she did not say but her eyes became so dark that they said it for her—because it is nice to possess, so nice to possess" (p. 95).

With the story of Little Flower, Lispector creates a comic parable of a native female power, sustained against all odds. The jungle inhabitant manages to retain the tranquil independence sought eagerly by city-bred women in their civilized world of enclosed spaces, prescribed behavior, and family ties. Lispector heaps on her protagonist multiple signs of powerlessness and oppression: membership in a black African tribe reminiscent of slavery and colonialism, the female sex, minute size, and the special dependence that pregnancy entails. She places her in opposition to a white male explorer (*explorador* in

Portuguese means both "explorer" and "exploiter"). Yet the most vulnerable of women is not a victim. Unlike Laura, who cannot keep the roses, and unlike Lispector's other protagonists, who cannot hold on to and use their insights to change the forces that bind them, the smallest woman in the world, alone in her tree house, possesses herself—Lispector's wry symbol of a successful development, though not of the means to attain it.

SANDRA FRIEDEN

Shadowing / Surfacing / Shedding: Contemporary German Writers in Search of a Female *Bildungsroman*

Until recently, many fictional heroes found their options determined by the two-hundred-year-old tradition of the German *Bildungsroman:* whether the world was prosaic or "the best of all possible worlds," the task of the hero was to integrate himself and his desires into the existing (dis)order.[1] The classic course of development took the hero from his typically rural environment out into the wide world. Forced to pull away from strong familial ties, he journeyed into risks and errors—although these risks were indirectly encouraged (and often secretly supported) by the very social structures that seemed hostile to his progress. He engaged in new love relationships which in themselves functioned as steps in his education. At last he made his choice of partner and profession, indicating thereby his integration into the social structure. Society was presented either as an ideal supportive guide and framework upon which the hero could establish his life or as a less-than-ideal but necessary structure to which he had to adapt himself.

Another eighteenth-century literary tradition that developed alongside the *Bildungsroman* was that of the autobiography, an outgrowth of Pietistic confessional fervor. The religious significance attached to the recounting of the past events of one's life (namely, sins) became secularized under the moralizing didacticism of Enlightenment philosophy. Autobiographical accounts, insistent upon the accuracy of their narrative content, came to serve an exemplary function, indicating the path one's life should take, either by explicit or implicit injunction. Together, the *Bildungsroman* and the autobiography acted as complementary counterparts of the same expressive role:[2] the fictional and the nonfictional account of the individual in his ("his" is, of course, being used in this context intentionally) development, in his struggle to integrate himself, his ideals, and his perspectives into an increasingly industrialized, materialistic, and alienating bourgeois society.

Although these two forms entered the twentieth century more or less intact, the original fiction/nonfiction distinction has become particularly blurred during the past decade in the heavily autobiographical novels of German-language literature. Historical, sociological, and psychological factors converged in an autobiographical impulse that expressed the postwar German crisis of identity and introspection;[3] the political *reportage* of the 1960s became, in the 1970s, the documentation of the self. The traditional autobiography was regarded more and more skeptically as a work in which "truth" could at best be embedded in self-told fictions.[4] "Fiction" writers, in turn, began infusing their narratives with "new-subjectivity" authenticity.[5] In such novels, authors trace their own experiences and development in the process of combating—or conforming to—their society. This autobiographical material is set within an ostensibly fictionalized framework that removes the work from the realm of the traditional autobiography. The moralizing tone has been discarded. These authors neither humbly portray their erring ways as a negative illustration nor self-righteously present themselves as exemplary.

Women authors, most noticeably, have evolved a new model that alters the socialization process depicted in the traditional *Bildungsroman* to correspond to the new awareness of women's roles. This model moves from the recognition of restrictive social roles, through a rejection of arbitrary standards, to the generation of a counter-figure who creates a new role and a new, positive life-style into which she becomes integrated. In works of this kind, style and structure reveal the new authorial consciousness shaping the conventional form and presenting a new claim upon it. I would like to examine this new literary type as it has found expression in some of the women's autobiographical writings in the German-language literature of the 1970s.

"For me, to become an adult means to come into the world in the middle of life with intensified birth pains," writes one German woman author.[6] In so doing, she locates the source and site of conflict for herself and many of her contemporaries: the contradiction between women's emerging sense of self and the social expectations imposed on her.

Frustrated by what they perceived as their exclusion from the student movement and from the intense political activity of the late 1960s, and influenced as well by emerging American radical feminist writings, these newly politicized women turned their sharpened awareness to themselves and to a culture they perceived as hostile. Those who expressed themselves in direct political activity became the founders of the German women's movement; those who expressed themselves as authors helped to create a literary support system. These writers took the responsibility for creating vocabulary and images that would give voice and coherence to the new consciousness and experience of women and thereby create a new role for an old genre: a female autobiographical novel of development.

Contemporary female authors find the conventional pattern of the hero's assimilation into the society inadequate, and perhaps it always was, for society has hardly encouraged women to strike out on a bold or treacherous path to self-discovery. Indeed, the occasional heroine of the *Bildungsroman* of the past generally found herself coerced by circumstances into accepting her "proper" societal role (Sophie von Laroche, *Geschichte des Fräuleins von Sternheim*, 1771–72), or trivialized into an account of the wayward, willful little girl who at last learns her lesson and becomes "civilized" (Magda Trott's "Trotzkopf"—stories for children at the beginning of this century). Today women writers who want to describe a developmental process choose precisely this bold path, but find no literary models through which they can formulate their experiences. Thus a counter-pattern has evolved in the attempts of women to "write themselves."[7] Setting out like her *Bildungsroman* brother, the new heroine departs from the scene of her cloistered upbringing, separating from familial ties only with great difficulty, since these persist in her own unexamined consciousness. The divergence from the old pattern becomes ever wider as the mistakes of the heroine along her journey are not remediable or socially condoned. Her love relationships generally play a role in her "education" only by strengthening her resolve not to accept the options they offer. The female literary figure who unsuccessfully traverses this path shatters upon realizing her inability to break away; those who do succeed make choices which irreparably sever their bonds with the social structure and propel them into a life without role models, a "conclusion" that is merely another step in the process of development.

The novels I have selected to discuss at length depict heroines who set out on this path and whose stories are narrated in language and forms that reflect the attempt to break through old patterns. In addition to yielding a coherent format for a female novel of development, these works—Ingeborg Bachmann's *Malina,* Brigitte Schwaiger's *Wie kommt das Salz ins Meer?,* and Verena Stefan's *Häutungen*—illustrate a progression in the process of coming to consciousness. We see in them the beginnings of an awareness that finds no social outlet, the initial emergence of such awareness as independent decisions, and the attempt to integrate new decisions into everyday existence.

Ingeborg Bachmann's *Malina*—misunderstood by established critics of the German literary scene when the novel first appeared in 1971[8]—is, on one level, the story of a love triangle told in the first person by a woman who identifies herself only as "Ich" and whose background reflects the life of the author. This narrator lives with a coldly rational and totally dependable man named Malina, who remembers everything, who pays her bills, who keeps her calm and who provides balance to her own extreme sensitivity. She is also having an affair with her neighbor Ivan, in whose presence she gropes for words, whose car she brushes lovingly as she walks past, and whose stimulating but undemanding demeanor affords her an emotional release. The narrator describes the development of both relationships as she tries to reconcile the contradictions in her own existence. In her attempt to comprehend this duality, she relates conversations in which word games and half-spoken phrases replace content, and thereby reveal the inadequacy of language to formulate her experiences and thoughts:

What I'm doing this evening?
No, if you can't
Oh, but you're
That's true, but I don't want to
But I think that's sorry.[9]

Through writing and recounting her dreams and visions, she then attempts to reach back into the shadows of her own past to solve a mystery about herself.

My father stands next to me and pulls his hand back from my shoulder, for the grave-digger has come over to us. My father looks at the man commandingly, the grave-digger turns timidly . . . to me. He wants to speak, but only moves his lips silently . . . , I hear only his last sentence: This is the cemetery of the murdered daughters. He shouldn't have said it to me, and I cry bitterly. [pp. 181–82]

Despite all her attempts, she is unable to incorporate her insights into her daily life. She says: "But during the night, and alone, come the erratic monologues which remain, for the human is a dark being, it is master over itself only in the darkness, and in the day it returns to its slavery" (p. 102). She gradually breaks with Ivan and, at the moment when she realizes that she is left only with the passionless Malina, she notices a crack in the wall:

I go into the wall, I hold my breath. . . . But the wall opens up, I'm in the wall, and for Malina, there's only the crack to be seen. . . . It was murder. [pp. 354–56]

Here, at the end of the novel, the story suddenly and necessarily opens up to other possibilities. For example, the other characters can now be seen as projections of the narrator. Malina, who is left behind after the "death" of the narrating figure, can be perceived as an alter ego—the rational, insensitive, practical, surviving aspect of the narrator's personality. Even the figure of Ivan can be interpreted as the representative of passionate expression condoned within the strict role-oriented confines of modern society. The narrator describes herself: "I need my double life, my Ivan-life and my Malina-field, I can't be somewhere that Ivan isn't, anymore so than I can come home to a place where Malina isn't there" (p. 299). The novel must be read on both levels at once. It realistically portrays the impossibility of human—specifically female/male—relationships set within a crumbling framework of social institutions. Simultaneously, it projects the associative, monologic narration of a single mind, split into its different and warring aspects, shattered by the weight of a society that demands such self-division of both its authors and citizens.

Ambiguous forms support these two readings. Conversations—some within the context of everyday reality, some set within a dream-framework—blend with presumably realistic narration, fantastic visions, legendary histories, and poetic passages.

> I think about Ivan.
> I think about love.
> About the injections of reality. . . .
> About the next, stronger injection. . . .
> It is incurable. And it's too late.
> But I live on and think.
> And I think, it won't be Ivan.
> Whatever comes, it will be something else.
> I live in Ivan.
> I will not outlive Ivan. [p. 43]

Such poetic passages contrast with the autobiographical reality inferred from correspondences with Bachmann's life. Indeed, the novel acknowledges such a plurality of forms that it becomes impossible to consider the work within a single set of generic conventions.

Form in *Malina* reflects the shattering of the narrator and the novel's ambiguity. The narrator—both autobiographical and fictional, formulating both external reality and internal experience, and employing a mixture of forms that enlightens and confuses—struggles through the hazy regions of her own past, trying to overcome the shadows that seem always to elude her. It is in the process of this struggle that a pattern takes shape which echoes the past through familiar, but considerably altered, reference points.

Bachmann's narrator follows a new course of consciousness, but exemplifies an unsuccessful attempt to break with an externally imposed identity that destroys rather than sustains. She recounts the details of her own *Bildung* through the Benedictine School and the Ursuline Gymnasium (pp. 20–21), and describes instructors who "consider questions immature" (p. 21). Her family ties still bind her, exerting their power over her in dream images: a father who puts her into a gas chamber (p. 182); a mother who lets herself be beaten like a dutiful dog (p. 197); the composite face of mother and father (p. 241). Risks and mistakes terrify her: even in writing letters, signed "an unknown woman" (p. 148), she tears up one attempt after another to express her undisguised thoughts and feelings. Both men in her life hinder her: one, from tapping her repressed emotions, the other from expressing her experiences directly. In her identity as a writer, each voice is stiffled by her emotional side, which prefers the gloss—"to write a beautiful book" (p. 53)—and by her intellectual side, which recognizes the "eternal war" (p. 247) raging inside and thus "disturbs her memory" (p. 24, 279), pushing toward expressions of the self-denial she has been taught to practice. Expression succeeds: she describes the narrow and equally stultifying options prescribed by her social role, but in so doing sees no new horizons, only a wall. She has gradually joined her own inner contradictions to their social roots, and has allowed the awareness of this conjunction to break through to consciousness. At the same time, she realizes that society does not tolerate the very contradictions it has created. Bachmann's figure perceives the nature of her dilemma and its causes, but cannot initiate change. Engulfed by the shadows of her self—past and present—she allows her identity to be swallowed up by a world that accommodates her only in providing a crack in the wall into which she can silently step and thus pass out of existence.

Brigitte Schwaiger's *Wie kommt das Salz ins Meer?* (How Does the Salt Get into the Sea?, 1977) describes in an uninterrupted inner monologue the breakthrough of consciousness in a newly married young woman. Impressions and reactions flow together with witnessed conversations to create a rhythm paralleling consciousness and exposing normally hidden processes. The arrangement of events in a confining and repetitive pattern generalizes the narrator's experience and reveals the larger implications of her struggle with her own socialization.

Occupation: housewife. . . . Set the table, clear the table, wash the dishes, shop, cook, set the table, . . . 365 times a year the question: what'll I cook for dinner? . . . call up Hilde, she'll give you advice, Hilde would be a nice friend for you, make friends with the wives of my friends! He's right, he brings home the money, he knows what the Israelis are doing wrong with the Arabs, . . . he knows what he has to do and therefore what I have to do, and so I'm frigid again—there has to be justice.[10]

The reader witnesses an unfolding awareness going back to childhood conversations and experiences.

How does the salt get into the sea? Mother laughs. The fishermen ride out, says Father, and they have packets, and they spread the salt carefully into the waves. Mother laughs and strokes me. [pp. 37–38]

Sheltered by her father's position as town doctor, the protagonist grows up observing her mother's anxieties, while she herself is given a false image of the world. Only later is she able to ask herself: "Father, Mother, why didn't you prepare me? . . . Why were you silent about so much?" (p. 118). Emerging from such protective surroundings, she carries with her in thought and behavior the lessons she learned in childhood, as she duplicates the subservient attitudes of her mother toward her father. Her husband, Rolf, approves of such submissiveness. Rather than encouraging her independence or self-confidence, he methodically "comforts" her into incertitude and timidity. His attention to her is oppressive and hinders her self-discovery.

You're keeping a diary? Rolf smiled. Why didn't you say you wanted something like that? I'll buy you a proper diary, with keys, then you can lock away your little secrets from me. Do you have secrets, anyway? No? Has something happened? What do you write in a diary, if nothing's happened?
Please, read.
No, God forbid, you should have your intimate sphere . . . I find it touching the way you sit there and look as though you were thinking about something important. [pp. 67–68]

Schwaiger's figure is able, however, to do more than conceptualize the limits of her situation. Bolstered by stories of her grandmother's former independence and warned by the image of her meek little dog who obediently licks Rolf's hand after having been beaten, she gradually recognizes her strength as she proceeds along the path of her development. At first participating, if ironically and subversively, in her own subjugation, the heroine moves gradually toward self-recognition by means of the interplay between the naive experiencing self and the perceptive narrating self. Gradually the narrator begins to trust her own perceptions and allows them to shape her behavior. Rather than measure herself against social expectations, she begins to act according to the truth of her own experience. She allows her marriage to dissolve and perceives that she has been the lifelong victim of a "trick" perpetrated on her by an entire society. The novel ends with the heroine shocked by the enormity of the conspiracy, but determined to battle her way through to dignity.

Like Bachmann, Schwaiger uses autobiographical material. In this work, however, the narration is unambiguous. Whereas the insights of Bachmann's narrator remain in the shadows of her consciousness, the comprehension gained by Schwaiger's figure crystallizes and surfaces within her own monologue and propels the action of the novel forward. As the narrator gradually dares to invest her own experience with metaphorical significance, the imagery becomes less elusive and the narrator is able to recount events and thoughts with more directness. This claiming of the right to create one's own imagery is bound up with the act of authorship, as suggested by the narrator's attempt at a diary. The autobiographical elements imply that perhaps this book *is* that diary. Thus, both Bachmann and Schwaiger problematize their role as writer and view the authorial act as essential to the expression of emerging consciousness—and, I would add, characteristic of the female novel of development. Schwaiger's narrative is able to portray the birth of awareness, a birth facilitated by the act of writing. Still, the end is open in both works: whereas in Bachmann's novel, it is only the wall—but thereby the structure of the work itself—that opens up for the narrating figure, in Schwaiger's work the protagonist's future remains open. Her new insights and perceptions, however, are untested.

Verena Stefan's *Häutungen* (*Shedding,* 1975) goes further than Schwaiger's novel. Published by a previously unknown feminist publishing house, Frauenoffensive, the book is in its fourteenth printing, having sold 165,000 copies—a testimony to the directness with which it addresses women's lives. The narrator is a young woman who relates her new, and still emerging, concept of self. She examines her sexuality and tries to discover the sources of the contradictions between her experiences and a socially imposed sexual role—shedding one-by-one old layers of skin imprinted with identities not her own. She recognizes the source of these false identities as "brainwashing,"[11] which she wants now to counteract. Bringing with her from childhood only a dimly remembered moment of being "intensely aware of every fiber" (p. 5)—a moment of intactness between body and self—she willingly sets out into the "jungle of the cities" (p. 22) as did her earlier male counterpart in the *Bildungsroman*. She chooses to risk the constant threats of violation and the "men's glances [which] assault" her (p 31). Far from supporting her attempted independence, society thwarts her continuously. Doctors to whom she turns for sexual counseling lecture her (p. 7). When she walks down the street or travels alone the men in her environment see her actions as statements of sexual availability. The men who presumably "believe" in women's equality treat her no differently: "The roles are left untouched" (p. 66). She attempts to reconcile her sense of self with the socially approved relationships she tries to maintain. "Our every day is filled with such schizophrenia. A woman alone can hardly survive if she is not willing to disown her self" (p. 20).

The lesbian relationships she forms bring their own difficulties. Without models of experience to guide her, she gropes for images, words, and ways to communicate that break out of the confining and damaging patterns of the "old" society.

> We found ourselves in empty space. We didn't want to imitate, we wanted to create new ways and means of behavior drawing on ourselves and on the untapped reserves of eroticism lying between us. The expanse of unexplored territory had a stupefying effect.
> The memory of old behavior patterns faded ever so slowly. The transition seemed to be at hand. [p. 74]

The work records her attempts to form relationships with nontraditional women and men. As she breaks away from the restrictive role demanded of her by society, she begins to notice changes: "Beneath the surface of my skin, new cracks were forming" (p. 22). She forces herself into uncomfortable new awarenesses, and she endeavors to live out these awarenesses despite society's resistance and hostility. " 'First of all it is a question of wanting to *fundamentally* change relationships between people, and this would imply, among other things, foregoing traditional relationships which are based on stereotypes' " (p. 77). She sheds her old skins as she goes along, "dappled" (p. 118) by the traces that remain, but never again to be so encased in bindings, nor forgetful of the feeling of confinement.

The emergence of awareness in Stefan's character is no stillbirth, as in Bachmann's work; and unlike Schwaiger's account, we see the narrator begin to implement her new perceptions in her immediate world. Here, too, the assertion of the authorial act is a necessary step and is made more explicitly, as Stefan describes her book as "autobiographical sketches   poems   dreams   analyses."[12] This open declaration of autobiographical "authenticity" parallels the narrator's implementation of her insights in the external world. Thus the manipulation of form and language is the literary means by which the narrator asserts the right to describe and interpret her own experience.

Indeed, Stefan attacks and dissects language as a factor in women's oppression: "in the process of writing, I bumped into the language," she writes in a foreword, describing the process by which women literally "in-corporate" the attitudes of the society.[13] By accepting vocabulary that implies the values of the system that creates it, women limit the possibilities of their own development and experience. Stefan tries to break through this barrier, rejecting alienating words and building new connections and associations to describe her experience. Rather than name her body parts, for instance, by the slang expressions "brutal and disdainful toward women," Stefan turns first to "clinical, . . . more neutral" terms, and then to her own more poetic innovations.[14] While the accepted name in German for the vulva is *Schamlippen,* meaning modesty-(or shame)lips, Stefan's narrator renames them "blossoming labella," (p. 91) imagery corresponding to that of Judy Chicago's *Dinner Party* designs.

Still, the narrator's new approaches and new relationships do not completely succeed in filling the gaps left by abandoning old values and roles. At the end of the work, the heroine must turn to fantasy—a vision of herself, described now in the third person, as a woman alone and satisfied with her self and her sexual identity. For Stefan, the goal does not yet lie within the realizable world, but at least can be envisioned. Another female author, describing a plan for the "developmental novel of a female soul," says that the central figure would of necessity be fictional: "no woman with a role" could possibly serve as a heroine.[15] Stefan's heroine sheds her limiting roles and tries to establish new identities, although an ultimate realization of such new identities is displaced into fantasy. We are left to draw the conclusion that the process depicted in the female novel of development cannot progress further than the society itself and cannot keep from entering the realm of futuristic vision.

Numerous other German-language works from the past decade could be considered in the category of the female novel of development. These are works by women who describe their repressive upbringing, with an ensuing split in consciousness, and who work through this dissociation to bring their own lives more into harmony. Christa Wolf, for example, explores the socialization process in her autobiographical account, *Kindheitsmuster* (1976). Wolf returns to the city of her early years and brings her childhood self back to life in order to explore her conditioning. She then attempts to deal with her new insights in the present. Other works focus on the problems of separation from parental ties. Elisabeth Plessen (*Mitteilung an den Adel,* 1976) and Ruth Rehmann (*Der Mann auf dem Kanzel,* 1979) both describe a daughter's confusion after the death of her father, whose imposing presence is still felt within the consciousness of the child, and whose values remain to be questioned. Gabriele Wohmann (*Ausflug mit der Mutter,* 1978) tries to become sensitive to the feelings of her mother, to deal with the natural but often untouched conflicts in the mother/daughter relationship. Another group of works deals with the coming-to-consciousness of a woman involved in a love relationship. Only gradually becoming aware of her self-imposed confinement, the woman slowly gathers her strength and severs the tie—although, as in Schwaiger's book, the future is uncertain. Such authors include Karin Struck (*Klassenliebe,* 1973), Hannelies Taschau (*Landfriede,* 1978) and Karin Petersen (*Das fette Jahr,* 1978).

Such works can scarcely be viewed as isolated from the society that produced their authors.[16] Elizabeth Bruss discusses this relationship between literary types and social origin.

A literary institution must reflect and give focus to some consistent need and sense of possibility in the community it serves, but at the same time, a genre helps to define what is possible and to specify the appropriate means for meeting an expressive need.[17]

This understanding of genre in its functional role within its own language community helps our investigation of the female novel of development; for when we use a traditional term such as *Bildungsroman* or autobiography in a new and expanded sense, we are necessarily recognizing a changed function for a genre which was historically adapted to other needs. The female novel of development in the hands of German authors has evolved accordingly. Departing from the developmental pattern traditionally prescribed in earlier centuries, these writers have employed new imagery and structures, asserting their prerogative to narrate in their own way. Consistent within their formal experiments is the need to express developing consciousness. Even though the ideological impetus for the original eighteenth-century forms of *Bildungsroman* and autobiography may well have changed in the twentieth century, the concern with individual growth in society has remained. Indeed, the quest for the self in women's fiction has become more open and more intense. And so, if the hero of the autobiographical *Bildungsroman* has now become a heroine, it is no coincidence.

Contributors

Elizabeth Abel is Assistant Professor of English at University of California, Berkeley. A former editor of *Critical Inquiry,* she has published articles on the relationship of psychoanalysis and female texts, particularly the novels of Rhys, Lessing, Woolf, Morrison, Christa Wolf. She is the editor of *Writing and Sexual Difference,* a collection of essays, and is now completing a manuscript on psychoanalytic and literary representations of female identity.

Elizabeth R. Baer is Assistant Dean of the College and Assistant Professor of English at Sweet Briar College in Virginia. In addition to her work on Jean Rhys, she has written on fairy-tale and quest motifs in the fiction of Margaret Atwood and Doris Lessing. She is currently engaged in research on children's literature and southern women writers.

Mary Anne Ferguson edited one of the first anthologies in women's studies, *Images of Women in Literature,* now in its third edition. Originally a medievalist, she also writes on women in contemporary fiction and has published articles on Tillie Olsen, Katherine Anne Porter, and Eudora Welty. She is Professor of English and chair of the English Department at the University of Massachusetts, Boston.

Sandra Frieden is Assistant Professor of German at the University of Houston. Her publications include articles on Christa Wolf, Elizabeth Plessen, Peter Handke, and Brigitte Schwaiger. A book on German-language autobiographical writings of the 1970s is forthcoming.

Blanche H. Gelfant is the author of *The American City Novel* and has written extensively on twentieth-century American themes and figures, specifically Faulkner, Hemingway, Cather, Paley, Beattie, and Le Seur. A Professor of English at Dartmouth College, she is at work on a study of women and the city.

Marianne Hirsch is Associate Professor of French and Italian and Comparative Literature at Dartmouth College. She has published articles on Michel Butor, Marguerite Duras, Madame de Lafayette and the novel of formation, and a book *Beyond the Single Vision: Henry James, Michel Butor, Uwe Johnson.* She coedited *Feminist Readings: French Texts/American*

Contexts, a special issue of *Yale French Studies,* and is currently writing a book on mother-daughter relationships in literature.

Margo Kasdan, Assistant Professor of Film Studies at San Francisco State University, reviews films for *Spokeswomen.* She has published pieces on Godard, Hitchcock, the *film noir,* and women in film.

Elizabeth Langland is Associate Professor of English and chair of the English Department at Converse College, Spartanburg, South Carolina. She coedited *A Feminist Perspective in the Academy,* a collection of essays about the impact of women's studies on the curriculum, and has authored a book entitled *Society in the Novel,* which will be published by the University of North Carolina Press. She has also published articles on Thomas Hardy, George Eliot, and Joseph Conrad.

Marta Peixoto has published articles on a number of Brazilian writers and has forthcoming a book on João Cabral de Melo Neto's poetry. Currently, she is working on contemporary Latin American women poets. She is Assistant Professor of Romance Languages at Princeton University.

Ellen Cronan Rose, Associate Professor of English at Haverford College, is the author of *The Tree Outside the Window: Doris Lessing's* Children of Violence, a study of Lessing's novel as Eriksonian *Bildungsroman.* She has also published a study of Margaret Drabble's fiction, *Equivocal Figures,* and numerous articles on women and literature.

Karen E. Rowe, Associate Professor of English at UCLA, has published on early American literature and women's literature. She is currently engaged in a book-length study of fairy tales and feminine fictions, a project supported by a National Endowment for the Humanities fellowship for independent study, 1977–78, during which time she was in residence at the Radcliffe Institute.

Susan J. Rosowski is an Associate Professor of English at the University of Nebraska, Lincoln. Her publications include studies on Willa Cather, Congreve, Joyce, and Atwood. She is coeditor of the anthology *Women and Western American Literature* (1982) and is currently writing a book on Willa Cather.

Brenda R. Silver has edited a number of Virginia Woolf manuscripts, including the recent *Virginia Woolf's Reading Notebooks.* She has also published articles on Virginia Woolf and is currently at work on an intellectual biography of Woolf in the 1930s based on the evolution of the manuscript of *Three Guineas.* She is Associate Professor of English and co-chair of Women's Studies at Dartmouth College.

Catharine R. Stimpson is Professor of English at Rutgers University and the Director of its Institute for Research on Women. A resident of New York City, she writes both fiction and nonfiction and is the author of the novel *Class Notes*. From 1974 to 1980, she was the founding editor of *Signs: Journal of Women in Culture and Society*.

Mary Helen Washington is editor of *Black-Eyed Susans* and *Midnight Birds*. Associate Professor of English and Black Studies at the University of Massachusetts, Boston, she has also written numerous essays on black women writers. Currently a Mellon Fellow at the Wellesley College Center for Research on Women, she is at work on a historical anthology of black women's fiction from 1850 to 1950.

Bonnie Zimmerman is Associate Professor of Women's Studies at San Diego State University where she teaches literature, humanities, popular culture, and lesbianism. She has published on George Eliot and on lesbian literature, critical theory, and pedagogy.

Notes

Introduction

1. Virginia Woolf, *The Voyage Out* (New York: Harcourt, Brace, & World, 1948), p. 341. Subsequent references will be cited in the text.

2. Although gender has been neglected in studies of the *Bildungsroman,* it has recently been included in studies of the picaresque. See Julio Rodriguez-Luis, "Picaras: A Modal Approach to the Picaresque," *Comparative Literature* 31, 1 (Winter 1979), 32–46.

3. Martin Swales, *The German Bildungsroman from Wieland to Hesse* (Princeton: Princeton University Press, 1978), p. 14.

4. Wilhelm Dilthey, *Das Erlebnis und die Dichtung* (Leipzig and Bern, 1913), p. 394.

5. See Jeffrey L. Sammons, "The Mystery of the Missing *Bildungsroman,* or: What Happened to Wilhelm Meister's Legacy?" *Genre* 14 (Summer 1981), 229–46.

6. For a definition of the *Bildungsroman* as a broader European genre, see Marianne Hirsch, "The Novel of Formation as Genre: Between *Great Expectations* and *Lost Illusions,*" *Genre* 12 (Fall 1979), 293–311.

7. Northrop Frye, *Anatomy of Criticism: Four Essays,* 1957; rpt. New York: Atheneum, 1969), p. 308. Many other theorists, most notably George Lukács, second the claim that the novel finds its distinctive form in depicting individuals within society.

8. Charlotte Brontë, *Jane Eyre,* ed. Richard Dunn (New York: Norton, 1971), p. 96.

9. Jerome Buckley specifies these "principal characteristics" in *Season of Youth: The Bildungsroman from Dickens to Golding* (Cambridge: Harvard University Press, 1974), p. 17. Subsequent quotations in this paragraph refer to the same page.

10. The heroine's strong relationship to nature, noted by several feminist critics and theorists, may be in part a compensation for exclusion from urban life. See Annis Pratt, "Women and Nature in Modern Fiction," *Contemporary Literature* 13, 4 (1972), 476–90, and her *Archetypal Patterns in Women's Fiction* (Bloomington: Indiana University Press, 1982), and Susan Griffin, *Women and Nature: The Roaring Inside Her* (New York: Harper and Row, 1978).

11. Critics have interpreted the heroine's isolation and inactivity in different ways. See Carol P. Christ's distinction between spiritual and social quest in *Diving Deep and Surfacing: Women Writers on Spiritual Quest* (Boston: Beacon Press, 1980). In "What Can a Heroine Do? Or Why Women Can't Write," *Images of Women in Fiction: Feminist Perspectives,* ed. Susan Koppelman Cornillon (Bowling Green, Ohio: Bowling Green University Popular

Press, 1972), pp. 3–210, Joanna Russ analyzes women's inactivity and their consequent exclusion from the central role in fiction. In *The Heroine's Text* (New York: Columbia University Press, 1980), Nancy K. Miller charts two typical female plots: the "euphoric," leading to social integration, and the "dysphoric," leading to exclusion and alienation. In nineteenth-century fictions of female development, the dysphoric plot predominates.

12. Charlotte Brontë, *Villette* (New York: Harper and Row, 1972), p. 30.

13. We borrow the phrase "long suicide" from Elizabeth Ermarth's essay, "Maggie Tulliver's Long Suicide," *Studies in English Literature* 14 (Fall 1974), 587–601. For other studies of the problematic nature of Eliot's plot, see Gillian Beer, "Beyond Determinism: George Eliot and Virginia Woolf," in *Women Writing and Writing About Women*, ed. Mary Jacobus (London: Croom Helm, 1979), and Mary Jacobus, "The Problem of Language: Men of Maxims and *The Mill on the Floss*," *Critical Inquiry* 8, 2 (Winter 1981), 207–22.

14. Diverse emphases and concerns clearly differentiate these theorists, yet they share numerous goals and assumptions. For some representative works, see Nancy Chodorow, *The Reproduction of Mothering: Psychoanalysis and the Sociology of Gender* (Berkeley: University of California Press, 1978); Dorothy Dinnerstein, *The Mermaid and the Minotaur: Sexual Arrangements and Human Malaise* (New York: Harper and Row, 1976); Jean Baker Miller, *Toward a New Psychology of Women* (Boston: Beacon Press, 1976); Jane Flax, "The Conflict Between Nurturance and Autonomy in Mother-Daughter Relationships and Within Feminism," *Feminist Studies* 4, 2 (June 1978), 171–91; Carol Gilligan, *In a Different Voice: Psychological Theory and Women's Development* (Cambridge: Harvard University Press, 1982).

15. Though Freud comments on female psychology throughout his writing, he presents the fullest exposition of female identity in his three late essays on femininity, "Some Psychical Consequences of the Anatomical Distinction Between the Sexes" (1925), "Female Sexuality" (1931), and "Femininity" (1933). These are conveniently collected in *Women and Analysis: Psychoanalytic Dialogues on Femininity*, ed. Jean Strouse (New York: Grossman Publishers, 1974).

16. Chodorow, *The Reproduction of Mothering*, p. 169.

17. Sigmund Freud, *Civilization and Its Discontents*, cited in Gilligan, *In a Different Voice*, p. 46; Miller, *Toward a New Psychology of Women*, p. 83.

18. Miller, *Toward a New Psychology of Women*, p. 61.

19. See Gilligan, *In a Different Voice*, for an in-depth exploration of the differences between male and female moral development.

20. For an exploration of adultery in fiction, see Tony Tanner, *Adultery in the Novel: Contract and Transgression* (Baltimore: Johns Hopkins University Press, 1979).

21. Our definition of the pattern of awakening differs from that of Susan Rosowski in "The Novel of Awakening," reprinted in this volume. Whereas Rosowski reserves the term "apprenticeship" for the male *Bildungsroman* and "awakening" for female versions, we attempt a fuller formal distinction within the female novel of development itself.

22. Like many feminist critics, we are indebted here to the theory of the palimpsestic female text enunciated by Sandra M. Gilbert and Susan Gubar in *The Madwoman in the Attic: The Woman Writer and the Nineteenth-Century Literary Imagination* (New Haven: Yale University Press, 1979).

23. Judith Kegan Gardiner proposes a theory of collective protagonists in women's fiction in "The (Us)es of (I)dentity: A Response to Abel's '(E)merging (I)dentities,'" *Signs: Journal of Women in Culture and Society* 6, 3 (Spring 1981), 436–42.

24. David H. Miles, "The Picaro's Journey to the Confessional: The Changing Image of the Hero in the German Bildungsroman," *PMLA* 89 (1974), 990.

25. Ellen Morgan, "Humanbecoming: Form and Focus in the Neo-Feminist Novel," in *Images of Women in Fiction: Feminist Perspectives,* ed. Susan Koppelman Cornillon, p. 185. Her claim is supported by feminist interest in the *Bildungsroman.* See, for example, Bonnie Braendlin, "Alther, Atwood, Ballantyne, and Gray: Secular Salvation in the Contemporary Feminist Bildungsroman," *Frontiers* 4 (1979), 18–22, and Braendlin's forthcoming anthology on the modern *Bildungsroman,* coedited with Sally Brett.

26. We are grateful to Jerald Jahn, Brenda R. Silver, Leo Spitzer, and Nancy J. Vickers for their suggestions on this introduction.

Hirsch: Spiritual *Bildung*

1. *The Second Sex,* trans. and ed. H. M. Parshley (New York: Bantam Books, rpt. 1970), pp. 271–72.

2. "The Antigone and Its Moral," *Leader* 7 (29 March 1856), 306.

3. Sophocles, *Antigone,* in *The Theban Plays,* trans. E. M. Watling (London: Penguin Books, 1980), p. 138.

4. Ibid., p. 140.

5. Ibid., p. 139. In *Speculum de l'autre femme* (Paris: Minuit, 1974), Luce Irigaray distinguishes between the "matriarchal line" that connects brother and sister in this unusual family where the mother of the husband is also his wife, and the "patriarchal power," whose representative is Creon, the maternal uncle. See also Josette Feral, "Antigone or the Irony of the Tribe," *Diacritics* (September 1978), 2.

6. Sophocles, *Antigone,* p. 150. Cf. Irigaray, p. 272: "And whatever her current debate with the laws of the city, another law attracts her to where she is going: the identification with her/the mother." Irigaray argues that Antigone assumes a maternal function, choosing her brother's eternal life over her actual one.

7. Jean Anouilh, in his modern-day *Antigone,* makes this allegiance to childhood even more explicit; his Antigone is an adolescent who refuses to grow up and to accept the disillusionments and degradations of adulthood.

8. Sophocles, *Antigone,* p. 150.

9. See especially "Female Sexuality" (1931), reprinted in *Women and Analysis,* ed. Jean Strouse (New York: Grossman Publishers, 1974).

10. For a more complete exposition of Freud's outline of female psychologi-

cal development in relation to the female novel of development, see Elizabeth Abel's "Narrative Structure(s) and Female Development: The Case of *Mrs. Dalloway,*" in this volume.

11. See especially Nancy Chodorow, *The Reproduction of Mothering: Psychoanalysis and the Sociology of Gender* (Berkeley: University of California Press, 1978); Jean Baker Miller, *Toward a New Psychology of Women* (Boston: Beacon Press, 1976); Dorothy Dinnerstein, *The Mermaid and the Minotaur: Sexual Arrangements and Human Malaise* (New York: Harper and Row, 1976); Jane Flax, "The Conflict Between Nurturance and Autonomy in Mother-Daughter Relationships and Within Feminism," *Feminist Studies* 4, 2 (June 1978), 171–91; Jessica Benjamin, "The Bonds of Love: Rational Violence and Erotic Domination," *Feminist Studies* 6, 1 (Spring 1980), 144–74. For a more complete overview of this literature, see Marianne Hirsch, "Mothers and Daughters: A Review Essay," *Signs* 7, 1 (Autumn 1981), 200–222.

12. For an analysis of different national traditions of the novel of development and the unique aspects of the German *Bildungsroman,* see Marianne Hirsch, "The Novel of Formation as Genre: Between Great Expectations and Lost Illusions," *Genre* 12 (Fall 1979), 293–311. As a feminist critic, it is important to explain my choice of texts for this essay. It might seem paradoxical to argue for the psychological specificity of female development on the one hand, and to ask the same questions of novels by male as well as female authors on the other. I believe, however, that it is valid to do so, that fictional heroines, whether their authors are male or female, encounter the same contradictions of psychological needs, social possibilities, and plot structures. Male and female writers often respond to these contradictions differently, and some differences emerge in my essay. Sometimes, however, their solutions can be quite similar: all four heroines analyzed here find death the only possible resolution.

13. See Carol P. Christ, *Diving Deep and Surfacing: Women Writers and the Spiritual Quest* (Boston: Beacon Press, 1980), for a useful distinction between patterns of social quest and patterns of spiritual quest in women's stories. Christ's religious/mystical description of the spiritual quest is quite different from the psychological language I use. However, in her brief analysis of *The Awakening,* she also sees the nineteenth-century pattern of female development as one of spiritual liberation and social defeat.

14. See David H. Miles, "The Picaro's Journey to the Confessional: The Changing Image of the Hero in the German Bildungsroman," *PMLA* 89 (1974), 982.

15. Ibid., 981.

16. Johann Wolfgang Goethe, *Wilhelm Meister's Lehrjahre,* 2 (Munich: Deutscher Taschenbuch Verlag, 1962), p. 74. Subsequent references will be cited in parentheses in the text. Translations are my own.

17. In "The Narcissistic Woman: Freud and Girard," *Diacritics* 10, 3 (Fall 1980), 36–45, Sarah Kofman reads Freud's essay "On Narcissism: An Introduction" (1914) as an analysis of the narcissistic woman who is self-sufficient, indifferent to men, autonomous, yet connected to the original paradise of childhood, a description Goethe's character fits remarkably.

18. I have found useful the excellent analysis of this aspect of the text in the terminology of contemporary German philosophy in Suzanne Zantop, "Reines Selbst und fremde Formen: Bewusstsein und Selbstbewusstsein in Goethe's 'Bekenntnissen einer schönen Seele,'" unpublished paper, Harvard University.

19. See, for example, Frederick Beharriell, "The Hidden Meaning of Goethe's 'Bekenntnissen einer schönen Seele,'" in *Lebendige Form: Interpretationen zur deutschen Literatur,* eds. Jeffrey Sammons and E. Schuerer (Munich: Fink Verlag, 1970), 37–63.

20. For a fuller analysis of this dialectic, see Martin Swales, *The German Bildungsroman from Wieland to Hesse* (Princeton: Princeton University Press, 1978).

21. George Eliot, *The Mill on the Floss,* ed. Gordon S. Haight (Boston: Houghton Mifflin, 1961), pp. 16, 17. Subsequent references will be cited in parentheses in the text.

22. In *A Literature of Their Own: British Women Novelists from Brontë to Lessing* (Princeton: Princeton University Press, 1977), p. 125, Elaine Showalter interprets this passage differently, seeing in it an option of "witch-like self-preservation," which Maggie, the "heroine of renunciation," does not take.

23. Eliot's depiction of the two sides of early childhood illustrates the movement from symbiotic fusion to separation and individuation stressed in child development theory.

24. See Elizabeth Ermarth's excellent article, "Maggie Tulliver's Long Suicide," *Studies in English Literature* 14 (Fall 1974), 587–601.

25. Gillian Beer, "Beyond Determinism: George Eliot and Virginia Woolf," in *Women Writing and Writing about Women,* ed. Mary Jacobus (London: Croom Helm, 1979), pp. 88, 89. See also Nancy K. Miller, "Emphasis Added: Plots and Plausibilities in Women's Fiction," *PMLA* 96, 1 (January 1981), 36–48.

26. Theodor Fontane, *Effi Briest,* trans. Douglas Parmée (London: Penguin Books, 1976), p. 157. All subsequent references will be cited in parentheses in the text.

27. Kate Chopin, *The Awakening and Selected Stories,* ed. Barbara H. Solomon (New York: New American Library, 1976), p. 14. All subsequent references will be cited in parentheses in the text.

28. Cynthia Griffin Wolff, in "Thanatos and Eros" in *The Awakening,* ed. Margaret Culley (New York: Norton, 1976), pp. 206–18, also sees the birth as an experience of separation that prevents Edna from continuing her life. Yet Wolff interprets the suicide as a regressive act, as Edna's inability to face the necessary accommodations of adulthood.

29. See Georg Lukács, *The Theory of the Novel,* trans. Anna Bostock (Cambridge, Mass.: MIT Press, 1971).

30. James Joyce, *A Portrait of the Artist as a Young Man* (New York: Viking Press, 1964), p. 253.

31. Sandra M. Gilbert and Susan Gubar, *The Madwoman in the Attic: The Woman Writer and the Nineteenth-Century Literary Imagination* (New Haven: Yale University Press, 1979), p. 99.

32.. I disagree here with the argument of Susan J. Rosowski, who, in "The Novel of Awakening" in this volume, describes the pattern of the novel of awakening as a "movement . . . inward, toward greater self-knowledge and . . . of the disparity between that self-knowledge and . . . the world."

33. *Persuasion,* chapter 23, quoted by Gilbert and Gubar, *Madwoman in the Attic,* p. 60.

34. Miller, "Emphasis Added," p. 40.

35. I wish to thank the two coeditors of this anthology, as well as Elizabeth Ermarth, Lincoln Hess, Marta Peixoto, Brenda Silver, and Leo Spitzer, for their helpful suggestions.

Rosowski: The Novel of Awakening

1. C. Hugh Holman, *A Handbook to Literature,* based on the original by William Flint Thrall and Addison Hibbard, 3rd ed. (New York: Odyssey Press, 1972).

2. Elizabeth Sabiston discusses this struggle in *Madame Bovary* as well as in *Emma, Middlemarch,* and *The Portrait of a Lady,* novels in which "romantic, imaginative, provincial heroines" try "against insurmountable odds" (p. 338) to realize their ideal selves, in "The Prison of Womanhood," *Comparative Literature,* 25 (1973), 336–51.

3. Gustave Flaubert, *Madame Bovary,* trans. Francis Steegmuller (New York: Random House, 1957), p. 45. Hereafter, page references in my text will be to this edition of the novel.

4. B. F. Bart discusses the "constantly shifting distances" between the reader and Emma Bovary in "Aesthetic Distance in *Madame Bovary,*" *PMLA,* 69 (1954), 1112–26.

5. *The Complete Works of Kate Chopin,* ed. Per Seyersted (Baton Rouge: Louisiana State University Press, 1970), 2, 882. Hereafter, page references in my text will be to this edition of the novel.

6. *Leader,* July 8, 1899, reprinted in *The World and the Parish: Willa Cather's Articles and Reviews, 1893–1902,* ed. William M. Curtin (Lincoln: University of Nebraska Press, 1970), 2, 698–99.

7. I have presented a more detailed discussion of the "expanding narrative consciousness [that lies] at the heart of *My Mortal Enemy*" in "Narrative Technique in Cather's *My Mortal Enemy,*" *The Journal of Narrative Technique,* 8 (1978), 141–49.

8. *My Mortal Enemy* (1926; rpt. New York: Vintage-Knopf, 1954), p. 11. Hereafter, page references in my text will be to this edition of the novel.

9. See the discussion of the complexity of Myra and the sides of her nature by Theodore S. Adams, "Willa Cather's *My Mortal Enemy:* The Concise Presentation of Scene, Character, and Theme," in *Colby Library Quarterly,* 10 (1973), 145.

10. Harry B. Eichorn, "A Falling Out with Love: *My Mortal Enemy,*" *Colby Library Quarterly,* 10 (1973), 138.

11. By recognizing Nellie Birdseye's role in the general theme of awakening, we may answer long-standing questions about the function of the narrator in *My Mortal Enemy.* Theodore S. Adams, for example, writes, "unlike the

narrator of *My Ántonia* and the window-character of *A Lost Lady,* Nellie does not present a study of her own development in parallel or contrast to that of her subject" (p. 141).

12. Agnes Smedley, *Daughter of Earth,* 2nd ed. (Old Westbury, N.Y.: The Feminist Press, 1976), p. 4. Hereafter, page references in my text will be to this edition of the novel.

13. George Eliot, *Middlemarch,* ed. Gordon S. Haight (Boston: Houghton Mifflin, Riverside Edition, 1956), p. 18. Hereafter, page references in my text will be to this edition of the novel.

14. In *George Eliot and Flaubert: Pioneers of the Modern Novel* (Athens: Ohio University Press, 1974), Barbara Smalley discusses the "counterpoint of inner vision with outer reality . . . [that] is central to the psychological realism of both Flaubert and George Eliot." (p. 128). Professor Smalley's chapter 4, *"Middlemarch:* Five Patterns of Romantic Egoism," is especially valuable as background to the novel of awakening.

Rowe: "Fairy-born and human-bred"

1. The perspective of the cultural functionalists is best represented by William Bascom, "Four Functions of Folklore," *Journal of American Folklore,* 67 (1954), 333–49; rpt. in *The Study of Folklore,* ed. Alan Dundes (Englewood Cliffs, N.J.: Prentice-Hall, 1965), pp. 279–98; William Bascom, "Folklore and Anthropology," *Journal of American Folklore,* 66 (1953), 283–90; rpt. in *The Study of Folklore,* pp. 25–33; and J. L. Fischer, "The Sociopsychological Analysis of Folktales," *Current Anthropology,* 4 (1963), 235–95. Bruno Bettelheim makes the case for a Freudian analysis in *The Uses of Enchantment: The Meaning and Importance of Fairy Tales* (New York: Knopf, 1976).

2. Madame d'Aulnoy's *Contes des fées* (1698) established the fairy tale as a literary genre and was republished in English as *A Collection of Novels and Tales, Written by that Celebrated Wit of France, The Countess D'Anois* (1721). Robert Samber's English redaction *Histories or Tales of Past Times* (1729) of Charles Perrault's 1697 French collection (*Histoires ou contes du temps passé*) also became one of the most popular works in England. Madame Marie Le Prince de Beaumont, who considered tales to be suitable for instruction of the young, published *Magasin des enfans, ou dialogues entre une sage Gouvernante et plusieurs des ses Elèves* (1756), subsequently translated as *The Young Misses Magazine* (1759). Folktales gained lasting respectability with Edgar Taylor's publication of *German Popular Stories* (1823–26) translated from the *Kinder- und Hausmärchen* (1812–22) of the Brothers Jacob and Wilhelm Grimm.

3. Bettelheim, *Uses of Enchantment,* pp. 183–93. Bettelheim argues that fairy tales, such as *Jack the Giant Killer,* "provide reassurance to children that they can eventually get the better of the giant—i.e., they can grow up to be like the giant and acquire the same powers. These are 'the mighty hopes that make us men!' " (pp. 27–28). And women?

4. See my essay on "Feminism and Fairy Tales," *Women's Studies,* 6 (1979), 237–57, which discusses the psychological and cultural paradigms

for women, as they are embodied in the most popular romantic tales. See also
Marcia R. Lieberman, " 'Some Day My Prince Will Come': Female Accul-
turation Through the Fairy Tale," *College English,* 34 (1972), 383–95; and
Kay Stone, "Things Walt Disney Never Told Us," *Journal of American
Folklore,* 88 (1975), 42–49.

5. Iona and Peter Opie, *The Classic Fairy Tales* (London: Oxford University Press, 1974). All further notations about tales refer to this edition,
which gives the texts of the "best-known fairy tales as they were first printed
in English, or in their earliest surviving or prepotent text" (p. 5).

6. Charlotte Brontë, *Jane Eyre* (New York: New American Library, 1960),
p. 31. All further references to *Jane Eyre* will be cited in the text.

7. Marthe Robert, "The Grimm Brothers," in *The Child's Part,* ed. Peter
Brooks (Boston: Beacon Press, 1972), pp. 44–56. Robert shows how in the
Grimms' versions, a "disturbing old woman," who in French would be called
a *sage femme* meaning "wise woman" or "midwife," replaces a "radiant
fairy" godmother: "Midwife, woman full of knowledge . . . the *sage femme*
informs us better than the romantic fairy of our country about the task with
which her model of ancient times was probably charged: to transmit to those
individuals whose need is greatest—children and adolescents—a knowledge of
the religious and social practices by which man can fit himself into the order
of things. . . . Perhaps the tale owes the continuation of its teaching to these
old women—good-natured souls or nurses—who, sitting by the hearth, transmitted it from generation to generation, and who modestly played (probably
without knowing it) the formerly prestigious role of the *sage femme* and the
fairy" (pp. 50, 52). In *The Life of Charlotte Brontë,* ed. Alan Shelston
(Middlesex, England: Penguin, 1975), pp. 110–11, Elizabeth Gaskell suggests
that Bessie also had a counterpart in Tabby, "an elderly woman of the village" who came to live at Haworth parsonage in 1825 "when Charlotte was
little more than nine years old."

8. See Richard Chase, "The Brontës, or Myth Domesticated," in *Forms of
Modern Fiction,* ed. William V. O'Connor (Minneapolis: University of Min-
nesota Press, 1948), pp. 102–19; Martin S. Day, "Central Concepts of Jane
Eyre," *Personalist,* 41 (1960), 495–505; Norman Sherry, *Charlotte and Emily
Brontë* (London: Evans Brothers, 1969), p. 52; Charles Burkhart, *Charlotte
Brontë: A Psychosexual Study of Her Novels* (London: Gallanz, 1973), pp.
69–73; Nina Auerbach, "Charlotte Brontë: The Two Countries," *University of
Toronto Quarterly,* 42 (1973), 328–42; and Sandra Gilbert, "Plain Jane's
Progress," *Signs,* 2 (1977), 779–804. In *Charlotte Brontë: The Self Conceived*
(New York: Norton, 1978), Helene Moglen illustrates the tendency of
critics to compare *Jane Eyre* with "Tales of the 'dispossessed princess' " who
"must pass through a number of trials . . . which test and prove her moral
worth" until "ultimately her lover . . . through marriage, bestows upon her
the family, wealth, and status which are the external signs and guarantees of
her true value" (p. 108).

9. Elaine Showalter, *A Literature of Their Own: British Women Novelists
from Brontë to Lessing* (Princeton: Princeton University Press, 1977), also
notes Jane's progress from "the nursery world of Lilliput to an encounter

with the threatening and Brobdingnagian Reverend Brocklehurst" (p. 115). Showalter links this incident to Jane's later "increasing Calvinist awareness of the 'vile body' that leads to the climactic encounter with Bertha, the female Yahoo in her foul den" (p. 115). As I suggest further, *Gulliver's Travels* contributes as much to structural movements in the novel as to precise incidents—so that Jane's confrontation with Bertha's animal sexuality becomes one of many such encounters with reality that break down Jane's romantic illusions based upon a rarefied purity (and puritanism) in fairy tales.

10. Paula Sullivan, "Fairy Tale Elements in *Jane Eyre*," *Journal of Popular Culture*, 12 (1978), 61–74. Sullivan emphasizes the "plot structure of cyclical journeys," whereby Jane "returns triumphant to her oppressive origins" and claims the "domestic idyll" promised to fairy tale heroines (pp. 61, 72). Representative of critics who view *Jane Eyre* as a "wish-fulfillment fantasy," Sullivan overlooks the novel's complex tensions between romance and sexuality which, I believe, signal Brontë's (and Jane's) disillusionment with fairy-tale patterns.

11. "La Barbe bleüe" was probably invented by Charles Perrault in *Histoires ou Contes du temps passé. Avec des Moralitez* (1697), becoming famous through Robert Samber's English translation (1729). As Sullivan notes, Tieck adopted this tale for a modern drama, which was described in *Blackwood's Edinburgh Magazine* (February 1833), to which Charlotte's father subscribed and which she read regularly.

12. For Brontë's use of English folklore, see Jacqueline Simpson, "The Function of Folklore in 'Jane Eyre' and 'Wuthering Heights,'" *Folklore*, 85 (1974), 47–61.

13. Madame de Beaumont's version of *Beauty and the Beast* appeared in English translation in *The Young Misses Magazine* (1759). Benjamin Tabart gathered this tale into his *Collection of Popular Stories for the Nursery* (London: Tabart & Co., 1804), and the revised edition, subtitled *A Lilliputian Library* (London: Sir Richard Phillips and Co., 1818), also contained *Cinderella* and *Bluebeard*. Charles Lamb transposed it into poetic form ("Beauty and the Beast: or, A Rough Outside with a Gentle Heart") in 1811, and Beaumont's narrative inspired early nineteenth-century pantomimes and stage melodramas.

14. The merchant's gift of a rose catapults Beauty into Beast's domain. But the Grimm brothers' title "Dornröschen" (1812) for *Sleeping Beauty,* denoting both the hedge of thorns and the rose, is the probable inspiration for Brontë's recurrent allusions. Recall the day before their wedding when Rochester questions Jane's coyness: " 'This is you; who have been as slippery as an eel the last month, and as thorny as a briar-rose?' " (p. 280). See *passim* pp. 101, 114, 218, 246, 261, 298, 365.

15. In *The Blue Beard* a forbidden room reveals mutilated bodies of previous wives, while the mystery in *Beauty and the Beast* is one of identity itself. Psychoanalytic interpreters equate this "secret" with masculine nature, sexual infidelities, or carnal knowledge into which the heroine gains entrance only paradoxically by defying prohibitions. See Bettelheim, *Uses of Enchantment,* pp, 277–309.

16. See Gilbert, "Plain Jane's Progress," pp. 792–98; Showalter, *A Literature of Their Own*, pp. 114–22, and Moglen, *Charlotte Brontë*, pp. 123–29, for interpretations of Bertha with which I substantially agree.

17. Moglen, *Charlotte Brontë*, jacket.

18. See Adrienne Rich, "Jane Eyre: The Temptations of a Motherless Woman," *Ms.*, 2 (1973), 106; reprinted in *Of Lies, Secrets and Silence* (New York: Norton, 1980).

19. Deprived of his train by Goneril and Regan, Lear first feels "Necessity's sharp pinch" (2.4.206) before he rages in his famous outburst, "O reason not the need" (2.4.250–81); he then recognizes amidst the heath's storm how "the art of our necessities is strange, / And can make vile things precious" (3.2.70–71). Robert Bernard Martin, *Charlotte Brontë's Novels: The Accents of Persuasion* (New York: Norton, 1966), pp. 84–85, also notes parallels with *King Lear*.

20. While I analyze the impact of "romance" elements from Milton and Shakespeare on Brontë's conclusion, Martin (*Charlotte Brontë's Novels*, p. 98) notes in passing the "Miltonic resonance of the lovers' walk back to Ferndean," then proceeds to a persuasive argument for Rochester's resemblances to the blinded Samson. Though my emphasis falls upon Lear and Gloucester as heroic models for Rochester, I concur with Martin's interpretation that Brontë's use of all such literary analogues gives "dignity and significance to the account of an individual who is part of the great archetypal pattern of sin, suffering, and redemption" (p. 99). See also *Paradise Lost*, Book 12, ll. 646–49.

Silver: The Reflecting Reader in *Villette*

1. Charlotte Brontë, *Villette* (New York: Harper Colophon, 1972), chap. 27; all subsequent references are to this edition. Earlier versions of this paper were presented to the Pacific Coast Conference on British Studies and the University Seminar for Feminist Inquiry at Dartmouth College. I am grateful to the members of the University Seminar and to Marianne Hirsch, Paula Mayhew, and Thomas Vargish for extremely useful criticism and suggestions.

2. The wording here reflects that in Wolfgang Iser's *The Implied Reader* (Baltimore: Johns Hopkins University Press, 1974), pp. 274–94, although the idea is common to reader-response criticism. For a collection of the classic essays in this field, see *Reader-Response Criticism: From Formalism to Post-Structuralism*, ed. Jane P. Tompkins (Baltimore: Johns Hopkins University Press, 1980); for more recent speculations, see *The Reader in the Text: Essays on Audience and Interpretation*, ed. Susan R. Soleiman and Inge Crossman (Princeton: Princeton University Press, 1980).

3. *Charlotte Brontë: The Self Conceived* (New York: Norton, 1978), pp. 196, 199.

4. "The Buried Letter: Feminism and Romanticism in *Villette*," in *Women Writing and Writing about Women*, ed. Mary Jacobus (London: Croom Helm, 1979), p. 43.

5. Sandra M. Gilbert and Susan Gubar, *The Madwoman in the Attic: The*

Woman Writer and the Nineteenth-Century Literary Imagination (New Haven: Yale University Press, 1979), pp. 418–19.

6. Tony Tanner shares this reading of the narrative. Lucy, he writes, "finds herself in 'bad' narrative in which she has effectively to create, or put together, her own ontology and value-system" ("Introduction," in Charlotte Brontë, *Villette* [New York: Penguin, 1979], p. 49).

7. *PMLA* 96, 1 (January 1981), 36–48. Hereafter, page references to Miller's essay appear in the text.

8. One need only recall Brontë's bitter comment in her explanation of why she and her sisters chose gender-ambiguous pseudonyms—"without at that time suspecting that our mode of writing and thinking was not what is called 'feminine' "—to measure the effect of criticism such as that in *The Christian Remembrancer*—"A book more unfeminine, both in its excellences and defects, it would be hard to find in the annals of female authorship"—and that of Elizabeth Rigby in the *Quarterly:* ". . . if we ascribe the book to a woman at all, we have no alternative but to ascribe it to one who has, for some sufficient reason, long forfeited the society of her own sex." (Charlotte Brontë's comment appears in the "Biographical Notice" to the 1850 edition of *Wuthering Heights* and *Agnes Grey,* quoted in Inga-Stina Ewbank, *Their Proper Sphere* [Cambridge, Mass.: Harvard University Press, 1968], p. 1; the reviews of *Jane Eyre* are quoted and discussed in Ewbank, pp. 43–46, and in Margot Peters, *Unquiet Soul: A Biography of Charlotte Brontë* [New York: Pocket Books, 1976], pp. 237–38.) Brontë was correct, moreover, to anticipate a similar response to *Villette:* Matthew Arnold, for example, found it "disagreeable . . . Because the writer's mind contains nothing but hunger, rebellion, and rage," and Thackeray criticized it as "rather vulgar—I don't make my *good women* ready to fall in love with two men at once" (quoted in Peters, p. 429). The most vicious attack, however, was Anne Mozley's anonymous review in *The Christian Remembrancer*. Although granting that the author of *Villette* had "gained both in amiability and propriety since she first presented herself to the world—soured, coarse, and grumbling; an alien, it might seem, from society, and amenable to none of its laws," her final judgment is severe. Brontë's "impersonations" are branded as "self-reliant" and "contemptuous of prescriptive decorum," and of Lucy she writes: "We will sympathise with Lucy Snowe as being fatherless and penniless . . . but we cannot offer even the affections of our fancy (the right and due of every legitimate heroine) to her unscrupulous and self-dependent intellect." Responding to this attack in a letter to the editor of the journal, Brontë consistently refers to the reviewer as "he." (The extracts from Mozley's review [June 1853] and Brontë's response [July 1853] appear in Thomas James Wise and John Alexander Symington, eds., *The Brontës: Their Lives, Friendships, and Correspondence* [Oxford: Shakespeare Head Press, 1932], vol. 4, pp. 78–79, and in Peters, *Unquiet Soul,* p. 428).

For a discussion of nineteenth-century criticism of women's fiction, including Brontë's, see Elaine Showalter's chapter "The Double Critical Standard," in *A Literature of Their Own: British Women Novelists from Brontë to Lessing* (Princeton: Princeton University Press, 1977).

9. For another reading of the "oddly assorted female Powers who people the novel's cosmos," see Nina Auerbach's chapter on *Villette* in *Communities of Women* (Cambridge: Harvard University Press, 1978), p. 110.

10. *Sexual Politics* (New York: Avon, 1971), p. 193.

11. Speaking of Mrs. Bretton's "patronage" of her, Lucy remarks, "it was not founded on conventional grounds of superior wealth or station (in the last particular there had never been any inequality; her degree was mine)" (chap. 16). I stress this point as a corrective to Terry Eagleton's analysis of Lucy's class anger and its effect on her psychological life, an analysis which overlooks the role of gender in connection with class (*Myths of Power: A Marxist Study of the Brontës* [New York: Barnes and Noble, 1975]).

12. M. Jeanne Peterson, "The Victorian Governess: Status Incongruence in Family and Society," in *Suffer and Be Still: Women in the Victorian Age*, ed. Martha Vicinus (Bloomington: Indiana University Press, 1973), p. 16.

13. Moglen interprets this linguistic pattern as part of Lucy's anesthetized reaction to the guilt of being a survivor, a way of not having to participate in life, and labels it neurotic (see, for example, pp. 196, 203). Eagleton, looking at this same language, reads it as part of Lucy's (and Jane Eyre's) need to see herself as a "meek, unworldly victim unable to act purposively" in order not to be accused of self-interested enterprise and the desire for social advancement (pp. 62–63). The truth is, however, that no matter how strong Lucy's energy and will, she would not have acquired her own school nearly as soon without Paul's gift, nor could she have expanded it as rapidly without Miss Marchmont's legacy. These are economic realities.

14. Miller is here quoting from Barbara Bellow Watson, "On Power and the Literary Text," *Signs*, 1 (1975), 113.

15. Jacobus argues that "The novel's real oddity lies in perversely withholding its true subject, Lucy Snowe, by an act of repression which mimics hers," and that "Lucy's invisibility is a calculated deception—a blank screen on which others project their view of her" (pp. 43, 44). The nun, on the other hand, forces the reader to experience the "uncanny" aspect of Lucy's narrative and becomes the true mirror of the hidden self (p. 52). I would argue that rather than perversely withholding its true subject, Lucy's narrative deliberately illustrates why the true subject is invisible to those with conventional social and fictional expectations. Lucy's true fiction is there from the beginning, created in part through the dialogue with the reader.

16. See, for example, the four addresses to the reader in chapter 18, "We Quarrel."

17. Observations about Ginevra and Polly continue to be addressed directly to the reader throughout the narrative, for here Lucy's perceptions do perhaps differ most radically from those of a society that might well find her merely jealous. Toward Ginevra she is continually sarcastic, but her attitude toward Polly is more complex. Ultimately, however, she underlines the conventional quality in Polly which leads the younger woman to respond to Lucy's understanding that "solitude is sadness" but not death. " 'Lucy, I wonder if anybody will ever comprehend you altogether' " (chap. 37).

Langland: Female Stories of Experience

1. Louisa May Alcott, *Little Women* (New York: Macmillan, 1962), pp. 115–16. All future citations will be to this edition and will be placed in parentheses in the text preceded by LW.

2. Nina Auerbach, *Communities of Women* (Cambridge: Harvard University Press, 1978), pp. 55–73, offers a perceptive analysis of the female community in *Little Women*. She is the first to analyze the richness and self-sufficiency of that community, a richness disrupted by the marriage plot. While Auerbach's illuminating reading focuses on the community of women in Alcott's novels, a concern of mine as well, my essay concentrates on the problems of female development, its stages and conclusions. I differ with Auerbach on developmental issues in that I see female community as a context in which to achieve maturity. Auerbach, in contrast, points out that Mrs. March allows her girls "a great freedom . . . the freedom to remain children" (p. 63). The family circle may prolong childhood, but I argue that it also stimulates maturity.

Auerbach is one of the first critics to perceive the complexity of *Little Women* and to begin to articulate it. She herself credits Elizabeth Janeway, *Between Myth and Morning* (New York: William Morrow, 1975), as the first "to make plain the high-spirited sedition behind the pieties of *Little Women*." Other feminist critics tend to see only the novel's conventional plot: a traditional story of girls growing up and marrying. See, for example, Patricia Meyer Spacks, *The Female Imagination* (New York: Avon, 1975), pp. 120–28, whose unsympathetic reading of Alcott's novel focuses entirely on surface patterns.

3. *The Madwoman in the Attic: The Woman Writer and the Nineteenth-Century Literary Imagination* (New Haven: Yale University Press, 1979), p. 76.

4. Jerome Buckley, *Season of Youth: The Bildungsroman from Dickens to Golding* (Cambridge: Harvard University Press, 1974), p. 17, defines the typical pattern of the *Bildungsroman* plot. The crucial developmental stages he describes are remarkably parallel to those of Christie's development.

5. *Work: A Story of Experience,* introd. Sarah Elbert (New York: Schocken Books, 1977), pp. 2, 8. All future citations will be to this edition and will be placed in parentheses in the text preceded by W.

6. *Louisa May: A Modern Biography* (New York: Avon, 1977), pp. 3–4.

7. Quoted in Madeline B. Stern, *Louisa May Alcott* (Norman: University of Oklahoma Press, 1950), pp. 189–90.

8. See Sexton, *Louisa May,* for a full development of Alcott's relationship to and role within her family.

9. *Literary Women: The Great Writers* (Garden City, N.Y.: Doubleday, 1977), p. 129.

10. In describing Beth, Alcott is drawing on a familiar nineteenth-century conception of ideal womanhood: the Angel. The Angel in the House always denies her own needs and identity for the sake of others. The ultimate self-denial is, of course, death. For one of the earliest feminist discussions of this image, see Susan Gorsky, "The Gentle Doubters: Images of Women in

Englishwomen's Novels, 1840–1920," in *Images of Women in Fiction: Feminist Perspectives,* ed. Susan Koppelman Cornillon (Bowling Green, Ohio: Bowling Green University Popular Press, 1972), pp. 34–38.

11. As quoted by Sarah Elbert, Introd., *Work,* p. xl.

12. Ellen Moers in *Literary Women* points out the significance of work in Alcott's novels, and she observes that Alcott's own unusual experiences as family breadwinner become a norm in the pages of her fiction and give her novels a "curious modernity": "For the working girls in Alcott, Jo and Meg as well as Christie, seem more like the college girl of today, working at menial pickup jobs without loss of respectability and class status, than like the Lucy Snowes and Maggie Tullivers who were their near contemporaries" (p. 133). This phenomenon helps account for the enduring appeal of Alcott's novels and further supports the presence of an alternative developmental pattern to that of marrying and bearing children.

13. Nina Auerbach, in *Communities of Women,* analyzes the association of death and marriage in *Little Women:* "The inclusion of young love among these upheavals implicitly defines it as more of a destroyer of sisterhood than an emotional progression beyond it; and the equation between the departures of marriage and of death continues in the last half of the book, where Beth's wasting illness and death run parallel to the marriages of the rest of the sisters. Both stress the loss of the childhood circle rather than the coming into an inheritance of fulfillment" (p. 63). Auerbach's perceptive analysis supports my argument that marriage marks the fulfillment only of the surface narrative. In the context of the submerged developmental narrative, marriage is disruptive and marks a death.

Baer: The Sisterhood of Jane Eyre and Antoinette Cosway

1. Adrienne Rich, "When We Dead Awaken: Writing as Re-Vision," *On Lies, Secrets, and Silences* (New York: W. W. Norton, 1979), p. 35.

2. Elizabeth Hardwick, *Seduction & Betrayal* (New York: Random House, 1974); Patricia Meyer Spacks, *The Female Imagination* (New York: Avon Books, 1972); Tillie Olsen, *Silences* (New York: Delta Books, 1979); Ellen Moers, *Literary Women: The Great Writers* (New York: Doubleday, 1977); Elaine Showalter, *A Literature of Their Own: British Women Novelists from Brontë to Lessing* (Princeton, N.J.: Princeton University Press, 1977); Sandra M. Gilbert and Susan Gubar, *The Madwoman in the Attic: The Woman Writer and the Nineteenth-Century Literary Imagination* (New Haven: Yale University Press, 1979).

3. Most criticism of the novel has been reductive in one way or another: Walter Allen, in a 1967 *New York Times Book Review* article, labeled the novel "Caribbean Gothic"; Kenneth Ramchaud's seven-page analysis of *Wide Sargasso Sea* in *The West Indian Novel and Its Background* (London: Faber and Faber, 1970) never once acknowledges its connections to *Jane Eyre;* many critics draw elaborate parallels between Rhys's writing and her life, claiming that her work is all autobiographical and hence derivative. But Rhys has also had her champions. Among the most sensitive interpretations her work has received are Thomas Staley's *Jean Rhys* (Austin: University of Texas Press,

1979) and Elizabeth Abel's first-rate article "Women and Schizophrenia: The Fiction of Jean Rhys," *Contemporary Literature,* 20, 2 (Spring 1969), 155–77.

4. Marcelle Bernstein, "The Inscrutable Miss Jean Rhys," *London Observer,* 1 June 1969, p. 50.

5. Hannah Carter, "Fated to Be Sad," *The Guardian,* 8 August 1968, p. 5.

6. I am indebted to Susan Gubar for this term; she suggested it to me in a telephone conversation in March 1981.

7. Here I will begin to use the name Rochester's first wife prefers in *Wide Sargasso Sea,* the name she has used her entire girlhood. Although Mr. Mason calls her "Bertha Antoinette Mason" in quoting from her marriage contract in *Jane Eyre* (New York: W. W. Norton, 1971, p. 255), Rhys asserts that Rochester has renamed her Bertha, thereby denying her identity.

8. Neville Braybrooke, "The Return of Jean Rhys," *Caribbean Quarterly,* 16, No. 4 (1970), 43–46; Dennis Porter, "Of Heroines and Victims: Jean Rhys and Jane Eyre," *Massachusetts Review,* 17 (1976), pp. 540–42; see also Walter Allen's review of *Wide Sargasso Sea* in *New York Times Book Review,* 18 June 1967, p. 5, which he entitled "Bertha the Doomed."

9. Greil Marcus, "Women as Losers: Jean Rhys in the 80's," *Rolling Stone,* 29 May 1980.

10. Although both Jane and Antoinette are orphans, the impact on Antoinette of having had a mother who gradually goes insane, is sexually exploited by her keepers, and finally dies must not be minimized. For an exploration of the function and result of a mother's death in twentieth-century fiction, see Judith Kegan Gardiner, "A Wake for Mother: The Maternal Deathbed in Women's Fiction," *Feminist Studies,* 4, 2 (June 1978), pp. 146–65.

11. Gilbert and Gubar, *The Madwoman in the Attic,* p. 364.

12. Otto Rank, *The Double* (New York: New American Library, 1978), pp. 8–33.

13. The classic pattern of the quest motif is elaborated in Joseph Campbell, *Hero of a Thousand Faces* (Princeton, N.J.: Princeton University Press, 1949).

14. Nancy Miller, "Emphasis Added: Plots and Plausibilities in Women's Fiction," *PMLA,* vol. 96, no. 1, p. 44.

15. Ibid., p. 46.

16. Ibid., p. 40.

17. Jean Rhys, *Wide Sargasso Sea* (New York: Popular Library Edition, 1966), p. 27; all subsequent references to this edition will be included in the text.

18. Charlotte Brontë, *Jane Eyre* (New York: W. W. Norton, 1971), p. 193; all subsequent references to this edition will be included in the text.

19. Rich, "Jane Eyre: The Temptations of a Motherless Woman," *On Lies,* pp. 89–106.

20. I owe this term to Judith Fetterley, *The Resisting Reader* (Bloomington: Indiana University Press, 1978).

Gelfant: Revolutionary Turnings

1. Jean Stafford, *The Mountain Lion* (New York: Harcourt, Brace and Company, 1947), p. 158. Subsequent citations to this volume will appear in the text.

2. Katherine Anne Porter, "Old Morality," *Pale Horse, Pale Rider* (New York: Random House, 1939), p. 81.

3. Charlotte Brontë, *Jane Eyre* (New York: Norton, 1971), p. 12.

4. In her recent book, *Poets in Their Youth: A Memoir* (New York: Random House, 1982), Eileeen Simpson reports a conversation in which Jean Stafford claims Molly's poem as her own, written when she was six: "Want to hear my first poem? [Stafford says]. It's called 'Gravel.' I've just given it to my character Molly in *The Mountain Lion*" (p. 123). Like Molly, Jean Stafford lived in Covina, California, her birthplace, and grew up in Boulder, Colorado. There her father wrote popular Westerns under various names; her mother ran a boardinghouse. As a girl, Stafford "resented her family's poverty," Simpson tells us, presumably repeating Stafford's confidence, "and had felt kinship only with her brother Dick, to whom she was very close" (p. 123). Apparently, Molly enacts some of Stafford's childhood fears and rituals, particularly those related to her aquaphobia.

In 1936, Stafford received a Master of Arts degree from the University of Boulder; subsequently, she studied philosophy at Heidelberg. She has been a teacher, a literary editor, a public lecturer, and an acclaimed fiction writer, the recipient of the Pulitzer Prize in 1970 for her collected stories. Some of the vicissitudes of her adult life, particularly the break-up of her marriage with the poet Robert Lowell, are presented in Simpson's memoir. She died in March 1976 at the age of sixty-one.

Abel: Narrative Structure(s) and Female Development

1. *A Writer's Diary* (London: The Hogarth Press, 1953), November 28, 1928, p. 139.

2. In *The Madwoman in the Attic: The Woman Writer and the Nineteenth-Century Literary Imagination* (New Haven: Yale University Press, 1979), Sandra M. Gilbert and Susan Gubar claim that "women from Jane Austen and Mary Shelley to Emily Brontë and Emily Dickinson produced literary works that are in some sense palimpsestic, works whose surface designs conceal or obscure deeper, less accessible (and less socially acceptable) levels of meaning. Thus these authors managed the difficult task of achieving true female literary authority by simultaneously conforming to and subverting patriarchal literary standards" (p. 73).

3. June 18, 1923, entry in Woolf's holograph notebook dated variously from November 9, 1922, to August 2, 1923; cited by Charles G. Hoffmann, "From Short Story to Novel: The Manuscript Revisions of Virginia Woolf's *Mrs. Dalloway*," *Modern Fiction Studies*, 14, 2 (Summer 1968), 183.

4. "Women Novelists," in *Women and Writing*, ed. Michèle Barrett (New York: Harcourt Brace Jovanovich, 1979), p. 71.

5. *A Room of One's Own* (New York: Harcourt Brace Jovanovich, 1957), pp. 76–77.

6. "Literary Criticism," *Signs,* 1, 2 (Winter 1975), 435.

7. On women novelists' dissatisfaction with the plot of romantic love, see Nancy K. Miller, "Emphasis Added: Plots and Plausibilities in Women's Fiction," *PMLA,* 96, 1 (January 1981), 36–48, and Marianne Hirsch, "A Mother's Discourse: Incorporation and Repetition in *La Princesse de Clèves,*" *Yale French Studies,* 62 (1981) 67–87. On the particular shift that took place in the early twentieth century, see Ellen Moers, *Literary Women* (Garden City: Doubleday, 1977), especially pp. 352–68; Jane Lilienfeld, "Reentering Paradise: Cather, Colette, Woolf and Their Mothers," in *The Lost Tradition: Mothers and Daughters in Literature,* ed. Cathy N. Davidson and E. M. Broner (New York: Frederick Ungar, 1980), pp. 160–75; and Louise Bernikow, *Among Women* (New York: Crown Publishers, 1980), pp. 155–93. In " 'Women Alone Stir My Imagination': Lesbianism and the Cultural Tradition," *Signs,* 4, 4 (Summer 1979), Blanche Wiesen Cook points out that "were all things equal, 1928 might be remembered as a banner year for lesbian publishing" (p. 718).

8. In his essay "Femininity," published the following year, Freud explicitly uses the metaphor of strata: "A woman's identification with her mother allows us to distinguish two strata: the pre-Oedipus one which rests on her affectionate attachment to her mother and takes her as a model, and the later one from the Oedipus complex which seeks to get rid of her mother and take her place with her father." The essay is reprinted in *Women and Analysis,* ed. Jean Strouse (New York: Grossman Publishers, 1974), p. 92.

9. Woolf's reaction to *Ulysses,* recorded in her journal entries in September and October 1922, suggests her interest in counteracting the perspective of this "callow school boy, full of wits and powers, but so self-conscious and egotistical that he loses his head" (*The Diary of Virginia Woolf,* vol. 2: 1920–1924, ed. Anne Olivier Bell [New York: Harcourt Brace Jovanovich, 1978]), September 6, 1922, p. 199. For structural echoes of *Ulysses* in *Mrs. Dalloway,* see Margaret Church, "Joycean Structure in *Jacob's Room* and *Mrs. Dalloway,*" *International Fiction Review,* 4, 2 (July 1977), 101–9.

10. The essay on Jane Austen in *The Common Reader* (1925) incorporates a review Woolf wrote just after completing *Mrs. Dalloway.* Woolf had also reviewed works by and about Austen in 1920 and 1922. In *The Common Reader* essay, Woolf tacitly assigns herself the role of Austen's heir by speculating that the novels Austen would have written in middle age would have manifested Woolf's aesthetic goals. The essay demonstrates a complex dialectic between Woolf's and Austen's concern with silence.

11. *The Diary of Virginia Woolf,* vol. 2: 1920–1924, ed. Anne Olivier Bell (New York: Harcourt Brace Jovanovich, 1978), August 30, 1923, p. 263.

12. In *"Mrs. Dalloway:* The Communion of Saints," *New Feminist Essays on Virginia Woolf,* ed. Jane Marcus (London: Macmillan; Lincoln: University of Nebraska Press, 1981), p. 136, Suzette A. Henke points out that in the manuscript version of the novel Sally Seton clearly reciprocates Clarissa's love. Until recently, Sally has been remarkably absent from critical commentary on

Mrs. Dalloway. Recent discussions include Judith McDaniel, "Lesbians and Literature," *Sinister Wisdom,* 1, 2 (Fall 1976), 20–23; Emily Jensen, "Clarissa Dalloway's Respectable Suicide," in *New Feminist Essays on Virginia Woolf,* ed. Jane Marcus. I am indebted to Tina Petrig, whose illuminating essay on female relationships in Woolf entitled "—all sorts of flowers that had never been seen together before—," first alerted me to the crucial role of Clarissa's relationship with Sally.

13. For the power and endurance of Woolf's relationships with women, see her letters, especially the letters to Violet Dickinson in volume 1; Jane Marcus, "Thinking Back Through Our Mothers," and Ellen Hawkes, "Woolf's Magical Garden of Women," in *New Feminist Essays on Virginia Woolf;* Phyllis Rose, *Woman of Letters: A Life of Virginia Woolf* (New York: Oxford University Press, 1978), pp. 109–24; and Jane Marcus, "Virginia Woolf and Her Violin: Mothering, Madness and Music" (unpublished). Although the relationship of Woolf's life to her fiction is much more pronounced in *To the Lighthouse,* there are quiet parallels between Woolf's biography and Clarissa's; the death of Clarissa's mother and sister cast Sally in the emotional role assumed by Vanessa Stephen, the primary nurturing figure throughout Woolf's life.

14. *Mrs. Dalloway* (New York: Harcourt, Brace & World, 1927), pp. 52–53. This passage suggests an analogy between the wrapped-up present of Sally's love and the buried subplot of female bonds. All future references to *Mrs. Dalloway* will be placed in parentheses in the text.

15. See, for example, Sigmund Freud, "Femininity," in *Women and Analysis,* ed. Jean Strouse, p. 89; Helene Deutsch, "Female Homosexuality," in *The Psycho-Analytic Reader: An Anthology of Essential Papers with Critical Introductions,* ed. Robert Fliess (New York: International Universities Press, 1948), pp. 208–30; Adrienne Rich, *Of Woman Born: Motherhood as Experience and Institution* (New York: W. W. Norton, 1976); Catharine Stimpson, "Zero Degree Deviancy," *Critical Inquiry* (forthcoming).

16. "Some Psychical Consequences of the Anatomical Distinction Between the Sexes," in Strouse, *Women and Analysis,* p. 24; "Female Sexuality," in Strouse, p. 42.

17. For an analysis of this scene as part of a pattern of interruption in *Mrs. Dalloway,* see Emily Jensen, "Clarissa Dalloway's Respectable Suicide," in *New Feminist Essays on Virginia Woolf,* ed. Jane Marcus. Jensen's point of view is similar to mine, though she does not adopt a psychoanalytic approach, and sees Clarissa's development in more purely negative terms than I.

18. "Mrs. Dalloway in Bond Street," in *Mrs. Dalloway's Party,* ed. Stella McNichol (New York: Harcourt Brace Jovanovich, 1975), p. 27.

19. Elizabeth Janeway suggests the resonance of this name in an essay entitled "Who Is Sylvia? On the Loss of Sexual Paradigms," *Signs* 5, 4 (Summer 1980), 573–89. She concludes the essay by asking, "Who is Sylvia, whose name carries an edge of wilderness and a hint of unexplored memory? We do not know, but we will surely recognize her when she comes."

20. The Hogarth Press began publication of Freud's *Collected Papers* in 1924; the first volume of the *Standard Edition,* translated by James Strachey and published in its entirety by the Hogarth Press, did not appear until 1948.

Woolf's review entitled "Freudian Fiction," in *Times Literary Supplement,* March 25, 1920, reveals that she was familiar with the essentials of Freudian theory, though opposed to a simplistic application of the theory in fiction.

21. "Female Sexuality," in Strouse, *Women and Analysis,* p. 42; "Femininity," in Strouse, p. 78.

22. "Femininity," p. 78.

23. For an analysis of this female sphere, see Carroll Smith-Rosenberg, "The Female World of Love and Ritual: Relations between Women in Nineteenth-Century America," *Signs,* 1, 1 (Autumn 1975), 1–30. In *The Reproduction of Mothering: Psychoanalysis and the Sociology of Gender* (Berkeley: University of California Press, 1978), Nancy Chodorow argues that the pre-Oedipal orientation is not terminated by the Oedipus complex, but continues as a powerful influence throughout a woman's life, triggering repeated conflicts between allegiances to women and men.

24. "Femininity," p. 77.

25. "Femininity," p. 85; "Female Sexuality," p. 43.

26. "Female Sexuality," p. 43.

27. This significant fact is also noted by Elizabeth Janeway, "On 'Female Sexuality'," in Strouse, p. 60, and Sarah Kofman, "The Narcissistic Woman: Freud and Girard," *Diacritics,* 10, 3 (Fall 1980), 45.

28. "Femininity," p. 87.

29. "Femininity," p. 92.

30. Phyllis Rose makes this point about Baron Marbot's *Memoirs* in *Woman of Letters: A Life of Virginia Woolf,* p. 144.

31. Catharine R. Stimpson implies a parallel between the coding of "aberrant" sexuality in the works of Gertrude Stein and Woolf. See "The Mind, the Body, and Gertrude Stein," *Critical Inquiry,* 3, 3 (Spring 1977), 505.

32. Another parallel between these women is established through the Shakespearean allusions. The recurrent lines from *Cymbeline* associate Clarissa with Imogen; Rezia's name (Lucrezia) recalls Shakespeare's narrative poem, *The Rape of Lucrece.* The situations in these works are remarkably similar: in both, men dispute one another's claims to possess the most chaste and beautiful of women, the dispute prompts one man to observe and/or test the virtue of the other's wife, and this encounter culminates in the real or pretended rape of the woman and eventually her actual or illusory death. The analogy between these Shakespearean heroines more closely allies Clarissa with Lucrezia in a realm external to but signaled by Woolf's text.

33. In her "Introduction" to the Modern Library edition of *Mrs. Dalloway* (1928), Woolf explains that "in the first version Septimus, who later is intended to be her double, had no existence. . . . Mrs. Dalloway was originally to kill herself or perhaps merely to die at the end of the party" (p. vi).

34. Emily Jensen also discusses the relationship between these passages in "Clarissa Dalloway's Respectable Suicide," *New Feminist Essays.*

35. Freud claims, for example, that "We can thus judge the so-called savage and semi-savage races; their psychic life assumes a peculiar interest for us, for we can recognize in their psychic life a well-preserved, early stage of our own development" (*Totem and Taboo,* trans. A. A. Brill [New York: Random House, 1946], p. 3).

36. In "*The Years* as Greek Drama, Domestic Novel, and Gotterdäm-merung," *Bulletin of the New York Public Library*, 80, 2 (Winter 1977), 276–301, Jane Marcus discusses the influence of Jane Harrison's work on Woolf's fiction. She points out that Woolf's library contained a copy of Harrison's *Ancient Art and Ritual* (1918), inscribed to Woolf by the author on Christmas, 1923. In "*Mrs. Dalloway:* The Communion of Saints," Suzette A. Henke mentions that Woolf's notes for *Mrs. Dalloway* are in a notebook that contains her earlier reflections on Aeschylus' *Choephoroi.* Woolf was reading Greek texts diligently in 1922 and 1923 in preparation for her essay "On Not Knowing Greek."

37. See, for example, Maria Di Battista, *Virginia Woolf's Major Novels: The Fables of Anonymous* (New Haven: Yale University Press, 1980); Phyllis Rose, *Woman of Letters;* J. Hillis Miller, "Virginia Woolf's All Souls' Day: The Omniscient Narrator in *Mrs. Dalloway,*" in *The Shaken Realist: Essays in Honor of Frederick J. Hoffman,* ed. Melvin J. Friedman and John Vickery (Baton Rouge: Louisiana State University Press, 1970), 100–127.

38. " 'Something Central which Permeated': Virginia Woolf and Mrs. Dalloway," in *The Fields of Light* (New York: Oxford University Press, 1951), p. 135. Brower also significantly omits Sally Seton from his summary of the novel's plot.

39. Xavière Gauthier, "Is There Such a Thing as Women's Writing?" *New French Feminisms,* ed. Elaine Marks and Isabelle de Courtivron (Amherst: University of Massachusetts Press, 1980), p. 164. The whole project of *écriture féminine* stresses the importance of representing women's silence and absence.

40. "Beyond Determinism: George Eliot and Virginia Woolf," *Women Writing and Writing about Women,* ed. Mary Jacobus (London: Croom Helm, 1979), p. 80. Beer analyzes Woolf's resistance to plot in *The Waves.*

41. I would like to thank the coeditors of this anthology, and Diane Middlebrook, Marta Peixoto, Lisa Ruddick, Sanford Schwartz, and Janet Silver for their helpful commentary on this essay.

Stimpson: Doris Lessing and the Parables of Growth

1. Doris Lessing, "The Small Personal Voice," *A Small Personal Voice: Essays, Reviews, Interviews,* ed. Paul Schlueter (New York: Alfred A. Knopf, 1974), p. 14. I will be using and quoting from the following editions of the *Children of Violence* novels: *Martha Quest* (1952; rpt. New York: New American Library, 1970); *A Proper Marriage* (1954; rpt. New York: New American Library, 1970) cited as APM; *A Ripple from the Storm* (1958; rpt. New York: New American Library, 1970) cited as RS; *Landlocked* (1965; rpt. New York: New American Library, 1970); *The Four-Gated City* (1969; rpt. New York: Bantam Books, 1970) cited as FGC. For a recent survey of Lessing criticism see Holly Beth King, "Criticism of Doris Lessing: A Selected Checklist," *Modern Fiction Studies: Special Issue, Doris Lessing,* 26, 1 (Spring 1980), 167–75.

2. "Introduction," *The Golden Notebook* (1962; rpt. New York: Bantam, 1973), p. xix.

3. "Afterword to *The Story of an African Farm*," *A Small Personal Voice*, p. 98.

4. Idries Shah, *The Way of the Sufi* (London: Jonathan Cape, 1968), p. 31.

5: George Lukács, *The Theory of the Novel: A Historico-Philosophical Essay on the Forms of Great Epic Literature* (1920), trans. Anna Bostock (Cambridge: MIT Press, 1971), p. 89.

6. Roy Pascal, *The German Novel* (Toronto: University of Toronto Press, 1956), p. 11. Comment on *The Four-Gated City* as a *Bildungsroman* is common. The most extensive is Ellen Cronan Rose, *The Tree Outside the Window: Doris Lessing's* Children of Violence (Hanover, N.H.: University Press of New England, 1976). Rose, seeing the series as a "novel of development or growth," adapts Erik H. Erikson's psychological theory to it. In "The Limits of Consciousness in the Novels of Doris Lessing," in *Doris Lessing: Critical Studies,* ed. Annis Pratt and L. S. Dembo (Madison: University of Wisconsin Press, 1974), pp. 119–32, Sydney Janet Kaplan compares Lessing to Dorothy Richardson. She too finds Lessing modifying the *Bildungsroman* through a self-conscious interest in such larger political issues as racism, class conflict, and war. In "Disorderly Company," in the same volume, pp. 74–97, Dagmar Barnouw says that *The Four-Gated City* becomes a collective *Bildungsroman*, its protagonists Mark, Lynda, and Martha. She cannot find the first volume a *Bildungsroman* in the strict sense of the word, for "Matty is neither moving toward a choice, a determining decision she will make at one time or the other, nor is the fact that she is incapable of such a choice integrated into the substance and structure of her developments" (pp. 83–84). I wonder. Matty moves toward the choice of leaving Africa, and her general difficulty of the will is one of Lessing's deep interests.

7. I adapt these terms from Frank Kermode, *The Sense of an Ending* (New York: Oxford University Press, 1967; pbk. 1968), pp. 6, 93.

8. Dorothy Brewster, *Doris Lessing* (New York: Twayne Publishers, 1965), p. 159, correctly compares Maggie Tulliver to the young Martha: "rebellious, adventurous, romantic, chafing against barriers of a narrow provincial society . . . and deeply influenced by books."

9. Lessing, "Afterword to *The Story of An African Farm*," *A Small Personal Voice*, p. 107. Of Lessing's critics, only Michael Thorpe has been sufficiently attentive to her African background, though he hurts himself through a programmatic disdain of feminists. He sees the need for a subgenre: *Bildungsromane* about colonized women, be they white, African, Asian, or aboriginal. See Michael Thorpe, *Doris Lessing* (London: Longman Group Ltd., 1973), and Michael Thorpe, *Doris Lessing's Africa* (London: Evans Brothers, Ltd., 1978). For a fine new biography of Olive Schreiner see Ruth First and Ann Scott, *Olive Schreiner: A Biography* (New York: Schocken Books, 1980).

10. Paul Schlueter, *The Novels of Doris Lessing* (Carbondale: Southern Illinois University Press, 1973), p. 75.

11. "The Small Personal Voice," *A Small Personal Voice*, p. 8.

12. Mary Ann Singleton, *The City and the Veld: The Fiction of Doris Lessing* (Lewisburg: Bucknell University Press, 1977), p. 166, makes a similar point.

13. Roberta Rubenstein, *The Novelistic Vision of Doris Lessing: Breaking the Forms of Consciousness* (Urbana: University of Illinois Press, 1979), p. 6.

14. For a fuller analysis, see Lynn Sukenick, "Feeling and Reason in Doris Lessing's Fiction," *Doris Lessing: Critical Studies,* pp. 98–118, and Elaine Showalter, *A Literature of Their Own: British Women Novelists from Brontë to Lessing* (Princeton, N.J.: Princeton University Press, 1977), p. 313.

15. "Introduction," *The Golden Notebook,* pp. viii–ix.

16. Brewster, *Doris Lessing,* p. 158.

17. "May" is a pun. Mrs. Quest might once have been capable of a quest; she is, after all, the woman whom Martha sees playing Chopin at night on her piano in the mud-and-thatch farmhouse. But she constricts herself. "May" is also Lessing's middle name. That she should assign it to Martha's mother surely reveals some unresolved dilemma. I say this while aware of Lessing's dislike of critics who reduce her texts to a series of autobiographical gestures.

18. Charlotte Brontë, *Shirley* (Baltimore: Penguin Books, 1974), p. 356.

19. Doris Lessing, *African Stories* (New York: Simon and Schuster, 1965), p. 6.

20. Sukenick, "Feeling and Reason," p. 114. Sukenick's tone is more sardonic than mine.

21. Rose, *The Tree Outside the Window,* p. 68. Carol P. Christ, more sympathetic, says that "Women's spiritual quest provides orientation of women's social quest and grounds it in something larger than individual or even collective achievements." See *Diving Deep and Surfacing: Women Writers on Spiritual Quest* (Boston: Beacon Press, 1980), p. 11. Her chapter on Lessing, pp. 55–73, is a fine reading of *Children of Violence* as such a quest, tactfully using Jungian and mythic materials. However, my point is that Martha is meant to represent both sexes. She has some special difficulties because she is a woman: sexuality, the limits of a middle-class role, male chauvinism. She is meant to work her way through this and to act in ways both men and women can emulate. Consciousness is sexless, like angels for Leonardo.

22. Shah, *The Way of the Sufi,* p. 222.

23. Northrop Frye, "Varieties of Literary Utopia," *Utopias and Utopian Thought,* ed. Frank E. Manuel (Boston: Houghton Mifflin, 1966), pp. 48–49.

Rose: Through the Looking Glass

1. Bruno Bettelheim, *The Uses of Enchantment* (New York: Alfred A. Knopf, 1976), p. 73. Further references will be included in the text.

2. Sandra M. Gilbert and Susan Gubar, *The Madwoman in the Attic: The Woman Writer and the Nineteenth-Century Literary Imagination* (New Haven: Yale University Press, 1979), p. 36. Further references will be included in the text.

3. Carol P. Christ, *Diving Deep and Surfacing: Women Writers on Spiritual Quest* (Boston: Beacon Press, 1980), p. 4.

4. Ibid., p. 1.

5. Ibid., p. 6. Note the covert allusion to Cinderella's step-sisters who, according to Grimm, lop off portions of their feet "to fit themselves" into the glass slipper the Prince proffers as a (happy) married conclusion to the story.

6. I borrow this phrase from the subtitle of the "polemical preface" to *The Sadeian Woman* (New York: Pantheon Books, 1978), an "exercise in cultural history" in which Angela Carter puts pornography "in the service of women."

7. Madonna Kolbenschlag, *Kiss Sleeping Beauty Good-Bye: Breaking the Spell of Feminine Myths and Models* (New York: Doubleday, 1979), p. 3.

8. Anne Sexton, *Transformations* (Boston: Houghton Mifflin, 1971); Olga Broumas, *Beginning with O* (New Haven: Yale University Press, 1977); Angela Carter, *The Bloody Chamber* (New York: Harper and Row, 1980).

9. "'A Woman Who Writes': A Feminist Approach to the Early Poetry of Anne Sexton," in *Anne Sexton: The Artist and Her Critics,* ed. J. D. McClatchy (Bloomington: Indiana University Press, 1978), pp. 216–18.

10. Adrienne Rich, *Of Woman Born* (New York: Norton, 1976), p. 96. Further references will be included in the text.

11. Even Bettelheim, p. 21n., compliments Sexton for thus noting the phallic significance of the dwarfs in Snow White's story.

12. Andrea Dworkin, *Woman Hating* (New York: E. P. Dutton, 1974), p. 41.

13. Katherine Hayles reminds me in a personal communication that according to the dictionary, a Goth is "any uncouth, uncivilized person; a barbarian," and suggests that Mother *Gothel* is outside (male) civilization.

14. Cf. the "bonefish" in "Snow White and the Seven Dwarfs."

15. Nor Hall, who believes that "the female void cannot be cured by conjunction with the male, but rather by an internal conjunction, by an integration of its own parts, by a remembering or a putting back together of the mother-daughter body," reminds us that "seduction is a kind of education. When you are educated, or educed, you are led *out*. When you are seduced, you are led *aside*. A girl's first seduction is when the separation from her mother begins." See *The Moon and the Virgin: Reflections on the Archetypal Feminine* (New York: Harper and Row, 1980), pp. 68, 76.

16. "Some Psychical Consequences of the Anatomical Distinction Between the Sexes" (1925), "Female Sexuality" (1931), and "Femininity" (1933), conveniently available in *Women and Analysis,* ed. Jean Strouse (New York: Grossman Publishers, 1974).

17. *The Reproduction of Mothering: Psychoanalysis and the Sociology of Gender* (Berkeley: University of California Press, 1978), p. 164.

18. "The Traffic in Women: Notes on the 'Political Economy' of Sex," in *Toward an Anthropology of Women,* ed. Rayna R. Reiter (New York and London: Monthly Review Press, 1975), pp. 157–210.

19. Note how uncannily this passage echoes Sexton's "Snow White and the Seven Dwarfs," with its reference to the virgin and the doll-maker.

20. It does, however, bring other stories to mind. Marianne Hirsch suggests, in a personal communication, that Carter alludes to Romulus and Remus, those wolf-reared children who are credited with founding Roman civilization. If Sexton's Mother Gothel is a feminist alternative to patriarchal civilization, so certainly is Carter's Wolf-Alice, who goes "through the looking glass" to discover an alternative to civilization.

21. Adrienne Rich, *The Dream of a Common Language* (New York: Norton, 1978), p. 3.

Ferguson: The Female Novel of Development and the Myth of Psyche

1. For discussion of male heroes, see Walter L. Reed, *Meditations on the Hero: A Study of the Romantic Hero in Nineteenth-Century Fiction* (New Haven: Yale University Press, 1974) and Ihab Hassan, *Radical Innocence: Studies in the Contemporary American Novel* (Princeton, N.J.: Princeton University Press, 1961). In *The Necessary Blankness: Women in Major American Fiction of the Sixties* (Bloomington: University of Indiana Press, 1976), Mary Allen points out that women are either absent or are negatively perceived as passive in works focused on alienated heroes.

2. Sandra M. Gilbert and Susan Gubar in *The Madwoman in the Attic: The Woman Writer and the Nineteenth-Century Literary Imagination* (New Haven: Yale University Press, 1979) point to women authors' recourse to metaphors of starvation, madness, and death when describing their heroines' attitudes toward their roles.

3. Though probably of more ancient provenience, the myth is first recorded in the second century A.D. in Lucius Apuleius' *Metamorphoses,* later called *The Golden Ass.* A convenient translation with important commentary appears in Erich Neumann's *Amor and Psyche: The Psychic Development of the Feminine* (Princeton, N.J.: Princeton University Press, 1956). Other important interpretations are those of Ann Ulanov in *The Feminine in Jungian Psychology and Christian Theology* (Evanston, Ill.: Northwestern University Press, 1971); Nor Hall, *The Moon and the Virgin: Reflections on the Archetypal Feminine* (New York: Harper and Row, 1980); and Lee Edwards, "The Labors of Psyche: Toward a Theory of Female Heroes," *Critical Inquiry,* 6 (Autumn 1979), 33–49. Edwards claims that Neumann's interpretation reflects patriarchal bias and suggests that Psyche's development is a myth of human development applicable to all cultures. In *Reinventing Womanhood* (New York: Norton, 1979), pp. 140ff., Carolyn Heilbrun also criticizes Neumann's view and sees in the Psyche story a gender-free paradigm of human development. Heilbrun points out that the majority of women writers "have failed to imagine autonomous women characters" (p. 71) and suggests the Psyche myth as a fruitful model. Rachel Blau DuPlessis points out that women poets have been concerned with "the invention of reevaluative quest myths," and shows specific parallels to the Psyche myth in the work of Denise Levertov. See her "The Critique of Consciousness and Myth in Levertov, Rich and Rukeyser," *Shakespeare's Sisters: Feminist Essays on Women Poets,* ed. Sandra M. Gilbert and Susan Gubar (Bloomington: Indiana University Press, 1979), pp. 280–300 (originally published in *Feminist Studies,* 3 [Fall 1975]). DuPlessis has also written an impressionistic critique of Neumann's interpretation; see her article "Psyche, or Wholeness," *Massachusetts Review,* 20 (Spring 1979), 77–96. DuPlessis focuses on the meaning of the four labors of Psyche, which, by performing, she acquires a knowledge of the entire cosmos—earth (both vegetable and animal), water, underworld. Thereby

Psyche finds a deeper knowledge. While I find her interpretation rich and valid, accepting it is not necessary to my argument.

4. Welty's "At the Landing" appeared in her collection *The Wide Net and Other Stories* (New York: Harcourt Brace, 1943); citations will be from this source. *Kinflicks*, first published by Knopf, will be cited from the paperback version of the New American Library. *Fanny* will be cited from the hardcover edition of New American Library.

5. Bruno Bettelheim in *The Uses of Enchantment* (New York: Knopf, 1976), discusses the fairy-tale versions of the Psyche myth in a section on animal bridegrooms. He sees the bride's acceptance of the lover as overcoming feminine repugnance for male sexuality, a liberation which feminists perceive as signifying also women's acceptance of their own sexuality and personhood. For suggestions about the relationship between myth and fairy tale, see Bettelheim and Jacques Barchilon, " 'Beauty and the Beast': From Myth to Fairy Tale," *Psychoanalysis and Psychoanalytic Review*, 46 (1959), 19–29. Joseph Campbell traces some of the history of the Psyche myth in *Myths to Live By* (New York: Bantam, 1973); he credits twelfth-century troubadours with the perception of *amor*, or noble love, as "discriminative—personal and specific—born of the eyes and the heart" (p. 162). For a feminist perspective, see Madonna Kolbenschlag, *Kiss Sleeping Beauty Good-Bye: Breaking the Spell of Feminine Myths and Models* (New York: Doubleday, 1979).

6. Hall makes the point that "Psyche divinized is consciousness raised" (p. 20). Kolbenschlag considers the image of the Terrible Mother to be a fantasized assessment of a real mother, a projection of our own fears" (p. 46). This description seems to apply to the image of a real mother presented in Nancy Friday's *My Mother, Myself: The Daughter's Search for Identity* (New York: Dell, 1977). For a recent feminist critique of Friday's view, see Linda Hunt, "Books about Women's Lives: The New Best Sellers," *Radical America*, 14 (Sept.–Oct. 1980), 45–52.

7. According to Hastings's *Encyclopedia of Religion and Ethics*, albinism is often viewed as a source of magical power. It may also reflect the mother as ghost.

8. Welty says that in all her works she has used the myth of the errand or search exemplified in the stories of Jason, Theseus, Osysseus, Dick Whittington, Don Quixote: "I drew on them as casually as I did on the daily newspaper," she says; "myth enters daily life openly, almost visibly." See "Looking Back at the First Story," *Georgia Review*, 33 (Winter 1979), 751–55. Though she does not mention the Psyche myth her allusion to the lovers as butterflies in "At the Landing" points specifically to Psyche, whose name in Greek means both "soul" and "butterfly."

9. By John Cleland, published in 1749, the same year in which Fielding's *Tom Jones* appeared. Imitating both these novels is part of Jong's wit in *Fanny*.

10. Neumann points out (p. 147) that Apuleius imputes knowledge of witchcraft and of the matriarchal mysteries to the old woman who tells the Psyche story. The story itself can thus be perceived as part of female lore to be transmitted through female networks.

11. This is an allusion to Greek images of Psyche or the soul as having wings—a butterfly, a winged woman, or a bird.

12. In their longitudinal study of women aged 35 to 55, psychologists Barnett and Baruch have found that 70 percent of their subjects never experienced the so-called Oedipal separation as traumatic; other research by them indicates that mothers may be positive models for the individuation of competent women. This research explodes the prevailing cultural stereotype of rebellious daughters fighting possessive mothers. See Rosalind C. Barnett and Grace K. Baruch, "Women in the Middle Years: A Critique of Research and Theory," *Psychology of Women Quarterly*, 3 (Winter 1978), 187–97; Caryl Rivers, Rosalind C. Barnett, and Grace K. Baruch, *Beyond Sugar and Spice: How Women Grow, Learn, and Thrive* (New York: Putnam, 1979); and Grace K. Baruch, Rosalind C. Barnett, and Caryl Rivers, *Life Prints: New Patterns of Love and Work for Today's Women* (New York: McGraw-Hill, forthcoming).

13. In her "Afterword" to *Fanny,* Jong credits anthropological and fairy-tale sources for the witchcraft material (p. 503). Erich Neumann points out that Apuleius in the larger work in which the Psyche myth is an episode pays tribute to female goddesses and rites. Jong's lore is appropriate to the myth; she has altered it to fit the eighteenth-century English setting in a way that affirms the living presence of myth. For an important overview about the persistence in our culture of Greek myths about women, see Christine Downing, *The Goddess: Mythological Images of the Feminine* (New York: Continuum Publishing Company, 1982).

14. Carol Gilligan argues brilliantly for a new theory of women's moral development as different from but not inferior to men's in *In a Different Voice: Psychological Theory and Women's Development* (Cambridge: Harvard University Press, 1982). Gilligan perceives women's priority for caring relationships as crucial to their development; this perception requires a rethinking of theories of human development.

15. In *Toward a New Psychology of Women* (Boston: Beacon Press, 1976).

16. Dorothy Dinnerstein, *The Mermaid and the Minotaur: Sexual Arrangements and Human Malaise* (New York: Harper and Row, 1976) and Nancy Chodorow, *The Reproduction of Mothering: Psychoanalysis and the Psychology of Gender* (Berkeley: University of California Press, 1978).

17. All theorists would agree that whether or not the presence of myth was intended by the author, the patterns are very much a part of works of art. For a review of various attitudes toward the relationship of myth and literature, see *Myth and Literature: Contemporary Theory and Practice,* ed. John B. Vickery (Lincoln: University of Nebraska Press, 1966). Recent studies include Bert O. States, "The Persistence of the Archetype," *Critical Inquiry,* 6 (Winter 1980), 333–44, and Rodney Needham, *Primordial Characters* (Charlottesville: University Press of Virginia, 1978), both of whom suggest that myths and archetypes are an aspect of the brain's functioning. Victor W. Turner, *Dramas, Fields, and Metaphors: Symbolic Action in Human Society* (Ithaca: Cornell University Press, 1974) uses the term "root paradigm"

to indicate "the cultural transliterations of genetic codes" (quoted by Lee Edwards in the article cited in n. 3 above).

18. *Powers of the Weak* (New York: Alfred A. Knopf, 1980).

Zimmerman: Exiting from Patriarchy

1. Karla Jay, "Coming Out as Process," in Ginny Vida, *Our Right to Love* (Englewood Cliffs, N.J.: Prentice-Hall, 1978), p. 29.

2. On the theme of "coming out," see Jane Gurko, "The Shape of Sameness: Contemporary Lesbian Autobiographical Narratives," unpublished paper presented to the Gay Rhetorical Panel at the Modern Language Association, Houston, December 1980. Also see Marilyn Frye, Review of *The Coming Out Stories, Sinister Wisdom* 14 (Summer 1980), 97–98.

3. Susan J. Rosowski, "The Novel of Awakening," in this volume.

4. Bonnie Hoover Braendlin, "Alther, Atwood, Ballantyne, and Gray: Secular Salvation in the Contemporary Feminist Bildungsroman," *Frontiers* 4, 1 (Spring 1979), 18–22.

5. This is the position of classic lesbian feminism or separatism. See, for example, Radicalesbians, "The Woman Identified Woman" and Anne Koedt's response to it, "Lesbianism and Feminism, in Koedt et al. *Radical Feminism* (New York: Quadrangle Books, 1973); Nancy Myron and Charlotte Bunch, *Lesbianism and the Women's Movement* (Baltimore: Diana Press, 1975); and Bunch, "Learning from Lesbian Separatism," *Ms,* November 1976.

6. Marianne Hirsch, "The Novel of Formation as Genre: Between Great Expectations and Lost Illusions," *Genre* 13, 3 (Fall 1979), p. 300.

7. I wish to thank Lillian Robinson for suggesting "the coming out novel" as the appropriate phrase for lesbian developmental fiction. This essay will not be able to treat all lesbian novels with developmental themes. The following novels are discussed in the text: June Arnold, *Sister Gin* (Plainfield, Vt.: Daughters Publishing Co., 1975); Sybille Bedford, *A Compass Error* (New York: Ballantine Books, 1968); Rita Mae Brown, *Rubyfruit Jungle* (Plainfield, Vt.: Daughters Publishing Co., 1973); Rosa Guy, *Ruby* (New York: Bantam Books, 1976); Radclyffe Hall, *The Well of Loneliness* (1928; rpt. New York: Pocket Books, 1950); Bertha Harris, *Confessions of Cherubino* (New York: Harcourt, Brace, Jovanovich, 1972); Sharon Isabell, *Yesterday's Lessons* (Oakland, Calif.: The Women's Press Collective, 1974); Elana Nachman, *Riverfinger Women* (Plainfield, Vt.: Daughters Publishing Co., 1974); Verena Stefan, *Shedding* (New York: Daughters Publishing Co., 1978); Dorothy Bussy (Strachey), *Olivia,* by Olivia (pseud.) (1949; rpt. New York: Arno Press, 1975); Christa Winsloe, *The Child Manuela* (1933; rpt. New York: Arno Press, 1975); Monique Wittig, *The Opoponax* (1966; rpt. Plainfield, Vt.: Daughters Publishing Co., 1976); Virginia Woolf, *Orlando* (New York: Harcourt, Brace, Jovanovich, 1928). All page references will be made in the text.

Two further points need to be made here. One is that differences often exist between novels written before and after the advent of the female and gay liberation movements of the past two decades. Although this paper argues for a similar overall pattern, it also points out these differences, particularly in endings. I will, therefore, use the terms "pre-feminist" and "feminist" lesbian novel to indicate those written before the current women's movement and those written after and influenced by it. The second point is that all of the novels I discuss, with the exception of *Ruby,* are by and about white lesbians. I know of only one other easily accessible novel by a lesbian of color (although poetry and short fiction exist in abundance) and that one—*Loving Her* by Ann Allen Shockley—is not a developmental novel. Since writing this paper, Elly Bulkin has informed me of a self-published novel by Red Arobateau, *The Bars Across Heaven,* but unfortunately I have never seen a copy of it. However, the evidence provided by short fiction indicates that we may expect shortly to see significant novels of development by lesbians of color: for example, *Lesbian Fiction: An Anthology,* edited by Elly Bulkin (Watertown, Mass.: Persephone Press, 1981).

8. The framework I am using for the classic *Bildungsroman* is provided by Jerome Buckley, *Season of Youth: The Bildungsroman from Dickens to Golding* (Cambridge: Harvard University Press, 1974).

9. Jay, "Coming Out as Process," p. 28.

10. Verena Stefan, *Shedding,* p. 74. Stefan, a European, conventionally identifies the new world, that is lesbianism, with America: "A year ago, shortly before I left for America, the venture with Fenna began to take shape. We came upon regions of human affection which had lain fallow until then" (p. 83). Of course, for other lesbian characters, America is also a fatherland, and the new world takes shape as a lesbian community.

11. Sexologists such as Krafft-Ebing and Havelock Ellis were responsible for developing the medical model of the homosexual as an invert, virtually a transsexual: a man trapped in a woman's body, or a woman trapped in a man's. In a number of early lesbian novels of development, especially Radclyffe Hall's *The Well of Loneliness,* the true self "as I really am" is identified with the masculine self; in fact, the protagonist is recognized as a potential lesbian by her predilection for "masculine" activities and feelings. Although masculine role-playing is still evident in contemporary lesbian novels of development, such tomboys as Sharon in *Yesterday's Lessons* and Molly in *Rubyfruit Jungle* are adamant that they are women. The connection between being a tomboy and being a lesbian in the feminist novel arises from the desire to be free and independent, not to be a man.

12. Adrienne Rich, "Introduction" to *The Coming Out Stories,* ed. Julia Penelope Stanley and Susan J. Wolfe (Watertown, Mass.: Persephone Press, 1980), p. xiii.

13. Adrienne Rich, *The Coming Out Stories,* p. xxii.

14. See also *Confessions of Cherubino,* p. 3, and *A Compass Error,* p. 1. In the latter, Flavia, during her first night with a woman, shapes into a long narrative the story of her life and her matrilineal heritage. Narratively, this digression is very ineffective, but it does focus the developmental theme of the novel.

15. One explanation for this focus is that the psychologists and sociologists in the twentieth century who defined lesbianism as an issue or "problem" of adolescent development heavily influenced many lesbians writing in eras prior

to the contemporary women's movement. Furthermore, the flowering of sexual identity, which is central to the lesbian novel, does often occur in adolescence, whereas the awakening of independent identity in the heterosexual woman usually occurs several years into a marriage. However, the lesbian protagonist need not always be an adolescent—as in the case of Su in *Sister Gin*—since coming out, the discovery or affirmation of one's lesbianism, is not a discrete event but a lifelong process.

16. In addition, the educational motif is of great importance in *The Well of Loneliness,* which is a classic apprenticeship novel or *Künstlerroman.*

17. See also *Confessions of Cherubino,* p. 109, and *Ruby,* p. 138.

18. "Smashes," "flames," or "crushes" among girls and women in all-female environments (schools, camps, gym classes) have been well-documented and even celebrated by contemporary feminists, as in Meg Christian's famous coming out song, "Ode to a Gym Teacher" (on *I Know You Know,* Olivia Records). See also, Carroll Smith-Rosenberg, "The Female World of Love and Ritual," *Signs* 1, 1 (Fall 1975), 1–29; and Nancy Sahli, "Smashing: Women's Relationships Before the Fall," *Chrysalis* 8 (Summer 1979), 17–27. In some pre-feminist literature, on the contrary, the influence of the all-female environment was considered to be pernicious, leading to such indictments as Clemence Dane's violently antilesbian novel, *Regiment of Women* (1917) or Dorothy Baker's *Trio* (1943). See also Havelock. Ellis's discussion of school-girl "flames" in *Sexual Inversion. Studies in the Psychology of Sex,* 3rd ed., Appendix D, "The School-Friendships of Girls" (Philadelphia: F. A. Davis, 1910). Most modern lesbian novelists have a relatively positive attitude toward these environments, and in feminist novels such as *Riverfinger Women,* the girl's school or dormitory (a necessary adjustment in the age of coeducation) becomes a metaphor for lesbian nation.

19. See also *The Child Manuela,* pp. 236, 244; *The Well of Loneliness,* p. 146; *A Compass Error,* p. 44; and *Sister Gin,* pp. 130, 148.

20. See also *Olivia; A Compass Error,* pp. 32, 34; *The Well of Loneliness,* p. 79; and *Ruby,* p. 138.

21. Les Avons was modeled after an actual school, Les Ruches, which also educated Natalie Barney. The historical Mlle. Julie later founded a new school, Allenswood, in England, where one of her students was Eleanor Roosevelt. Dorothy Bussy was a teacher there at the time.

22. Denis de Rougemont, *Love in the Western World* (New York: Harcourt, Brace, and Co., 1940), p. 19.

23. This accommodation may also account for the absence of the ironic tone characteristic of the developmental novel's narrator. See Hirsch, "The Novel of Formation as Genre," p. 298.

24. Adrienne Rich, "It Is the Lesbian in Us . . . ," *On Lies, Secrets, and Silence* (New York: W. W. Norton, 1979), p. 199.

25. *Riverfinger Women,* p. 170.

Kasdan: "Why are you afraid to have me at your side?"

1. Molly Haskell, *From Reverence to Rape* (New York: Holt, Rinehart, Winston, 1974), p. 207.

2. Ibid., p. 40.

3. Herbert Biberman, *Salt of the Earth: The Making of the Film* (Boston: Beacon Press, 1965).

4. The original screenplay, written by Michael Wilson, published in *California Quarterly* (vol. 2, 4, Summer 1953), makes the suppression of women more explicit. After the request for equal plumbing is made, Sal Ruiz rises and says, "Just for the record, brothers, I want you to know I didn't ask my wife to bring this up." And after the proposal has been tabled, Ramon asks Esperanza why she has come. She answers defensively that "they" talked her into it. He says, "You're not needed here . . . [kisses his sleeping daughter]. But this one needs you . . . [pats her back gently]. And this one, straining to be born, this one needs you . . . [kisses her cheek]. And I need you—for what you are" (p. 18).

5. Michael Wilson, *Salt of the Earth* (Old Westbury, N.Y.: Feminist Press, 1978), p. 54.

6. Ibid., p. 74.

7. Ibid., p. 32.

8. The gun, as Deborah Rosenfelt points out in her comments on *Salt of the Earth* (in Wilson, *Salt of the Earth*, p. 151), is significant because "Guns . . . become icons for both a crude machismo and the power of the ruling class. As the ruling class oppresses the worker, so the man oppresses the woman." She goes on to say that the president of the company is shown in the magazine photo in a safari outfit with a rifle across his chest. I would add that the hunting trip is decided upon after the men see the photo: they go hunting for food while the company president hunts for pleasure.

9. Esperanza dominates the composition in the frame, standing while Ramon sits. Although she is shot from a high angle, as women so often are (the point of view of a man looking down at them), the close-ups and the strength of her verbalized position help maintain her dominance.

10. In the original screenplay, Ramon's memory of Esperanza's words is absent. He returns home because he suddenly pieces together the strategy of the bosses: "An idea dawns on him . . . Evictions" (*California Quarterly*, p. 55). The important element of his recognition of Esperanza's truths and her participation in his understanding is thus more fully and logically developed in the final version.

11. Ellen Morgan, "Humanbecoming: Form and Focus in the Neo-Feminist Novel," in *Images of Women in Fiction: Feminist Perspectives*, ed. Susan Koppelman Cornillon (Bowling Green, Ohio: Bowling Green University Popular Press, 1972), p. 185.

12. Laura Mulvey, "Visual Pleasure and Narrative Cinema," in *Women and the Cinema*, ed. Karyn Kay and Gerald Peary (New York: E. P. Dutton, 1977), p. 420.

13. Ibid., p. 419.

14. Ibid., p. 421.

Washington: Plain, Black, and Decently Wild

1. *A Voice From the South by a Black Woman of the South* (Xenia, Ohio: The Aldine Printing House, 1892), p. 133.

2. Chapter 1 in *A Voice From the South.*

3. Jacqueline Grant's essay, "Black Women and the Church," in *But Some of Us Are Brave* (Old Westbury, N.Y.: Feminist Press, 1982) shows historically how black women were excluded from preaching in the black church. The black churches have oppressed women in ways that range from separate seating in certain sections to denial of ordination for women. In the essay I wrote for the Radcliffe papers in April 1980 entitled "These Self-Invented Women: A Theoretical Framework for a Literary History of Black Women," I catalogued many of the ways black women were excluded from the Afro-American literary canon.

4. Ann Jones, "Pheoby's Hungry Listening: Zora Neale Hurston's *Their Eyes Were Watching God,* paper presented at the National Women's Studies Association, Humboldt State University, Arcata, Calif., June 1982.

5. "In Search of Our Mothers' Gardens: The Creativity of the Black Woman in the South," *Ms,* May 1974.

6. "Introduction: Women, Blacks, History," to *Black Women in Nineteenth-Century American Life,* ed. Bert Loewenberg and Ruth Bogin (University Park: Pennsylvania State University Press, 1976), p. 4.

7. Sandra M. Gilbert and Susan Gubar describe this crucial struggle for literary power in chapter 2, "Infection in the Sentence: The Woman Writer and the Anxiety of Authorship," *Madwoman in the Attic: The Woman Writer and the Nineteenth-Century Literary Imagination* (New Haven: Yale University Press, 1979), pp. 83–92.

8. *Maud Martha* (1953; rpt. New York: AMS Press Reprint, 1974). All references are to this edition.

9. 1952 reviews of *Invisible Man:* George Mayberry, "Underground Notes," in *New Republic* (April 21, 1952), 600 words; Irving Howe, "A Negro in America," *Nation* (May 10, 1952), 950 words; Anthony West, "Black Man's Burden," *New Yorker* (May 31, 1952), 2,100 words; C. J. Rolo, "Candide in Harlem," *Atlantic* (July 1952), 450 words; Wright Morris, "The World Below," *New York Times Book Review* (April 13, 1952), 900 words; "Black & Blue," *Time* (April 14, 1952), 850 words; J. E. Cassidy "A Brother Betrayed," *Commonweal* (May 2, 1952) 850 words.

1953 reviews of *Maud Martha: New Yorker* (October 10, 1953), 160 words; Hubert Creekmore, "Daydreams in Flight," *New York Times Book Review* (October 4, 1953), 400 words; Nicolas Monjo "Young Girl Growing Up," *Saturday Review* (October 31, 1953), 140 words; Coleman Rosenberger, *New York Herald Tribune* (October 18, 1953), 600 words.

The diction of the reviews, too, is revealing. The tone of *Invisible Man* was defined as "vigorous, imaginative, violently humorous and quietly tragic" (New R), "searing and exalted" (Nation), while *Maud Martha* drew "freshness, warm cheerfulness . . . (and) vitality" (NYT), "ingratiating" (Sat R). Several reviews of Ellison used "gusto," for Brooks, "liveliness." Brooks's "Negro heroine" (NYT) was characterized as a "young colored

woman" (Sat R) and a "spunky and sophisticated Negro girl" (NY); Ellison's character as a "hero" and "pilgrim" (New R).

Matters of style received mixed response in both novels. *MM*'s "impressionistic style" was deemed "not quite sharp or firm enough" and her "remarkable gift" was seen (in the same review) as "mimicry" and an "ability
to turn unhappiness and anger into a joke"—a gift which her style did not
engender (NY). The Sat R said: "Its form is no more than a random narration of loosely assembled incidents" and called its "framework . . . somewhat ramshackle." Only the *New York Times* noticed a significance in her
style, and likened the "flashes . . . of sensitive lightness" to Imagist poetics,
as well as commenting on the "finer qualities of insight and rhythm."

Both authors are criticized along the same lines concerning form and style,
but in the reviews of Brooks, her style is that topic which draws the most
attention, and the review is favorable or unfavorable depending upon
whether or not the reviewer is personally attracted to "impressionism." Ellison's novel is treated more seriously than Brooks's because his novel is seen as
addressing a broader range of issues, despite his sometimes "hysterical" style.

This position is most apparent in Howe's review in the *Nation*. Howe asks
serious questions about traditional literary devices, such as narrative stance
and voice, and method of characterization, despite the book's lack of "finish."
(Ellison's first-person narration is discussed by all reviewers, while Brooks's
narrative style is hardly mentioned in any review.) Implicit in Howe's stance
toward *IM* is an assumption that this is a serious novel to be investigated
rigorously in accordance with the (high) standards of the academy. Despite
those qualities of tone and style which Howe criticizes it for, *IM* is important,
finally, because it fits into the literary tradition of the epic journey of discovery. Howe calls it a "searing and exalted record of a Negro's journey toward contemporary America in search of success, companionship, and finally
himself."

10. The most egregious example of the condescension toward black women in
the 1950s is the *Negro Digest's* (August 1950) article covering Brooks's winning of the Pulitzer Prize. The entire piece is an act of sabotage. It begins
with a list of all the people who didn't believe Brooks had won the prize. It
catalogs all the negative experiences Brooks had after winning the prize. It
mentions her husband briefly—as a poet who cannot devote time to writing
because he feels "no one family can support two poets." The article includes
a poem written by the poet's nine-year-old son (but not a line from the poet
who has just won the Pulitzer Prize!) and ends with the son's complaint that
his mother's fame has upset his life so much that he is glad the attention is
wearing off so he can have some peace. The article focuses entirely on the
negativity of Brooks's literary achievement and so absolutely ignores the work
of the poet that one can only infer the article's author had little respect for
the achievement. A similar article on Ralph Ellison, in *The Crisis* in March
1953, focuses on the professional achievement of the writer.

11. "Vesuvius at Home: The Power of Emily Dickinson," in *On Lies, Secrets
and Silences: Selected Prose 1966–1978* (New York: W. W. Norton, 1979).

12. A line from Brooks's poems in *Annie Allen* in *The World of Gwendolyn Brooks* (New York: Harper & Row, 1971), p. 121.

13. Gilbert and Gubar, *Madwoman in the Attic*, p. 75. In this passage the authors refer to ideas in Patricia Spacks's *The Female Imagination* and to discussions of women's literature by Carolyn Heilbrun and Catharine R. Stimpson.

14. Brooks has commented on the autobiographical character of *Maud Martha* in many places. In her own autobiography, *Report From Part One* (Detroit: Broadside Press, 1972) she says: "Much that happened to Maud Martha has not happened to me—and she is a nice and a better coordinated creature than I am. But it is true that much in the 'story' was taken out of my life, and twisted, highlighted or dulled, dressed up or down" (p. 191).

15. *Report From Part One*, p. 72.

16. In *The Second Sex* Simone de Beauvoir maintains that the reproductive process is not the same as the creative process, that reproduction is passive, creativity active. She insists that women cannot achieve self-realization through having a child and that an independent person cannot be used as her justification for existence. While I agree with de Beauvoir that a child cannot be a substitute for creative and fulfilling work, I think she is limited to understanding the meaning of motherhood in a European culture. African cultures view childbearing differently, and Maud's attitude is more closely akin to that culture's view.

17. "Update on *Part One:* An Interview with Gwendolyn Brooks," *CLA Journal,* 21 (1977), 26.

18. *Annie Allen* (1949) in *Selected Poems* (Harper & Row, 1963). George Kent suggests in his analysis of Brooks's poetry ("The Poetry of Gwendolyn Brooks," in *Blackness and the Adventure of Western Civilization* [Chicago: Third World Press, 1972], 104–38) that Annie Allen's life justifies its epic title and grand language, and I agree because that combination creates a powerful irony.

19. I wonder if Brooks is restrained from allowing Maud a more dynamic role in the community by her own ambivalence (understandable in terms of the restrictions of women in the 1950s) toward women as heroic figures. When Brooks chooses heroic characters for her poetry she outlines tasks for them that generally only men can perform. From the dapper hustler Satin-Legs Smith to the renegade Way-out Morgan or the soldier in "Negro Hero" or the armed man defending his family against a white mob, Brooks selects the heroic strategies of men and the ritual grounds on which men typically perform. With her men characters, Brooks sculpts bold designs out of the rawest material—the pool players at the Golden Shovel have a swaggering brashness; the half-mad prophet, Way-out Morgan, displays a kind of divine fanaticism in his determination to carry out his radical purposes: while the little yellow-woman he "postpones" in his bed is a vulnerable sexual creature (unnamed), associated with "wetnesses and little cries and stomachings." Even a plain man like Rudolph Reed has a moment of glory as he runs out into the street "with a thirty-four / And a beastly butcher knife." He dies in defense of his family while his wife, who has been passive throughout the entire ballad, stands by mutely and does nothing "But change the bloody gauze."

Brooks betrays a tremendous resistance to endowing women with the power, integrity, or magnificence of her male figures. Sometimes Brooks's women manage to be "decently wild" as girls, but they grow up to be worrisome and fearful, fretful over the loss of a man. They wither in back yards, afraid to tackle life, they are done in by dark skin; and like "estimable Mable," they are often incapable of estimating their worth without the tape measure of a man's interest in them.

Peixoto: *Family Ties*

1. Clarice Lispector, born in the Ukraine in 1925, immigrated with her parents to Brazil while still an infant. She lived in Recife (a major port in the northeast of Brazil) until age twelve, when her family moved to Rio de Janeiro. While attending law school she published her first novel and married a fellow student who later became a diplomat. With her husband, Lispector spent the better part of the next fifteen years living in Europe and the United States. She published two novels and a collection of short stories during this period and had two sons, born in Bern and Washington. From 1959, when she separated from her husband, until her death in 1977, she lived in Rio, working occasionally as a journalist and translator, and continued to publish fiction.

2. Emir Rodríguez Monegal, "The Contemporary Brazilian Novel," *Daedalus* 95, no. 4 (Fall, 1966), p. 1001.

3. In one interview, Lispector emphasized that both male and female writers in Brazil imitated her works, and in another maintained that "it just happened" that the sole character of her novel *The Passion According to G. H.* was female. By avoiding in literary matters an unambiguous identification with her sex, she no doubt hoped to avoid membership in a subgroup of writers of supposedly inferior talent, a strategy other women writers have been known to use. Interviews with María Ester Gilio, "Tristes Trópicos," *Crisis* 4, no. 39 (Buenos Aires, July 1976), p. 44, and with Maryvonne Laponge and Clelia Pisa, in *Brasileiras: voix, écrits du Brésil* (Paris: des femmes, 1977), p. 198.

4. Affonso Romano de Sant'anna, "Laços de Família e Legião Estrangeira," in *Análise Estrutural de Romances Brasileiros* (Petrópolis: Vozes, 1973), p. 198.

5. Hélène Cixous, "L'approche de Clarice Lispector," *Poétique* 40 (November 1979), 408–17. See also Naomi Lindstrom, "Clarice Lispector: Articulating Woman's Experience," *Chasqui* 8, 1 (1978), 43–52.

6. A. R. Sant'anna, *Análise Estrutural de Romances Brasileiros*, p. 187.

7. Ibid., p. 199.

8. Translations are my own and have been in part based on Giovanni Pontiero's. Page numbers refer to his translation of the collection: Clarice Lispector, *Family Ties* (Austin: University of Texas Press, 1972).

9. I use here Jean Baker Miller's terms and her view of female development from *Toward a New Psychology of Women* (Boston: Beacon Press, 1976), p. 83.

10. Susan J. Rosowski, "The Novel of Awakening," in this volume.

11. Ibid.

12. Ibid.

13. Clarice Lispector, "O Ovo e a Galinha," in *A Legião Estrangeira* (Rio de Janeiro: Editora do Autor, 1964), p. 63.

14. Carolyn G. Heilbrun, *Reinventing Womanhood* (New York: W. W. Norton, 1979), p. 71.

15. "Uma História de Tanto Amor," in *Seleta de Clarice Lispector,* ed. Renato Cordeiro Gomes and Amariles Guimarães Hill (Rio de Janeiro: José Olympio, 1976), pp. 7–8.

16. Ellen Moers, *Literary Women: The Great Writers* (New York: Doubleday, 1976), p. 245.

17. Quoted by Amariles G. Hill, "A Experiência de Existir Narrando," in *Seleta de Clarice Lispector,* p. 141.

Frieden: Shadowing / Surfacing / Shedding

1. See David Miles, "The Picaro's Journey to the Confessional: The Changing Image of the Hero in the German *Bildungsroman,*" *PMLA* 89 (1974), 980–92, for a discussion of characteristics of the traditional *Bildungsroman.*

2. Jürgen Jacobs, *Wilhelm Meister und seine Brüder: Untersuchungen zum deutschen Bildungsroman* (Munich: Fink, 1972), p. 17.

3. For a more extensive discussion of this phenomenon, see my forthcoming book *Autobiography: Self into Form. German-language Autobiographical Writings of the 1970's* (Frankfurt am Main: Peter Lang Verlag).

4. Although titles as early as Goethe's *Dichtung und Wahrheit* (*Poetry and Truth*) betray skepticism toward autobiographical reliability, Roy Pascal provides one of the earliest critical acknowledgments of the truths contained in the fictions of autobiography in his 1960 work *Design and Truth in Autobiography* (Cambridge: Harvard University Press). Pascal worked predominantly in German literature, but the skepticism toward the "non-fictional" nature of autobiography reached beyond the German-language literary community.

5. A similar turn to the literary authentication of personal experience had occurred earlier in other language communities, as seen by the examples of Michel Leiris's *L'Age d'Homme* in 1939 and William Burroughs's *Naked Lunch* in 1959. The delayed appearance of such a self-revelatory autobiographical mode into German-language literature resulted from a number of factors, not the least of which was the trauma of postwar recovery. See n. 3, and also Peter Beicken, " 'Neue Subjektivität': Zur Prosa der siebziger Jahre," in *Deutsche Literatur in der Bundesrepublik seit 1965,* eds. Paul Michael Lützeler and Egon Schwarz (Königstein/Ts.: Athenäum, 1980), pp. 164–81.

6. Jutta Heinrich, *Das Geschlecht der Gedanken* (Munich: Frauenoffensive, 1977), pp. 130–31. This and all subsequent translations of quotations from cited German texts are my own.

7. Hélène Cixous, "The Laugh of the Medusa," trans. Keith Cohen and Paula Cohen, *Signs* 1, no. 4 (Summer 1976), 875–93.

8. That the critical reception of this work—as well as that of the two others I discuss here—would be problematic is hardly surprising, given the formal

and thematic subversion of literary and social norms undertaken by Bachmann (as well as by Schwaiger and Stefan) from the perspective of female
experience. Bachmann's earlier reputation as a poet, essayist, and scholar as-
sured at least the publication of her work (*Malina*); yet the work received
(until quite recently) amazingly little serious consideration and was regarded
as disjointed and incoherent. The frequent discounting of the female perspective in critical reviews and the popular success enjoyed by both Schwaiger
and Stefan led to a dominant critical assertion of triviality in regard to their
works. Such difficulties of literary-critical reception for women's writings are,
of course, not unique to the German-language community.

9. Ingeborg Bachmann, *Malina* (Frankfurt/Main: Suhrkamp, 1971), pp.
41–42. All subsequent page references for quotations from this work appear
in the text.

10. Brigitte Schwaiger, *Wie kommt das Salz ins Meer?* (Vienna: Zsolnay,
1977), p. 44. All subsequent page references for quotations from this work
appear in the text.

11. Verena Stefan, *Shedding*, trans. Johanna Moore and Beth Weckmueller
(New York: Daughters Publishing Co., 1978), p. 66. All subsequent page
references for quotations from this work appear in the text.

12. Verena Stefan, *Häutungen* (Munich: Frauenoffensive, 1975), Introduction, p. 1, my translation.

13. Ibid., p. 4, my translation.

14. Ibid., p. 3, my translation.

15. Hannelies Taschau, *Landfriede* (Zürich: Benziger, 1978), p. 35.

16. While similar social problems for women exist in numerous countries—
a situation that has generated both an international women's movement and
an international women's literature—still, the unique circumstances within
each country, the literary-historical boundaries within which each author
writes, the literary-critical climate confronting each new book, and the varying factors of literary production and distribution in each country's book mar-
ket lead to works which show the influence of their origins. Thus we can find
works that concentrate on one area of experience—such as psychological
breakdown, as in Hannah Green's *I Never Promised You A Rose Garden*
(New York: Holt, Rinehart, and Winston, 1964), Maria Erlenberger's *Der
Hunger Nach Wahnsinn* (The Hunger for Madness) (Reinbek: Rowohlt,
1977), and Marie Cardinal's *Les Mots pour le dire* (The Words for Speaking) (Paris: Grasset et Fasquelle, 1975)—that are quite similar in form and
content. Yet there are works which enjoy considerable popularity in their
own countries and to a great extent reflect their origins: the dialectic engagement of the heroine with her society in *Häutungen;* the melodramatic unfolding of realistically portrayed experience in *The Women's Room* by Marilyn
French (New York: Summit, 1977); and the theoretical experimentation
with form, language, and fantasy in Monique Wittig's *Les Guérillères* (Paris:
Les éditions de minuit, 1969).

17. Elizabeth Bruss, *Autobiographical Acts* (Baltimore: Johns Hopkins
University Press, 1976), p. 7.

Fictions of Female Development

Cited in This Volume

Alcott, Louisa May. *Little Women*. 1868.
———. *Work: A Story of Experience*. 1873.
Alther, Lisa. *Kinflicks*. 1975.
Arnold, June. *Sister Gin*. 1975.
Arobateau, Red. *The Bars Across Heaven*. n.d.
Atwood, Margaret. *Lady Oracle*. 1977.
Austen, Jane. *Emma*. 1816.
———. *Northanger Abbey*. 1818.
———. *Pride and Prejudice*. 1813.
Bachmann, Ingeborg. *Malina*. 1971.
Bedford, Sybille. *A Compass Error*. 1968.
Biberman, Herbert. *Salt of the Earth*. 1953. (Screenplay by Michael Wilson, 1953.)
Brontë, Charlotte. *Jane Eyre*. 1847.
———. *Shirley*. 1849.
———. *Villette*. 1853.
Brontë, Emily. *Wuthering Heights,* 1847.
Brooks, Gwendolyn. *Maud Martha*. 1953.
Broumas, Olga. *Beginning with O*. 1977.
Brown, Rita Mae. *Rubyfruit Jungle*. 1973.
Bussy, Dorothy (Strachey). *Olivia*. 1949.
Cardinal, Marie. *The Words for Speaking* (*Les Mots pour le dire*). 1975.*
Carter, Angela. *The Bloody Chamber*. 1980.
Cather, Willa. *A Lost Lady*. 1924.
———. *My Mortal Enemy*. 1926.
———. *Obscure Destinies*. 1932.
Chopin, Kate. *The Awakening*. 1899.
Colette, Sidonie Gabrielle. *Break of Day* (*La Naissance du jour*). 1928.
———. *Claudine at School* (*Claudine à l'école*). 1900.
———. *My Mother's House* (*La Maison de Claudine*). 1922.
———. *Sido*. 1929.
Eliot, George, *Middlemarch*. 1872.
———. *The Mill on the Floss*. 1860.

* Works marked with an asterisk do not exist in English translation; title translations are our own.

Erlenberger, Maria. *The Hunger for Madness* (*Der Hunger nach Wahnsinn*). 1977.*

Flaubert, Gustave. *Madame Bovary.* 1856.

Fontane, Theodor. *Effi Briest.* 1896.

French, Marilyn. *The Women's Room.* 1977.

Gray, Francine du Plessix. *Lovers and Tyrants.* 1967.

Green, Hannah. *I Never Promised You a Rose Garden.* 1963.

Grumbach, Doris. *Chamber Music.* 1980.

Guy, Rosa. *Ruby.* 1976.

Hall, Radclyffe. *The Well of Loneliness.* 1928.

Hardy, Thomas. *Tess of the d'Ubervilles.* 1891.

Harris, Bertha. *Confessions of Cherubino.* 1972.

Hurston, Zora Neale. *Their Eyes Were Watching God.* 1937.

Isabell, Sharon. *Yesterday's Lessons.* 1974.

James, Henry. *Portrait of a Lady.* 1881.

Jong, Erica. *Fanny: Being the True Story of the Adventures of Fanny Hackabout-Jones.* 1980.

———. *Fear of Flying.* 1973.

Lafayette, Marie Madeleine. *The Princess of Clèves* (*La Princesse de Clèves*). 1678.

Laroche, Sophie von. *The Story of Fraülein von Sternheim* (*Geschichte des Fraüleins von Sternheim*). 1771.

Larsen, Nella. *Quicksand.* 1928.

Leduc, Violette. *Thérèse and Isabelle* (*Thérèse et Isabelle*). 1970.*

Lessing, Doris. *African Stories.* 1965.

———. *The Four-Gated City.* 1969.

———. *The Golden Notebook.* 1964.

———. *Landlocked.* 1965.

———. *Martha Quest.* 1952.

———. *A Proper Marriage.* 1954.

———. *A Ripple from the Storm.* 1958.

———. *The Summer Before the Dark.* 1973.

Lispector, Clarice. *Close to the Heart* (*Perto do Selvagem*). 1944.

———. *Family Ties* (*Laços de Familia*). 1960.

Millett, Kate. *Flying.* 1974.

———. *Sita.* 1978.

Morrison, Toni. *Sula.* 1973.

Nachman, Elana. *Riverfinger Women.* 1974.

Petersen, Karin. *The Fat Year* (*Das fette Jahr*). 1978.*

Piercy, Marge. *Small Changes.* 1978.

Plessen, Elisabeth. *Message to the Gentry* (*Mitteilung an den Adel*). 1976.*

Porter, Katherine Ann. *The Collected Stories.* 1979.

Radcliffe, Ann. *The Mysteries of Udolpho.* 1794.
Rehmann, Ruth. *The Man on the Pulpit (Der Mann auf dem Kanzel).* 1979.*
Rhys, Jean. *After Leaving Mr. Mackenzie.* 1930.
———. *Good Morning, Midnight.* 1939.
———. *Quartet.* 1928.
———. *Voyage in the Dark.* 1934.
———. *Wide Sargasso Sea.* 1966.
Schreiner, Olive. *The Story of an African Farm.* 1883.
Schwaiger, Brigitte. *How Does the Salt Get into the Sea? (Wie kommt das Salz ins Meer?).* 1977.*
Sexton, Anne. *Transformations.* 1971.
Shockley, Ann Allen. *Loving Her.* 1978.
Smedley, Agnes. *Daughter of Earth.* 1929.
Stafford, Jean. *Boston Adventure.* 1944.
———. *The Catherine Wheel.* 1952.
———. *The Mountain Lion.* 1947.
Stefan, Verena. *Shedding (Häutungen).* 1975.
Stimpson, Kate. *Class Notes.* 1979.
Struck, Karin. *Class Love (Klassenliebe).* 1973.*
Taschau, Hennelies. *Public Peace (Landfriede).* 1978.*
Tolstoi, Leo. *Anna Karenina.* 1904.
Welty, Eudora. *The Wide Net and Other Stories.* 1943.
West, Dorothy. *The Living Is Easy.* 1948.
Wharton, Edith. *The House of Mirth.* 1905.
Winsloe, Christa. *The Child Manuela.* 1933.
Wittig, Monique. *The Guérillères (Les Guérillères).* 1969.
———. *The Opoponax (L'Opoponax).* 1966.
Wohmann, Gabriele. *An Outing with Mother (Ausflug mit der Mutter).* 1978.*
Wolf, Christa. *A Model Childhood (Kindheitsmuster).* 1976.
Woolf, Virginia. *Mrs. Dalloway.* 1925.
———. *Orlando.* 1928.
———. *The Voyage Out.* 1915.

Index